THE HEAVENLY ROSE-GARDEN

A History of Shirvan & Daghestan

by

'Abbas Qoli Aqa Bakikhanov

Introduced, Translated and Annotated by

WILLEM FLOOR & HASAN JAVADI

MAGE
PUBLISHERS

Copyright © 2009 Willem Floor and Hasan Javadi

All rights reserved.
No part of this book may be reproduced
or retransmitted in any manner whatsoever,
except in the form of a review, without the
written permission of the publisher.

Library of Congress Cataloging-in-Publication Data

Bakikhanov, Abbas-Kuli-aga, 1794-1847.
  [Gulistan-i iram. English]
  The heavenly rose-garden : a history of Shirvan & Daghestan / by
'Abbas Qoli Aqa Bakikhanov ; introduced, translated and annotated
  by Willem Floor & Hasan Javadi.
       p. cm.
  ISBN 978-1-933823-27-0 (soft cover : alk. paper)
  1. Shirvan (Kingdom)--History. 2. Dagestan (Russia)--History. I.
  Floor, Willem M. II. Javadi, Hasan. III. Title.
        DK697.1.B3513 2009
        947.5'2--dc22
                                              2008047495

Printed and Manufactured in the United States

Mage books are available at bookstores,
through the internet, or directly from the publisher:
Mage Publishers, 1032 29th Street, NW, Washington, DC 20007
202-342-1642 • as@mage.com • 800-962-0922
visit Mage Publishers online at
www.mage.com

CONTENTS

INTRODUCTION *by Willem Floor & Hasan Javadi* . . . . *vii–xvii*

PREFACE OF *The Heavenly Rose-Garden* 1

INTRODUCTION 5
    Describing the borders, lands, reason for their names, the situation, languages and religions of the country of Shirvan and Daghestan

CHAPTER ONE 21
    Describing the ancient events of the province of Shirvan and Daghestan until the time of the invasion of the Arabs after the advent of Islam.

CHAPTER TWO 41
    From the beginning of the coming of the Arab army until the time of the Mongol invasion

CHAPTER THREE 65
    From the time of the Mongol invasion until the advent of the Safavids as well as the situation of the rule the Shirvanshahs
        CONCERNING THE KINGSHIP AND LINEAGE OF THE SHIRVANSHAHS . . . 77

CHAPTER FOUR 83
    From the Rise of the Safavids until the Death of Nader Shah
        THE STORY OF NADER 122

CHAPTER FIVE 135
    From the death of Nader until the treaty of the government of Russia and Iran in the village of Golestan

CONCLUSION 169
    On the lives of the people of the province of Shirvan and its neighboring regions who are authors or who have other accomplishments that are worthy to record

APPENDIX 1 200
APPENDIX II 202
INDEX 203

PRE-SAFAVID AZERBAIJAN

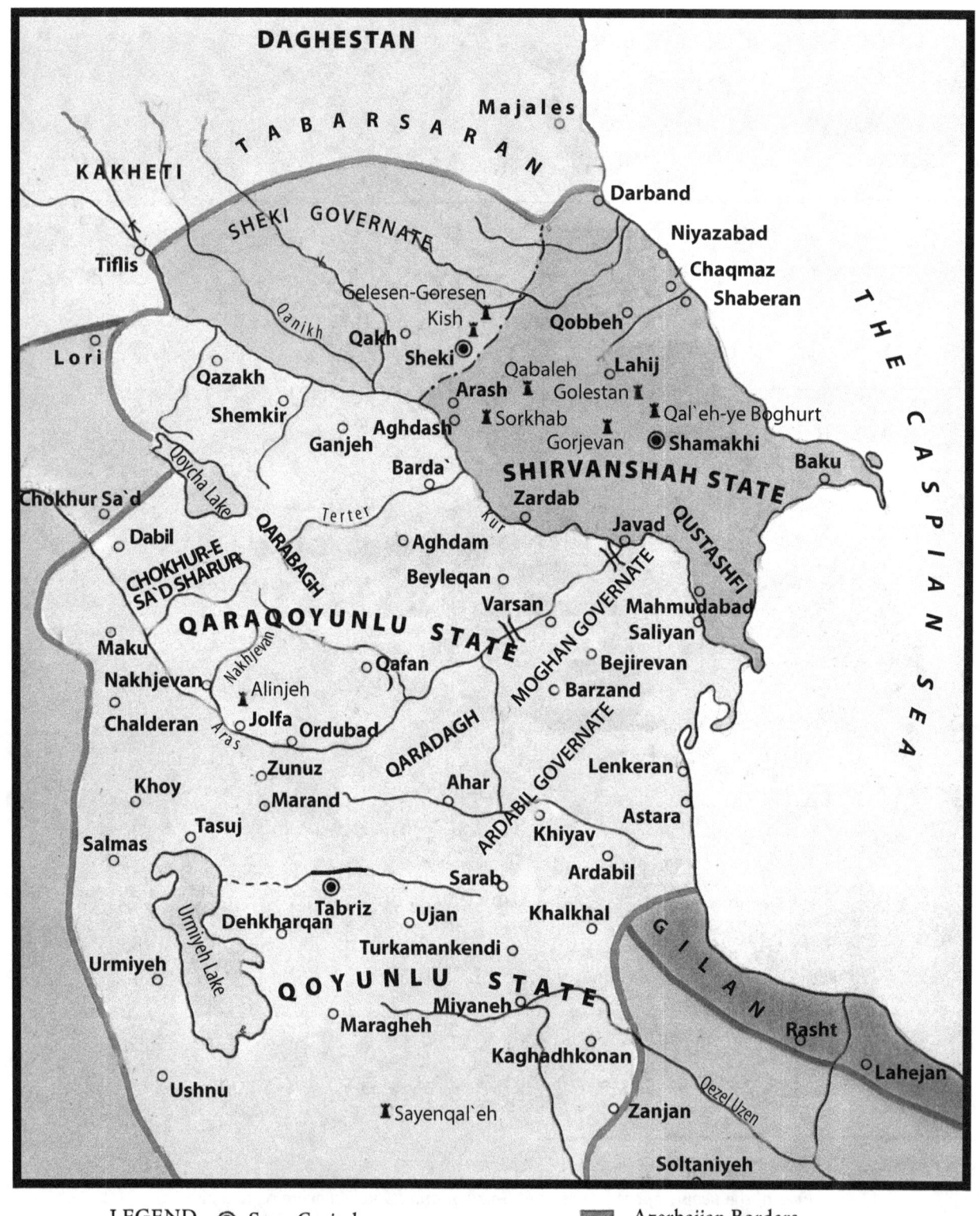

INTRODUCTION

'Abbas Qoli Aqa Bakikhanov, also known under the pen-name Qodsi, was an Azerbaijani writer, historian, journalist, linguist, poet and philosopher. He was born on Thursday, the 4th Dhu'l-Hejjeh 1208 *hijri*, or the 10th of June in the year 1794 in the village of Amir Hajan near Baku. Bakikhanov was a scion of the ruling dynasty of the Khanate of Baku, being the nephew of the last khan of Baku. His father Mirza Mohammad Khan II was the ninth Khan of Baku and was driven from his throne by his brother Mohammad Qoli Khan. 'Abbas Qoli Aqa became an officer in the Imperial Russian army in 1820 and participated in the Russo-Persian war of 1826-28. He later retired and lived in Qobbeh, but traveled extensively in Russia and the Caucasus, meeting such important literary figures as Pushkin and Akhundzadeh.[1]

Bakikhanov's childhood coincided with one of the most decisive and turbulent periods of the history of the Caucasus—the era of battles between Russia and Persia over the political domination in the region. Beginning a traditional education at home at the age of seven, he later moved to Qobbeh where he learnt Persian and Arabic and other customary academic subjects of the time for ten more years. It was here that 'Abbas Qoli Aqa excelled in Persian and made a thorough study of the great poets of Persian literature. After learning Persian and Arabic, he learnt Russian, followed later by French. 'Abbas Qoli Aqa's mother Sophia was Georgian and, when he moved to Tiflis at the age of 26, he lived with his maternal uncle in this city. In 1820, two years after his move to Tiflis, he was employed as the Oriental interpreter for general Yermelov, the head of the Russian forces

---

1. For a detailed biography of Bakikhanov the reader is referred to Rahim Ra'is-niya, "Godhari bar andishehha va athar-e 'Abbas Qoli-ye Aqa Qodsi [Bakikhanov]," *Tarikh-e ravabet-e khareji* 3/12 (1381/2002), pp. 177-224. Also see Vali Habib Ogli, *Abbas Quli Aga Bakixanov*, (Baki 1992); and Hasan Javadi, "Abbas Quli Aqa Bakikhanov" in *Encyclopaedia Iranica*; and Anvar M. Ahmadov, *A. K. Bakikhanov: epokha zhizh', dejatel'nost'* (Baku: Elm', 1989)

in the Caucasus, and except for eight years (1834-1842) when he lived on the estate of his father in Qobbeh, he remained in the service of the Russian government until 1845.

Tiflis at this period was the cultural center of the Caucasus. Mirza Shafi' Vazeh (1792-1852), the great Azerbaijani poet whose *ghazal*s became famous in the German adaptation of Bodenstedt, Akhundzadeh (1812-78), the Azeri playwright and reformer, Gribayedov (1795-1829), the Russian playwright and ambassador to Iran, who was killed in Tehran, Khachatur Abovyan (1805-48), the founder of modern Armenian literature, and the Georgians Ilia Chavchavadse (1786-1846), Nikoloz Baratashvili (1817-45), and Grigol Orbeliani (1804-83), all lived around this time in that city. Lermantov, the great and liberal poet of Russia, joined this group when he was exiled to Tiflis for writing an elegy on the death of Pushkin.

At the time that Bakikhanov was in Tiflis he frequented two literary societies: one was at the house of Chavchavadse, the founder of modern Georgian literature, where Akhundzadeh, Baratashvili, and Lermantov would come regularly. The second was the literary and philosophical coterie called *Divan-e hekmat neh Divan-e 'Aql*,[2] which was formed by Mirza Shafi'. Friedrich Bodenstedt during his stay in Tiflis also frequented it. After staying for three years in Moscow, Bodenstedt moved to Tiflis to teach Latin and French at its Gymnasium (1844-46), where he came to know Mirza Shafi' and Bakikhanov. Bodenstedt studied Persian and Azerbaijani (or Tatar) and translated the poems of Mirza Shafi',[3] which made him famous. Apparently he also wanted to translate some of the poetry of Bakikhanov and make it into a separate book since he wrote in his Diaries (24 November 1861): "More than Mirza Shafi', 'Abbas Qoli deserves to be a representative of Oriental poetry."[4] Three years later Bodenstedt published some poems from the "Divan of 'Abbas Quli Khan" and one of them is a *ghazal* that is found at the end of *Golestan-e Eram*.[5]

Bakikhanov's government service began in 1820 under General Aleksey Yermelov, who, after a trip to Tehran where he met with Fath 'Ali Shah, had become the commander-in-chief of Russian forces in the Caucasus. Although he was adored by the soldiers, he was not liked by the Caucasians. Apparently, he had a condescending attitude towards them and Bakikhanov, who worked under him as a secretary and interpreter, did not rise higher than the rank of captain after eleven years of service under him. It was in 1827 that General Ivan Paskevich replaced Yermelov after the latter suffered some setbacks in the Russo-Persian of 1826-28. Bakikhanov's career took a turn for the better during the five-year commandership of Paskevich, which included the Russo-Persian war that led to the treaty of Turkmanchay and the Russo-Ottoman war of 1829-29. Bakikhanov actively participated in all of its military campaigns, and, on account of his valor in the battle of Erevan and Nakhjevan he received a special medal and was promoted to the rank of major. Referring to Bakikhanov, Paskevich wrote in his memoirs: "After coming to Georgia I

---

2. Fereydun-e Adamiyyat, *Andishehha-ye Mirza Fathali Akhundzadeh* (Tehran, 1349/1970), p. 17.
3. Friedrich Bodenstedt, *Die Lieder des Mirza-Schaffy* (Berlin, 1851).
4. Ra'is-niya, "Godhari bar andishehha," p. 193.
5. Vali Habib Oghlu, *Abbas Quli Aga Bakikhanov* (Baku, 1992), p. 341.

found him very capable and with good qualities and benefited from him in political affairs with full confidence."[6] After the Russian forces crossed the Aras and entered Tabriz on October 24, 1827, Bakikhanov was in Tabriz and remained there until the signing of the treaty of Turkmanchay on February 22, 1828. He was Gribayedov's interpreter during the negotiations of this treaty in Dekharqan (Turfargan), and received one hundred silver manats from Paskevich and a Lion and Sun Medal from 'Abbas Mirza.[7] According to Mirza Mas'ud Ishliqi Ansari, the interpreter of 'Abbas Mirza, Bakikhanov was present as the interpreter of "Colonel Gribayedov and General Paskevich" in all the negotiations.[8]

Apart from taking part in these military campaigns as an interpreter or a Russian officer, Bakikhanov was always involved in literary and scholarly activities. In 1823, he assisted in gathering ethnographic information for the *Description of the Province of Karabakh*. In the Persian expedition apparently Bakikhanov was one of the officials who selected manuscripts from the library of the tomb of Sheikh Safi in Ardabil and sent them to St. Petersburg. When the Russian forces crossed the Aras River, the head of the Oriental Institute of St. Petersburg University, Osip Ivanovich Senkoveski, asked General Paskevich that the precious manuscripts of the libraries in Azerbaijan should not be destroyed and be sent to St. Petersburg. Paskevich entrusted this task to Gribayedov, and he in turn involved Bakikhanov. The librarian and custodian of the shrine were not in the position to preserve the precious collection of books, and perforce relinquished it as a "loan" to be returned after having been transcribed. According to Habib Oghlu, 166 manuscripts were chosen with the help of Bakikhanov and sent under special guard to the Imperial Library at St. Petersburg.[9] While serving in the Russo-Ottoman war of 1828-29, in which he was awarded the fourth Degree Medal of St. Vladimir for participating in the siege of Kars, Bakikhanov was also entrusted with the task of selecting books from the mosque library of Akhatalisk (now in Georgia). He also purchased manuscripts for the Imperial Library in St. Petersburg. Throughout his life Bakikhanov gathered a valuable collection of Persian, Turkish and Arabic manuscripts, of which the Russian Orientalist Bérézine speaks with admiration, and after the death of Bakikhanov, his wife Sonya made a gift of them to the same library.

Soon after returning from Iran, Bakikhanov participated in the Russo-Ottoman wars, which ended in September 1829. In April of that year he was promoted to the rank of colonel, and apparently it was during this campaign that he came to know Pushkin who was visiting Erzerum. After the replacement of Paskevich in the Caucasus with Baron Rosen, whose policies were not very much in accord with Bakikhanov's ideas, he requested a two-year leave of absence and traveled widely in Russia and Poland. At the end of the *Golestan-e Eram* he writes:

---

6. Habib Oghlu, *Abbas Quli Aga*, p. 186.
7. Habib Oghlu, *Abbas Quli Aga*, p. 214.
8. Mas'ud Ansari, "Tarikh-e Ahval-e 'Abbas Mirza Nayeb al-Saltanah," in Khosrow Mirza, *Safarnameh-ye Khosrow Mirza* ed. Mas'ud Ansari (Tehran, 1349/1970), p. 69.
9. Habib Oghlu, *Abbas Quli Aga*, p. 218. See also Hesari, "Sarnevesht-e malal-angiz-e ketabkhaneh-ye Ardabil," *Keyhan-e Farhangi* (Dey 1365/January 1987), p. 4.

> In the year 1248/1833, I went on mission and for nearly two years I was traveling through the steppes, Tana, Ukraine and the Russian lands, Livonia, Lithuania, and Poland and I had contacts with the leading scholars of Europe. I saw many wondrous and strange things. In every land I gained some experience. Gradually my ignorance was reduced and the absurdity of what I had imagined became apparent. I saw that the great functions of the world are very low and great accomplishment [at the most] is to learn from experience.

For seven months he stayed in Warsaw, where he was honored by Paskevich who was now the governor of Poland. It was here that Bakikhanov met the famous Azeri novelist and writer Ismail Bey Gutgashynli, who, like himself, was a high ranking officer, the Russian army. After a short stay in St. Petersburg, he returned to Tiflis. It was here that he met Fathali Akhundzadeh, who was twenty-two in 1834, and, according to Fereydun Adamiyyat, took him under his wing. Their friendship continued for many years, but Bakikhanov, at this time, did not have an official position to help his young friend in his career. In fact, Akhundzadeh was appointed as the Oriental Interpreter of the governor of the Caucasus, the same job that Bakikhanov had some years earlier.

In 1836 Bakikhanov returned to Qobbeh and most of the time lived on the estate of his father in the village of Amsar. In Qobbeh he began writing the *Golestan-e Eram* and some of his other works, and he also established a literary circle called *Golestan*. Many eminent scholars and writers visited him, among them the French traveler de Suzannet, the German botanist Koch, and the Russian orientalist Bérézine, who all mention him in their works. A year later the peace and quiet of the life in the village of Amsar was broken by a large peasant uprising against the Tzar's government, and, though ruthlessly suppressed, it put an end to the governorship of Baron Rosen. Given the relationship between Rosen and Bakikhanov, he was bound to be called for interrogation. He was summoned to Tiflis and was not allowed to go back until the rebellion had been put down. Although Bakikhanov did not have any dealings with the rebels, he opposed the harsh autocratic rule of Baron Rosen. He wrote a report in Russian entitled 'Edifications' for the committee that was investigating the causes of the uprising, and it is recorded on October 19, 1837, as "the manifesto of Colonel Abbasquli against Baron Rosen."[10]

While living in Amsar at least three European travelers visited Bakikhanov. The French traveler Comte de Suzannet visited him in Qobbeh in 1840 and mentions him in his *Souvenirs de voyages. Les provinces du Caucase, l'empire du Bresil* (Paris, 1846) as a well-read and knowledgeable historian of the Caucasus. He in particular says that Bakikhanov was trying hard to publish his *Golestan-e Eram*. The German botanist Karl Koch, who traveled twice in Russia and the Caucasus before and after 1840, also refers to "his historical work in Persian that he himself has translated into Russian and has been waiting

---

10. For the text see Suleyman Alyarov, *Azarbycan Tarixi Uzra Qaynaqlar* (Baku, 1889), pp. 306-09.

for its publication by the Academy of St. Petersburg."[11] Lastly, the well-known Russian orientalist Ilya Nikolaevitch Bérézine, who, at the beginning of his career, visited Daghestan, Caucasus and Persia, and stayed with Bakikhanov for two days in the early 1840's and enjoyed his incomparable "Oriental hospitality."[12] Bérézine says: "Bakikhanov is busy writing the story of the whole of Daghestan based on Oriental authors, a most important work, which unfortunately remains unpublished."[13] They had lively scholarly discussions on a variety of subjects. Bérézine wrote that Bakikhanov had a deep love for the people of Qobbeh, whom he considered to be "the descendants of the ancients Algons or Alans and the latter are the descendants of the Massagetes, basing himself, among others, on the fact that some inhabitants of Qobbeh speak an incomprehensible language, which must be the Alan language."[14] Bakikhanov displays his interest in archeology and says that he believes "there is a submerged Shahr-e Yunan near Baku." He said that once the chief-commander of Georgia at his request had examined the site, but nothing was found.[15]

It seems that for a long time before beginning *Golestan-e Eram*, Bakikhanov was contemplating writing a history of Shirvan and Darband, and he had gradually gathered materials for it. In 1829, the weekly *Tiflisskii domoisty* published an article about a forthcoming translation of the *Darband-nameh* by Bakikhanov, and it printed some passages from it. It seems that a few months after the Golestan treaty of 1813 Bakikhanov had begun working on a Russian translation of the *Darband-nameh*, and wanted to prepare its text for publication as well.[16] Bakikhanov often refers to this work in the *Golestan-e Eram*, but his Russian translation was never published. Furthermore, at the request of General Paskevitch, from 1829 Bakikhanov was a member of the research committee on Trans-Caucasia, and he had easy access to government documents and related historical works. Apparently, he wrote at least four articles or reports on the history of the Caucasus, although none of them have survived. One was "The Origin of the Caucasian Tribes," the other "A Look at the History of the Lands Acquired by Russia." His biographer Habib Oghlu mentions two other works, which were written after 1837. They are "Notes on the Administration of the Moslem Lands of Caucasia," which was undertaken at recommendation of the above-mentioned committee investigating the rebellion of 1837. "The History of the Baku Khanate" was another work devoted to the history of his own family, and his forefathers[17].

It was the military commander of Daghestan, Moisey Zakharavich Arguinski Dolgorukov, who urged Bakikhanov to write a comprehensive history of Shirvan, Dagh-

---

11. C. H. E. Koch, *Reise durch Russland nach dem kaukischen Isthmus, in den Jahren 1836, 1837 und 1838.* (Stuttgart-Tubingen, 1842).
12. Ilya Nikolaevitch Bérézine, *Puteshestvie po Severnoi Persii* (Kazan, 1852) the first part of which has been translated into French by Jacqueline Calmard-Compas as *Voyage au Daghestan et en Transcaucasie* (Paris, 2006).
13. Bérézine, *Voyage*, p. 142.
14. Bérézine, *Voyage*, p. 148.
15. Bérézine, *Voyage*, p. 189.
16. Ra'isniya, "Gozari," p. 213.
17. Habib Oghlu, *Abbas Quli Aga*, pp. 264-65, 77.

estan and Darband, from the ancient times until 1813, the work that later on was called *Golestan-e Eram*. Obviously after the treaties of Turkmanchay and Golestan, the Russian domination was a new chapter in the history of the Caucasus, and the family of Bakikhanov had no small role in this history. He himself had been actively involved in the treaty of Golestan and it is the ending point of his history. Hence, the name of *Golestan-e Eram*. Golestan is the village in Qarabagh, where the treaty was signed in 1813. Henceforth Iran lost all its territories to the north of the Aras River and was forced to recognize Russia's authority over them. Sir Gore Ouseley, the British envoy to Iran served as mediator and it was signed by Mirza Abol-Hasan Khan Ilchi and Nikolai Fyodorovich Rtischev, respectively for the Persian and Russian side.

It took him almost a year and half to finish the *Golestan-e Eram*. This was 1838 when General E.A. Golovin had replaced Baron Rosen, and Bakikhanov was recalled to service, and soon thereafter he became a colonel. It was an opportunity for him to try and publish his work. While living in Tiflis in 1843, Bakikhanov translated the *Golestan-e Eram* into Russian with the help of a Polish officer and friend, Zabloteski as "The History of Eastern Caucasia."[18] This translation was submitted for publication to General Pendgart, who had replaced Golovin, and eventually, with a recommendation from the Minister of Defense, it went to the Secretariat of Tzar Nicolas I in March 1845. The book was well received and a diamond ring, worth 800 *manats*, was given to Bakikhanov as an award. The royal favor did not result in publication. The work was sent for evaluation to two professors at the Imperial Academy of Sciences in St Petersburg, B.A. Dorn and M.F. Brosset, who were experts on the history and affairs of the Caucasus. Bakikhanov had initially asked for 3,000 *manats* for the publication of his history, but after a year of deliberation, it was announced that as "this work could not stand up to European scholarly criticism, it is not wise to be published by Russian governmental institutions. But the author can publish it at his own expense."[19]

In 1845, while Bakikhanov was trying to publish his work in Tiflis, he managed to get a year's leave of absence from the Office of the Military Commander of the Caucasus to which he still was affiliated. In the following year, in the company of his friend Hajji Molla Abdollah, the qadi of Qobbeh, and a few of his literary friends, he decided to undertake the pilgrimage to Mecca. They traveled via Ardabil, Tabriz and Tehran. It is said that Bakikhanov stayed one month in Tabriz and more than two months in Tehran, where he was admitted to the audience of Mohammad Shah and was awarded a medal of the order of the Lion and the Sun.[20] Bakikhanov wanted to continue his journey via Baghdad but apparently at the advice of Prince Dimitri Dolgorukov (known in Persian as Kinyaz Dalguroki), the Russian minister to Persia in 1846-54, he goes to Istanbul and after traveling to Cairo he went to Mecca. He reached Istanbul in September 1846 and met with 'Abdul-Majid I and dedicated the book that he had written on astronomy in Arabic (*Asrar al-Malakut* or Celestial Secrets) to him. Two years later this book, along with its

---

18. *Istoriya Vostochnoy Chasti Kavkaza.*
19. Habib Oghlu, *Abbas Quli Aga*, p. 77.
20. Habib Oghlu, *Abbas Quli Aga*, p. 344.

Turkish translation, was published in Istanbul.²¹ After performing the pilgrimage, on his way back to the Caucasus, Bakikhanov died in January 1847 of the plague in a place called Wadi Fatimah, between Mecca and Medina and was buried there.

It is interesting to compare Bakikhanov and Akhundzadeh, the two very first Azeri pro-western intellectuals and writers in the nineteenth century. Though very liberal-minded and against the fanaticism of the religious masses as well as of the clergy, Bakikhanov was a religious man and especially fond of Sufism. On the contrary, Akhundzadeh gave a materialistic interpretation to the works of a man like Rumi. As Rahim Ra'is-niya puts it: "While 'Abbas Qoli Aqa like Akhundzadeh believes in the salvation of mankind from backwardness through science and learning, unlike him [Bakikhanov] believes in the harmony between science and faith. In other words, with a foot in the past he was facing the future."²² Although both men were influenced by Russian culture and its government, it would seem that this was less so in Bakikhanov's case. Akhundzadeh in his plays often propagates Russian rule, while Bakikhanov wrote a report criticizing the repressive rule of Baron Rosen. After his retirement from political and military life, Bakikhanov devoted himself to scholarship, which indicates a disillusion with the government, though he could not openly display it. At one time, he wanted to establish a Moslem college in Baku and an Oriental languages school in Tiflis. In 1832, he proposed that the government establish a school for Moslems where modern subjects would be taught in Russian as well as Azeri and Persian. But given Bakikhanov's relations with Baron Rosen it never materialized. The project was sent to the governor of the Caucasus for approval but unfortunately was disregarded and never looked into. Bakikhanov also translated several fables by Ivan Krylov into Azeri; however, only one has been preserved. His greatest accomplishment in the field of education was writing *Qanun-e Qodsi*, the first Persian grammar manual published in history.

In many ways Bakikhanov and Akhundzadeh were similar. Akhundzadeh was the first Azeri playwright and tried in his plays as well as his other prose works to criticize the social injustices and vices connected with the feudal governments of the East as well as the ignorance and fanaticism of the people. Satirical plays for him were a means of reform. He said: "In the experience of European philosophers nothing is more effective in uprooting vices and evils than criticism, derision and ridicule."²³ Also, Akhundzadeh devised a new alphabet to make learning in Azeri and Persian easier, and a number of intellectuals and writers followed him. Bakikhanov tried to bring about reform through education. After submitting his proposal for schools in Baku and Tiflis, he went further, and wrote a number of text books through which students were expected to learn Persian in a shorter time.²⁴ Among his nine works that he enumerates at the end of the *Golestan-e*

---

21. Mohammad 'Ali Tarbiyat, *Daneshmandan-e Azerbaijan*, ed. Gholam-Reza Tabataba'i Majid, (Tehran, 1375/1996), p. 442. The Turkish translation is entitled *Afkar-e Jabarut*.
22. Ra'isniya, "Gozari," p. 208.
23. Hasan Javadi, *Satire in Persian Literature* (London, Fairleigh Dickensen University Press, 1988), p. 257.
24. On this subject see E.R. Yaqubi, "A. Bakikhanov və Savad Tə'limi məsəlisi" in *Professor Məmməd Mübariz Əlizadənin Anadan Olmasının 90 illiyi Münasibətil Materialları* (Baku, 2001), pp. 249 ff.

Eram is *Qanun-e Qodsi*, on teaching Persian grammar to the students, to be used both in Azeri and Russian schools. He wrote it in 1831 and translated it into Russian in 1841. It was the third printed Azeri book to be published in Tiflis in 1831.[25] He has a number of other educational works, *Asar-e Malakut*, mentioned earlier. Originally it was written in Persian and then translated into Arabic. Similarly his work on "Geography" was written in Persian. These two works on astronomy and geography respectively, compared the ideas of the ancients with the insights of modern science. *Kashf al-Ghara'eb* or 'Discovery of Wonders' is about the discovery of America. He wrote another work entitled *Tahdhib al-Akhlaq*, or 'Moral Purity,' which discusses Islamic teachings and compares them with Greek philosophy and Western values. In most of these works Bakikhanov tries to find a middle ground between Western and Eastern values and teachings.

His most outstanding work is the *Golestan-e Eram*, which may be said to constitute a new beginning in Azerbaijani and perhaps in Persian historiography. Bakikhanov divided the *Golestan-e Eram* into five sections: the first covers the earliest times to the Arab conquest; the second part takes the history of Shirvan and Daghestan to the Mongol invasion; the third period takes us to the establishment of the Safavid state and the demise of the Shirvanshah dynasty; the fourth covers the Safavid state and the reign of Nader Shah; and the last part takes us from the death of this king to the Golestan treaty of 1813, and the peace between Russia and Iran. Although dynastic rules and wars between various kings and khans play an important role in these divisions, the settlement of different ethnic groups and tribes, as well as their languages, customs, religions, and ethnic qualities are given much prominence.

He was very much influenced by European and Russian historiography. According to Adamiyyat, he was particularly influenced by the Russian historian Nicholas Karamazin (1766-1826). Concerning the Avars, Turks, Khazars, Russians, etc. Bakikhanov quotes him several times, and follows his methodology. As Karamazin prepared himself to write his twelve-volume history of Russia by reading Livy and Tacitus, Bakikhanov made use of Classical sources, especially Plutarch and Strabo, in giving an account of the ancient Caucasus. But these were not the only sources he used. He had access to Persian, Arabic, Turkish, Russian, Georgian and Armenian sources. He made use of coins, architectural remains and whatever document he could find. Obviously, since this period was prior to the advancement in the study of ancient Iran, like the deciphering of the cuneiform script and the publication of the Avesta, Bakikhanov depended on the then-available sources in these areas. His account of the Pishdadi kings of Iran is mostly taken from the *Shahnamah*, and his descriptions of the exploits of Alexander in the Caucasus are based on the Alexander romance by Nezami of Ganjeh and on Islamic traditions, which ultimately come from the Pseudo-Callisthenes tradition of *Eskander-namehs*. In the case Babak Khorramdin, he just follows the Islamic traditions and simply states that he was a follower of the Magi. In short, in areas such as these, which constitute the very first part of the book, he follows the

---

25. See Hasan Javadi, "Azeri Publications in Iran", *Critique,* Spring 1996, pp. 79-88.

traditional historians, whereas in the remainder of the book he judiciously tries to put all available sources together.

At the very beginning Bakikhanov describes his method of historiography which is very revealing:

> I gathered different subjects, connected them and whatever was remaining compared it with oral history. When writing a book it is necessary to present the subject in a simple and concise manner, give the events sequentially, and connect them properly and avoid national prejudice and siding with your own country. Also to provide references to every subject from trustworthy sources, as well as to correspondence and edicts of the kings, coins, remains of buildings, and different sayings of different people on related subjects I tried as much as possible, and resolved the points of difference with conjectures and logical assumptions.

Of particular interest are "not siding with your own country" and "avoiding national prejudice" (*ejtenab az ta'assob-e mellat*). The latter in reality means "religious prejudice" because "nation" in this period means *mellat-e Islam*. It is to his credit that, as a historian, Bakikhanov tries to be above partisanship. This reminds one of the saying of that classical Persian historian Beyhaqi who said: "When I decided to write this history I made sure that what I wrote would be after my own examination or from a trustworthy source."

Although Dorn and Brosset considered the *Golestan-e Eram* to be of insufficient scholarly quality to be published by the Russian government, other scholars were more positive about Bakikhanov's work. Barthold referred to Bakikhanov's *Golestan-e Eram* and its Russian version in his work on 'The Regions around the Caspian in Islamic History', and he furthermore states that the Azeri scholar Hasan Effendi al-Qaderi in his work 'Traces of Daghestan's Past' (*Athari az Daghestan-e Gozashteh*) (1890) also had used Bakikhanov's work.[26] Minorsky commented that Bakikhanov had used "ancient classical, Russian and Western European sources. He did not succeed in bringing them into harmony with the Oriental sources, but these latter he has presented in a coherent digest with valuable additions for the eighteenth-nineteenth centuries." He further noted that Bakikhanov had provided new identification for place names mentioned in the *Darband-nameh*.[27]

As the editor of the *Golestan-e Eram*, Abdul-Karim Alizadeh, points out, apart from dealing with the history of Daghestan and Shirvan, Bakikhanov carried out interesting researches on Baku and its Apsheron Peninsula. Based on Pliny and Strabo's information, Bakikhanov concludes that the name of the village Zekh is derived from the name of a tribe with the same name, and similarly the name of the village Mashgata' is associated with the ancient Massagets. He also compares and contrasts the customs and manners of

---

26. Vasilii Vladimirovich Barthold, *Mesto prikaspiiskikh oblastei istorii musul'manskogo mira* (Moscow, 1963) translated into Persian by Layla Robensheh as *Jayegah-e manateq-e atraf-e darya-ye Khazar dar tarikh-e jahan-e Islam* (Tehran, 1375/1996), p. 160.
27. Vladimir Minorsky, *A History of Sharvan and Darband* (Cambridge, 1958), p. 9.

different people and localities. Bakikhanov goes into the origins of villages such as Bilgah, Zirah, Bibi-Heybat and others. For instance, he discusses a paved road which had existed between Baku and some off-shore islands, which later were submerged under the waters of the Caspian Sea. This came to light while drilling a well in Baku, which went below the sea level. Bakikhanov also suggests that there was a submerged town in the distance of eight miles from the coast between Baku and Saliyan.

The importance of Bakikhanov's work, in our view, is that for the first time there was a book by a native from the Caucasus who critically assessed and analyzed the history of his multi-ethnic region and did so in an admirable manner. Furthermore, as Minorsky also had observed, he provided much interesting information on the history of the Caucasus in the eighteenth and nineteenth century that was not available elsewhere. Also, the work may not have met the academic standards of Dorn and Brosset, but neither they nor anybody else has written a history of Shirvan and Daghestan and, to this day, it remains virtually the only book available on the subject. There are certainly better books or articles on specific subjects dealt with by Bakikhanov, but anybody who wants to read only one book on the history of Shirvan and Daghestan has no choice but this one. Moreover, his final chapter is still a mine of information for any scholar dealing with this period, for there is no better alternative. Finally, Bakikhanov also showed that despite the differences in language, religion, and ethnicity all the peoples living in the Caucasus shared a common history and to a certain extent also an identity that was different from the populations of the adjacent larger states such as that of the Ottoman Turks and the Persians, although they shared religious and historical ties with them a lesson that seems to have been lost on the current generation inhabiting the same geographical area.[28]

Although this is an English translation we have nevertheless decided to provide the Persian, Arabic and Azeri texts of the poems that Bakikhanov has offered, so that readers may better enjoy these, as our rendering of these poems are unfortunately not equal to the poetic quality of the original. Also, we have indicated in the English translation, in bold numbers, the end of each page in the Persian original[29] so that those readers may easily refer to this text.

We have kept the footnotes to a minimum and rather than provide detailed explanations we refer the reader to relevant literature that is provided in the footnote concerned. We also, where possible, have tried to provide references to English language materials,

---

28. This certainly is the case with Zia Bunyatov, who has made an incomplete and defective Russian translation of Bakikhanov's text. Not only has he not translated any of the poems in the text, but he does not even mention that he has not done so, while he does not translate certain other prose parts of the text without indicating this and why. This is in particular disturbing because he suppresses, for example, the mention of territory inhabited by Armenians, thus not only falsifying history, but also not respecting Bakikhanov's dictum that a historian should write without prejudice, whether religious, ethnic, political or otherwise. See George A. Bournoutian, *Two Chronicles on the History of Qarabagh* (Costa Mesa, 2004), pp. 265-69.

29. We have used the Baku edition of the *Golestan-e Eram*, ed. Abd al-Karim Ali-zada (Baku, 1970) as the basis for our translation. There is also a Tehran reprint of this edition (*Golestan-e Eram. Tarikh-e Shirvan va Daghestan* (Tehran, 1382/2003 and 1383/2004), but it has a different pagination.

and only when no relevant book or article is available in English we list materials in other languages. If the text of a footnote is by Bakikhanov then this is indicated at the end of the note by [B]. The Baku editor of the *Golestan-e Eram* on occasion gives variant readings from the different manuscripts used for his edition. The manuscript source concerned for each variant reading is indicated by T or B; both manuscripts are kept in the National Archives in Baku and for their precise identification we refer the reader to the English introduction of the Persian text edition.

Because the governors of Darband play such an important role in this text we have provided a list of the known governors of Darband as an appendix, as well as, of the chiefs (*Nowsal*) of the Avars, who also are mentioned. For information on the Shamkhal, the ruler of the Qomuq and of the Usmi, the ruler of the Qeytaq, who were major players in local Caucasian politics, the reader is referred to Willem Floor's forthcoming article entitled, "Who were the Shamkhal and the Usmi?"

Without the help of Rahim Ra'is-niya (Tabriz), Moharram Ghasemov (Baku), and Rafael Huseynov (Baku) and Mohammad Tajahmady (Paris) we would not have been able to provide many particulars about the life of Bakikhanov or to understand the difficult Azeri poems. We also would like to thank Turkhan Gerb (Baku) and John Emerson (Boston) for providing some of the illustrations.

Willem Floor and Hasan Javadi,
January 2009

PREFACE OF
THE HEAVENLY ROSE-GARDEN

In the Name of God, the Merciful and the Compassionate

Oh God, praising you should be in such a way that you know best. In describing you this much suffices that you are not in need of it. What can we do, because our praise, according to our understanding, explaining and describing of you, is but an illusion.

> *Quatrain*
> Knowing you is fathoming difficulties
> Defining your qualities is describing your essence.
> We do not acknowledge our ignorance
> As that is the foundation of the glory of existence.

دانش بتو عین مشکلات است
تعیین صفت بیان ذات است
اقرار بجهل هم نیاریم
کان پایه فخر کاینات است

Furthermore, our nature, without reservation, is inclined to the science of history, and, regardless of real events, is also inclined to legends, and makes mankind acquainted with virtues and learning as well as with the ways of life, tolerance and civilization.

Therefore, history has been considered to be one of the most spiritual sciences. We can say that it is a system of governance without oppression and tyranny that makes mankind adhere to its rules. In the school of its learning the learned teachers are like starting children and history is life-inspiring that in one moment brings to life the dead of millennia past. People of different centuries like on the day of resurrection each one in its own dress, manner, character and tradition, row in row, having their life accounts in their hands, come to account for themselves. Without bias, they will receive the result of their good and bad deeds, whether with approval or disapproval, from the viewers. It is a silent speaker, who gives the recommendation of the ancestors to the descendants with details and explains the reasons of poverty and wealth as well as of rise and decline. The nature of the future he gives in the form of the past, so that you may take a lesson from it. Indeed, the manner of the past is the manual for the future, because a deed based on learning lasts forever. Beginning a work without knowing the changes of time [1] is like passing through a desert without roads, which is dangerous. A person who gains experience in the short time of his life profits tremendously from it. The science of history gives us the life experience of the world. What better than this? Especially the history of every nation about the land that it inhabits is valuable from the point of view of knowing the nature of the land and the characteristics of the people, information about the neighboring peoples, results of relations with different groups, and good and bad pertaining to them. Therefore, this humble author without much accomplishment, who is always eager to improve himself, 'Abbas Qoli, known as Qodsi, son of Mirza Mohammad Khan the Second of Baku, has collected the events that have occurred in different ages in Shirvan and Daghestan, and neighboring lands, and, in spite of being aware of the difficulties of the work, has proceeded with writing this book. I hope that the learned readers to forgive its shortcomings due to its author's lack of capability, upheavals in his life, shortness of time, and that they will try to improve it:

It is a good habit to cover the faults of others
This magnificent dress covers everyone's faults.

پوشیدن عیب دگران خصلت خوبست
این خلعت فاخر همه را ستر عیوبست

Histories and remains of no land can describe in proper detail the events of the past. This land especially, because of the coming and going of many different peoples, was the place of disturbances, chaos and upheaval, and many books and documents and buildings and artifacts have perished. The books of other nations have not explained these matters in a suitable manner. However, according to the famous saying, "if you do not comprehend all of it, it does not mean that you are abandoning all of it." Therefore, from whatever was available I gathered different subjects, connected them and whatever was remaining compared it with oral history. When writing a book it is necessary to present the subject in a simple and concise manner, give the events sequentially, and connect them properly and avoid national prejudice and siding with your own country. Also to provide references to every subject from [2] trustworthy sources, as well as to correspondence and edicts of the kings, coins, remains of buildings, and different sayings of different people on related subjects I tried as much as possible to resolve the points of difference with conjectures and logical assumptions. I organized the book with one introduction and five chapters and one conclusion.

This manuscript dated 1257 [1841], which is the date of its composition and I called it Golestan-e Eram.

INTRODUCTION

> Describing the borders, lands, the reason for the names, the situation, languages, and religions of the country of Shirvan and Daghestan.

FIRST CHAPTER.

> Concerning the description of ancient events of Shirvan and Daghestan until the coming of the Arab army and after the advent of Islam.

SECOND CHAPTER.

> From the time of the arrival of the Arabs until the time of the Mongols.

THIRD CHAPTER.

> From the time of the Mongol invasion until the rise of the Safavids and the Shirvani dynasty.

FOURTH CHAPTER.

> From the time of the Safavids to the death of Nader Shah.

FIFTH CHAPTER.

> From the death of Nader Shah until the signing of the Treaty between Russia and Iran in the village of Golestan.

CONCLUSION.

> Concerning the people of the country of Shirvan and neighboring places who are authors or have distinguished themselves by other accomplishments.

The Bayat Gate at the southern entrance of the city of Darband.
From: A. V. Williams Jackson, *From Constantinople to the Home of Omar Khayyam*.

INTRODUCTION

Describing the borders, lands, reason for their names, the situation, languages and religions of the country of Shirvan and Daghestan. [4]

The country of Shirvan to the east borders on the Caspian Sea, and to the south on the river Kur, which separates it from the provinces of Moghan and Armenia.[1] From the north-west on the river Qaneq and with an undefined line it goes to the region of Ilisu and the high mountains of the Caucasus. The mountain chain that distinguishes the region of the Kur and Tabarsaran from the land of the Ghazi-Qomuq and the Qeytaq continues from the course of the river Darvaq until the place where it joins the Caspian Sea borders on the sea, from the estuary of the river Kur until the estuary of the Darvaq from 39 to 43 degrees North and from the estuary of the Qaneq to the top of the mountains of Afsharan from 64 to 68 degrees Eastern longitude. The distance of each degree is nearly 15 geographical miles and every geographical mile is seven Russian versts, or 1.5 *farsakh*. Every *farsakh* is three Islamic *mil*, and every Islamic *mil* is 96,000 *angosht*. Each *angosht* is on average six barley corns (*jov*), if they are put one after the other.[2]

Thus, present day Shirvan with Saliyan, Sheki, Baku, Qobbeh, Darband, Tabarsaran and Kur and the region of Samuriyeh and some parts of lower Ilisu is part of that and constitutes the largest and the best part of this country. The big mountain chain of the Caucasus, which faces the south-east and faces the winter-quarters that have good weather and grazing, wonderful streams and many rivers, which flow down from both its sides and mostly into the vast and fertile valleys on the shore of the sea and the banks of the river

---

1. For the geography of Shirvan see Minorsky, *A History of Sharvan*, pp. 75-77. Abbas-Kuli-aga Bakikhanov, *Giulistan-i Iram* translated and with commentary by Zia M. Bunyatov (Baku, 1991), p. 11, where the translator has deleted the words `and Armenia' from the text, which shows, as indicated in the Introduction, that his translation should be used with circumspection, because this is not the only example of omissions from Bakikhanov's text.
2. For more information on Islamic weights and measurements see Walther Hinz, *Islamische Masse und Gewichte* (Leiden, 1971). For the weights and measures used in Iran see Willem Floor, "Weights and Measures in Qajar Iran," *Studia Iranica* 37 (2008), pp. 57-115.

Kur, are the cause of abundance of wheat, forests, orchards and other products. Because of their existence near the sea, between Russia and Iran and the many tribes of Daghestan, the affairs of trade are very brisk.

The author[3] of the *Taqvim al-Boldan* says that Shirvan was built by the Sasanian [king] Anushirvan [4] the Just[4] and [bore his name]; therefore, by dropping the letter 'anu' [from his name], due to long usage [its name] has become Shirvan. Some people say that it is called Shirvand, i.e., the place of lions, and eventually [it became] Shirvan. In the history of Moses of Khoren[5] and the book of Zand-Avesta it is known as Shiruvan. Amir Ahmad in his book *Haft Eqlim*[6] says that Shirvan was first the name of the city; after that it became the name of the province. Chamchiyan in the Armenian history[7] calls the province of Shirvan Aghvan, which borders on [the lands of the] Alans, that is, Daghestan.[8] First, it was the wall of Alghun and then the wall of Darband. In an edict that Soltan Ya'qub b. Hasan the Turkman king has given in the year 892/1487 to the Armenian Katholikos it is called Aghvan.[9] The land of Daghestan extends from 42 to 44 degrees Northern latitude and from 63 to 66 degrees Eastern longitude: from the east to the Caspian Sea and from the north to the river Terek and from the east to the land of the Circassians and the Ossetians and from the south-west to Georgia. From the south-east it is bordered by Shirvan. The north-western part of it is known for its good situation and its abundance of live necessities, especially on the sea shore and the banks of the river Terek. Because of inundation by the rivers and the coming and going of people it is known for agriculture and advantages of trade. In the other part, which is a mountain chain, life is extremely dif-

---

3. Abu'l-Feda Esma'il b. 'Ali (1273 - 1331), *Taqvim al-Boldan*, translated into Persian by 'Abdol-Mohammad Ayati (Tehran, 1349/1970).

4. Khosrow I Anushirvan the Just (r. 531 - 579) is the most famous of the Sasanian kings. On the Sasanian dynasty see Ehsan Yarshater ed. *The Cambridge History of Iran* (henceforth cited as *CHI*), vol. 3, The Seleucid, Parthian and Sasanian Periods (Cambridge, 1983).

5. Moses Khorenats'i, *Patmuti'wn Hayots'* translated into English as *The History of the Armenians* by Robert W. Thompson (Cambridge, 1978).

6. Amin Ahmad al-Razi, *Haft Iqlim, the geographical and biographical encyclopedia* ed. E. Denison Ross et al. 3 vols. (Calcutta, 1919-1939).

7. Ch'amch'yants' Mik'ayel, *Patmuti'wn Hayots'* (Erevan, 1984-85), originally published in (Venetik: Petros Vaghvazeants', 1784-1786) and translated from the original Armenian into English by Johannes Avdall as: Father Michaele Chamich. *History of Armenia; from B. C. 2247 to the year of Christ 1780, or 1229 of the Armenian era, To which is appended a continuation of the history by the translator from the year 1780 to the present date.* 2 vols. (Calcutta, Printed at Bishop's College Press, by H. Townsend, 1827).

8. Caucasian Albania, Aghbania or Aghvan was an ancient kingdom in what is now southern Daghestan and most of Azerbaijan. See Movses Daskhurants'i, *History of the Caucasian Albanians*, translated by C.J.F. Dowsett (London, 1961).

9. For the Persian text of this decree see A. D. Papaziyan, *Persidskie dokumenty Matenadarana* (Erivan, 1956), p. 254 (doc. 6). Soltan Ya'qub (r. 1478 - 1490) was the last king of the Aq-Qoyunlu dynasty who reigned over an undivided realm, for after his death a succession war broke out. For more information see John E. Woods, *The Aqquyunlu. Clan, Federation, Empire* (Minneapolis, 1976).

ficult, although it has some fertile lands in some valleys and good winter quarters. According to Mas'udi,[10] in the year 332/922 this land consisted of three kingdoms.

First, the kingdom of the Qeytaq, which is situated between Darband and the North.[11] Its capital is Samandar. Anushirvan built it and it became the capital of the Khazar Khaqans.[12] When Salman b. Rabi'eh took it the *Khaqan* moved his capital to Atal.[13] Most of the people of Samandar [5] are Khazars, Moslems and Jews. Ibn Hawqal[14] says that the people of Rus in the year 358/969 took Samandar which had many buildings and gardens and destroyed them all.

The second kingdom is that of Sarir, which is in the north-west and at three stages from Darband and it has 12,000 families. The king of Sarir is called Filanshah who is a Christian.[15] According to some, Yazdegerd the Sasanian[16] who was defeated by the Arabs and went to Khorasan took his golden throne with other treasures and sent them with one of his officials, who was of the lineage of Bahram Chubin,[17] to conquer the Mountains of Victories, i.e., the Caucasus. He conquered the land, which is now known as Sarir [meaning, throne], and left it to his descendants. The reason for calling it this, according to Nezami, is because of the crown and throne of Key Khosrow, which were here in a cave. Some say that the rulers of this land used to sit on a golden throne and governed. The Amir of Sarir considered his subjects his slaves and he attacked the Khazars. Because the mountain people are more courageous than the people of the plains they raided them. Near the capital of the king there are makers of chain-mail, who are now called *kupechi*.[18] They are Moslems, Christians and Jews.

The third kingdom is that of the Qomuq Mountains,[19] which border in the north on Sarir and in the west on Qeytaq. They are Christians who obeyed lords and they do not

---

10. Al-Mas'udi, *Muruj al-Dhahab va ma'adin al-jowhar* 4 vols. (Beirut, 1973) translated as *The Meadows of Gold, The Abbasids* by Paul Lunde and Caroline Stone (London and New York, 1989). For an English translation of Mas'udi's chapter XVII on the Caucasus see Minorsky, *A History of Sharvan*, Annex III, pp. 142-65.

11. On the Qeytaq see Minorsky, *A History of Sharvan*, pp. 92-95 and Samuel Gottlieb Gmelin, *Reise durch Ruszland zur Untersuchung der drey Naturreiche* 4 vols. (St. Petersburg, 1770-1784), of which vols. 3 and 4 have been translated into English by Willem Floor as *Travels through Northern Persia 1770-1774* (Washington DC, 2007), pp. 303-06.

12. On the Khazars see W. Barthold, "Khazar," *Encyclopedia of Islam* and Minorsky, *A History of Sharvan*, pp. 105-07. On Samandar see Douglas Morton Dunlop, "Samandar," *Encyclopedia Judaica*.

13. On Salman b. Rabi'eh see Minorsky, *A History of Sharvan*, pp. 13, 18, 106, 146. On Atal or Itil see Douglas Morton Dunlop, *The History of the Jewish Khazars* (Princeton, 1954); Ibid., "Itil," *Encyclopedia Judaica*.

14. Mohammad Ibn Hawqal, *Kitab Surat al-Ard* translated into French by J.H. Kramers and G. Wiet as *La configuration de la terre* 2 vols. (Paris, 1964).

15. See Minorsky, *A History of Sharvan*, pp. 97-101, 155.

16. Yazdegerd III (r. 632 - 651) was the last Sasanian king.

17. Bahram VI Chubin (r. 590 - 591) was an army general and head of the house of Mehran and, although not a member of the royal Sasanian family, became a usurper king of Iran. For more information see A. Sh. Shahbazi, "Bahram", *Encyclopedia Iranica*.

18. See Minorsky, *A History of Sharvan*, pp. 92, 155.

19. On the Qomuq or Kumyk see Minorsky, *A History of Sharvan*, pp. 96-97.

have a king. From here they go to the lands of the Alans, which is very fertile.[20] The villages are so near that when a cock crows all the cocks crow together. They called the king of the Alans Gergerandaj or Kergendaj. His wife was called Maghas. He had 30,000 troops. One of his forefathers in the first century [*hijri*] in the time of the 'Abbasid caliphs accepted Christianity; before that he was a fireworshipper. In the year 320/932, he abandoned this religion and expelled the priests that the Byzantine emperor had sent him. Between the Alans and the Victory Mountains (*Fath*) there is a fort on the top of a mountain and beside a river that has a bridge, [6] which is called *Hesn Bab al-Alan* (Fort of the Alan Gate) and the passage to the mountain is only possible through it. This was one of the strongest forts and Persian poets have described it many times. It was built by the order of Esfandiyar. When Maslameh b. 'Abdol-Malek conquered most of the Caucasus he put Arab guards there to whom until this day provisions and wages are sent from the border town, which is Tiflis. The gate of Lazeqeh is in the region of Georgia and its king is a Moslem. On the western side of the Alans is the tribe of the Kashak, who are idol worshippers, and the kingdom of the Kashak extends from the Victory Mountains until the Pontus, i.e. the Black Sea. They are handsome and they make a fabric called *tala*, which is better than that of Egypt.[21] The merchants travel between the Kashak and Trabson by sea. They have ports on the coast and when the Alans invade them they take refuge there. They are numerous and scattered and if they were united they would conquer everyone. On the other side of their land are seven cities. The present author says that the Alan Gate, according to the Arabs, would be Daryal, of which the bridge and fort are still in existence up there.[22] There are many indications of Persian occupation of these lands. One of them is Daryal itself, which is an old Persian word, and [another is] the mountain Kishavar, which originally was Kuh-e Shapur or Kishapur as well as the place called Pasnavar, which was Pasin Avar. The Ossetians (Us) still have many old Persian names and verbs in their language, which they use with slight changes. They call themselves Iruni and their country Irunistan, just like the people of Fars call Irani in popular parlance Iruni.

The Kashak people are Circassians. Old Russian historians call them Kasog and the Ossetians are still called Kasaq. According to Mohammad Rafi' b. 'Abdol-Rahim Shirvani's *History*,[23] their land also consists of three countries. First is the valley, then Zerehgaran, and the third one is Avar, which, judging by their way of life and roads is one of the most inaccessible places. Chamchiyan in his history names four kingdoms. They are Alan, Baslas, Heptaq and Hun. The author of the *Darbandnameh*,[24] according to the division made by Esfandiyar and Anushirvan, writes that it is divided into four kingdoms. They are Golbakh, Molk-e Tumanshah [7], Qeytaq and the Qomuq Mountains. These

---

20. On this ethnic group see Agustí Alemany, *Sources on the Alans: A Critical Compilation* (Leiden, 2000) and Minorsky, *A History of Sharvan*, p. 107.
21. Kashak or Cherkes, see Minorsky, *A History of Sharvan*, pp. 157-58.
22. On the Daryal pass see Minorsky, *A History of Sharvan*, pp. 87, 107, 143, 161, 169.
23. This history is only known in excerpt and appended by Kazem-Beg to his translation of the *Derbend-nameh*, see next note. Minorsky, *A History of Sharvan*, p. 8.
24. Anonymous, *Derbend-nameh, or the History of Derbend* translated by Aleksandr Kazem-Beg (St. Petersburg, 1851).

divisions are in correspondence with to-day's division. The first kingdom is that of Alan or Golbakh-e Qomuq, which is on the other side of Sulaq, Machgach and Qobbehrti Minor. The second kingdom is that of Molk-e Tumanshah or Heptaq or Qeytaq, where the land of the Shamkhal is; the first part and the lower part is the land of the Usmi. The third land is that of the Qomuq Mountains or Hun or Avar. It is the land of the Ghazi-Qomuq or Avaristan. The fourth country is that of Baslas, Zerehgaran, Sarir or Qeytaq. According to the last division, the upper districts are considered to be Qeytaq, Aqusheh and Surhi. The name of the city of Bashli is the distorted form of Baslas. Qomuq, according to Ptolemy, is the remainder of the tribe of Kam and Kamak and the name of the land has been derived from it. According to the author of the *Rowzat al-Safa*[25] and others, they are of the lineage of Kamak or Kamari, who was the son of Jafeth. In a place called after his son the Bolghars are living and perhaps that is the place called Bolghar, which is situated in Qabarti minor. The people of Bolghar and its region, consisting of Chekam along with Khasan and Bezenki and others, are still speaking Turkish, in the Qomuq dialect. It seems that they are all from one tribe and this has been confirmed by the *Habib al-Siyar*[26] and other histories. After Emir Timur had defeated Toqtamesh Khan he brought the leaders of the army to the river Qomari and he gave them many presents. In the Isthmus of Qom he made his winter quarters. The name of this river has been derived from Komari and in Turkish is pronounced as Qomi [meaning sandy], as they say it now, and in Russian as Quma. The change of Alef to Vaf and Qaf to Ghaf and Gheyn is not impossible. One can imagine that Qeytaq and Heptaq have the same meaning and that they have been derived from one another, or from Tagh (Mountain), which, in general, was applied to Daghestan. The land of the Shamkhal is called Heptaq, which has been derived from Hep, i.e. 'all' and the country of the Usmi is called Keytaq due to the attribution to the Kayani kings[27] or in the meaning of 'big' and 'high.' Over [8] time, 'ta' has been changed to 'dal' and 'gheyn' to 'qaf' and in reverse.

The Hun people would be the same as Ghun and, according to Moses of Khoren,[28] in the fifth century AD they were living on the western shore of the Caspian Sea. The city of Varchan, whose site is now not known, was one of their big cities. These people were ugly, blood-thirsty, plunderers, and courageous. In ancient times they came from China to the Qebchaq steppe and from there to the area between the Black and the Caspian Sea. They committed many atrocities and their king Attila had utmost power and authority. He was devoid of greed and laziness. After a succession of victories he subjugated different peoples until he reached Vangaria. He received tribute from Constantinople. He died in the year 454.[29] Because of discord between his sons the state of the Huns came to an end.

---

25. Mohammad b. Khavandshah Mir Khvand, *Rowzat al-Safa fi sirat al anbiya' va'l-moluk va'l-kholafa* partially translated into English as *History of the early kings of Persia* (London, 1832) by David Shea.
26. Khvandamir. *Habib al-Seyar*, 4 vols. ed. Mohammad Dabir-Siyaqi. (Tehran, 1362/1983 [3rd. ed.])
27. The Kayanid or Sasanian dynasty ruled Iran from 226-651.
28. He is considered to be the Father of Armenian literature.
29. On the Huns see, for example, Otto Maenchen-Helfen, *World of the Huns; studies in their history and culture* (Berkeley, 1973).

Ammianus Marcellinus,[30] the historian of the fourth century AD, writes that "the tribe of Huns cut themselves with a knife so that they would not grow beards. They are mostly ugly and they have thick necks like animals. They eat the roots and leaves of trees and they put raw meat under their saddle to heat it and then they eat it. They do not have houses and they do not want them. They live in deserts, mountains and forests. Their clothes are from cotton and of animal skin, which rot on their body. They are accustomed to heat, cold, hunger and thirst. They come down from the back of their horse when they have a general meeting. They do not have any shame or good manners. They are plunderers, blood-thirsty, lawless, liars and faithless." Priscus,[31] who was one of the emissaries of Constantinople (*Rum*), says: "we met him in the camp and he very haughtily accepted the presents of the emperor and told us to follow him to a town, where we would rest. There girls in long white dresses came to welcome him. They were singing songs in the Scythian language. They had a building made of wood situated on a high place and it was surrounded by a wooden palisade. Every day he would sit in that house and he would attend to the people's business. During the day he would receive the emissaries of different peoples and at night he would banquet with them. The people gathered there would eat and drink from silver dishes and golden cups, but he himself would drink and eat from wooden utensils. After the banquets poets of the Huns would come forward [9] and recite poems celebrating his victories. His army would express joy and the old men, because of weaknesses and not being able to fight would weep in grief. Attila always was of a sour countenance, thoughtful, taciturn, and would caress his young son who was young and of whom astrologers had predicted that he would inherit all the arts of his father. The horse and armor of his generals were decorated with gold and precious stones, but he himself was devoid of all such ornaments. The Hun people, but also all the peoples under him, because of his justice and other great characteristics, loved him. Many Byzantines had come into his service. Atilla himself was not ugly and he was known because of his courage and magnanimity. He knew that one of the Byzantine emissaries wanted to kill him, but he did not punish him in order to humiliate him. Perhaps the Atal River is named after him, or he has been named after the river."

The reason that the people of the mountains are called Lezgi is because of the intermingling with the Laz people who at the end of the third century AD lived in Colchis and the king of the Sarmatians came from the Qebchaq steppe and defeated them. In the fifth century, with the Albanians and Iberians,[32] they were involved in the long Perso-Roman wars. Their kingdom still existed in the sixth and seventh century, and of their kings Ghubaz and Khuriyan were famous. The remainder of this people still inhabits the shores of the eastern Black sea. In their writings they call themselves Lazegi.[33] Most his-

---

30. Ammianus Marcellinus (325/330 - after 391) was a historian; whose great work was the history of the Roman Empire (*Res Gestae Libri XXXI*), translated into English as *The Later Roman Empire (354-378)* (Harmondsworth, 1986) by Walter Hamilton.
31. For details see [http://en.wikipedia.org/wiki/Priscus].
32. The Georgian kingdom of Kartli was called Iberia by the Greeks and Romans.
33. The Laz people are related to the Mingrelians (Georgians) and live in Lazona, a land later also known as the kingdom of Colchis, which encompassed modern Western Georgia and the Turkish provinces of Trabson and Rize. When the Romans conquered Colchis they turned it into the province of Lazicum, with Phasis (Poti) as its major center. For more

torians of Armenia, Iberia Colchis and Albania have not properly differentiated them and thus there is confusion. By comparing the sources it is very probable that the right bank of the river Kur, until where the Aras flows into it, was called Armenia. As Pliny and Ptolemy also have written the northern part of Armenia extends to the river Kur. The right bank of the river Kur where Tiflis, Domanisi, Bolnisi, and others are situated is called Sumokht, which in the Georgian language means Armenia. The Armenian people there are more numerous than the Georgians. According to the *Habib al-Siyar*, Habib b. Salami conquered Tiflis, which was inside Armenia in the time of the caliphate of Othman and it was always under the control of the caliphate as appears from the coins struck by the Arabs in Tiflis. Iberia was in the western mountains of Daghestan and the eastern side was Bash Achoq, just like the old Armenian historians call the ancient Georgians Ivuros[34] which means 'mountain.' According to Yaqut,[35] from the end of the fifth century *hijri*, the Georgians started to plunder and kill people on the right bank of the river Kur because of disturbances in the affairs of Iran. Until the time that Soltan Mahmud and Soltan Mas'ud,[36] the sons of Mohammad Saljuqi, were fighting with one another, [10] it was occupied by the Georgians. The plain lands of Bash Achoq,[37] Mingrelia,[38] Guria,[39] and Colchis may be counted among them and Shirvan and Daghestan together were considered to be Albania.

In the case of the Alans this much is known that the inhabitants of this place had special kings. Because of the affinity of the word Alan and Alban one can imagine that one is taken from the other; or Albania in the Latin (*Rumi*) word Alba, which alludes to freedom, and the lands of Shirvan and Daghestan were known as the land of free men.[40] In the words of Ammianus Marcellinus, the Alans are descended from the ancient Massagetes,[41] who originally came from Tartarestan, expelled the Scythian people from the eastern shore of the Caspian Sea and settled here. The Scythians crossed the Atal River (Volga) and occupied the lands from the river Don until the Danube. They are different tribes, wild and nomadic. The southern historians have called all the inhabitants of those places Scythians. Herodotus says that from the intermingling of the Scythians with the daughters of the

---

information see David Braun, *Georgia in antiquity: a history of Colchis and Transcaucasian Iberia 550 BC – AD 562* (Oxford, 1994).

34. Ivuros is derived from Iberi, the Greek name for Georgia, which in Georgian became Iveri and in Armenian Vêra.

35. Yaqut b. 'Abdallah al-Hamavi, *Mu`jam al-Buldan* partially translated as *Dictionnaire geographique, historique et litteraire de la Perse et des contrees adjacentes* by C.A. Barbier de Meynard (Paris, 1861).

36. See for details the *CHI*, vol. 5, pp. 113-20.

37. Bash Achoq, meaning uncovered head, is the Ottoman name for the Georgian land of Imereti situated in the upper Rioni river basin.

38. Mingrelia or Samegrelo, the low lands of Western Georgia, which border on the Black Sea.

39. Guriya is a region in the western part of Georgia, bordering on the Black Sea.

40. The word Albania may come from the Latin (*altus* or high) or from a non-Indo European root (*alb* or mountain) and in both cases means 'mountainous land.' For more information see M.L. Chamont, "Albania," *Encyclopedia Iranica*.

41. For more information see [http://en.wikipedia.org/wiki/Massagetae]. See also Minorsky, *A History of Sharvan*, p. 78.

Amazons the Sarmathians came into being.[42] But Gatterer[43] proves that the Sarmathians came 80 years BCE to Europe and in the neighborhood of the river Don mixed with the Scythians. Gradually the name Scythians was lost and the Sarmathians became famous. The people of Alan came; they put to flight the Sarmathians and occupied their lands. The Alans had the religion of sword worship, because they stuck it into the earth and worshipped it. In most of their customs they were like the Hun people.[44] Procopius[45] considers the Alans to be descended from the Massagetes, and the Massagetes are of the line of Get or Getov, which means Get Maior. In the book of the prophet Ezekiel, chapter 38, Masubiyan is known to be from the lineage of Masub, the son of Yafeth. They are a famous people among the North-eastern peoples. It may be that the Massagetae are from this tribe or from an intermingling of the Masub people and the Get. De Guignes[46] considers the word Alan to be from the word *alin*, which was a mountain, where a tribe of the Massagetes, in the old days when they were in the mountains of the Altai, were known as such. Moses Khorenats'i writes that the Alans were near the Caucasus and they were known from the time of Ptolemy until the fourteenth century in the northwestern mountains of the Caucasus. According to Mas'udi, the Alan Gate of the present day must be in Daryal in Georgia. But the author of the *Darband-nameh* says that the Alan gate was the Alghun wall, which was built by Esfandiyar and repaired by Anushirvan. The remains of that wall and the place of the gate and the ruins of the city can still be seen on the west bank of the river Kalhin[47] in the district of Shabaran of Qobbeh. The place of the fort above the hill on the right bank of the river still exists. This wall starts from the sea [**11**] and from the top of the village of 'Ali Khanlu, which probably originally was Alghunlu, and is close to the said city; it joins with the fort called Cheragh. From there to the mountain Ateh, where the ruins of a big city are to be seen; it passes above the village of Qunaq kend and goes to Baba-daghi. To verify that there were two versions it can be imagined that the Alan Gate was and is in both Georgia and in Shirvan. Because the Alans, who were in the north of the Caucasus, invaded from every side and the name Alan, and because of its popularity in most books of the Armenians, was applied to the mountain dwellers of the eastern sides of the Caucasus. Even the northern part of the plains of Moghan, which is considered to be

---

42. On the Scythians and the related Sarmatians, both nomadic peoples speaking an Indo-European language, who lived in the Pontic steppe see Sulimirski, T. "The Scyths", in *Cambridge History of Iran*, vol. 2, pp. 149-99.

43. Johann Christoph Gatterer (1727 - 1799), German historian and author of *Versuch einer allgemeinen Weltgeschichte* (Göttingen, 1792).

44. According to Ammianus Marcellinus, *The Roman History*, Book XXXI, Loeb's Classical Library edition, vol. 3 (Cambridge, 1939), p. 395, "a naked sword is fixed in the ground and they reverently worship it as their god of war."

45. Procopius, [*Anekdota*]. *Arcana historia, qui est liber nonus Historiarum* translated into English as *The Secret History* by G.A. Williamson (Harmondsworth, 1966).

46. Joseph de Guignes (1721 - 1800), French orientalist and author of *Histoire générale des Huns, des Turcs, des Mogols, et des autres Tartares occidentaux, ... avant depuis Jesus-Christ jusqu'a present : ouvrage tiré des livres Chinois, et de manuscrits orientaux de la Bibliotheque du Roi ; suite des memoires de l'Academie Royale des Inscriptions et Belles-Lettres* (Paris, 1756-58).

47. Bunyatov identifies this river as the Gigilchay.

the border of Shirvan in ancient texts, is known as Old Alan and their city of Alban that historians have situated between the river Albanus and Qasi, which, because of the natural situation, must have been Darband. The river Albanus is the Samur and the river Qasi is the Manas, which flows between Tarkhu and Buynaq. The passage of many centuries has not changed the names of some of these places. The city of Shamakhi is the same as Kamakhi or Ksamakhi. Qabaleh is the same place as Khabala, which is mentioned by Ptolemy. In the country of Qobbeh there is a village called Alpan, which is the distorted form of Alban and the very old fort, which is situated at the top of the mountain, is called Qal'eh-ye Ashgebush. Ashkabus, according to Ferdowsi, was a famous Turkish hero (*pahlavan*) who went to fight the *Khaqan* and was killed by Rostam.[48] The village of Zar Qobad with the same description, which is mentioned by Hamdollah in *Majma' al-Buldan*,[49] perhaps is the same as the city of Firuz Qobad.[50] The village of Sa'dan gets its name from the name of the Sa'dan of Baku. The place of Khazargan might be the same as Khazaran Kuh, which is mentioned in the *Eskander-nameh*.[51] The [names of the] village of Jaghatay in Qobbeh and of Jangutay in Daghestan are both Mongol words, [12] which originate from the names of their old residences and the village of Bayan is Machgach, which originates from Bayan Khan, a famous Avar.[52] The town of Nakhu, because of the name and its natural situation, might be Shahr-e Nakhiya or Naghiya, which has been named in the ancient histories as one of the old cities of the land of Shirvan. In olden times a people named Qaspi used to live on the shore of the sea on the right bank of the Kur river, and therefore it is known as the Caspian Sea among the Greeks (*Rumi*). Among the Moslems, due to the provinces situated on its shore, it is known as the Khazar Sea or the Georgian sea or the Gorgan Sea, or the Gilan Sea or the Shirvan Sea. The word Qafqaz has been derived from the Qaspi name. The Qaf Mountain is mentioned in the holy Koran[53] and is a place of wonders, and in the books of legends it is the dwelling place of the elves (*divs*) and fairies (*paris*). In these same books, the king of the fairies is called Shahbal and the author of the *Darband-nameh* gives the name of the Arab emir who was appointed to [head] the army of the Arabs in Daghestan as Shahbal or Sha'bal. In the land of the Shamkhal, the beautiful women of one of the villages, who are known allover Daghestan, are still called *par aval*, which means the ten fairies (*paris*). *Golestan-e Eram*, which is situated near Mount Qaf, has been described as an exceptionally beautiful place full of streams and fruit trees, which could be the same as the beautiful place of Shaberan of Qobbeh. This place is well-known among the people

---

48. This story is told in the national epic of Iran, *Shahnameh: The Persian Book of Kings* translated into English by Dick Davis (New York, 2006). For various miniatures depicting this battle see Google/Ashkabus.

49. This must be a mistake and rather refers to Yaqut's *Majma' al-Boldan*.

50. This perhaps is the current town of Qobbeh; see Minorsky, *The History of Shirvan*, p. 164.

51. Nezami Ganjavi, *Eskandarnameh* translated into English by Minoo S. Southgate as *Iskandarnamah: a Persian medieval Alexander romance* (New York, 1978).

52. Bayan Khan I, Khaqan of the Avars (r. 562 - 602).

53. Mount Qaf is not mentioned in the Koran; only the Surat al-Qaf occurs there. However, some Moslem commentators on the Koran have interpreted a number of verses as referring to these mountains. See Dehkhoda, *Loghatnameh*, q.v. Qaf.

and some say that Golestan-e Eram is the place called Golestan in Qarabagh, where the treaty of Golestan between Russia and Iran was signed in the year 1228/1813. There are winter quarters in the mountains above that place, which are called Golestan-e Eram.

Most Moslem historians called the Caucasus Mountains the Elburz Mountains. Kateb Chelebi in his book *Jahan-nama*[54] says that the Elburz is situated to the west of Bab al-Abvab, the Gate of gates, i.e., Darband and it is a mountain joining the mountain chain going from Turkestan to the Hejaz. It is more than 1,000 *mils* long. This is why some believed it to be the same as the Qaf Mountains. Near Darband there are two mountain ranges. One [13] is called the Big Qaf and the other is the Small Qaf. In the old Arab geographies this same mountain chain, because of the wars and victories that have happened there, are called the Victory Mountains. Many circumstances, other than those mentioned, also bear proof that the Qaf Mountains are the same as the Caucasus Mountains. Some characteristics attributed to in traditions such as metaphors and other allusions are due to ignorance, because the ancients did not have accurate knowledge about the interior and the situation of the northern parts of these mountains filled with wonder. If for this reason they considered it to be the end of the civilized world, and imagined its strong-bodied and wild inhabitants as elves, and the beautiful creatures there who are famous all over the world for their beauty and good manner as fairies, it is not improbable. Now that many travelers have frequently gone to the far corners of the world and have traversed the western and eastern hemispheres and the other half of the world, i.e., America, has become known in detail, the Qaf Mountains can no longer be described in this manner, in which only simple-minded people believe, because it does not exist anywhere. Since pre-historic times many diverse peoples have frequented the Caucasus from south to north and back again and they have fought many battles and won many victories and they have conquered many lands and settled there. The refugees and the oppressed people of different nations have rested from the hands of their enemy in those inaccessible places. The ancient kings of Iran, especially Yazdagerd, son of Bahram Gur,[55] and Anushirvan, son of Qobad,[56] brought many peoples from different provinces and they have constructed many forts and buildings in these lands, and many of its ruins still exist. Many peoples from Greece, Rome, Persia, Armenia, Huns, Avars, Turks, Rus, Khazars, Arabs, Mongols, and Tartars have conquered most of these places. In particular, the province of Shirvan more than any other was the scene of rebellion. In the age of the Safavids, the armies of Iran and of the Ottomans one after the other have occupied it. It thus becomes evident that these people are a mixture of many peoples. The traces and remains, languages, and habits of different peoples, are still in existence and the characteristics and the capabilities of the people are a good indication thereof. But defining them with certainty is not possible. So much can be said that the inhabitants of some parts of Tabarsaran, the western region of Qobbeh, and the region of Samuriyeh and Kur are mostly of ancient stock, being a mixture of different peoples and the inhabitants of

---

54. Katib Chelebi, *Cihan-numa* (Constantinople: Ibrahim Muteferrika, 1732).
55. Yazdegerd II (r. 438 - 457) son of Bahram V (r. 421 - 438), was the 15th Sasanian king.
56. Khosrow I Anushirvan the Just was the son and successor of Kavadh (r. 488 - 531)

Darband and most of Tabarsaran and the eastern part of Qobbeh, Sheki, Baku, Shirvan [**14**] and Saliyan are a mixture of Persian, Arabs, Mongols and Tartars. The Armenians and the Jews who were there as well gradually have mixed with the Moslems. More have remained [unmixed] in the lands of Tabarsaran, Darband, Baku, Qobbeh, Kur and very few in Shirvan and Sheki. They have their own religions and languages, because the peoples and villages still have kept the original names and languages, which is an obvious indication of the intermingling of people.

In the land of Baku, the village of Zekh, and in Daghestan, Miyatulu, are the remnants of the people of Zekh and Miyat, who are mentioned as the old inhabitants of these places by Pliny and Strabo. [The name of the village of] Odilu in Sheki and Shirvan and Qobbeh originates from the inhabitants of the city of Odi[57] that in the 3rd century AD was the capital of Armenia. They were originally the inhabitants of a place in Enderey, which is called Tumanler, which still exists on the right bank of Quy-su until Timur-quyi, where they have properties and streams. The inhabitants of the village of Tumanlar near Bashli would be the remnants of the people of Tumanshah, who Anushirvan moved there. According to one tradition,[58] the ancestors of the people of Kubachi were descended from some Genoans and Greeks who had come to trade. They had built workshops there and gradually they became a different people. Because most of the people of Tabarsaran were brought by Anushirvan from Tabarestan and Isfahan, the name of that region is the distorted form of Tabarsaran [sic; properly Tabarestan].[59] There are two villages in Qobbeh, one village in Darband and two villages in Sheki and a large tribe in Shirvan who among themselves still speak Arabic.[60] The village people of Darvaq in Tabarsaran also spoke Arabic; they have abandoned it in recent years. Some old people of that village still remember that language. Apart from the lands of Kur, Tabarsaran and the district of Samuriyeh like most of Daghestan, use the Arabic language and script in their books and writings. The district of Barmak in Qobbeh [derives its name] from the tribe of Ja'far Barmaki, the vizier of Harun al-Rashid. After the [**15**] killing of Ja'far they came and settled there. It is obvious that tribes such as the Zanganeh,[61] Khalillu, Kangarlu in Qobbeh and Shirvan; the Qaramanlu, the Tekellu, Shamlu and Chakerlu in Shirvan; and the Usalu, 'Arshlu, Ostajalu, and the Qajar in Qobbeh; the Bayat in Qobbeh, Darband and Shirvan; the Qara-Qoyunlu and Khalaj in Sheki and Shirvan and many others like them are from different

---

57. Reference is made to Utik or Owtik, which was a province of the kingdom of Armenia and Caucasian Albania. It is now partly situated in the Republic of Azerbaijan, immediately west of the Kur River and partly in Tavush province in Armenia. The Armenian name Owtik was also rendered as Outi and Otena and its population as Udini in Latin sources and as Utioi in Greek sources.

58. The text has "according to their ancestors," which does not make sense. It is quite likely that the words *beh qowl-e aslaf-e ishan* should be read as *beh qowli-ye aslaf-e ishan*.

59. This is highly unlikely as the people of Tabarsaran speak an ergative language that is a member of the Lezgian subfamily of Northeast Caucasian languages.

60. Crossed out and written in the margin in a different handwriting: There are many tribes, especially in Qabestan [Qobestan], and Khanchupan who are Arabic speakers.

61. It would seem that this is a mistake as the Zanganeh are a Kurdish tribe. It is possible, of course, that one section of this tribe had become Turkified.

Turkic tribes such as the Turkman and other nomads living in Iran and Anatolia (*Rum*), who have come here.

The [people of the] village of Chaghatay in Qobbeh are a remnant of the Mongols. The [people of the] village of Maskanjeh in the region of Samuriyeh are from the region of Astarabad, and Shah Tahmasp I brought them there; they are Shi'ites.[62] The people of the village of Hazreh, which is the distorted form of Hezrat [meaning Holy], were brought by the king of Iran from Iran to Qobbeh and he settled them near the shrine of his ancestor Sheikh Joneyd. Although they are Sunnis one district is still Shi'ite. The people of the village of Mikragh in the Samuriyeh region and most people of Ghazi-Qomuq as it is known are descended from the Rus. They have come during the period of the rule of Khazars. Moreover, their appearance and habits are an indication of that. The people of Ghazi-Qomuq when they meet each other still take their hats off and say to each other 'izrov,' which is a vulgar version [of the Russian] 'zdarov.'[63] In the town of Ghazi-Qomuq and some of those places scattered around this town there are still three other peoples living. They are the Ghachi, Mecheh, and Qomuq. It is probable that the Qachis are descended from the Huns, Slavs, Avars and Khazars. The Mecheh are descended from the Mekkeh, who are descendants of the Qoreysh tribe. The Qomuq are from the old Kamak and likewise the other peoples of this province and districts of Aqusheh, Qeytaq and the land of the Shamkhal, which is on the right bank of the Sulaq, which are mostly a mixture of old peoples of Armenians, [16] Persians, Arabs and Turks. The Qomuq people on the other bank of the Sulaq River, the Machgach and the Avars and many free people are from ancient stock mixed with northern tribes. In short, in these glorious mountains every unknown people with their own unintelligible language can be the remainder of an ancient tribe,[64] who for many centuries were known for their victories and power and now have been utterly wiped out and their names have remained as a memory in the histories.

According to Karamzin[65] and others, the Avars in the Turkestan steppe were powerful and famous. According to Chinese historians, the Huns were their neighbors.[66] In the second century they fled from the Turks and came to the southern lands, where they mixed with other tribes, and their Khan, who was named Diz I, became famous like

---

62. Between the line and the margin the following has been added: After Shah Esma'il turned away from his ancestral religion and established sectarianism among the Moslem nation and introduced Shi`ism here. In places such as Maskanjeh, Lahij, Besqal and other districts of Shirvan people of Shi`ite belief are settled. The people of Hazreh, which is situated near the shrine of Sheikh Joneyd, are the followers and the faithful of that saintly person. They have come in his company from Ardabil to Shirvan. From there they have gone to Qobbeh and settled there. They adhere to Sunnism and are still Sunnis. They cannot co-exist, because for the Shi`ites saintly attributions are not acceptable and except for the 12 Imams nobody else of the prophet's family or others is acceptable to them.

63. Meaning `hello, how are you,' and the like.

64. According to a well-known Caucasian tradition, when God was creating the Caucasus he put different languages in a bag. The bag had a hole in it and while creating these languages dropped down on the Caucasus reason why there are so many languages there.

65. The Russian author and historian Nikolai Mikhailovich Karamazin (1766 - 1826) is meant here and Bakikhanov refers to his *Socheneniia* 8 vols. (Moscow: V tipograf i S. Selivanovskago, 1803-1804), vol. 5.

66. For more information see [http://en.wikipedia.org/wiki/Eurasian_Avars].

Attila. In the Altai mountain chain, in a tent decorated with silk rugs and golden vases, he received the envoys of the Byzantine emperor Justinian and made peace with them. But he fought well with the Persians. According to Byzantine historians, the envoys of Diz I, who in appearance and habits were similar to their king, kept their hair long and overall were similar to Huns. In the time of Atilla they astonished people who looked at them. In the year 568, they came to Constantinople to make peace and told emperor Justinian that "the courageous and invincible people of Avar have come to seek your friendship. They are desirous of your friendship as well as good rewards, emoluments, and good places for living from you." He did not dare to refuse any of these requests. Bayan, the bloodthirsty khan of the Avars, defeated the Bolghars and did not spare anyone in killing and plundering. He conquered Moravia and Bohemia (Bughmiyar) where the Cheh people and other Slavs were living. He put Sigebert the king of the Franks to flight.[67] He came to the Tuna River and he united with the Longobards and destroyed the Gepid state. He conquered Hungary and then wanted to occupy Italy. In the year 568, the kingdom of the Avars extended from the Elba River until the Atal [Volga]. In the year 580, Bayan Khan took the northern shores of the Black Sea from the Turks. The next year, with 60,000 horsemen, he came to plunder and kill and subdued the people of Salavan on the banks of the Don, who were lawless and independent. According to Nestor,[68] the historian of the Khan of the Avars, [17] in the year 619 he defeated Heraclius, the emperor of Byzantium (*Rum*)[69], in such a way that he was nearly captured. In the years 624 -26, he laid siege to Constantinople, but without having achieved anything he returned. This people thereafter in different periods fought different tribes and gradually became weak. In the early years of the 9th century they became unknown, because they mixed with other tribes. From precious objects obtained from their graves it has become clear that they were not that uncivilized and that they had trade relations with Byzantium, China and Iran. A group of them, who are now in the Caucasus Mountains, has a separate language, their own emirs and their own habits. The Khan of these Avars is also called Usmi.[70] In the year 1140/1727, he came to the army camp of the Russians and said that one of his ancestors, who had lost his kingdom, had retaken his kingship with the help of the Russian king. His edict still exists. But when it was examined it became apparent that it was from Batu, son of Juji, son of Jenghiz Khan, who occupied Russia in the 7th century.

The [people of the] village of Ghunubb, with double 'b,' that sometimes is dropped, are the remainder of the ugly-faced tribe of the Ghun or Hun. This village is situated in the area of 'Andalal on an inaccessible mountain, which has pastures, streams, trees and has nearly 100 families and these people are known for their bad temper. Often they fight with each other. They are distinguished by their short stature and ugly face.

---

67. For more information see [http://en.wikipedia.org/wiki/Sigebert_I]
68. Nestor, *Povesta vremennykh let* translated into German as *Die altrussische Nestorchronik* (Leipzig, 1931) by Reinhold Trautman.
69. Heraclius (r. 610 - 641).
70. Usmi is also the title of the chief of the Qeytaq.

There are eight villages in Tabarsaran,[71] which are: Jalqan, Rukal, Maqatir, Kamakh, Ridiyan, Homeydi, Mata'i, and Bilhadi. They are in the environs of a city that Anushirvan built near the wall of Darband. Its remains are still there. They speak the Tat language, which is one of the languages of old Persia. It is clear that they are from the people of Fars and after its destruction they settled in those villages. In that city, which is near the village of Bilhadi, there is a gate with a strange device that is still in existence, which very likely was that same Iron Gate (Bab al-Hadid). The village's name [18] over time has become Bilhadi. The districts situated between the two cities of Shamakhi and Qodyal, which is now the city of Qobbeh, include Howz, Lahej, and Qoshunlu in Shirvan and Barmak, Shehshpareh and the lower part of Boduq in Qobbeh, and all of the country of Baku, except six villages of Turkman, speak Tat. It becomes apparent from this that they originate from Fars. The western part of the country of Qobbeh, except the village of Khenaleq, which has a diferrent language, and the region of Samuriyeh and Kur, two districts of Tabarsaran, which are Derreh and Ahmarlu, have different languages and they call the Turkic speaking people Mongols. According to the *Darband-nameh* and other indications, these people are descended from the Alan Massagetes. The people of the village of Mashqata' in Baku, changing 's' to 'sh,' are from the same people. In spite of the fact that they have adopted the language of the people of Baku, their habits and manners are from a different country.

The remaining districts of Tabarsaran have different languages. Four other villages, which are Magharti, Maragheh, Khucheni and Cheragh, and all the villages of Olus and the Turkman, which are on both sides of Darband, and that city itself, and the districts of Tip, Moskur, Shabaran, and the very city of Qobbeh, the remaining districts, and the city of Shirvan with Saliyan, and with six villages of Turkman in Baku, and all the land of Sheki are Turkic speaking, and they are mostly of Turkman, Tatar and Mongol stock. Some of them have come during the wars between the Ottomans and the Iranians during the Safavid period and some afterwards. Their Turkish is the same as in all the provinces of Armenia, Azerbaijan and most of Iran, which is in between the Ottoman language, Chaghatay, Kalmyk and Noghay. But the way in which it is written, and the orthography and grammar of this language, have not yet been defined.[72] The numerous emirates and peoples of Daghestan [19] have innumerable languages and expressions. Among them there are five languages that are commonly used. First, the Turkic language or so-called Qomuq, which is used in all the lower parts of Qeytaq and the land of the Shamkhal and Qomuq. Most other people know this language. Second, the Avar language, which is prevalent in the land of the Avars, and many other communities use it and others know it as well. Third, the language of the five districts of Aqusheh [Akusha], which is spoken in Suri and each of the districts of upper Qeytaq and the village of Kupchi, with different dialects and variants. Fourth is the language of Ghazi-Qomuq, which is peculiar to this land

---

71. On Tabarsaran see Minorsky, *A History of Sharvan*, pp. 91-92.
72. The Azeri language is based on the Oghuz language, which came into western Iran and the Causasus with the Seljuqs in the 11th century CE and gradually replaced the older Iranian (Tat and Pahlavi) and various Caucasian languages. Azeri consequently contains many Tat and Pahlavi loanwords.

only. Fifth is the language of Machgach, which is peculiar to this land and its upper parts like Shebut, Jarbelleh [Jarak] and others. The people of Zamtal, Baqtolal, Jamalal and 'Andeb, Qapuchay, Ansukh, Jineq, Zakhur, Akvakh, Qabalal and the village of Kapuchi and Gharchub, which belong to Ghazi-Qomuq, and many others have different languages and a multitude of dialects. Their description requires a separate study.[73]

All the people of Shirvan, except the Armenians and Jews, have the faith of Islam; some are Shi'ites and some are Sunnis. The country of Baku is completely Shi'ite and so is Darband mostly, and half of Shirvan, all of Saliyan and the port of Sheki and Qobbeh. Half of Shirvan, most of Sheki and Qobbeh, and a small part of Darband, and all of Tabarsaran and Kur and the district of Samuriyeh, except for Miskindzheh, and all of Daghestan are Sunni. This faith here has two branches; one is Hanafite and the other Shafi'i.[74] In Qobbeh, Sheki and Shirvan they are mixed; in the region of Samuriyeh, the mountains of Tabarsaran, and the Sunni part of Darband, and all of Daghestan are Shafi'i. If the characteristics of the villages, tribes and buildings and all the ancient ruins of these places are examined properly very likely many of them will show the origin of the population. [20]

---

73. For more information see [http://en.wikipedia.org/wiki/Caucasian_languages]and the Atlas of Caucasian Languages [http://linguarium.iling-ran.ru/publications/caucas/alw_cau_content.shtml]. See also map on page 20.

74. There are four so-called schools of jurisprudence recognized by Sunni Islam, to wit: the Hanafi, Shafi`i, Maliki and and Hanbali school.

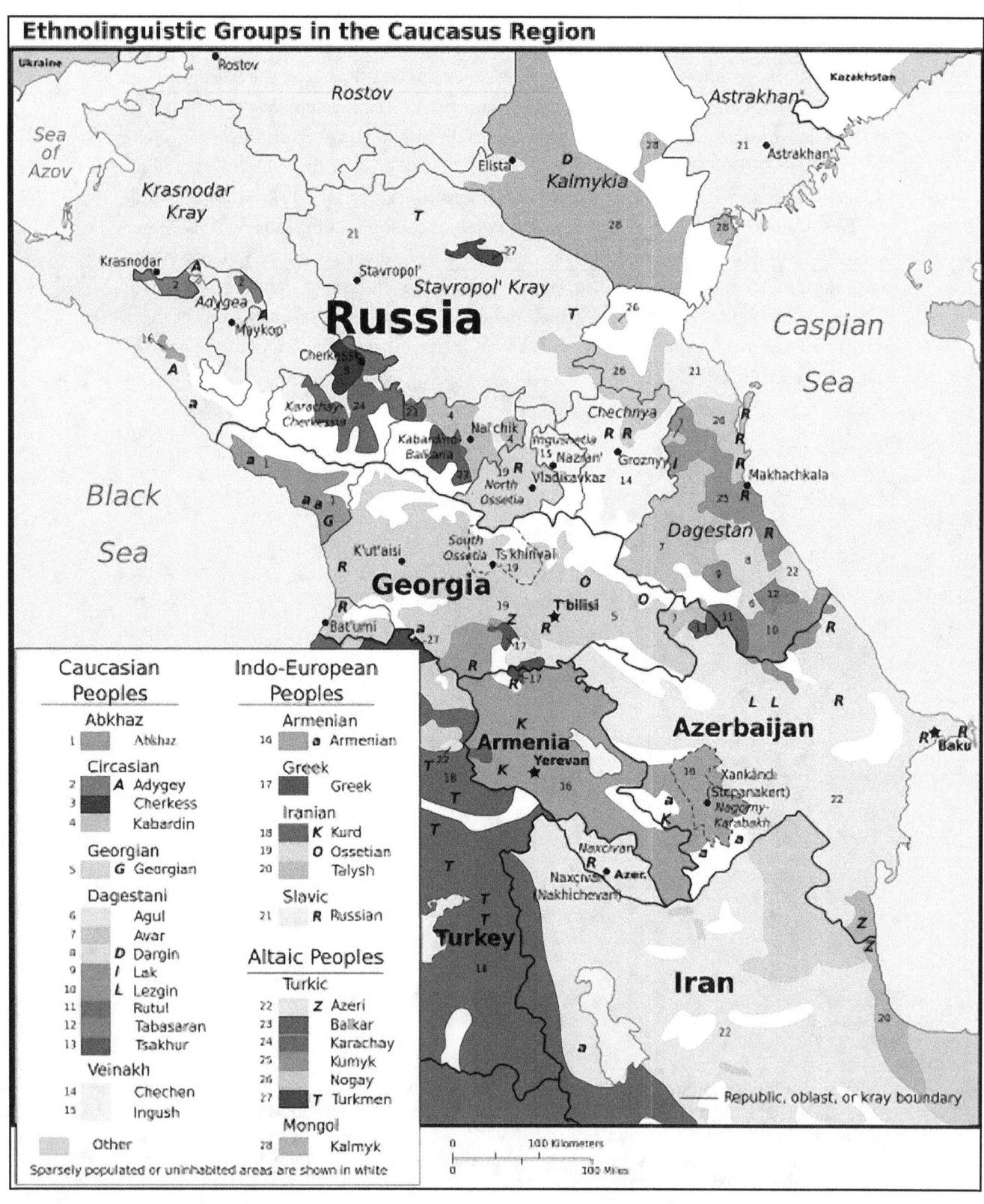

CHAPTER ONE

Describing the ancient events of the province of Shirvan and Daghestan until the time of the invasion of the Arabs after the advent of Islam.

According to most historians, it appears that the first site of habitation of mankind was Babylonia. The deluge of Noah has also taken place there. Mohammad b. Jarir Tabari in his *History*[1] says that the Magi do not believe in a universal deluge. Some Moslem historians believe that it took place in Babylonia, Iraq and from Syria until Yemen. Ahmad b. Hamdollah in the *Tarikh-e Gozideh* says that the deluge, according to some historians, was in the Arab peninsula. The people of China and some Turks deny the deluge. In a book of dynasties, which is the genealogy of the Ottoman Emperors, their lineage goes back to the Khans of the Turks and from there directly to Noah and then to Adam. In any case, the cause of the deluge is some unknown event, or after many generations the population of the southern parts in search of a better life spread out over the different inhabited parts of the world. The Eastern and the Northern part became that of the race of Jafeth, and the hot areas of Africa and India of the sons of Ham, and the Arab lands, Iran and Turkey (*Rum*) became that of the sons of Sam. According to the *Rowzat al-Safa*,[2] which was written at the end of 9th century *hijri*, the limit of the inhabited world is the fourteenth degree southern latitude. Its people were of the lineage of Sam. All these three, who are the sons of Noah, are, according to some, considered to be the chiefs of different peoples. Although they were all alone they would not have traveled such a long distance. Some consider Jafeth the first king of the Turks, who was a contemporary of Gayomarth, the king of Iran.[3] Or they consider all of them of the lineage of Sam. According to the author of the *Gozideh* and

---

1. Tabari, *Ta'rikh al-rusul va'l-muluk* translated into English by various authors as *The History of al-Tabari* 50 vols. (New York, 1989 -2006); in this case see vol. 1, *From the Creation to the Flood* by Franz Rosenthal.
2. Mir Khvand, Mohammad b. Khavandshah, *Tarikh-e Rowzat al-Safa* 10 vols. (Tehran, 1339/1960).
3. Gayomarth, the first man created by Ahura Mazda and the first king in the world.

of the *Kholasat al-Akhbar*,[4] Jafeth had eight sons and according to *Rowzat al-Safa* he had eleven sons. [21]

THE FIRST Turk was the eldest of his sons and his heir-apparent, who was a justice-loving and subject-caring king. His name and the names of all tribes [which are descended] from Jafeth have become known as Turks. After the death of his father, he chose Turkestan with its pastures and many streams of hot and cold water. First, he made a hut for himself from wood, reed and plants. After that he made a tent from animal skins. He called that place Suluq. In the *Zafarnameh*[5] it is called Suluqay. According to the writings of Karamzin and others, the Turkish tribes ruled on the banks of the river Irtish and Yayq. They invaded China and Iran. In the year 580 AD they had conquered the N.E. coast of the Black Sea until the Crimea. They lost it in the fight with the Avars in the same year. The Byzantine emperor Tiberius[6] came to the khan of the Turks expressing friendship and the latter said: "Are you not the same who speaks ten languages and cheat all people equally? He said, we are Turks and do not lie and cheat. Be aware, I will find the means to get revenge on your king. He assures me of his friendship, but he gives protection to our fugitive subjects, to our Avars. You say that the only way of going to Constantinople is via the Caucasus. I will find out from the course of the Don and Dniepr rivers, wherefrom the Avars have come, how they have gone to the Byzantine Empire and I also will find out about your power. All the word from East to West obeys me." In the year 581, the country of the Turks was divided in a western and eastern part and both of them were in the hands of weak tribes until they appeared again and made the world full of turmoil and calamity.

Two. Khazar, who after many travels and treks settled with his tribe on the banks of the Atal River. He built a city there and they became fishermen. The beginning of apiculture is attributed to them. They say that a son of Khazar died and that, accompanied by music, during a tribal gathering, they burnt his body in fire, which is the opposite of water, because Yafeth had died in the sea. The Khazar people are of Turkish descent. In the books of the Armenians of the 3rd century and the European books of the 4th century it is written that they were condemned [to live] in the deserts of Astrakhan at the time of the domination of Attila's Huns. D'Anville[7] says that [22] in the 5th century a Tartar emir called Tulun or Turun gave himself the title of *Khaqan* of the Khazars. In the year 626, the Khazars joined Heraclius, emperor of Byzantium,[8] in the war against the Iranians. It was in the same year that Heraclius called the *Khaqan* his own son and put a crown on his head. Justinian II, the Byzantine emperor, fled from Tiberius and went to the *Khaqan*

---

4. Ghiyath al-Din b. Homam al-Din Khvand Mir, *Ma'ather al-Moluk, beh zamimeh-ye khatemeh-ye Kholasat al-Akhbar va Qanun-e Homayuni* (Tehran, 1373/1994).
5. Sharaf al-Din Yazdi, *Zafarnameh* 2 vols. ed. Mohammad 'Abbasi (Tehran, 1336/1957).
6. The Baku as well as the Tehran edition have Tiuri, which is an error of the editor, because the person meant is Tiberius II Constantine (574 - 582); the quotation is from the Byzantine historian Menander Protector.
7. Jean-Baptiste Bourguignon d'Anville, *Géographie ancienne abrégée* (Paris: Chez Merlin, 1769) translated as *Compendium of Ancient Geography* (New York, 1814). Bakikhanov most likely used the original French edition of this work.
8. Flavius Heraclius Augustus (r. 610-641)

and married his daughter. Emperor Leo also took a daughter of the *Khaqan* for his son Constantine, and from her Emperor Leo the Khazar was born.[9] The Khazars took the land between the two seas and many tribes of Slavs and others were subjugated. They were friendly with the Byzantine emperors and they went from the Caucasus to Armenia and Azerbaijan and fought with the king of Persia and Arabia. According to Kamrazin, the town of Atal on the river Atal was the *Khaqan*'s capital, which was built by Anushirvan. The Khazars, unlike the Huns and other Turkic tribes, were inclined to build things. The fort of Sarkel in the land of the Cossacks of the river Don and the city of the *Khaqan* near the city of Kharkov and other places are attributed to the Khazars. Their unknown city must have been located in the vicinity of Varanaj.

The Khazars were first idol worshippers. In the 8th century they accepted Judaism. In the year 243/858 they accepted Christianity. According to Mas'udi, someone called Bola, one of the *Khaqan*s of the Khazars, accepted this religion in the year 121/740. Abu'l-Feda says that the *Khaqan* must be of the lineage of kings, and, except for special permission, nobody can see him. When going into his presence you had to prostate yourself. Without his permission getting up or speaking was not permitted. When you were passing in front of the tomb of the *Khaqan*s you had to get off your horse and bow. Whenever the *Khaqan* told any official "go and die" he went immediately to his house and killed himself. Even the poor of that nation attained kingship in their turn. I heard that a young man had a haberdashery shop and people would say that after this *Khaqan* he would be king. But he was a Moslem and the *Khaqan* has to be [23] a Jew. With the *Khaqan* two people would arrive at the people's assembly at the same time. They could be Moslem, Jew, Christian, or an idol worshipper. Most of the people of this place are Moslem and Christian and a few are Jews. The most notable ones are Moslems, and most of the merchants. Most of their food consists of rice and fish. The environs of the town extend 10 *farsakh*s and are fertile plains. With the river that passes through the city, ships come with goods from Khvarezm. Other ships from the Burtas kingdom[10] bring black fox pelts that the kings of the nomads buy at high expense to make hats from. From other lands red, black, and white pelts arrive, which they call Arabic. They are cheaper. From here they take them not only to Darband, Barda', and Khorasan, but also to Europe and Spain. The houses of this place are made of wood and reed. The palace of the *Khaqan* on the left bank of the river is made of bricks. In the Khazar kingdom there is a city called Asmid that has beautiful gardens. In the way it is written 'ya' is changed to 'nun', and 'ra' is dropped. So it was Smid or Samandar or Ismandar, and all the way from Darband to Sarir is full of orchards, where grapes grow.

---

9. The Byzantine emperor Leo III (r. 717- 775) married his son Constantine (later Constantine V Kopronymous, r. 741- 750) to the Khazar princess Tzitzak, daughter of the Khaqan Bihar. After she had been baptized the princess was renamed Irene (meaning `peace'). Their son Leo IV was commonly known as Leo the Khazar (775 - 780).

10. The Burtas or Bortas (Bortaslar) were a tribe living north of the Caspian. The ethno-linguistic affiliation is unknown; some think they were related to the Alans, others hold that they were a Finno-Ugrian group.

THIRD, Rus was a restless man. After many wanderings he sent an envoy to Khazar to ask to settle there. Khazar gave him some of the islands of that region that had a good climate. Rus [again] started complaining and asked for justice. The custom of the Rus is that they give all the money to the daughter and give nothing to the son except their sword and they say: "this is your portion." According to the writings of Karamzin and other Russian historians, in the year 247/862, at the proposal of the Northern Slavic tribe who were in rebellion and disorderly, three brothers of the Rus people, who are mentioned in the history of the Franks[11] in the year 235/850, came from the other side of the Baltic Sea and their chief, Rurik, became king. From that time the government of the Rus was established and every day by adding several different Slavic tribes and by intermingling with Hun, Khazar, Avar, Turk, Mongol and Tartar tribes they have increased in number. Thus, an unknown and weak tribe that had been defeated by most others [24] became the independent ruler of the eastern and northern lands. After this, apart from the above-mentioned history and descriptions, the Rus people and their arts are mentioned in many strange legends. A friendly letter from Alexander of Greece to them is famous and shows how old they are. Also, in the book of Ezekiel the prophet, chapter 38, and the book of Jeremiah the prophet, chapter 25 the name of the Rus is mentioned among the eastern tribes.

FOURTH. Ghazeh, he was a cunning man. He came with his people in the land of Bulghar and settled there. Between him and the Turks there was a fierce battle. Bighur, the son of Ghazeh, was killed and they say that the enmity between them remains. According to Moses of Khorents'i, the people of Bolghar are mentioned in the histories of 100 years BCE.

FIFTH, Kamari who is also called Kamak. He was well-natured and a hunting-loving man. He reached the place where the Bolghars are now. He had two sons. One is Bolghar and the other Partas. Each one became chief of a tribe. The Qomuq tribe is descended from this lineage and the name is a distortion of Kamak. Ptolemy[12] calls these people in the same region Kam and Kamak.

SIXTH, Saqlab, who also had many tribes and who was wandering in search of a place [to settle]. He had a son. Because of the death of the mother he was fed the milk of a dog. When he grew up, like dogs he would attack people. The father gave one of his relatives in marriage to him. She bore a son who was called Saqlab. When he became big and the chief of the tribe he sent envoys to Rus and Khazar and asked for a place to settle. They, because of his huge herds, did not accept and they fought. Saqlab was defeated and

---

11. Rashid al-Din Tabib, *Die Frankengeschichte der Rashid al-Din* translated by Karl Jahn (Vienna, 1977).
12. Ptolemy, *Geography,* Book Six, Middle East, Central and North Asia, China (Wiesbaden, 1998) by Helmut Humbach and Susanne Ziegler (Greek text with German and English translation).

went to the North and stayed around the 64 latitude and because of the severe cold they made underground dwellings.

SEVENTH, Chin, he remained in a city that Jafeth had made in his name. The making of different products like silk, cloth, colors, painting, the production of musk, and many other things are attributed to him. [25]

EIGHTH, the Barij are a Frankish people; some of the Byzantines are related to them.

NINTH, Mosk. The Mongols, Yajuj [and Majuj] (Gog and Magog) are descended from him. The fate of the other sons of Jafeth has remained unknown. In the Thorah of Moses, Jafeth has eight sons and their names are: Kasamsar, Makuk, Madi, Yaval, Elisiya, Fowul, Musuq, and Firas.[13] Makuk (Magog) in Arabic was Majuj. Komer and Musuq could be the same as Kamari and Mosk.[14] This author says the resemblance between the different languages of the peoples of the North and South from the point of view of their basic verbs and nouns indicates that they are from the same stock. Humankind in the early stage was wild and naked. They inhabited the southern parts. It is obvious that without suitable clothes, warm houses and provisions living in the northern parts was not possible. As gradually the means of living were provided and because of the growth in the number of people they needed to look for provisions, to hunt animals and to have more grazing lands for the herds. So they came to the northern parts and their passage took place in particular via the Caucasus and especially via Shirvan and Daghestan. Because in those days they did not have ships, passage across the sea from the western side was difficult. From the eastern side passage was also difficult because the Qebchaq desert was without water and grass. These [northern] lands were full of grazing pastures, streams and warm valleys filled with forests and fruit trees suitable for habitation by those wild tribes. After that, according to most historians from unknown ancient times, the Iranians kings and others with the intention of fighting or seeking pleasure, or while they were fleeing from the enemy, passed through this land of the Caucasus full of wonders. Especially the province of Shirvan has not rested from the continuous invasions of southern and northern tribes. [26] In the histories of ancient nations such as Babylonia and Assyria there is no clear description of the Caucasus. But in Iranian histories it is said that Fereydun, son of Farrokh, one of the Pishdadi kings,[15] and Qey Qobad, the founder of the Kayani dynasty,[16]

---

13. The names of the sons of Jafeth according to the Bible are: Gomer, Magog, Madai, Javan, Tubal, Meshech, and Tiras. For more information see [http://en.wikipedia.org/wiki/Japheth].
14. This name may refer to the Iron Age Mushki people in eastern Anatolia or the Georgian tribe of the Meshki. See, e.g., [http://en.wikipedia.org/wiki/Mushki].
15. Gayomarth, the first human being created, was also the first so-called king of the Pishdad dynasty. Fereydun was one of the mythical kings.
16. The Kayanids or Kayanians are a mythical dynasty, the heroes of the Avesta, the holy book of the Zoroastrians, and of Ferdowsi's *Shah-nameh*, the Iranian national epic.

were hidden from the enemy during their youth and they were living in the region of the Caucasus. Fereydun was saved by Kaveh the Blacksmith[17] and Qey Qobad was saved by Rostam of Zabul. Both of them were installed on the throne of Iran. The Persian historians say that Fereydun was the king of all civilized lands and he divided his kingdom among his three sons. He gave the western part to Salam, the eastern part to Tur, and the middle part, which was prosperous, to Iraj, which is the Arabicized form of Irak, and he was his crown-prince. After a while Salam and Tur, who were envious of Iraj, invited him for consultations and talks. They killed him near Qarabagh. From that time onwards there was enmity among their family. The eastern part is known as Turan and the middle part as Iran. Near Estakhr, in Fars, there is a place that still is called Iraj. About 700 years BCE, the Greeks, especially the Milesians, built the cities of Phanagoria, Harmunas [?], and Dioskurias on the north-eastern shore of the Black Sea. They had trade relations with the people of the Caucasus. According to the Greek historian Herodotus, who lived about 450 BCE, the Cimmerians[18] had fled before the Scythians and had occupied Lydia. The Scythians in 636 BCE followed them and after a period of conquest of 28 years they returned to Europe. It was obvious that their passage went via the Caucasus. However, the first occupation and the last conquest were also in these lands, because there are many ancient remains in Shirvan and Daghestan from the Greeks and the Scythians. [27] Herodotus has described the expedition of Key Khosrow the Kayanid[19] to make war on the Scythian Massagetes and their queen Tomiris, and he has written that it is the same Albania. He says that Cyrus after having crossed the Aras without any impediment reached the confluence of the river Kur. Without fear he went to a narrow ravine and the people of the mountains defeated him with all his army. There is a difference between the European and Asian historians, whether Key Khosrow went to a mountain and disappeared. The description of the cave and his golden throne near a mountain close to Darband that Sheikh Nezami of Ganjeh has described corresponds to this. In short, Key Khosrow after crossing the Aras, if he wanted to go to Georgia as some people have assumed, should not have come to the passage of Javad, which is the place of the confluence of two rivers. From this it becomes clear that his march was to Albania. This alleged event happened in a ravine that passes from the mouth of the Rubas River through Tabarsaran, Darvaq, and Qeytaq, which is a very inaccessible place. The valley of Su, which is well-known in the old books, could be the same. The reason for its name is because of the proximity of the wall that extends from Darband, because *su* in Arabic is a fort and probably it is from the root *sul* or from the city of Sul, which Anushirvan built at three *farsakh* from Darband at the mouth of this ravine. It has been named after that and gradually, because of the passage of time, 'ar' has changed to 'el' and then they have been interchanged. Another possibility is that this has happened in one of the ravines of the place called Surhi, between many tribes of the Qeytaq, Aqusheh and Ghazi-Qomuq, because the name Sur with the addition of the word '*hey*' is still in existence in this district. The fact that in some places they have written that the defeat of

---

17. Kaveh the Blacksmith is a mythical figure who lead an uprising against the evil foreign king Zahhak.
18. For information on the Cimmerians see [http://en.wikipedia.org/wiki/Cimmerian].
19. This probably is Cyrus.

Key Khosrow was in a place near the fort of Ganjeh does not seem to be right, because it is a flat place and there is no ravine there. Mohammad Khavandshah in the *Rowzat al-Safa* and Khvondamir in the *Kholasat al-Akhbar* and other historians have mentioned that Goshtasb after returning from the lands of Rum acceded to his father's throne. He moved the capital of Iran from Balkh to Estakhr, which he had built himself and spread the Zoroastrian religion in Iran. He had sent somebody to Arjasb, the governor of the Turks, to also invite him to this [28] religion. Therefore between him and the Turks, who had formerly been in agreement, discord arose. Arjasb with a huge army went to Iran. Goshtasb with his brave son Esfandiyar came to oppose him. The Turks fled and he returned to Fars. He ordered Esfandiyar to go and conquer Armenia and Azerbaijan. The second time that Arjasb came to Iran Esfandiyar defeated him and he himself went to the land of the Turks and he was victorious many times. Goshtasb at the end of his life gave his kingship to Bahman son of Esfandiyar and became a recluse.[20] Looking at the events, the description that has been written about his conquests, expeditions to the Caucasus, journey to Rome and the adoption of the Zoroastrian religion, the founding of the city of Estakhr under the name of Cyrus seems to be more appropriate to Goshtasb than Key Khosrow. But because of conflicting reports and scarcity of documents it is difficult to determine this with certainty. According to Karamzin, Darius, the king of Iran, with the intention of punishing the Scythians, who were plundering and killing in the provinces of Armenia and Azerbaijan and thereabouts, launched an expedition to their vast steppes, but he could not do anything and it almost happened that his whole army would have perished. In an old Persian book, which is a pseudo-history of Alexander, called *Eskandar-nameh*, it has been mentioned that Alexander reached Baku while campaigning and the Sa'dan of Baku, who was one of the most courageous men of his time, embellished the city and with the notables and the dignitaries went to welcome him. He performed the necessary services and since Alexander's army was in need of good horses he said that in this region in a place called Khazran-Kuh there is an old man called Firuz, who has a herd of numerous horses, which was started by King Bahman. After him, Homay and Dara asked [for a horse], but he declined. Alexander sent someone called Badpay as a scout (*'ayyar*) to find out about Firuz's situation. Badpay went and saw that there were multi-colored tents erected around the mountain and there is a tent of Chinese silk and some people had gathered around it and an old red-haired man, who was from Turan, with a caftan of leopard skin and a head of tiger skin with a golden chain around it was sitting and had a big staff in his hand. In short, the next day Firuz with 40,000 men that he had gathered came to fight Alexander, but after finding out about the splendor and glory of that king he came and submitted the herd to him. Also, in that book it is written that Alexander reached the city of Yunan, which was a big city. Because they did not submit to him he wanted to destroy it. Since the city was seaward-looking and there was an iron mountain in between, Aristotle in his wisdom made a potion in the amount of 700 *mann*, which softened the rock like lime. In this way he opened the waterway and drowned the city. Some people, who were saved, founded the city of Gilan. This author says that although you cannot trust this book, it could be that

---

20. This tale is told in the *Shahnameh*.

this has happened in another way. Since most of the Iranian people attribute great works to Alexander they have attributed this one to him as well. You cannot deny the fact that in the land of Baku in the villages of Bilgah, Zireh, and [29] Bibi Heyat and others and also in some of the islands the road for carts on the rocks facing the sea can still be seen. Opposite the city of Baku there are buildings, towers, and forts, which can be seen under water. In the city of Baku when they were digging a well in the house of Hajji Baba b. Hajji Aqa Hoseyn a paved road made of stone appeared whose level was under the sea bed. Between Baku and Saliyan about eight geographic miles offshore there is a town below the sea. In the Moskur district of Qobbeh from the Samur River to the Shaberan districts a well-known hill extends about two *farsakh* above sea level. According to people's descriptions and water traces, you can clearly see that up to that place the sea water came.

After the conquest of Mo'ammari, which was mentioned, it had fallen and had joined the Caspian Sea. This situation can also be seen in some locations in the land of the Qomuq at the seaside. This may also be concluded from the multitude of branches and swamps of the river Atal and the lower level of the Caspian Sea compared to the Black Sea. The authors of the *Masalek va Mamalek* [21] and the *Majma' al-Boldan* type of books and others have written that "the confluence of the two seas"[22] has been mentioned in the Koran as being in the country of Shirvan. The rock of Moses and Khedhr is also there. Taking into consideration the names and signs, it is the rock of the living Khedhr, who is known among the people.[23] Thus, from the land of Baku towards Turkmenistan there was a land road and the people of the eastern shores would come to plunder here. Although considering the remains of the towers and the forts and the tombstones that have emerged from the sea opposite the city of Baku and according to the descriptions of the historians about the city's past it becomes evident that 400 to 500 years ago the places that were prosperous in those areas are in ruins now. Possibly after a short while they will return [to their original stage]. I recall that 40 years [30] ago the wall of this castle was two cubits into the water. After that, especially in the last 45 years the sea gradually has gone down by three cubits and it is still going down. However, attributing all these above mentioned remains to these activities and passing definite judgment about them is difficult and is still dependent on further observation and studies. Nezami of Ganjeh in his poetic composition *Eskandernameh* says that Alexander during his conquest reached Armenia, whose inhabitants were fire worshippers. During a hunting expedition he passed through the land of Barda', the remains of the city is still in evidence near Qarabagh, near the banks of the Kur river. It is said that it is one of the buildings of Fereydun of the Pishdad dynasty. The governor of that place was a woman called Noshabeh, who was wealthy and powerful. She did not spare anything in entertaining Alexander and whatever was needed she would continuously send to the army camp. Since Alexander had heard of the beauty and accomplishments of Noshabeh many times he disguised himself as a messenger and went to see to

---

21. Such as by Ibn Khordadhbih, Ibn Fazlollah al-'Omari, and Ibrahim b. Mohammad al-Istakhri.
22. Surat al-Rahman, 19-22.
23. Khedr or the Green One, symbolizes Life and is associated with the Water of Life. On the prophets Moses and Khidr see [http://en.wikipedia.org/wiki/Al-Khidr].

her. Noshabeh recognized him on sight and she honored him greatly and hospitably. She got pledges of protection for herself from him. Since Alexander returned to his camp the next day Noshabeh with her daughters came to Alexander and she spent the night at his court drinking and feasting. The love between Alexander and Noshabeh grew strong.[24] He then went to the Elburz Mountain, passed Shirvan and came to the passage of Darband. There was no city there. There was only a small fort on the mountain in a difficult narrow pass with many provisions and a few guards, who stopped those coming to that road. Alexander called them many times to come and obey him. They refused and he gave the order to take and destroy it. It was so strong that the entire army for 40 days and nights tried to do so, but it could not do anything. Eventually the people of the fort could not resist any longer and submitted. Alexander gave them other fiefs and repaired the destroyed parts of the fort and put troops there. At this time the people inhabiting those mountains complained to the king that the wild tribes of Qebchaq committed much destruction in these lands and they asked him to fill the crevices of the mountain and build a wall. Alexander gathered many workers and ordered that all the crevices of that mountain be filled and the wall be made. When he was returning, at the first stage he was told that nearby there is a well-equipped and very beautiful fort known as Sarir, where the throne, crown, and arsenal of Key Khosrow was hidden in a cave [31] and that a prince of his lineage was ruling there. Alexander went to the fort and the place of Key Khosrow's throne, which was also known as Darvazeh. The emir of Sarir went to welcome him and Alexander saw the golden throne, the cave, and the mountains as well as many wonders. One week later he was hunting; after that via Rudbar he went to Khalkhal and from there to Gilan and also from there to Rey. While he was building cities in Mesopotamia he received news that the Rus tribe with many Qebchaq people had found their way into Darband and its neighboring lands and also that they had attacked that place with boats from the sea. They had plundered that land, killed many, destroyed Barda' and had taken Noshabeh with all her daughters as captives. Alexander with a huge army came to the Qebchaq steppe via Khvarezm. The beautiful women of that land never cover their faces from men. He came down to a vast plane near a big river. Qontal who was the chief of the Rus tribe came to confront him with a large army of 900,000 that was composed of seven tribes of Rus, Aysu, Partaz, Pechenegh,[25] Alans, Ilaqs, and Khazars. A fierce battle ensued lasting a few days. Eventually Alexander was victorious. Qontal was captured with 10,000 people and made peace and returned Noshabeh and the captives with many things. After imposing a contribution on Qontal he released the other captives and returned. Quintus Curtius in the *History of Alexander*,[26] which was written 400 years after him, has described most of these events with variants. Noshabeh is the same Amazone queen who fell in love with Alexander. She

---

24. This love story is described by Nezami in his *Sharaf-Nameh*, Vahid Dastgirdi ed. (Tehran, 1937). See also Sayyed Hasan Safavi, *Eskander va Adabiyat-e Iran va Shakhsiyat-e Madhhabi-ye Eskander* (Tehran, 1364/1985).

25. Pecheneg or Bijanak, a Turkish tribe; see Minorsky, *The History of Sharvan*, p. 160. The other tribes, other than the Rus, Alans and Khazars, who are mentioned above, are unknown to us.

26. Quintus Curtius Rufius, *Historia Alexandria Magni* translated into English as *The History of Alexander* (Harmondsworth, 1984) by John Yardley.

came to his camp and the big river is the river Atal or river Don. The Scythians would be these seven tribes, because the ancient historians call all the tribes of the northern region Scythians. The fort of Darband is the same as the small fort, whose conquest has been mentioned earlier. In the *Darband-nameh* and also in other sources there is a description of Alexander's construction of the wall of Darband. Among the people Darband it is still known as [32] Alexander's wall. If you read the Holy Koran carefully it also describes the same subject.[27]

View of a street in Baku circa 1900

The purport of the verses is that Dhu'l-Qarneyn took a road until he reached the West, where the sun sets, and found it going down into a warm spring. He continued until he reached the rising place of the sun and found it shining upon a people, who were not protected against it. He continued again and reached [an area] between two walls and he found a people who could not understand speech and they said: "Oh Dhu'l-Qarneyn, the Gog and Magog are evil-doers in this land. Should we give you a contribution so that you may establish a wall between them and us?" He said: "whatever my God has given me and I possess is enough for me." Then he ordered workers and pieces of iron so that

---

27. "They asked thee concerning Dhu'l-Qarnayn. Say, `I will rehearse to you something of his story and then verily we established his power on earth and we gave him the ways and the means to all ends. Once such way he followed until when he reached the setting of the sun he found it set in a spring of murky water, near it he found a people, we said `Oh Dhu'l-Qarneyn (Thou hast authority) either to punish them or treat them with kindness. He said `Whoever thus does wrong, Him shall we punish; then shall he be sent back to his Lord; and He will punish him with a punishment unheard of [before]." Sura 18/83-88 *al-Kahf*.

a wall between the two sides was established, so that they could not go over and through it. According to writings of many commentators and famous historians, Dhu'l-Qarneyn is the same as Alexander of Macedonia, the king of Greece, Iran, and of the West and the East, who took Africa as well as the steppes of the Qebchaq. They say that his crown looked like two horns, which could have been an allusion to two aigrettes. Also, this could mean running water and it can be an allusion to the western sea. Because of the proximity of the realms of Cancer (*Sartan*), the climate and the water of the sea is warm. Also, Alexander's march to the Western lands went through endless hot sand deserts that lead to the sanctuary of Jupiter. The writings of Greek historians acknowledge this point and the wild inhabitants of the bare Qebchaq desert in reality had no cover in the way of buildings, forests and gardens to protect them from the sun. The third road between east and west must be towards the north, because the one which is towards the south is the sea. The two walls (*sa'deyn*) were the two ranges of the mountains of Armenia and Azerbaijan or between the Caspian and the Black Sea. The people who were not able to understand speech are the inhabitants of the Southern Caucasus, whose language was not comprehensible, because of the strangeness and the multitude of languages or because of their lack of education. The Gog and Magog were wild plundering tribes of the North and sons of Jafeth. They say that the Gog are Turkish and the Magog are from the mountains.[28]

The same subject is mentioned in the Torah, viz. that the Scythian people are descended from the lineage of the Magog, the son of Jafeth, the Scythian people. They inhabit the slopes of the Caucasus Mountains. They had a city there that was called Magog; it was also called Yarapul. Magog was also the name of one of the sons of Israel; the king Hadehgarar [?] was also called Gog. According to the book of Jeremiah[29] and others, the Magog lived close to the coast [33] of the Caspian Sea and the Gog lived farther away towards the north. Both tribes were Scythians. The wall is the same wall of Darband in which lots of iron had been used. These two walls are opposite the Caspian Sea and the Qeytaq Mountain or the Caspian and the Black Sea. Akhund Mohammad Baqer in the book *Hayat al-Qolub*[30] writes that a man came to the Lord of the Believers 'Ali, who asked him, "where are you from?" He said, "from Darband." 'Ali said: "is that the same as the *Bab* [gate] that was built by Dhu'l-Qarneyn?" The man answered: "yes, that is true." The present author says that because the coming of Alexander to Armenia and Gilan and his conquest from the Venetian Sea [i.e. the Mediterranean] until the Ganges and from the Southern Sea to the Black and Caspian Seas has been proven, and, because he came to the land of the Caucasus, which is in those parts and near to the regions that he has traveled, and which most of the ancient writers have considered to be the last border of the inhabited world and a place of wonders, it is not too far-fetched that he had built a wall or had

---

28. On these two walls see Minorsky, *A History of Sharvan*, pp. 86-89.

29. Jeremiah 25:9 [B]. This text does not mention the Gog and Magog, but only that the people of the North would destroy Babylon. As the Gog and Magog lived in the North, he concluded that this text also referred to them, see Ezechiel 38, 1-6.

30. Mohammad Baqer b. Mohammad Taqi Majlesi, *Hayat al-Qolub* of which there is an abridged translation into English of its second part as *The Life and religion of Mohammad as contained in the Sheeah traditions of the Hyat ul-Kuloob* (Boston, 1850) by James L. Merrick.

taken other measures to protect the country of Iran from the wild tribes of the North. In spite of the writings of many Moslem and Armenian historians and in spite of the confirmation by the Koran, which apart from being the divine word is also closer to the historical events that have happened more than 1,200 years ago, the existence of the remains of the wall and its fame among people and other indications as well as the fact that Alexander's expedition to the Caucasus has been mentioned by Quintus Curtius, although it might not be geographically accurate, fully indicates that Alexander has come to this land and that the wall has been made by his order. It is the mistake of some commentators and historians that they do not have accurate information about this issue and they have fabricated it and in this way they have falsified the history books and documents. Kateb Chelebi definitely says in the *Jahan-nama* that Alexander of Macedonia is not the same as Dhu'l-Qarneyn, because he was a king from Himyar in Yemen, a contemporary of Abraham. He traveled to the east and the west of the world and built a wall at the end of the known world in the north-east in an unknown location. He also says about the wall of Darband that it cannot have been constructed by Alexander, because it was built [34] by Anushirvan in order to stop the tribes of the Khazars and other Turkic tribes who used to come and plunder the provinces of Shirvan, Armenia and Azerbaijan and kill people there. The kings of Fars always fought with them. They say that the first one who constructed it was Esfandiyar, son of Goshtasb. The *Nohzat al-Qolub* has attributed it to Lohrasb, father of Goshtasb, and states that Anushirvan repaired it. It is odd that such an author has not brought any evidence for his statement and openly denies this [i.e. the previous statement]. Imam Fakhr al-Razi, Qadi Beyzabi and others say that Alexander of Macedonia has been called Dhu'l-Qarneyn and that the fort of Darband has been called the wall of the Gog and Magog, but they say this is an error. They do not believe that its construction could have occurred before Anushirvan and be attributed to either Esfandiyar or Alexander. Assuming that Dhu'l-Qarneyn of Himyar had built it and that it had fallen into disrepair, its repair by Alexander is not far-fetched.[31] Because Abraham became prophet 2,543 years ago and the crowning of Alexander was 958 years before the *hijra*, there is a difference of 1,500 years between them. It is also possible that in the valleys and the mountains each one of these kings has made separate constructions or repairs and after they had fallen into ruin Anushirvan repaired all the existing fortifications. The wild tribes of Turkic lands, who were evil-doers and plunderers, do not want to be called Gog and Magog, because there is no definite proof about this or [if there is then] it is by allusion and they leave the existing wall here and refer to an imaginary wall, which does not exist at all. Considering the size of the army that according to Plutarch[32] and Strabo[33] had gone from Albania to fight Pompey one can imagine that Albania in 65 BCE [35] was a powerful and rich state. Pompey is one of the first Roman generals who defeated Mithridates, the king of Pontus, and subjugated Tigranes, the king of Armenia, and wanted to cross the Cauca-

---

31. On Dhu'l-Qarneyn see W. Montgomery Watt, "al-Iskandar," *Encyclopedia of Islam*.
32. Plutarch, *Fall of the Roman Republic* (London, 2005) translated by Rex Warner and Robin Seager.
33. Strabo, *The Geography* (London/Cambridge, Mass, 1960-70) translated by Horace Leonard Jones.

sus Mountains and pursue Mithridates who had gone to the north-east of the Black Sea.[34] It was in this quest that he wanted a passage through Albania and Iberia.[35] They at first accepted it, but since it was winter, he decided to have his winter quarters on the banks of the Kur River. Suddenly, the Albanians came to fight him with 40,000 troops. Although he had the force to stop them from passing he did not do so. They crossed the Kur River and then he fought and defeated them badly. After this event, the king of Albania, who was called Orozoes, was forced to ask for peace, which was not denied. Pompey pursued the expedition that he had already decided upon. When he arrived at Colchis it was reported that the Albanians had gathered. He returned the same way that he had gone and after the crossing of the river Kur and the waterless desert, which is between the Kur and the Aras, with many difficulties he met the Albanian army, which consisted of 60,000 foot and 12,000 horse, on the banks of the river Abazeh and defeated it again. He himself killed the son of the Albanian king, Cosis, who was commanding the army.[36] He wanted to cross the Aras River and pursue the Albanians until the sea which was at three days stages distance, but he was dissuaded by the many poisonous snakes in those areas. From there he returned to Armenia Minor. In the early stages of the Roman Empire, when the emperors were called Ceasar, the people of Albania and the king of Iberia were allies. They interfered in the conflicts of the Parfan tribe, which is Kurdestan, against the Romans. According to Tacitus,[37] the historian of those events, whose writings are better known [than others], Ceasar Tiberius[38] in the time of his reign appointed Mithridates as the governor of Armenia, who was the brother of Farazman who ruled in Iberia. But the king of the Parfan, who claimed the kingdom of Armenia, [36] was against this appointment. Farazman with the Albanians were helping Mithridates. Via Daghestan, Shirvan and the valley of Qarabagh, which is now the land of Ganjeh, they brought an army to help him consisting of Sarmathians, which affair ended well. This was in a time when most of the lands of Iran were in the hands of the kings of Parfan and Armenia. Albania also was occupied or under the dominance of the Armenians. The Armenian historian Chamichian says that the king of Armenia, Artashes b. Senatrak[39] in the year 88 AD fought with the people of the Alans, of Daghestan and of the Mountains and some of the Iberians,[40] who gathered in the Alan steppe, i.e. the Moghan. He defeated them and captured Saten, the son of the king of the Alans. Part of the Armenian troops had already passed to the left bank of the Kur. The king of the Alans then sued for peace; his daughter Satenik came to

---

34. Tigranes the Great (r. 95-55 BCE), king of Armenia and Mithridates VI (r. 120 - 63 BCE), king of Pontus (in northern Anatolia) were defeated in 66-65 BCE by Pompey the Great (106 - 48 BCE), a leading Roman general and statesman. On Tigranes the Great see Hakob H. Manandyan, *Tigranes II and Rome* translated into English by George A. Bournoutian (Costa Mesa, 2007).
35. The Georgian kingdom of Kartli was referred to as Iberia.
36. He was the king's brother, see Plutarch, *The Parallel Lives. Pompey*, 35.
37. Tacitus Cornelius, *The Annals & the Histories* (New York, 2003), translated by Alfred John Church and William Jackson Brodribb.
38. Tiberius Caesar Augustus (r. 14 - 37 CE), emperor of the Roman Empire.
39. Artaxias in Greek and Roman sources.
40. Iberia is the old Greek name for the Georgian kingdom of Kartli. In Georgian this became Ivoria. Its habitants, therefore, were called Iberians or Iverians.

the bank of the Kur and through an interpreter she started talking with Ardashest, who was on the other bank. She said: "Oh powerful and wise king, it is not right that because of the killing of my brother a permanent feud should exist between two powerful kings." Ardashest crossed the Kur River and talked with her and was smitten by her beauty and accomplishments. He therefore sent the general of his army called Sombat[41] to her father the king of the Alans. The marriage took place. Saten was set free and the two kings returned to their kingdoms. After some time the king of the Alans died and one of his generals became the king. Saten fled and went to Ardahesht. He sent Sombat [37] with a big army to help him. A fierce battle ensued; the usurper was defeated and took refuge in the land of the Turks. Sombat pursued him until Darband. He was victorious and some of his soldiers were killed and captured and he settled them in Armenia near the mountain of Arghi. Saten became independent in his inherited lands. As an indication of this event near the city of Ghazi-Qomuq there is a village and a mountain called Sonbat.

Since Anak killed his cousin Khosrow the king of Armenia by treachery near the city of Udi in the year 258 AD,[42] the heirs of Khosrow killed Anak with most of his sons and followers. Two small sons of Anak were taken by their tutors and the eldest one who was St. Gregory[43] was brought to Qeysariyeh. The other one who was called Suren was taken to his aunt, who was the wife of king Javanshir of Hiptak [=Qeytaq]. After a while, Suren reigned in Darband for 39 years. After the killing of Khosrow, when disturbances had broken out in Armenia, king Ardashir the Sasanian[44] occupied that land and destroyed the lineage of Khosrow. Someone called Artavaz, an Armenian chief, took Tiridates,[45] the son of Khosrow and fled to Caesarea (Kayseri). Tiridates, who was very strong and brave, became famous through his military activities. Eventually, he came with a Roman army and took Armenia. After that, in the years 289 and 290 AD, he occupied Iberia, Aghvan[46] and Massagethia. He sent a man called Sombat, from the lineage of the previous Sombat, and took in marriage the daughter of the king of the Alans, called Eshken, and Khosrow II was born of that union.[47] Again the Aghvanians rose up, and again Tiridates came and huge armies from both sides gathered and a fierce battle ensued in the plains of Moghan. Artavaz who was an old man and a great general of the Armenians was killed, which enraged Tiridates who continued fighting. [38] Katarhun, the king of Baslas, who was from the Alans and was very brave, threw his lasso to capture Tiridates,

---

41. In Armenian Smbat.
42. The date of 258 probably is a copyist's error and should be 238 CE, given the regnal dates of Khosrow I (r. 197 - 238), king of Armenia.
43. St. Gregory the Illuminator (ca. 257 - ca. 337), the apostle and patron saint of Armenia. He converted Tiridates to Christianity.
44. Anak had acted at the order of Ardashir I (r. 226 - 241), founder of the Sasanian dynasty and king of Iran.
45. Trdad III or Tiridates III, also called the Great (r. 286 - 330), son of Khosrow I (d. 287), king of Armenia. In 301 he proclaimed Christianity in Armenia and thus made it the first Christian state in the world.
46. Caucasian Albania, Aghbania or Aghvan was an ancient kingdom in what is now southern Daghestan and most of Azerbaijan.
47. Khosrow II (r. 330 - 339), also called the Small, because of his small size, founded the city of Dvin, the later capital of Armenia.

who cut it and killed him. In short, the Aghavians were defeated. Tiridates pursued them and subdued the Alans, Baslas, Heptaq, and Huns who, because they were intermingled, were considered as one people, and he took hostages from them and returned. After that Shapur, son of Hormuz the Sasanian, fought and conquered Azerbaijan and then made peace. At the early stage when Tiridates came from Kayseri to Armenia, St. Gregory was one of his close friends. Since he did not accept the religion of fire worshipping he bothered him constantly and, as a result, he became deformed[48] and because of the prayer of that saint he was saved and was converted to Christianity. In the year 301 AD, St. Gregory built the church of Uch Kalisa in the city of Veghar-shabat, which had been built by Vagharsh, the king of Armenia, at the end of the 2nd century AD.[49] Until the death of Tiridates it was the capital of Armenia. Until now it is the See of the Catholicus of Armenia. It was built according to the Saint's wishes and at the end he became a recluse and in the year 331 he died and the shepherds found his body in the mountains of Armenia and buried him in Uch-Kalisa. According to the Armenians, one of his hands has been cast in silver and it is still there. A girl named Nina, who converted the Georgians to Christianity, was a contemporary of that saint.[50]

Mohammad Lavabi Aqtashi says in the *Darband-nameh*, which, at the request of Chupan Bey Bingeray Khan Shamkhal, was summarized and translated from Persian into Turkish in the early part of the 11th century *hijri*[51] in the village of Enderey, that there was continuous fighting between the Turks and the Persians and the hand of tyranny and destruction reached to the provinces of Shirvan, Armenia [39] and Azerbaijan. The Sasanian king Qobad, son of Firuz, the king of Iran,[52] made peace with the *Khaqan* of the Khazars, whose capital was at mouth of the Atal River. Moscow and Noqrat, which probably is Novgorod, as well as all Rus, gave tribute to the *Khaqan* who had 400,000 troops and Qobad married his daughter. After that Qobad sent an envoy because he wanted to build a wall between the two countries and the *Khaqan* agreed. Qobad had seen in the histories that in Darband, which is a sacred place, there was this wall of Alexander Dhu'l-Qarneyn. They say that the wall in the length of one *mil* started in the Caspian Sea and it continued until the Black Sea. Therefore he ordered the excavation of that construction from the earth and sand and he repaired the fortification. He extended it until the upper part of Tabarsaran and then he put iron gates there. Then he established the southern walls of Darband. He laid the foundation of the city and this was all done in seven years. After

---

48. Tiridates fell ill and, according to legend, he adopted a pig-like behavior and was aimlessly wandering around in the forest and was cured of his illness by St. Gregory.
49. King Vagarsh (r.117 - 140) ordered the name of the old town of Vardkesavan to be changed into Vagharshapat, which a few decades later became the capital of Armenia. St. Gregory built a cathedral in that town, which became the spiritual and political center of Armenia after the fall of the kingdom of Armenia and is called Edzmiazin. In Turkish the town is called Uch Kalisa meaning Three Churches.
50. St. Nino or Nina (ca. 296 - ca. 338) introduced Christianity into Georgia and was a relative of St. George, the dragon slayer.
51. Minorsky, *A History of Shirvan*, p. 9 rightly strongly doubts whether this early date is correct.
52. Kavadh I (r. 488 - 531), son of Peroz I (r. 457 - 484).

finishing the work, he was certain that the Khazars in spite of their strong army could not penetrate that wall. He sent the daughter of the *Khaqan* to her father's house so that, because of the marriage, the affairs of state would not suffer. They say that before Qobad, Yazdegerd son of Bahram Gur, had constructed this wall. It was completed in the time of Anushirvan. Qobad and Anushirvan both moved many people to these lands and constructed many cities and fortifications in them. Anushirvan in the time of his father had stayed a long time in this land. Before the wall of Darband, which is the wall of the Khazars, the ruined places of the wall of Alghun constructed by Esfandiyar, son of Goshtasb, extended from the sea until the mountains. Anushirvan repaired it and he put a gate in it, called the Alan Gate, and he himself stayed there. After that with the permission of his father he built 360 forts around the city of Darband and neighboring places. Its people he brought from different parts of Iran and moved them there. The land from the Alghun wall until Ahran he divided into seven provinces and for each he assigned a governor.

First, Kolbakh in which the city of Ahran on the right bank of the river Quy-su is situated, in the place which is now Chehel Yurt, and he built Sorkhab in Qezelyar [Kizliar] [40] in the lower part of Enderey, and Kachi Majar in the district of Chumlu, higher than Enderey, and Ulu Majar [Upper Majar], which later on was called Tatar Tup and is now called Menarat, in the land of the Cherkes.

Second, the land of Tumanshah, [where he established] the fort of Samandar at the location of the town Tarkhu and the fort of Enji at a distance of three *farsakh* from the seaside and its ruins can still be seen. He constructed the fort of Keyvan, which was between Tarkhu and Enderey, and the city of Balkh and the mouth of the river Ahran, that is to say Quy-su, which was the place for the army. It was situated on the left bank of that river on the northern side of the town where he also constructed several forts. All this until the border of Hamri he gave to an emir of the Tuman tribe, whom he had moved there and called him Tumanshah. Since Esfandiyar sat on the golden throne in Ahran he made Ahran the seat of that land. A silver mine, at the mouth of the river Terek, and a copper mine at Ahran belonged to the generals of Ahran. A warm water spring, which is on the left bank of the Quy-su and higher than Chehel Yurt, is now called Ab-e Garm Kalbakh.[53]

Third, Qeytaq, where, by making many forts, appointing emirs and moving many people from Gilan and Kashan, he put its affairs in order, and Zerehgaran, which they now call Kubachi, is one of the forts.

Fourth, the Qomuq Mountains and their environs, which now consist of Ghazi-Qomuq, the districts of Aqusheh and some of the Avars and others, to which in the same way he assigned an emir and called him Filanshah.

Fifth, Tabarsaran, whose people were skirmishers and they were the best of the army of Darband; they had come from Isfahan and Tabarestan. Their emir was called Hejran Shah.

---

53. *Gal bakh* in Turkish means "come and see."

SIXTH, Masqateh in lower Tabarsaran and the Qomuq mountains whose people are Alans and they were fewer in number than others.[54] Their emir was called Tiyun [or Botun] Shah.

SEVENTH, Shabaran and Moskur, which comprises the city of Shabaran, Baghdad-Kerker, and at one *farsakh*'s distance there is Shahr-e Abad and in Moskur there is the city of Kesran, and at three *farsakh* from Darband there is the city of Sul or Sur.[55] He built cities and forts and in [**41**] Moskur, Kur and Akhti he settled some people from Fars and appointed an emir from his family.

Since Anushirvan had organized the affairs of the country in this manner and the defense of the borders in a strong fashion he returned home from these lands. The *Khaqan* conquered the province of Kalbakh and he placed the commander of his army in Ahran. They say before Anushirvan, Esfandiyar had built the same forts and shrines. He had made seven provinces and had moved the people of the forts around Ahran, whom he had brought from Khorasan. It is written in the *Akhti-nameh*[56] that an emir called Shahbani from the Sasanid dynasty at the order of Anushirvan came and settled in the place of Akhti with 60,000 families from Fars and 300 troops, and he built a fort whose remains can still be seen on the top of the mountain and he settled there. He spent 1,500 gold coins (*ashrafis*). In the warm springs of Akhti he made a bath and imposed a tax on it. In the year 560 AD when Anushirvan after 30 years of reign was called 'the Just', the chiefs of the different places gathered and took council. They asked Shahbani to intercede with Anushirvan so that he would lift the tax on the baths. He sent his son Shah Asan to Anushirvan, who was at that time in Azerbaijan, to discuss the matter, which the latter accepted. After that Shahbani ruled for 15 years and died; his son Shah Asan replaced him and ruled for 12 years. The author of the *Tarikh-e Gozideh* writes in the year 730/1330 *hijri* some of the titles and honorifics that Anushirvan had given to his emirs in the region of Darband that are still in existence, such as Filanshah and Shirvanshah. 'Omar b. Vardi in the *Khariteh al-'Ajayeb* (Map of Wonders),[57] which is an old geographical Arabic work,

---

54. According to Minorsky, *The History of Sharvan*, p. 78, "Maskut or Mashkut, from the Massagetai, who were settled there" was situated on the Samur River. As some authors mention that the Alans were the ancient Massagets these settlers indeed may have been Alans.

55. See Minorsky, *The History of Sharvan*, p. 86.

56. The *Akhti-nameh* is a local history, probably "only of interest for the Samur basin," of which Minorsky further reported in 1958 that it had been discovered recently. "It is very likely that Khanikov's pseudo-*Darband-nama* is only an excerpt from the *Akhti-nama*." Vladimir Minorsky, *A History of Sharvan and Darband* (Cambridge, 1958), p. 9, n. 1. It seems that it has not yet been published.

57. Isma'il b. 'Ali Abu'l-Fida, *Abulfeda Tabula Syriae cum excerpto geographico ex Ibn ol Wardii Geographia et historia naturali, arabice nunc primum ed., latine vertit notis explanavit Io. Bernhardus Koehler, accessera io. Iacabi Reiskii Animadversiones ad abulfedam et Prodidagmata ad historiam et geographiam orientalem* (Lipsiae: Litteris Schonermarkii, 1766). Zeyn al-Din 'Omar b. Mozaffar Ibn al-Wardi. *Fragmentum libri Margarita mirabilium prooemium, caput secundum, tertium, quartum et quintum continens* 2 parts, translated into Latin by C.T. Tornberg (Upsala, 1835 - 38). See also J. de Guignes, "Perles des merveilles, mélanges de géographie et d'histoire naturelle par Ebn al-Ouardi," in *Notices et extraits de la Bibliothèque du Roi* 14 vols. (Paris, 1787 - 1843), vol. 2, pp. 19-59.

says that Bab al-Abvab is a town in the northern part of Iran that Anushirvan built on the coast of the Caspian Sea and that it has many fruit orchards. It stands opposite the Khazar people and the Gates are in the mountain ranges of [42] Qeytaq, like the Bab al-Sul, Bab-e Alan, Bab al-Shaberan, Bab-e Lazeqeh, Bab al-Sajasi, Bab-e Saheb al-Sarir, Bab-e Filanshah, Bab-e Kardemanshah, Bab-e Iranshah, Bab-e Liyanshah, and since Darband is on the sea and situated on the road and is the largest of the forts it is called Bab al-Abvab. The range of its forts extends to the high mountains, which prevents people from coming and going. In these mountains there are many forts. Abu'l-Hasan Mas'udi says that in these lands there are 300 towns and each speaks a different language, which is not similar to the others. Ibn Hawqal says, "I was denying this until I saw it myself after checking it. Among the many kingdoms of this land is the kingdom of Shirvanshah, which is very large and has many villages and buildings. Its inhabitants are rebellious and they do not obey anyone. The kingdom of the Shirvanshahs was established by Anushirvan." The authors of *Rowzat al-Safa* and *Kholasat al-Akhbar* and many other historians say that the daughter of the *Khaqan* was married to Anushirvan and he did not sent her back to her father's house and she bore him two sons, Nushirzad and Hormozd. This woman did not accept Zoroastrianism. Nushirzad when he came to the age of adolescence could not accept fire worshipping either. Therefore he was imprisoned at the orders of his father. While Anushirvan was in Syria and made conquests there, news of his sudden sickness, which was not true, reached Nushirzad. He came out of prison, gathered some people around him and with the representatives of his father from Fars and Ahvaz he left to conquer Iraq. Anushirvan hearing of this gave orders to Ran Barzin, who was the commander of the army of Iran, to go and suppress his son's revolt. He came and advised the prince, but with no result. In the battle Nushirzad was killed by an arrow. When Anushirvan in the year 578 AD, 44 years before the *hijrah* [43] and after 48 years of reign, died, the other son of that wife became king of Iran, the reason why he is called the Turk.[58] The author of *Rowzat al-Safa* says that in the time of Hormuzd the Khazars passed the wall of Darband and pillaged the provinces of Armenia and Azerbaijan. This plundering occurred in the fourth year of the *hijra*. In the years 624 to 626 the emperor of Byzantium, Heraclius, encouraged the Khazars to fight Iran. The author of the *Tarikh-e Gozideh* and others say, since Hormuzd became a tyrant the people rebelled and struck coins in the name of his son Khosrow Parviz.[59] For this reason he became afraid of his father and came to Azerbaijan. When Khosrow was in Moghan and Bajarvan, Mahin Banu the aunt of Shirin, the princess of Barda', came and took him to Barda' and received him with great hospitality. Khosrow fell in love with Shirin and eventually married her. This event is described by Sheikh Nezami in his book *Khosrow and Shirin*, which is one of his famous five books jointly known as *Khamseh* and which describes it in great beauty and detail.[60] After Anushirvan there is no independent

---

58. Hormozd IV the Turk (r. 579 - 590).
59. Khosrow II Parviz (the Victorious) (r. 590 - 628).
60. Nezami Ganjavi, *Khosrow va Shirin, matn-e 'elmi va enteqadi*. ed. Barat Zanjani (Tehran, 1377/1998). There is no English translation of this text, but there is one in French, three in Russian, one in German and one in Japanese. *Roman de Chosroès et Chirin*. Henri Massé translator (Paris, G.-P. Maisonneuve & Larose, 1970); *Khosrov i Shirin: poema; perevod s persidskogo* translator K. Lipskerova (Moskva: Gos. izd-vo khudozh. lit-ry, 1955)

information [about this region] except that due to the dominance of the Khazars and the disorder of the affairs of Iran it was a place of disturbance and unrest, until the time of the coming of the Arab army that in numerous battles vanquished the northern tribes and ruled this province.

---

and Chosrou und Schirin; *Ubertragung aus dem Persischen, Nachwort und Erlauterungen* by J. Christoph Bürgel (Zürich: Manesse, 1980).

View of The Maiden Tower (Qis Qalasi) from Baku's inner city (Icheri Shahar)

CHAPTER TWO

From the beginning of the coming of the Arab army until the time of the Mongol invasion

In the histories of Tabari, *Gozideh* and the *Rowz al-Mi'tar*[1] it is mentioned that 'Omar b. al-Khattab in the time of his caliphate, during his conquest of the kingdom of Iran, sent Saraqeh b. 'Amr to conquer Azerbaijan. After conquering that province in the year 22 *hijri*/644 AD, the latter sent Bakr b. 'Abdollah to Shirvan and he himself followed; 'Abdol-Rahman b. Rabi'eh led the vanguard of the army going to that place. 'Abdol-Rahman from the side of Moghan and Bakr from the side of Armenia conquered most of the lands by fighting and some by peace. Bakr constructed the Khoda-Afarin bridge across the river Aras. Most of the Armenians[2] of Qarabagh, who are still living in inaccessible places, took refuge from the Arab army and did not want to oppose them. The town of Barda' from that time onwards fell into ruins. In short, when Bakr and 'Abdol-Rahman reached the vicinity of Shirvan, a certain Shahriyar, who was royalty, ruled there. He asked for amnesty, submitted and made peace, provided he would not have to pay tax and poll-tax. Instead he spent that money for the army to expel the Turks and the followers of different religions. They wrote of this incident to Saraqeh b. 'Amr and he reported it to 'Omar b. al-Khattab. The request was accepted. This rule [44] was always applied to the Shirvanis. Saraqeh sent each one of the chiefs with some troops to the narrow passes and the towns that were in the mountains. He fortified all the forts of the Khazars and Alans and settled Moslems there. When Saraqeh died 'Abdol-Rahman replaced him by the order of 'Omar. With an army he took a fort, which was 200 *farsakh* away, and converted the people of many towns to Islam. Although he made peace with Georgia on condition that it paid poll-tax, he converted some to Islam and then returned to Darband. He remained there during the reign

---

1. Muhammad ibn `Abdallah Himyari, *Kitab al-Rawz al-Mi`tar fi khabar al-iqtar*. Ihsan `Abbas ed. (Beirut, 1975).
2. Bunyatov translated here 'most of the population,' which is yet another example of his tampering with Bakikhanov's text.

of 'Othman and then he died. In the *History* of Tabari it is written that 'Abdol-Rahman one day saw on the finger of Shahriyar a ruby ring, which was unique in color and light. It was valued at 200,000 *derham*. Shahriyar gave it to 'Abdol-Rahman, but he did not accept it. Shahriyar said: "whoever of the kings of Iran had learnt of this ring would have taken it from me, but I am giving it to you and you do not accept it. You with this kind of faith and without any greed will conquer the entire world." In the *Habib al-Siyar* it is said that Habib b. Salameh with an Arab army and at the orders of 'Othman b. 'Affan came to Armenia, Azerbaijan, Moghan and Shirvan and made peace with most of the rebellious people. After him until the death of 'Othman, Hodheyfeh b. al-Yaman, Mogheyreh b. Sho'beh and Ash'ath b. Qeys were governors of this region. The author of the *Darband-nameh* says that since most of the Companions of the Prophet had heard from him that Darband is a holy place and is the cause of peace in the southern Caucasus, whoever fights there to preserve it will gain the blessing and benediction of God. Most of the people wanted to gain this blessing. In the year 41/662 Salman and Rabi'eh al-Baheli who were among the followers of the prophet with 4,000 brave troops, while making holy war, went to Darband. The Khazars had retaken it and the guards of the keep of the citadel (*narin-qal'eh*) of Darband fled to the fort of Hamri as soon as the army of Islam entered the city. The Moslems took the fort and city of Darband and the *Khaqan*, the king of the Khazars, came with [45] a huge army to oppose them. The Moslems confronted it on the banks of the Darvaq River where they fought each other. The *Khaqan* did not want to fight, since he had heard much about the courage of the Arabs. He believed that arms would not penetrate their bodies. At that time one of the Khazars came to the sea coast and killed a Moslem who was making his ablutions there. He cut his head and brought it to the *Khaqan*. After this incident they found the courage to fight. Five days from morning until evening fierce battle ensued and many people on both sides were killed. On the sixth day, the *Khaqan* criticized his army and said: "whoever flees from battle will be punished by me." On the other hand the Moslems were fighting with the fervor of holy war. Salman and Rabi'eh with 40 volunteers in the vanguard of the army attacked the enemy. A fierce battle ensued and several thousand men of the *Khaqan*'s army were killed. Salman and Rabi'eh with those 40 people were martyred and their graves, called *qerkhlar* [meaning the forty], situated near the town of Darband, still are a place of pilgrimage. The remainder of the army of Islam was vanquished and wounded and went to Darband and then to Syria. The *Khaqan* left 3,000 people for the protection of the city of Darband and returned to his capital. When Valid 'Abdol-Malek the Omayyad in the year 86/705 became the caliph he sent his brother Maslameh with 40,000 brave troops to conquer Darband. First Maslameh took the town of Julah (Jolfa), which is in Nakhjevan and its ruins can be seen near the river Aras. Then he took the city of Lahjan (Lajan) and he also destroyed it. Then he came to Shirvan and conquered the lands as far as Moskur, and for each of them he assigned a governor. After that he came to Darband and laid siege to it. He despaired of getting it and wanted to return. One night someone came from the fort and told him that if he gave him enough money to give him peace of mind he would show him a secret passage so that he could lead the army into the fort. Maslameh asked for volunteers, but nobody came forward, except for 'Abdol-'Aziz Baheli with his two sons and 100 brave men from his tribe, with the provision that apart from one-fifth (*khoms*) of the booty, which belonged to the *Bayt al-Mal*,[3] [46] nothing would be given to the others. Six thousand people also followed him onto the mountainside. With the help of this guide they went underground through a door, which had been made on the bank of the Darvaq River and led to a tunnel, and then in some way they entered into the fort. None of the guards became aware of them and the battle began at mid-night. The Khazars wanted to save their lives and families. Until morning confusion and fighting continued. In the morning the Moslems opened the gate so that the entire army of Islam entered. All the booty taken, after deduction of one-fifth (*khoms*), was given to 'Abdol-'Aziz and he divided it among the army of 6,000 that had taken the fort. That man of the city was given much money and a position. Maslameh out of fear that after him the Khazars would take the fort thought it wise to destroy it. The chiefs of his army approved this, but 'Abdol-'Aziz said that this was wrong, because the Khazars would return and build it better than before. If Darband were in their hands the provinces of Armenia and Azerbaijan would not be safe. Maslameh did not accept his advice and ordered the wall of the fort to be destroyed on both sides. He left 'Abdol-'Aziz in charge of the province of Armenia and Azerbaijan and returned to Syria. Again the Khazars came to Darband, but they did not repair the fort. Every year they would invade it and plunder Armenia and Azerbaijan and kill people. Because of continuous complaints by the inhabitants of these lands Maslameh again came with 40,000 troops to Darband. He repaired the fort, left 5,000 troops there and returned to Syria.

A few years passed. The guards of the fort out of fear of the Khazars could not go out of the fort and the Khazars would go through the pass and plunder Armenia and Azerbaijan. 'Abdol-'Aziz Baheli the governor of Armenia and Shirvan occasionally would defend them, but he did not have the strength to defeat the Khazars. The armies of the Arabs and Turks were fighting all the time. One of them was JamJam the Great, who was one of the great generals of Islam. According to Georgian historians, he came to Georgia in the year 100/719 and killed the ruler of that place called Archel[4] by torturing him. It seems that he displayed much bravery in the region of Shirvan and Daghestan, because wondrous stories about his deeds have been composed in Persian verse at an unknown date. His grave is outside Darband towards the south under the name of Soltan Jamjameh.[5]

---

3. *Bayt al-Mal*, literally 'house of money', but generally used to refer to the treasury of revenues, gifts and spoils etc., which are supposed to be used for the common weal of all Moslems.

4. Archil II (Eristavi son of Stephanoz) (r. 668 - 718).

5. Ilya Nikolaevitch Bérézine, *Puteshestvie po Severnoi Persii* (Kazan, 1852) the first part of which has been translated into French by Jacqueline Calmard-Compas as *Voyage au Daghestan et en Transcaucasie* (Paris, 2006), p. 325 reports that the inhabitants of Darband told him that the Arab commander "Djamdjama" was buried in the ancient cemetery just outside Darband. He further reports that the *Darband-nameh* mentions a "Soltan Chumcha" as a martyr, while Olearius also mentions that "king Tzümtzume" is buried in the Darband cemetery of which he gives the location on the accompanying plate depicting Darband and its cemetery. Olearius further relates a fantastical story about "Tzümtzume", whose fame was sung by the poet Fuzuli. Adam Olearius, *Vermehrte newe Beschreibung der moscowitischen und persischen Reyse*, ed. D. Lohmeier (Schleswig, 1656 [Tübingen, 1971]), p. 720; see also for further information M. Brosset, *Histoire de la Géorgia*. 2 vols in 4 (St. Petersburg, 1849), vol. 1/1, p. 253.

As in the year 103/722 'Abdol-'Aziz died the caliph of the time, Yazid b. 'Abdol-Malek,[6] [47] sent Abu 'Obeydeh Jarrah with 6,000 troops to help the guards of the fort of Darband.[7] The son of the *Khaqan* came to Hamri with an army. Abu 'Obeydeh Jarrah had come to Moskur and he gathered all the troops that were in the forts of those parts and met on the banks of the Rubas River with the emirs of Tabarsaran and Qeytaq, who had not yet converted to Islam. He said, "I have come from Arabia to fight the Khazars and I want you to help me." A certain Artanish who was one of the Lezgi chiefs secretly reported this conversation to the son the *Khaqan*. Abu 'Obeydeh Jarrah heard of this. Apparently he said that he would stay for three days in that place, but at night with the light of torches he crossed the river Rubas and passed the city of Darband. From the spring of Ava'in he brought the emir of the right flank 12,000 heads of cattle and sheep and 700 captives and the commander of the left flank 40,000 animals, horses and sheep and 2,000 captives with many other things and all this booty, after deducting *khoms*, was divided among the army. The Khazar prince after hearing this news, intending to give battle, moved from Hamri. Abu 'Obeydeh hurried to confront him. At the mouth of the river Darvaq the two armies met, and Abu 'Obeydeh in front of his army gave a speech and said: "Oh Moslems, the homeland is very far, there is nothing but struggle, if you try and become victorious you will find much wealth, but if you are killed your reward in the other world will be even more. It will be better than life in this world." From both sides the battle drums were struck, banners were raised, a fierce battle ensued and many were killed on both sides. Eventually the Khazar army could no longer hold their ground and, leaving all its heavy equipment, fled. The Moslems pursued them and they did not hold back in killing and plundering. On that day 7,000 men from the Khazars and 2,000 Moslems were killed and the son of the *Khaqan* with a thousand difficulties managed to get to the city of Anji and said "the foe that I have seen is extremely strong, if no help is coming, escape to save yourself." From there he went to Balkh.[8] The government of Balkh, Upper Majar (Ulu Majar), Little Majar (Kechi Majar), Qezelyar [Kizliar], and others were entrusted to the governor of Ahran. He took the [48] necessary military precautions which were required to protect his country. He himself returned to the capital city. Abu 'Obeydeh Jarrah took fort Hasin, which is near the village of Ghiyeh-kend above a hill overlooking the sea. He went to the city of Samandar, which is now called Tarkhu [Tarki]. The people of that place submitted themselves. From there he came to Fort Enji, which on one side is protected by the mountains and on the other side by the sea. In between there is a strong fortification. The people of that place, relying on its inaccessibility and having plenty of water and provisions, defended the fort. The Moslem army after a few days of siege had no hope for victory and wanted to return. Two people, called 'Abdollah and Ebrahim shouted, "Oh Moslems we exchange our lives for heaven." The army gathered around them and they said we will do the same. Then they gathered 12,000 carts from all around on which they stacked timber

---

6. Yazid II (r. 720 - 724).

7. A.k.a. Al Jarrah ibn Abdallah; for details see al-Tabari, *History*, vol. 24 "The Empire in Transition," translated by David Stephan Powers (Albany, 1989).

8. Balkh of the Lazk (Lezgis); its exact location is unknown. Minorsky, *The History of Sharvan*, p. 83.

and behind which the army entered the city. Emir Enji took refuge in the citadel and he was there until morning and with a few of his chiefs and soldiers he fled to Fort Keyvan, which was between Enji and Balkh. In the morning the Moslems invited the people of Enji to convert to Islam. Whoever did not accept was killed or enslaved. They destroyed the fort of Enji. In the *Rowzat al-Safa* and *Tarikh-e Gozideh* it is written that Abu 'Obeydeh Jarrah killed people and plundered the land of the Khazars. When he returned to Azerbaijan the *Khaqan* supported by several Turkic tribes gathered an army of 300,000 men. Peshang, the son of the *Khaqan*, passed Darband with that army and alighted at the confluence of the two rivers Kur and Aras. He sent his army to pillage the countryside. The army of Abu 'Obeydeh at that time was dispersed and he himself had gone to the plains of Ujan to destroy a fire temple. He confronted them with as many men as he had and there was a fierce battle and the Moslems were defeated, and Abu 'Obeydeh himself was killed and his wife was captured. A man from the notables of Azerbaijan, called Mardanshah, who was accompanying the army of Islam, was also killed.

The fire-temple (Atashgah) at Sorkhan, near Baku

The Turkish army started killing people and plundering in the provinces of Armenia and Azerbaijan, but from the coinage of Armenia it is clear that at this time of the revolt this province had not slipped out of the hands of the caliphs. When the news reached the caliph of that time, Hesham b. 'Abdol-Malek,[9] in the year 114/733 he sent Sa'id b. 'Amr Harshi with a large force to fight the Turks. After some victories he reached Bileqan in Qarabagh. There he heard that the son of the *Khaqan* had surrounded one of

---

9. Hesham b. 'Abdol-Malik (r. 723 - 743); for information on his activities see al-Tabari, *History* vol. 25 "The End of Expansion," translated by Khalid Yahya Blankinship (Albany, 1989).

the forts of the Moslems and that they were about to surrender. Therefore, he sent one of the princes of Fars, who was known as the master of a piebald horse and who knew the language of the Khazars, to notify the people of the fort that he was coming. The next day the Khazars captured the prince and asked who he was and where he was going. He said: "the Arab general [**49**] has sent me to notify the people of the fort that he is coming." They told him, "if you want to be saved go to the fort and say that the Arab army is very far." When the prince came to the gate he shouted: "You Moslems, you know me, the good news is that Sa'id Harshi is with a huge army in Bileqan and in few days he will be here. Be brave." The Moslems said "Allahu Akbar." The prince was torn into pieces by the Turks. They themselves moved and went to Ardabil. At this time someone with clothes and a white horse came to Sa'id and said that 2,000 Khazars with 5,000 Moslem captives are in such-and-such a place. Sa'id sent a spy and he found that what he was saying was true. At the end of the night he suddenly fell upon them and killed most of them and freed the captives. The remainder of the army fled to the son of the *Khaqan* and Sa'id returned with much booty. The owner of the white horse came again. Sa'id said: "where were you, good adviser, for I have kept a good reward for you." He replied: "it will be even better if the emir keeps it, for I would like now to take you to another bounty. A number of Khazars are in such-and-such place with captives and much baggage, and they are going to their own land." A number of Moslems went to that location and shouting "Allahu Akbar" attacked. Many Turks were killed and the captives and the booty fell into their hands. Sa'id honored the relatives of Abu 'Obeydeh Jarrah and gave them much property. After this event the son of the *Khaqan* was down-cast and went to fight and Sa'id sent couriers to Bileqan, Barda' and other towns that obeyed him and called for recruits. Once again the man with the white horse appeared and greeted him. Sa'id answered him with great joy and said: "You are a blessed man; you are a felicitous man. I have won two victories because of you. I have kept very many rewards for you, why don't you accept them?" He said: "when I want I will get them, now prepare for battle, because the son of the *Khaqan* with 40,000 troops is coming towards you." Sa'id put his army in battle order and in the afternoon the two armies clashed and battle ensued. In the evening the Turks fled, many were killed and Sa'id returned to his camp ground. In the morning the man of the white horse came and said, "Oh Emir, the son of the *Khaqan* has gathered his scattered army with the intention to give battle." Sa'id ordered some to guard the heavy baggage and he himself set off with the majority of the army. After the armies reached each other he asked, "where is Peshang, the son of the *Khaqan* standing?" They said, "in a place where a head is on a stake." He said: "whose head is that?" They said, "the head of Abu 'Obeydeh Jarrah." Sa'id attacked that side with the courageous army and struck the crown from the head of the *Khaqan*'s son, who fell from his horse. A number of people gathered around him and put him on his horse again. The fire of battle was aflame; at the end the Turks left the battleground and much booty fell into the hands of the people of Islam. Sa'id sent one-fifth to Hesham b. 'Abdol-Malek and the rest of the booty [**50**] he divided among 40,000 people and to each person 1,700 dinars was allotted.

After that, in the year 115/734, Hesham gave the provinces of Armenia, Azerbaijan and Shirvan to his brother Abu Moslem. He sent him with 24,000 soldiers from Syria and Iraq to put the affairs of Daghestan in order. It appears to the present author that Abu Moslem is the same as Maslameh b. 'Abdol-Malek. Perhaps in writing there was a mistake, or, as it is the fashion with the Arabs, Abu Moslem is the patronymic and Maslameh is his name and he was known by both.[10] At any rate, Abu Moslem came to Darband where he repaired the destroyed parts of the fort and the wall. He destroyed a big building that was called Sahranj, which was in the keep of the citadel (*narin-qal'eh*) and dated from the time of Anushirvan, and instead built an arsenal and reservoirs for water, oil (*naft*), and provisions. He reinforced the keep of the citadel and he improved the Qeyd palace, whose wall he extended more than 100 cubits into the sea. The present writer says that when three or four years ago that Qeyd building was opened up from one side, there appeared big stones which were joined together with iron bars and between them they had molten lead. He ordered that the taxes of all of Daghestan, in cash and in kind, be stored in storehouses and when it was needed it was to be divided between the guards and the people of Darband. In short, he settled most of the people of Darband who were Moslem, in seven quarters and for each one he built a mosque. They were called after each people, so that the first one was the Khazar Mosque; the second the Palestinian Mosque; the third, the Damascus mosque; the fourth, the Homs mosque; the fifth, the Kayseri mosque; the sixth, the Jazayer [S. Iraq] mosque, and the seventh, the Mosul mosque. In addition, he built a big Friday mosque, which still exists. He gave the town six gates. The first is the Bab al-Mohajer (Traveler's Gate), which is now known as Jarchi Qapu (Herald's gate). The second, Bab al-Jehad (Jehad gate), which is now known as Qerkhler Qapu (The Gate of the Forty). The third is the Bab al-Khoms (The One-Fifth Gate), which they now call Yengi Qapu (New Gate). Fourth is the Bab al-Saghir (Small Gate), which is now known as Turkman Qapu (Turkman Gate). Fifth is the Bab al-Maktub (Gate of the Book), which is now called Bayat Qapu (Bayat Gate). Sixth is the Bab al-'Alqameh ('Alqameh Gate),[11] which is now known as Narin-Qal'eh Qapu (Citadel Gate). After putting all that in order he went to Qomuq. The people there after many fights sued for peace and were converted to Islam. A Friday Mosque was constructed in the middle of the town of Ghazi-Qomuq, which is still in existence. He made Shahbal or Shah Ba'l b. 'Abdollah b. Qasem b. 'Abdollah b. 'Abbas b. 'Abdol-Motalleb governor over them and he appointed a qadi to teach them the doctrine of Islam. After that he came to Qeytaq. The people there after many fights and many of them being killed accepted Islam. He made an Emir called Hamzeh, [51] one of his own people, governor there. Then he went to Tabarsaran where most of the people were Jews or without religion. At first they wanted to defend themselves, but when the governor and many of them were killed or captured they were converted to Islam. He made a man called Mohammad Ma'sum, who was a righteous and charitable person, governor there and left two judges to teach the religious law of Islam. He said that "all the people of Tabarsaran should do as Mohammad Ma'sum and the two Qadis would require." After settling the

---

10. This is a correct conclusion by Bakikhanov. See Minorsky, *The History of Sharvan*, p. 6.
11. 'Alqameh is the name of one of the Companions of the prophet Mohammad.

affairs of all of these places he went to the people of Tav, i.e. the mountain (*tagh*), and to the Avars and with his sword he converted them to Islam. He built mosques and appointed qadis. Aqusheh is now the most important place in Tav as Khomzaq is in the Avar country. He ordered all the governors and judges of Daghestan, from Georgia up to the steppes of Qebchaq, to be under Shahbal. He said that if the Khazars come to Darband you should confront them. The merchants who came from the Khazars had to stop at one *farsakh* from the city and after buying and selling they had to return. Anyone from Darband who went for trade to the Khazar would pay one-tenth of his goods. If an envoy came they would blindfold his eyes and would take him out the same way, so that the Khazars would not have knowledge about Darband. He imposed payment of taxes (*kharaj*) on all of Daghestan and ordered that the people of Tabarsaran, Kupchi and Qeytaq would bring it every year and deliver it to the governor of Darband. He would deduct his own and Emir Hamzeh's salary; the remainder would be kept in the store-house to be used for the guards and the poor of Darband. If he took more than had been assigned to him and was unjust the army commanders would dismiss him. The people of Hamri, Kur, Qobbeh, Qolhan [Golechan], Qorah, Akhti, Knov, Rotul, Zakhur and all of Qomuq, Avar, Qarakh, Hedat, Tarkhu [Tarki], Ahran, and Enderey paid the taxes to Shahbal. If an enemy would come to Shahbal or he would go to fight the unbelievers, the governors of Qeytaq and Tabarsaran would help him with their troops. The governor of the city guarded the city all the time and did not go anywhere. Every Friday he would lead the prayer in the Friday Mosque. Kateb Chelebi in the *Jahannama* quotes Abu Hamed that after organizing the affairs of Darband Hesham himself had come to that city and in accordance with the request of the people left his sword near Darband as a souvenir, which now is a place of pilgrimage. The present author says that, according to the sayings of trustworthy persons from among the people of Upper Tabarsaran, there is a dagger inside a cave near the village of Jurdaf in the district of Kharaq. [52] People of that place go there to make pilgrimage and give alms. They consider the area around it, in a circumference of one *farsakh*, as sanctuary, so that property there is safe from confiscation and a killer safe from having to pay blood-money and one cannot even cut a branch from the trees of the forest in that place. One can say that the sword of Hesham is that same dagger; because of the length of time and the vast distance it is known as a sword.

In the year 120/739, Marwan b. Mohammad was sent by Hesham as the governor of Darband and he acted according to the regulations which had been fixed by Abu Moslem. Every year, the people of Tabarsaran would clean the streets and lanes of Darband. Because in the year 132/751 the caliphate went from the Ommayads to the Abbasids, Abu 'Abbas Saffah was doing his best to keep Darband and its environs in order. When in the year 136/755 Abu Ja'far Mansur became the caliph[12] he appointed Yazid b. Asad as governor of Darband. In his time, the Khazars came with a huge army and laid siege to Darband and one night they stacked up a lot of wood so that they could climb up to the fort. The guards of the fort became aware of this and poured oil (*naft*) and set fire to them. The Khazars returned without any success. Abu Ja'far Mansur asked Yazid b. Asad

---

12. Abu Ja'far Abdallah b. Muhammad al-Mansur (r. 754 - 775), the second Abbasid caliph.

to come to him and said: "how can we get rid of the Khazars?" Yazid replied that around Darband there were many forts that were in ruins. If they would be repaired and guards put there, defending Darband would be easier. In accordance with the order of the caliph, Yazid returned and started repairing the places and forts. Among them were the forts of Sovar, Mota', Kamakh and Fort Sofnan, which is now called Cherkeni. He repaired Darvaq, Yersi, and Homeydi and he brought 7,000 families from Iraq, Syria and Mosul and settled them there. He also built two forts named Yazidiyeh and Sarmakiyeh. He settled some of his own people there and developed Maqatir and Mahraqeh. He put troops everywhere and in this way he kept Darband safe, for the Khazars could not cross the Quy-su.

In the year 170/787 Harun al-Rashid[13] appointed Jayun b. Najm as the governor of Darband. He maintained the place in accordance with the previous order. Jayun because of being confident in the strength of the fort and the walls became a tyrant and lived a life of debauchery. He neglected the affairs of the country. Many of the people of Darband went away. This news reached Harun in Baghdad and he appointed Rabi'eh al-Baheli as governor of Darband, who put Jayun in chains and sent him to Baghdad.

In the year 173/790, Khozeymeh b. Jazem with 12,000 troops of Harun al-Rashid's army came to Darband. He built many towers and forts. [53] After a while Harun al-Rashid himself came to Darband and looked after its affairs. He rerouted a stream from the river Rubas to Darband and constructed many gardens, orchards and mills, whose income he endowed to the poor of Darband. He appointed Hafseh b. 'Omar to the governorship of Darband and he gave him the necessary instructions and orders, and then returned to Baghdad. They say that there is a stone dome opposite the Kerkhlar Gate on the northern side of Darband, where the son of Harun al-Rashid is buried. It is known that Zobeydeh Khatun, daughter of Abu Ja'far Mansur, the esteemed wife of Harun al-Rashid, because she had been cured of a chronic fever in a place known as Tab-riz, which is known for its good climate, repaired the ruins of an old city in the year 175/792, which dated from the time of the kings of Fars, and called that town Tabriz. From this event and the death of the son of Harun al-Rashid it is very likely that Zobeydeh had come with her husband.

In the year 180/797, the Khazars again invaded and occupied all of Daghestan, Darband and Shirvan. According to Kateb Chelebi, 140,000 Moslems were killed during this conflict. Such a catastrophe had never happened before in the time of Islam. Thus it must be assumed that the children of the children of king Ba'l, Amir Hamzeh and Ma'sum, who had been appointed governor by Abu Moslem, perished during this conflict and no sign of them is left. The tribes of Daghestan who had been converted to Islam, because of the dominance of the Khazars and the weakness of the Moslems, returned to their idol worshipping faith. In every place an emir and in every corner a wicked person started to make trouble. At that time, Farrokhzad b. Akhshiyan was the king of Shirvan. In a mosque, in the village of Bibi Heybat near Baku, which had been built at his orders, his title is inscribed as 'The Great Soltan Naser, Lord of the Believers'. From this it becomes

---

13. Harun al-Rashid (r. 786 - 808).

evident that that the Moslems were obedient to the Abbasid caliph. After him Filanshah became king.[14]

In the year 210/826 [**54**] a certain Babak from the Magians rose up in the region of Bileqan and founded one of the branches of fire worshipping, which is called Khorramkish, which in fact is another form of Mazdak's hedonistic religion, and many gathered around him.[15] He brought about much immorality. They say that the number of people killed because of him is more than one million. In continuous battles he conquered Azerbaijan as well as Hamadan and Isfahan. The caliph Mo'tasim[16] sent Eshaq b. Ebrahim b. Mos'eb with a big army to Persian Iraq. He killed 60,000 people, but no success was achieved. Eventually in the year 221/836 Heydar b. Kavus known as Aqshin[17] one of the rulers of Central Asia, with a large army was appointed to oppose Babak and the war lasted two years. Babak suffered a major defeat and he fled with a number of people to Armenia to Sahl b. Sonbat. Aqshin sent a trusted person with 4,000 troops to get him. Sahl put him in chains and sent him to Afshin. Sahl was given extra favors and Babak was taken to Baghdad and was killed with great humiliation.

Azerbaijan is perhaps the Arabicized form of Azerbaigan and the name is derived from him or another Babak. It is well-known that in the beginning the faith of fire worshipping was prevalent in this land. The author of *Riyaz al-Siyaha* [18] says that Azerbaijan is the Arabic form of Azerbigan, which in old Persian meant fire temple.[19] In short, in this way the provinces of Azerbaijan and Armenia came into the possession of the caliph, and the city of Barzan in the Moghan, which was destroyed, was made prosperous by Afshin. Now it is in ruins again.

---

14. From the year [blank] to the year [blank] to the year [blank] is written in this way. In Azerbaijan there was a man called Babak, from the Majus tribe, who rebelled. For a period of time he was engaged in seditious practices, the killing of the faithful, the destruction of towns and the propagation of the faith of Fire worship. Mo'tasim, son of Harun al-Rashid, became caliph in the year 218/834. He sent his slave Aqshin [=Afshin] with a large army to fight Babak. Babak fled to Armenia and Afshin with 4,000 troops asked for him from the governor of Armenia Sahl b. Sonbat. Sahl caught him and brought to him Afshin, who sent him to Baghdad where he was killed. [B]

15. The date of 826 is wrong and must be due to a copyist's error, given that Babak Khorrami's uprising started around the year 816 CE and was quelled in 837 and he himself was executed in 838. For more information see [http://www.cais-soas.com/CAIS/History/Post-Sasanian/babak_khorrami.htm]

16. al-Mu'tasim (r. 833 - 842).

17. Khaydar b. Kavus Afshin. His name was Arabicized as Haydar. The use of Aqshin in the text must be due to a copyist's error, for Afshin was a hereditary title of the rulers of Oshrusana in Transoxiania. For more information see [http://www.cais-soas.com/CAIS/History/Post-Sasanian/afshin.htm].

18. Zeyn al-'Abedin al-Shirvani, *Riyaz al-Siyaha* ed. by Sa'id Tabataba'i Na'ini (Isfahan, 1339/1920).

19. Azerbaijan is believed to have been derived from the name of Atropates, the governor of Media, and after the death of Alexander the Great (323 BCE), independent ruler of a region in N. W. Iran called Atropatene, whose name means 'protected by fire'; see L. Chamont, "Atropates," *Encyclopedia Iranica*.

In the time of the caliph Vathiq bi'llah,[20] son of Mu'tasim, around 230/845, Filanshah Shirvani pledged allegiance to the caliph and Darband came into the possession of the caliph. In the year 270/884, at the orders of caliph Mu'tamid[21] the oil and salt mines of Baku were assigned to the guards and the people of Darband. Mohammad b. 'Ammar was the revenue collector. Every year he divided the income of the mines according to the allotment. In 290/903, a certain Hashem was appointed to the governorship of Darband. Because caliph Muktafi[22] was at war with the Carmathians[23] there was major disorder in the affairs of the caliphate. The total of pensions and incomes of the mines and the produce of the villages that the people of Darband were entitled to he took for himself. The people of Darband were forced to engage in trade and crafts, and corruption and debauchery became prevalent among them. The Khazars came and made a major effort to seize Darband. Finally, Moslems from inside and outside [55] attacked and put them to flight. At this time, the tribe of the Rus, having been promised shared spoils of whatever they would get, received permission from the king of the Khazars to ferry 50,000 of them in 500 boats across the Atal River, and entered the Caspian Sea where they killed and plundered towns and places from Mazandaran until Darband that had been safe from the attacks of the Khazars, because they did not have ships.

Abu'l-Qasem Yusof b. Abi al-Saj had become the governor of Armenia and Azerbaijan at the orders of caliph Muqtadir bi'llah[24] from the year 296/909 for ten years. He was also governing Shirvan and he gathered his people at the oil coast, i.e. Baku, which was inside the province of Shirvan and under the governorship of 'Ali b. Heysham. The Rus after pillaging and killing people settled in the islands near Baku. Some remains of their presence can still be seen in those places. The army of Islam went to them in boats, defeated them and killed many, and returned. The remaining Rus stayed there and plundered the coastal area for a while. After having gathered enough booty they returned and gave half of it to the *Khaqan*. A group of Moslems who lived among the Khazars attacked the Rus to take revenge; eventually the Rus were defeated and went to the kingdom of the Portas and from there to Bolghar. The Moslems of that land behaved in the same manner and 30,000 Rus were killed during this battle. Mas'udi who in the year 333/944 wrote about this event says that the Rus after that did not invade those lands anymore. But Ibn Athir in his *History*[25] does not mention this event and says that the tribe of the Rus in the year 332/944 came from the sea and the river Kur to take Barda', the capital of Arran. The governor of that town with 5,000 people hurried to defend it and then was defeated and returned. The Rus took Barda' and spared the life of the people. Since they were opposing

---

20. Vathiq b. Mu'tasim (r. 842 - 847).
21. al-Mu'tamid (r. 870 - 892).
22. al-Muktafi (r. 902 - 908).
23. The Carmathians were an Isma'ili sect with its power base in Bahrain and eastern Arabia, where they established a utopian community in 899 CE and started a revolt against the Abbasid caliphate.
24. Al-Muqtadir (908 - 932).
25. Abi al-Hasan 'Ali b. Abi al-Karam Muhammad al-Shibani Ibn al-Athir, *al-Kamil fi'l-Ta'rikh* 8 vols., edited by Abi al-Fida 'Abdullah al-Qadi, Muhammad Yusuf al-Daqaq & Ibrahim Shams al-Din (Beirut, 2003).

them the Rus ordered them to vacate the city within one week and whoever was left would be killed or enslaved. Every slave was sold for 20 *derham*. Nineteen thousand captives, men and women, were in their hands. The governor of Azerbaijan, Mohammad b. Mosafer, known as Marzban, came to fight the Rus with 30,000 troops but he was defeated. The Rus remained there for more than one year. They marched to Maragheh and because of eating too much fruit they all became ill. Marzban feigned as if he wanted to give battle, but after some resistance he fled. The Rus pursued him and Marzban turned around and attacked and an army that [**56**] had been waiting in ambush attacked them from behind. The Rus were defeated and many of them along with their commander were killed. Those remaining took refuge in the citadel of Barda', which at that time was called Shahrestan. Marzban, because of this event, went with his army to Salmas and left part of the army to lay siege to the Shahrestan. The Rus who were desparate because of sickness and lack of provisions took their precious things and went to the bank of the river Kur. They took to their boats and returned to their homeland.[26] The present author says that it is probable that these two events may have happened in the same campaign and the historians because of differences in their view have written it in a different way. According to Mas'udi, in the year 232/944, 'Abdol-Malek was governor of Darband; he was the nephew of the emir of Tabarsaran. After that, gradually, due to the passage of time, rebellions and disturbances came to the lands of Islam and the caliphs of Baghdad could not manage their own army, and the affairs of this land became disrupted. The forts and places which were under Darband became rebellious and the emirs of Daghestan began fighting each other and the kings of Deylam of the lineage of Mardavij b. Ziyad, who were from the dynasty of the old kings of Gilan, in the year 315/927 rebelled in Tabarestan, and six of them were ruling most of the provinces of Iran for a period of 150 years.[27] It seems that they had some dominance in these parts, because Shamgir b. Ziyad, the second king of that dynasty, acceded to the throne in the year 323/935 and reigned for 35 years. He constructed the city of Shamgir, which is near Ganjeh, and he placed tall minarets with two entrances at the mosque. The remains of that city, the fort and the bridge still are in existence. This city was prosperous in the time of Emir Timur Gurgan and thereafter. In the *Akhti-nameh* it is mentioned that in the time of the occupation of Shirvan by the Khazars one of their chiefs, a certain Samsam, stayed with his emirs and some people in a place, which is now called the village of Mikragh. A certain Emir Kaghi who was originally from Syria became his vizier. Another city was built on the left bank of the river Samur to help Samsam. The people there, called Tarsa, had been brought from a place that is now called Qezlar. Samsam wanted to take the fort of Shahbani and to kill a certain Darvisha'i, who was from the lineage of the Shahbani emir. Darvisha'i sent 3,000 gold coins and induced the emirs of Tarsa to come to his side. Samsam laid siege three times, but he had to return without success. The first time, the time of the siege lasted one month. Getting water from the river

---

26. On these events see, e.g., Boris Andreevich Dorn, *Caspia; über die Einfalle der alten Russen in Tabaristan, nebst Zugaben über andere von ihnen auf dem Kaspischen Meere und in den anliegenden Ländern ausgeführte Unternehmungen* (St.-Petersbourg, Eggers, 1875).
27. For the reign of this dynasty known as the Buyids see *CHI*, vol. 5.

Akhti was difficult for the people of the fort and they brought water with great difficulty from the river Samur. After the return of Samsam, Darvisha'i made a secret road from the fort [57] to the river Akhti in three months' time, whose remains and tower at its beginning still can be seen. The second time it lasted six months and the state of the people in the fort did not become desperate. After three years he came for the third time from above and remained at Sar-e Hammam for seven years. Darvisha'i perforce asked the chiefs of Tarsa to come to his help with experienced people from the Rotul, Jonoq, Rofuq [tribes]. They battled for seven more months. Many people on both sides, including Qasem, the son of Darvisha'i, were killed. Eventually Samsam was defeated. There was peace for 15 years. Suddenly one night he attacked the village of Tarsa; he killed everyone and took their property and their wives. Nine years had passed when Darvisha'i came to Darband to Abu Moslem and asked for help. He gave his sister Omm al-Mo'manat to Darvisha'i who was a Moslem and sent an army to conquer the city of Samsam and defeat the Khazars. For seven months the war continued, but there was no progress. Darvisha'i came to the tent of Sheikh Shah Elborzi, who was from the tribe of the Qoreysh, but, because he lived in the lands of Elborz he was known by this title. A mountain on whose slope he stayed was called after him. Because of this and the frequency of usage it is known as Shalborz. He secretly sent somebody to Emir Kaghi, the vizier of Samsam, who was from Syria. They deliberated and came to an agreement. Emir Kaghi informed his followers in the city and Darvisha'i with 6,000 troops on Friday night came to the gate and the followers of Emir Kaghi took them into the city. Emir Kaghi went with 10 people and killed Samsam; Darvisha'i came to Government House and asked the people to convert to Islam. Those who became Moslem received special treatment; those who did not become Moslem were killed and their property, goods and family were taken. The city was known as Emir Kaghi and gradually was changed and was known as Mokragh. Then Darvisha'i and Emir Kaghi and Shah Elborzi went to see Abu Moslem in Darband and he gave them a very warm welcome and called the village of Shahbani after the name of his sister, Okhti, which because of the frequent usage has become Akhti. According to the people, the prayer niche of the mosque of Akhti is a remnant of the construction by Abu Moslem. At this time five relatives of Samsam, who had fled, attacked Shah Elborzi and killed one of his sons and took captive two of his daughters. His wife with another son fled. Therefore, Shah Elborzi took 30 families from the town of Mir Kaghi and made Qoreysh his residence. Because of frequent usage, this has become Qorush and on [58] the left bank of the river Samur opposite Kalleh-e Kureh in a place called Qepchah there are ruins of a city, which, according to the accounts of the locals, was the place of residence of the emir of Tarsa. The reason why this place is called Qepchah may be that the name of their original homeland was Qebchaq. It is very likely that this event took place in the time of Sheikh Abu Moslem in the 5th century *hijri*, because he was living with his family and herds in this place. His tomb in the city of Khomzaq is a dome made of rock, which is famous. Abu Moslem, the brother of the caliph, came with his army and then returned. Bringing the sister and giving her in marriage here is very unlikely. In a history written by Mohammad b. Rafi' b. 'Abdol-Rahim Shirvani in the year 712/1313 and transcribed in 1030/1617, it is clear from documents and old letters and also from an another manuscript written in 118/931 that Sheik Abu

Eshaq Ebrahim, Sheikh Ahmad, and Sheikh 'Ali from the lineage of the paternal aunts of the daughter of Hamzeh had come in the company of Sheikh Mohammad and Sheikh Naser al-Din from the lineage of 'Abbas b. 'Abdol-Motalleb of the Qoreysh in the year 200/816 from the holy places (Mekka and Medina) to Syria with 2,000 of their followers and relatives. After several years they had gone with 5,000 people to Egypt and after having stayed there for several years and after having traveled to several countries they had come to the land of Cherkes, which at that time was Dar al-Harb (enemy country). They had tried very hard to kill Emir Azal and they took his goods and family as booty. From there they had come to the land of the Qeytaq. They killed the Emir there, called Ghazanfar, and took his goods and treasures and converted the inhabitants to Islam. According to their customs, whoever was old in age would become emir and others without controversy and differences would follow him. At that time Emir Chuban b. Soltan 'Ali Bey was their emir. After most of the people of Tabarsaran had been converted to Islam he gave his daughter to Ma'sum Bey, the Emir of Tabarsaran, and married his daughter. He built many villages in Qeytaq and signed a treaty with the Emirs of the Qomuq. After a while, he broke his treaty and suddenly attacked and killed many of them and took their city and converted them to Islam. One of his relatives, a certain Shamkhal, who was called after the name of the birthplace of his ancestors in the village of Khal in the country of Sham [Syria], was appointed as emir. Then he came towards the southern mountains and conquered the town of Madhara which is considered as part of the Qabaleh district [59] and made it his residence. The males and females of that village were his property. *Madha lafz* is an Arabic phrase, which means "what is this." He destroyed many villages in the neighborhood that belonged to the infidels. He made a pact with the emirs of Qorush who were Esma'il Bey and Hasan Bey and he collected tax, poll-tax and tithe from all the people of the Mountains until the region of Shamakhi. By sending correspondence and envoys to Soltan Fereydun Shirvanshah he made friendly relations and gave his daughter to the former's son, Soltan Key Qobad, and the former's daughter to his own son, Soltan Soleyman. For a while there was friendship and cordiality between them. Eventually, because of taxes and tithe enmity arose between them and for a while they were fighting with each other and then they made peace again. In another manuscript, Hasan 'Alavi-ye Safavi, the Qadi of Qomuq, quotes in great detail and with some differences from another text which is in the handwriting of the abovementioned Mohammad b. Rafi', written when the town of Qomuq was being destroyed by the Turks, and there are several copies of this manuscript in Daghestan, that apart from what was said earlier that in the town of Tanus, the old capital of the Avars, which is now a village, near Qamzaq, a powerful and strong emir known as Seraqeh had converted to Islam and had changed his name to Nowsal. The Avars called their kings by this name. The present author believes that his lineage as it was recorded, because of some discrepancies in events and names, does not seem to be trustworthy. At any rate, this Seraqeh[28] who was the son of Saretan b. Oruskhan b. 'Omma Khan b. Firuzshah from the lineage of 'Araskani held sway over an area of Shamakhi until

---

28. Bunyatov (p. 226, n. 87), following Bakikhanov's Russian translation, writes that among the Avars he is known as Surakat. See also appendix II.

the land of the Cherkes. From all the governorships and people except for the small town of 'Akari he would collect taxes in different forms and monies from cultivation, herds, textiles, fruits and even eggs. The regulations were as follows: every family would give three silver *dirhams* or its value in gold and from the most prevalent form of cultivation one *keyl*, and from merchants two rolls of silk and two rolls of cotton fabric (*karbas*), and from each garden one sack of grapes, and from every murderer 100 sheep and from every criminal and thief one cow, and from each village to celebrate the accession of the new king five fox pelts, one of which black and four yellow, and five rams, and for the burial of the deceased king one horse, and for every marriage in the family one cow and two rams.[29] The kingdom of Qomuq had other emirs and the Qeytaq also had separate emirs, whose chief with full authority and power was called Ghazanfar [meaning lion]. The descendants of Hamzeh and 'Abbas who had come from Egypt and Syria fighting their way to the land of Byzantium and India eventually had come to Shirvan and they had made preparations for the campaign, and with good elephants, camels [**60**] and horses went to Daghestan to make holy war. The people of Daghestan and the tribe of the Rus on account of the news of their approach all gathered in the vicinity of the town of Chur or Sur. The Moslems sent 100 of their brave men to reconnoiter the state of the enemy and because of their number and strength they became very frightened, and therefore they had recourse to a stratagem. They cooked many dishes and mixed them with a poisonous herb, which, along with a few goods, they left in the camp and when the fighting began they fled. The enemy's army took the camp and ate the food and many of them were killed and then they fled. The Moslems then initiated a number of conquests. First, they destroyed the province of Qeytaq and occupied it. Emir Chupan b. Soltan 'Ali Bey became the governor there. Among the many villages that he built was the fort of Qoreysh. He made it the center of his government. From there he went to Avar. Its emir Bayat b. Seraqeh fled to the neighborhood of Tush, which was part of his kingdom. The Moslems by continuous fighting extended their conquest in length and width. Their descendants gradually took hold of the Crimea. In short, many villages in Avar were destroyed and the town of Khamzaq was taken by force, its men were killed and their wives and property were taken as booty. All of that land came into the possession of the Moslems and the people were converted to Islam. A certain Ma'sum Bey, one of the descendants of Sheikh Ahmad, became emir, and Sheikh Abu Moslem, who was the most learned scholar, became the qadi and imam of that country. Since all of Daghestan came into their possession, some parts by destruction and killing and some parts by peace, a certain Shamkhal among them in the town of Qomuq became the chief emir of Daghestan. His name has become the name for a position, because all his successors are called Shamkhal. He received all the taxes from the land, poll-taxes from the protected religious minorities, and tithe from the traders, and *zakat* from the Moslems, and took one fifth for himself. The remaining four-fifths he divided equally among the sons of Hamzeh and 'Abbas. According to another text, the presents that the caliph of Baghdad sent continuously he also divided in the same manner. People whom over time would descend from this family were exempted from all government taxes. Nothing is

---

29. On fiscal regulations in Shirvan see also Minorsky, *The History of Sharvan*, pp. 117-18.

known about the life and the lineage of Hajji Mohammad, Abu'l-Qasem, Sheikh 'Ali, Mansur, and Hasan who are the descendants of 'Abbas and who lived at that time. According to the thinking of the present author, the regular taxes of the Shamkhal of Daghestan in the ninth [61] or tenth century *hijri* were as follows:

> For grazing the herds from the people of Hebelel every four years each household one sheep;

every year from the people of Qarakhi 500;

from the people of Kerkhi 300 sheep;

for the Crimea whose heir-apparent is still called Ghrim-Shamkhal 400 sheep;

from another mountainous region in Kerkhi 1,000 sheep;

for the Crimea 30;

from the people of Jamalal 500 sheep;

from the district of Tandeb 20 cows;

from the village of 'Archub, which now belongs to Ghazi-Qomuq 130 sheep, and for the Crimea 30 rams.

In the second year 10 sheep from the district of Khomzaq, 700 rams and 700 *keyl* of wheat and 60 *keyl*[30] of honey;

from the region of 'Andeb one cow and 8 felt floor covers.

From the towns of Ghadar and Horkus half of what they were getting from Khomzaq;

from the people of Tumel, who in the parlance of Avar are the people of Ghazi-Qomuq, from each household one ram and one *keyl* of wheat;

from Machqach, which was the private property of the Shamkhal, each household one sheep;

from the town of Kostak-sar each household one fish;

from the town of Tarkhu [Tarki] each household two *sa*[31] of rice;

from the village of Guyden 100 rams;

from the people of Qeytaq 150 buffaloes;

from the village of Aqusheh and Esisheh 100 cows;

from Zuqar 50 cows and from Surhi each house one *dirham*;

from the village of Jomjuqat and Kakoba, probably Shokoba, they are now part of Ghazi-Qomuq, six donkey loads of cooking oil (*rowghan*).

From the village of Zerehgaran 30 guns;

from Sombat Mountain 50 rams;

---

30. One *keyl* weighs between 6.5 and 22 liters depending on the location.
31. One *sa`* weighs 3.245 kg.

from the village of Erhani from each household one *keyl* of the usual cultivation;

from Zhentab Mountain 80 sheep;

from the people of Baqtolal 30 cows and 30 lambs;

from the Zakhuri and Gholdi Moutain, i.e. Jar, which is the private land of the Shamkhal, 50 sheep;

from the people of Res'or, which now is under Ghazi-Qomuq, and Mokroq 70 rams;

from [**62**] Koralal, which is also called Kur, 100 horses and 100 mares.

For a long time the land of Avar was in the hands of the descendants of Hamzeh until Emir Soltan b. Biyar b. Seraqeh, who had his residence in Tush, gathered an army from the beginning of Zomtal until the end of 'Arishti, and secretly in a dark night came to the region of Khomzaq and allied himself with some people who had not really accepted Islam and who were supporters of his family, hid his army in their houses, and in the morning Abu Moslem b. Yusof b. Mohammad b. Sheikh Abu Moslem, because of a dream that he had, and they say that it was concerning this event, fled to Qomuq. The following night, before day-break, Emir Soltan with the army entered Khomzaq, killed the emir of the Moslems Ahmad b. Chuban b. Soltan b. Ma'sum and cut off his head and hung it from the wall of the fort. All Moslems who were residing there were slaughtered. Emir Soltan sat on the throne of his ancestors and returned the people of that land who had been converted to Islam to heresy. There were many battles between them and the Moslems for a period of 24 years and eventually the people of Avar, because of the difficulty of living and the scarcity of provisions, were fed up and converted to Islam. In this way enmity turned into peace. For a long time they lived in peace and comfort. Eventually, because of temptation of the carnal soul, enmity appeared among the emirs of Qeytaq and differences appeared among the descendants of 'Abbas and Hamzeh. From the emirs of Qeytaq, Mohammad Khan and Emir Khan, Emir Hamzeh went to the king of the Avars asking for help. They signed a treaty of friendship. For many years they were fighting the emirs of Qomuq. Eventually, Saratan the king of the Avars sent envoys to Kothar Shah the Turk, whose tribe had been converted to Islam in the time of 'Omar b. al-Khattab, and they concluded a treaty of friendship. Kothar Shah asked for the hand of the daughter of King Saretan for his son and gave his sister in marriage to his son. Because of this relationship the bonds between them became strong. Kothar Shah attacked Qomuq with the Turkish army from the east and Malek Saratan with the Avar army and the emirs of Qeytaq from the west. This event happened in the time of Sheikh Najm al-Din.[32] In Fort Balay-Masjed [meaning small mosque] of Kekeli 70 young men fought and sacrificed their lives. The town of Qomuq was destroyed and its emirs fled. Kothar Shah and Malek Saratan returned. The Soltan of Qeytaq became independent in his hereditary lands. According to the present author, Emir Chuban lived at the end of the 5th century, because in the genealogy of the year 1030 he is put at the 10th level, whereas Sheikh Abu Eshaq Ebrahim is

---

32. Najm al-Din II (1294 - 1312), the Artaqid ruler of Mardin is possibly meant here, see *CHI*, vol. 5, pp. 393-94.

put at the 19th level. In short, after Harun al-Rashid, the 'Abbasids went into decline [63] and emirs of Islam everywhere became tyrants. Outwardly they were obeying the caliphs, but the caliphs were not able to defend themselves against the emirs and were reduced to giving them a title to their kingdom. Therefore, the affairs [of the state] had fallen into disorder and the tribes of the east and the north were invading most of the provinces, especially Shirvan and Daghestan. The Moslems were defending themselves, but unfortunately proper information about these periods is not available until the Seljuq kings became powerful in Iran.[33] Most of these kings had control over Shirvan and Daghestan. In their time, most of the people of the mountains were converted to Islam.

According to the most outstanding historians, Seljuq was a chief of a Tatar tribe, whose sons Mika'il and Israfil, with the permission of Soltan Mahmud the Ghaznavid, had come to the other side of the Oxus with numerous tribes.[34] In the year 432/1041 Toghrul Bey, son of Mika'il, who was son of Seljuq, defeated Soltan Mas'ud the Ghaznavid and became the king of Khorasan, Fars, Iraq, Kurdestan, and Azerbaijan. After his death in the year 443/1051 his brother's son Alp Arsalan became king of Iran and received the title of 'Ezz al-Din from the caliph Qa'im bi'amrollah.[35] He made some conquests in Georgia and its environs and went to the province of Armenia and made peace with its king and took his daughter in marriage. After his death in the year 454/1062 Malekshah b. Alp Arsalan put the country in good order and became extremely independent as a result of the wise counsel and endeavors of his father's vizier, [64] Nezam al-Molk.[36] Malekshah gave his daughter in marriage to the caliph Moqtadi bi'llah and in the company of Nezam al-Molk sent her to Baghdad.[37] They say that there were 130 camels with gold-wrought covers, precious fabrics, gold and silver utensils, six camels laden with silver boxes full of valuable jewels, 33 horses with saddles studded with pearls and rubies and other precious stones, and three studded howdahs on big camels with studded bridles and anklets. When the daughter of the Soltan with all this pomp and luxury entered Baghdad they made a big wedding for her in which 40,000 *man* of sugar were consumed. Malekshah launched many campaigns in areas near Byzantium (Rum), Georgia and Shirvan and the reign of this king was one of the best times, and the country was prosperous and the nation was entirely at peace. The unrivalled vizier Nezam al-Molk was firmly in control of the state. He talked with scholars and poets and sometimes he would write poems himself. This poem is by him:

---

33. It is known that the northern tribes were continuously in revolt and were plundering and killing people. The armies of the caliphs of Baghdad and the kings of Shirvan and the descendants of Hamzeh and 'Abbas, who had been established in Daghestan from the 5th century or 4th century, were trying to repel them.

34. On the rise and fall of the Seljuqs and the succession of rulers see *CHI*, vol. 5.

35. al-Qa'im (r. 1031 - 1075).

36. Abu Ali al-Hasan al-Tusi Nizam al-Mulk (1018 - 1092), vizier of Alp Arsalan and Malekshah.

37. al-Muqtadi (r. 1075 - 1094). In the B. version of the manuscript this paragraph has been added: In the year 482 (1089), Malekshah campaigned much in the regions of Anatolia and Shirvan and he was killed in the year 485 (1092) by the hands of one of the Assassins. He left the throne to his son Berk-Yareq. Berk-Yareq's younger brother was the ruler of this region and resided in Ganjeh, which he left to oppose his brother in 492 (1099), and met him in battle. Soltan Borkyareq came to face his brother. One day, the emirs of his army killed Majd al-Din Qomi in the palace, who was the state comptroller.

Quatrain:

Last night the beloved kissed me on the eyes

She went away leaving me with tearful eyes

My beloved kissed me on the eyes because

She saw her own face in my eyes

بوسی زد یار دوش بر دیدهٔ من
او رفت و ازو بماند تر دیدهٔ من
زآن داد برین دیده نگارینم بوس
کو چهرهٔ خویش دید در دیدهٔ من

During his life Hasan Sabbah[38] introduced the abominable religion of heresy, which in many respects was based on the religion of the Khorramkishan.[39] He brought together many suicidal devotees. Through corrupt practices he increased his authority and tyranny. Eventually, Torkan Khatun, the older wife of Malekshah, turned the Soltan against Nezam al-Molk with much bad-mouthing, and he had been dismissed for more than one year when he was killed by the dagger of the devotees of Hasan Sabbah, and while he was dying he wrote this poem for the king:

Fragment:

Forty years[40] lo King of young fortune

I wiped away the dust of tyranny from the face of the world

As my age came to ninety-six

In this journey I died from a single knife. [65]

The edict of good name and the signature of felicity

In your signature I took them to the Lord of Kingdom

I left all this service to my son

And entrusted to God and to my Lord.

چل سال باقبال تو ای شاه جوان بخت
گرد ستم از چهرهٔ آفاق ستردم
چون شد زقضا مدت عمرم نود و شش
اندر سفر از ضربت یک کارد بمردم

منشور نکو نامی و طغرای سعادت
پیش ملک العرش به توقیع تو بردم
بگذاشتیم این خدمت دیرینه بفرزند
او را بخدا و بخداوند سپردم

---

38. Hasan Sabah (ca. 1024 - 1134), the 'Old Man of the Mountain', was a Persian Isma'ili Nizari missionary, who led a community of adherents in the Alamut, in the Elburz mountains, from where he sent trained assassins to kill political figures. For more information see Farhad Daftary, *The Assassin Legends: Myths of the Isma'ilis* (London, 1994).

39. For the doctrine of the Khorramiyeh movement see Browne, *History*, vol. 1, pp. 323-29.

40. Nezam al-Molk was vizier from 1063-1092, thus thirty not 40 years. For a slightly different version of this poem see Browne, *Literary History*, vol. 2, p. 188-89.

Forty days after Nezam al-Molk Malekshah was also killed in the vicinity of Baghdad. In the year 482/1089 he went to the eternal world. His eldest son Berk-Yaruq acceded to the throne and Mahmud b. Malekshah was appointed as governor of Azerbaijan, Armenia and other districts, and he resided in Ganjeh. He opposed his brother and Soltan Berk-Yaruq defeated him. One day the chiefs of his army revolted and killed Majd al-Din, the comptroller of the *divan*, in his court. He became afraid by this dastardly deed. From Qohestan in Iraq he fled to Rey and Mohammad without any impediment or trouble acceded to the throne. After that there was four times war between the brothers. Both sometimes were defeated and sometimes were victorious. Eventually they made peace and the provinces of Syria, Diyarbekr, Azerbaijan, Moghan, Shirvan, and Armenia went to Mohammad and the other provinces of Iran belonged to Berk-Yaruq. In the year 489/1096 Berk-Yaruq died[41] and Soltan Mohammad became the king of the entire kingdom and he went to Baghdad.[42] In the year 491/1098 he received the title of Naser Amir al-Mo'menin from the caliph Mostahzar bi'llah.[43] After his death in the year 502/1109 Soltan Sanjar b. Malekshah, titled Borhan Amir al-Mo'menin, acceded to the throne and reigned for 40 years independently.[44]

In the *Tadhkereh* of Dowlatshah Samarqandi it is mentioned that Prince Mahmud, son of Soltan Mohammad, at the order of Soltan Sanjar ruled Iraq, Armenia and Azerbaijan for eight years, and according to the *Rowzat al-Safa*, [66] for eleven years, and the affairs of Shirvan and Daghestan were also in his hands. Eventually, in the year 519/1126, he rebelled against his uncle and was defeated. Soltan Sanjar forgave him and made him the governor of the abovementioned provinces as well as of the province of Syria. He gave his two daughters, one after the death of the other, in marriage to him.[45] He himself was in Khorasan and Transoxiania. When Soltan Mahmud became king his younger brother Mas'ud rose up against him. The two brothers sometimes fought against each other. They were the cause of the disorder in the affairs and the ruination of these lands. The Geor-

---

41. This date is wrong as Berk-Yaruq ruled from 1092 to 1105 CE. For this date and the confused situation of rivals and usurpers see *CHI* vol. 5, pp. 102-12.

42. Soltan Mohammad (r. 1105 - 18).

43. al-Mustahzir (r. 1094 - 1118).

44. Soltan Sanjar (r. 1118 - 56).

45. Variant: He also gave his own daughter to him and he himself was in Khorasan and Transoxiania until he became the prisoner of the Ghuzz tribe; weak and old and one year after his release he passed away. Mas'ud b. Mohammad was at war with Soltan Mahmud. Until the year 525/1131 his son Toghrol b. Mahmud acceded to the throne and in the year 529/1135 he died in the city of Hamadan. After him Mas'ud b. Mohammad b. Malekshah acceded to the throne. He was a just, generous, brave and famous king and Mostarshed bi'llah fought him, was defeated and taken captive. Because of the reproachful advice that Soltan Sanjar had sent from Khorasan Soltan Mas'ud sent the caliph with honor to Baghdad. But some of the heretics found an opportunity underway and killed the caliph. They themselves were punished by the Soltan. Soltan Mas'ud sent a son of his brother, Davud b. Mahmud, to Azerbaijan to eradicate evil and terror. He quelled the rebellion and died in the year 547/1143. After him Malekshah b. Mahmud acceded to the throne and because of excessive debauchery and drinking he neglected the affairs of state and his brother Mohammad acceded to the throne. He defeated his uncle Soleyman b. Soltan Mohammad near the river Aras. Because of some incidents there was enmity between him and the caliph. After a few days of siege of Baghdad the caliph gave his daughter Kerman Khatun in marriage and made peace. [B]

gians took possession of Tiflis and its environs. Soltan Mahmud died and his son Toghrol acceded to the throne and he also soon died in the city of Hamadan and Soltan Mas'ud became the sole king. During his lifetime the devotees of Hasan Sabbah started their reign of evil and terror in the lands of Iraq and Azerbaijan. The caliph Mustarshid bi'llah[46] in the year 534/1140 marched against them to suppress them, which was the cause of resentment between him and Soltan Mas'ud. This led to war between them in which the caliph was defeated and taken captive. Because of the reproach [67] and advice that Soltan Sanjar had written from Khorasan Soltan Mas'ud sent the caliph with proper honor to Baghdad. A group of devotees underway found an opportunity and killed the caliph by knifing him, and they were punished by the king. According to some historians, the killing of the caliph was at the instigation of Soltan Mas'ud, but it was rumored that he was killed by the devotees. In short, as soon as this news reached Baghdad, Rashed bi'llah son of Mostarshed bi'llah, became caliph[47]. Soltan Mas'ud went to Baghdad and Rashed bi'llah, who could not defend the city, went to Mosul. After one year of wandering in Azerbaijan and Persian Iraq he was knifed by devotees outside the city of Isfahan and died. As soon as he entered Baghdad Soltan Mas'ud appointed Muqtafi li'Amrollah[48] as caliph and he himself made the pledge of allegiance to him, but in reality he himself was the ruler. It is said that he asked through a messenger how much the caliph needed for his expenditures. The caliph replied that every day 40 mules for bringing water and other life necessities should be assigned. The Soltan said: "What a splendid Lord have we appointed to the caliphate. May God remove his calamity from the heads of the Moslems." At the end of the reign of Sanjar the tribe of Ghuzz crossed the Oxus and he went to fight them, but he was defeated and captured. After a while he fled and wanted to take revenge, but he died in the year 543/1148.[49] While he was dying he composed this poem:

Fragment:
With the world-conquering sword and the fort-opening mace
I conquered the world as I was conquered by wisdom
Many forts I opened with the show of one hand
Many battles I won by putting down a single foot
When death assailed me it was of no use
Existence is only God's and the kingdom is God's kingdom

به ضرب تیغ جهانگیر و گرزقلعه گشای
جهان مسخر من شد چومن مسخر رای
بسی حصار گشودم به یک نمودن دست
بسی مصاف شکستم به یک فشردن پای
اجل چو تاختن آورد هیچ سود نداشت
بقا بقای خدای است و مُلک مُلک خدای

---

46. al-Mustarshid (r. 1118 - 35).
47. al-Rashid (r. 1135 - 36).
48. al-Muqtafi (r. 1136 - 60).
49. This date is wrong. See above.

After this, Soltan Mas'ud reigned for 12 years independently and he was known for bravery, justice and consideration for his subjects. At the end of his reign, Malekshah b. Soltan Mahmud rose up and rebelled against him in Hamadan. The king came and suppressed the rebellion. In the year 554/1159 he died. Malekshah II, son of Mahmud, acceded to the throne. Because of his excess in debauchery and drinking he neglected the affairs of the country and his brother Mohammad II acceded to the throne. He fought with his uncle Soleyman, son of Soltan Mohammad, [68] near the river Aras and defeated him. Because of some incidents there existed enmity between him and the caliph Mostanjed bi'llah, son of Muqtafi Bi'llah.[50] After Baghdad had been besieged for a few days the caliph gave his daughter Kerman Khatun in marriage to him and made peace. After him in the year 556/1161 Soleyman b. Mohammad b. Malekshah acceded to the throne, but after six months, because of spouting profanities and a hedonistic life, he was imprisoned. Arsalan b. Toghrol b. Mahmud acceded to the throne and he was the patron of the poets Nezami, Zahir and Anvari.[51] He was a learned, just, charitable, experienced and wise king. After him in the year 571/1176 his son Toghrol b. Arsalan acceded to the throne and his uncle, Mohammad b. Toghrol, was his minister. After Mohammad's death his brother Qezel Arsalan replaced him. Eventually friendship was replaced by enmity and Qezel Arsalan, helping the caliph, defeated Toghrol and imprisoned him. After the death of Qezel Arsalan, Toghrol again acceded to the throne. He was an art-loving king and they say that he sometimes composed poetry. This poem is by him:

Quatrain:
Yesterday such a life-inspiring union
To-day such as world-burning separation
Alas, that in the scroll of my life the passage of time
Writes this and that one as a single day

دیروز چنان وصال جان افروزی
امروز چنین فراق عالم سوزی
افسوس که در دفتر عمرم ایام
آن را روزی نویسد این را روزی

In the year 590/1194 he was killed in the war with Takesh Khan, the Khvarezm Shah, and the kingship of this dynasty was transferred to the Khvarezmshahs who a few years before had become the ruler of Khvarezm and Fars. The situation of this dynasty in short is: a certain Anushtakin, one of the slaves of Malekshah Seljuqi, was appointed

---

50. al-Mustanjid (r. 1160 - 70).
51. Zahir-e Faryabi (ca. 1156 - 1201) is well-known for his panegyrics. He imitated Anvari and Khaqani and was imitated by later poets. Owhad al-Din Anvari (ca. 1126 - 1190) was master of panegyrics and he described the terrible Ghuzz invasion into Khorasan in 1153.

to the governorship of Khvarezm and after his death his son Qotb al-Din Mohammad [**69**] remained in this position and was given the title of Khvorazmshah. When Soltan Sanjar was taken captive by the Ghuzz tribe he struck coins and had the *khotbeh* read in his name. After him his son Atsiz and his son Soltan Shah, then Takesh Khan and Il Arsalan one after the other ruled. In the year 596/1200 Mohammad b. Takesh Khvarezmshah acceded to the throne, and because of Chengiz Khan's invasion, which had begun in the year 617/1221 and had continued for four years, he fled and died on the island of Abeskun in Mazandaran [in 1221]. His oldest son Jalal al-Din acceded to the throne and when he came to conquer Georgia it is not clear whether his kingdom included Shirvan and Daghestan.

A view of the Maiden Tower (Qiz Qalasi) part of the former city walls of Baku circa 1900

CHAPTER THREE

From the time of the Mongol invasion until the advent of the Safavids as well as the situation of the rule the Shirvanshahs

In the year 656/1258, during the reign of his brother Mangu Qa'an, Hulagu Khan b. Tuli b. Chengiz Khan, after he had come to Iran, killed caliph Musta'sam bi'llah[1] and put an end to the rule of the 'Abbasids. He settled two hundred thousand Turkic families that he had brought with him in different parts of Iran and most of the tribes of Iran, except the Lors and Kurds, are descended from them. The area from Syria to the Oxus and from Oman to Darband was under his rule. Hulagu Khan was very powerful and he had many virtues and qualities. He revered men of learning and philosophy and constructed many philanthropic institutions and buildings. In Tabriz, which was his capital, he built splendid buildings, and Khvajeh Naser al-Din Mohammad Tusi who was very close to him built an observatory in Maragheh in accordance with his orders.[2] In the year 663/1265, he left his kingship to his son Abaqa Khan [**70**] and died. Abaqa gave the governorship of Shirvan, Armenia and Azerbaijan to his brother Prince Yashmat. Meanwhile, Borkeh Khan, son of Chaghatay Khan, the king of the Qebchaq steppe sent Prince Buqa via Daghestan to conquer Azerbaijan. In early 664/1266, Yashmat defeated him near Darband and expelled him. After his defeat Borkeh Khan with 300,000 cavalry came via Darband and he did not stop until he arrived at the river Kur. Abaqa Khan also alighted near the Kur with many troops to cut off his passage. Borkeh Khan in order to cross the bridge turned to Tiflis, but he died underway because of sickness. His army dispersed and returned home. Abaqa Khan died in the year 681/1282. Takudar b. Hulagu, who after he had been converted to Islam was known as Soltan Ahmad in Iraq and Azerbaijan, acceded to the throne and spread justice. After two years, Arghun the son of Aqaba Khan killed him and acceded to the throne. He was a tyrannous and evil king. In the year 690/1291 he died and his brother Qeykhatu was enthroned. He spent his time in debauchery and drinking and he

---

1. al-Musta`sim (r. 1252 - 58).
2. See H. Daiber and F.J. Ragep, "Naser al-Tusi," *Encyclcopedia of Islam*2.

had affairs with the wives of his emirs. At the instigation of the emirs, Beydu b. Toraqay b. Hulagu came with his army from Baghdad and Qeykhatu fled to the Moghan. The emirs pursued him at the orders of Beydu Khan and in the year 694/1295 he was captured and killed. After this event Ghazan, son of Arghun Khan, who was governor of Khorasan and had been converted to Islam and was known as Soltan Mahmud,[3] seeking to avenge Qeykhatu came to fight with Beydu Khan. First they made peace and then war. The Khan fled and was killed near Nakhjevan at the hands of Emir Nowruz. Ghazan Khan acceded to the throne. They say he was a wisdom-loving king and one of his sayings [71] is that: 'The most difficult thing in the world is living, which is the reason for all hardship and trouble.' In the year 703/1304, after his death, Oljeytu Mohammad Khodabandeh, son of Arghun Khan, acceded to the throne and built Soltaniyeh and made it his capital. Some of the towers and mosques that he constructed can still be seen in the city of Baku and he was very interested in the research of scholars and the companionship of the olama. Because of his choosing Shi'a Islam he ordered coins to be struck with the names of the twelve Imams. He said many wise maxims that were taken down by scholars. One of his maxims is: "Kingship deserves a man who sets slaves free and enslaves the free by good deeds. [72] An ornament worthy of both men and women is truth. The reason for prayer is mentioning God and the reason for *zakat* is taking away the passion for worldly goods. The reason for fasting is strengthening the soul and preventing it from sinning. The reason

---

3. This passage has been added in the margin: Ghazan Khan was the reviver of Islam in the 6th century. Since Islam had become weak because of the dominance of infidels God caused Ghazan Khan to be converted along with 100,000 Turks en masse in the plains of Lar by Sheikh Ebrahim Hamavi, may God rest him in peace. They were converted to Islam and they all pronounced: "There is no God but God and Mohammad is his prophet." The signs of unbelief and heresy were removed. He spread Islamic law over the towns and districts. They are the guardians of the Book, commentators of the divine revelation and the keepers of the religious law of Mohammad. When the Soltan uttered these words everyone praised the prophet and his descendants. Then the Soltan said that the first proof of the descent from the prophet is 'Ali and the last is the Mahdi, the expected one. And so I cannot take possession of the kingdom of Mohammad without the consent of his descendants otherwise I will be a usurper. Since all olama accepted this he ordered the *khotbeh* to be read in the name of the household of the prophet and coins to be struck in their name. ... The reviver of the 7th century is Oljeytu, son of Arghun Khan, who became known as Soltan Mohammad Khodabandeh and in that abovementioned year, after the death of his brother, he acceded to the throne. Since he was informed that the religion of Mohammad had become so weak that in the prayers after the salutations, they did not say "peace be upon Mohammad and his family". He therefore came to the Friday Mosque of Soltaniyeh and ordered all the olama of Islam to be present and asked about the virtue of saying "Peace be on Mohammad and his family." Some olama said Imam Shafi'i has considered prayer without supplications invalid. Others said, according to Abu Hanifa prayer without supplications is undesirable, but not invalid. He said: "why do you not say supplications to the prophets and their family and only mention the prophet Mohammad in the supplications?" Since the olama remained silent and could not answer, the king said: "although I am young, two answers come to my mind. The first one is that since the enemies called him without [male] issue God caused them to be without sons so that their line was cut off and if there would be a trace of them they are unknown. Whereas the descendents of the prophet are so many that their number is only known to God and saying supplications for those following the prophet, they also are saluted. Another point is that the religions of all other prophets are abrogated and the religion of Mohammad will last until the Day of Resurrection. Therefore it is necessary for the community [of Moslems] to give supplications to these descendants following the example of the prophet, so that it becomes clear to the community who are the defenders of the religion of Mohammad." [B]

for pilgrimage (*hajj*) is seeing the man of perfection and acquiring good characteristics and knowledge. Whoever does not have these characteristics does not perform any of these religious acts properly."

After him, in the year 716/1317, his brave son Abu Sa'id, who was 13 years old, acceded to the throne. It was in his time that the king of the steppes of Qebchaq, Uzbeg Khan, from the lineage of Jurjin, son of Chenghiz, and from whom the Uzbeg tribe is descended, came via Darband to conquer Azerbaijan in the year 718/1319. Soltan Abu Sa'id went to confront him and in the plains of Qarabagh made his winter quarters. The Uzbeg army in Shirvan started killing and pillaging until Emir Chuban with 20,000 troops came to help him. The Uzbeg army could not withstand them and fled. Emir Chuban pursued them and killed many of them. The Uzbeg king came again in the year 735/1335 and via the same route to Azerbaijan. Abu Sa'id came to oppose him, but because of the heat and infection he fell ill in Shirvan and died in the year 736/1336. His contemporaries in the passage about his death say that he died in Qarabagh. Since Qarabagh is on the way to Shirvan therefore in the history books his place of death is known as Shirvan. In the introduction of the *Zafar-nameh* it is said that his wife Baghdad Khatun was the daughter of Emir Chuban, the previous wife of Hasan Ilkhani,[4] with whom the Soltan had fallen in love. He was forced to divorce her and then the Soltan married her. He also had her brother and father killed. At the instigation of Uzbeg she poisoned him. After him Arpa Khan of the lineage of Tuli b. Jenghiz acceded to the throne and defeated Uzbeg and expelled him from Shirvan and Darband. Meanwhile, Musa b 'Ali b. Beydu Khan rebelled and killed Arpa Khan. A certain Mohammad, also from the lineage of Hulagu, rose against him. After this several people from this dynasty fought each other and the result was the discontinuation of their lineage and the ruination of the state. Their strong government in Iran, Iraq and Azerbaijan passed to the Ilkhans.

The story of this dynasty is that Aq Buqa b. Ilkan b. Jalayer in the time of Keykhaytu was the commander of the army, and when Beydu Khan was killed his son Emir Hoseyn took the daughter of Arghun Khan as his wife. [73] His son Sheikh Hasan was the governor of Rum in the time of Soltan Abu Sa'id. After his death, Delshah Khatun, daughter of Khvajeh Demashq, son of Emir Chuban, married him and he rose to power. Sheikh Oweys, who was known for being very handsome, while in music, astronomy, and painting he was outstanding in his time, was born from Delshad Khatun. In the year 757/1356 he acceded to the throne of Iraq.[5] In the time when the rule of the descendents of Hulagu was in turmoil and the Ilkhans still were not independent, Sheikh Hasan, son of Teymurtash, son of the abovementioned Amir Chuban, ruled Tabriz and some other places for seven years and after the death of his ill-fortuned tyrant brother Emir Ashraf for another 13 years. Ashraf committed unimaginable tyrannous acts and gathered incredible wealth. Qadi Mohiy al-Din of Barda' went to the steppes of Qebchaq and requested Jani Bey Khan of the lineage of Juji, son of Chengiz Khan, who was a just and virtuous king, to come and punish and destroy Ashraf the tyrant. Jani Bey came with 30,000 troops via

---

4. See, e.g., the poem in Browne, *History*, vol. 3, p. 60.
5. See J.B. van Loon ed., *Ta'rikh-i Shaikh Uwais (History of Shaikh Uwais) an important source for the history of Adharbaija n in the fourteenth century* (The Hague, 1954).

Darband and Qabus, and the son of Qey Qobad the Shirvanshah rendered good services to him in this campaign. Although pillaging is in the nature of the Mongol and Tatar people, nobody took a single grain of wheat during harvest time. Jani Bey came to Tabriz, killed Ashraf and took his treasures. This proverb is well-known among the people:

Poem

Did you see what Ashraf the ass did

He took the sins and Jani the treasures

دیدی که چه کرد اشرف خر   او مظلمه برد جانی بیک زر

After that Jani Bey left his son Berdi Bey as deputy of Azerbaijan and returned to his kingdom. Berdi Bey, hearing that his father was gravely ill, left as his deputy a Mongol called Akhi Juq in Tabriz and left. Akhi Juq ruled Tabriz for about 15 years and revived the evil tradition of Ashraf and oppressed the Tabrizis. They asked for justice. Mo'ezz al-Din Oweys Ilkhani came with a large army. Akhi Juq went to confront him. He was defeated [74] and he fled to Nakhjevan and from there to Qarabagh. Soltan Oweys pursued him, captured him and cut off his head. In the year 775/1374, he came into possession of Persian Iraq and Azerbaijan and Hushang, son of Kavus, the governor of Shirvan, came to pledge his allegiance. But Soltan Oweys fell ill during this campaign and returned to Baghdad. The next year he died, while he was still young. When he was dying he composed this poem:

Strophe

From the capital of the soul when I went to the province of the body

I was a stranger there; I stopped for a few days and then went home

ز دارالملک جان وقتی به شهرستان تن رفتم
غریبی بودم اینجا چند روزی در وطن رفتم

His son Soltan Hoseyn succeeded him. As he was engaged in debauchery and hedonism and neglected the affairs of the country and the army, his brother Soltan Ahmad in the year 784/1383 with the help of the Qara-Qoyunlu Turkman made him despair of his life and kingdom. He also overcame his brother Sheikh 'Ali and with Soltan Bayazid his other brother in Azerbaijan; with the help of Hushang, son of Kavus the governor of Shirvan, he made peace and acceded to the throne. Meanwhile Sahebqeran, the World Conqueror Emir Timur Gurgan arose.[6]

Strophe

His name was Tamur which means iron[7]

His characteristic was strong fortitude

---

6. See, e.g., Beatrice Forbes Manz, *Rise and rule of Tamerlane* (Cambridge, 1989).
7. In modern Turkish iron is *damır*.

CHAPTER 3 ﴾ FROM THE MONGOLS TO THE SAFAVIDS ﴾ 69

تمور نام او بود یعنی حدید   و من شانه فیه باس شدید

According to most historians, he was the son of Emir Taraqay, who was one of the Mongol Barlas emirs, the great grandson of Qarajar Nuyan, who was one of the important emirs of Chengiz. He was born in the town of Sabz, in the district of Kesh, in the year 736/1336. He rose quickly to power and defeated his father-in-law, Emir Hoseyn, the reason why he was known as Guragan (meaning son-in-law). When he was 35 he became the ruler of Transoxiania. After taking possession of Mongolia and of most of the provinces of Iran and even Gilan and Azerbaijan he returned to Transoxiania. In the winter of the year 787/1386, according to the *Zobdat al-Tavarikh*, Toqtamesh Khan, one of the descendants of Chengiz Khan, came with 90,000 troops via Darband to Shirvan and Azerbaijan. Previously he had been defeated by Orus Khan and with the help of Emir Timur had become the ruler of the Qebchaq steppe in the year 782/1381. After pillaging and destroying he returned via the same way. The following year when Emir Timur wanted to go to Iran the news reached him in Khorasan that Soltan Ahmad Jalayer Ilkhani [75] was coming from Baghdad to Tabriz. Timur appointed a certain Hajji Seyf al-Din to go and confront him with some troops. In the salt desert of Nakhjevan he gave battle to Soltan Ahmad, who, because of the fame of Timur, intended to return. Soltan Ahmad saved himself by fleeing. Some of his troops were killed and his camp was plundered. Emir Timur then came to Tabriz and fined and killed most of the notables of Tabriz. He took the most famous craftsmen of that city and sent them to Samarqand to live there. In the autumn he conquered and destroyed the forts of Nakhjevan and Qars and then went to Georgia. Emir Boqrat the ruler there came to oppose him and he was defeated and captured. From there he went to Qarabagh and Emir Boqrat who [by this time] had converted to Islam returned to his hereditary lands. Emir Ebrahim, the ruler of Shirvan, had come into his presence with precious gifts to save his kingdom and was favored by Timur, who gave him the title of Shirvanshah. In the spring, when Timur's retinue had moved from the banks of the Aras to Ganjeh, news arrived that a huge army led by Toqtamesh Khan was coming to Shirvan. Timur appointed his son Miranshah to oppose him and he defeated and pursued him until the other side of Darband. He seized much booty. Dowlatshah Samarqandi in his *Tadhkereh al-Sho'ara* says that Soltan Ahmad Jalayeri apart from outward splendor had many virtues in the art of writing, composing Arabic and Persian poetry and painting, inlaying mosaics (*khatam-bandi*) etc., in astronomy and music, and he was the author of many works. In spite of all this he was untrustworthy, ill-behaved, an opium eater, whimsical, and a tormentor of people. Mowlana Khvajeh Mohammad Hafez Shirazi says in a *ghazal* about him:

Ghazal:
I praised God for the justice of the king
Ahmad, the son of Sheikh Oweys, the son of Hasan Ilkhani;

Lineage, virtue and love are all yours by right

The evil eye be away from you because you are my soul and beloved

Curl your locks in Turkish fashion for in thy fortune lie

The empire of Khosrow and the status of Chengiz Khan

احمد الله علی معدله السلطانی

احمد شیخ اویس حسن ایلخانی

نسب و فضل و محبت همه در حق تواند

چشم بد دور که جانی و هم جانانی

بر شکن کاکل ترکانه که در طالع تست

دولت کسروی و منصب چنگیزخانی

From the last line it becomes clear that Hafez had his virtues and evil characteristics in mind and his famous praise [76] referred to his evil side. His possession of Baghdad is likened to the possession by the infidels;[8] otherwise it would have been more appropriate to say the state of the Sasanians, Abassids and Chingizids. In short, because of his evil deeds his subjects and his army despaired of him and sought help from Emir Timur. Since in the year 791/1389 Timur went to Baghdad Soltan Ahmad then wrote a piece of poetry that he sent to him:

Why do we bear the hardships of the world

Why do we suffer for a small affair

Like a Simorgh we should bring land and sea under our wings

And leave the seas and mountains and pass over them

Either we will put our foot on the top of the world with our goal achieved

Or we will lose our head over our goal like a man.

گردن چرا نهیم جفای زمانه را

زحمت چرا کشیم بهر کار مختصر

---

8. The line concerning the possession of Baghdad has not been given by the author, but can be found in the *divan* of Hafez and is as follows: "No rose-bud of delight bloomed for me from the earth of Fars: O, for the tigress of Baghdad and the spiritual wine!" For this longer version of the poem see Browne, *Literary History*, vol. 3, p. 285.

دریا و کوه را بگذاریم بگذریم

سیمرغ وار زیر پر آریم بحر و بر

یا بر مراد بر سر گردون نهیم پای

یا مرد وار بر سر همت دهیم سر

Timur regretted that he did not have poetic talent and ordered that one of his children should write his answer. Miranshah and some say Soltan Khalil wrote the answer:

We have to bear the hardship of the world
You cannot belittle a major work
Though you aim like Simorgh to reach Mount Qaf
Be small like a sparrow, shed your feathers
Banish the idea of the impossible from your head
So that for the sake of your head 100,000 heads will not fall

گردن نهادنی است جفای زمانه را

کار بزرگ را نتوان داشت مختصر

سیمرغ وار ارچه کنی قصد کوه قاف

چون صعوه خرد باش و فرو ریز بال و پر

بیرون کن از دماغ خیال محال را

تا در سرت نه شود صد هزار سر

Soltan Ahmad did not think it wise to stay and fled to Rum, and Baghdad was taken by Timur. He appointed Khvajeh Ahmad Mas'ud Sarbadar as its governor. After this campaign Emir Timur went to the capital Samarqand. In the year 793/1191, he went to the Qebchaq steppe and defeated Toqtamesh Khan in a place called Qonduzjeh. The Jiji tribe was the victim of the usual killing, capturing and pillaging. In the year 796/1394, he went again to Georgia and plundered and conquered Sheki, and he made his winterquarters in Mahmudabad in Shirvan, which had been built by Soltan Mahmud Ghazan between two branches of the Kur and the sea. Then news arrived that some of the army of Toqtamesh Khan had passed Darband and were pillaging that region. Therefore, in the spring of 997/1395 via Darband, he went with a large army to punish [77] Toqtamesh Khan. According to the *Habib al-Siyar*, when he arrived at the Samur at a distance of five *farsakh* from the sea he pitched camp and sent Shams al-Din Almaleqi with a letter to

Toqtamesh Khan, who returned with an unfriendly letter. Timur reviewed his army and he had never seen it in such order and multitude before. From there he left to his destination. Underway when he encountered any of the followers of Toqtamesh Khan he did not spare them and pillaged and killed them. In short, on the banks of the river Ab-e Ghuri, which is now called the Terek, the two armies clashed. A battle whose like had not been seen in many centuries took place. It was like the day of judgement and the signs of defeat appeared in the army of Timur, but by the great efforts and counsel of that victorious king the battle changed. Toqtamesh Khan with his huge army fled in complete distress. Emir Timur praised the commanders of his army on the banks of the river Qomari and gave rewards and he pursued the enemy until the Atal River. He appointed Qoveyzijan b. Orus Khan as king of the Qebchaq steppe, and Toqtamesh Khan with some other people fled to the forests. Emir Timur traversed the southern lands of Russia until the river Uqa [Oki] and laid waste to them. Because of the approaching winter he chose to return. On the coast of the Black Sea he conquered the city of Azaq and he made some other conquests in the land of Cherkesia and the Elburz Mountains, and in the Isthmus of Qom he took up winter-quarters. In the heart of winter he went himself to Astrakhan and destroyed and burnt it and properly punished his opponents. According to the saying of most of the people of Daghestan, Emir Timur subdued the tribe of Qomuq between the Terek and the Sulaq. From Machgach he went to the city of Almaq, which had about 7,000 families, and after severe battles occupied and destroyed it. Now only a village has remained, which has about 100 families. From there via a road across the Sala-Tav [Sala Mountain], which is still called Timurshah-yolu [the road of king Timur] he went to the inaccessible forts and houses of Berk-Tav [Berk Mountain], Alkhas-Tav [Alkhas Mountain], Chuban-Tav [Shepherd Mountain] and Batluq [marshland], whose wondrous remains can still be seen. The people of Sala-Tav had taken refuge in them; he went there, occupied them, and removed the people and settled them in a lower part. Because of the passage of time these people were scattered and most of them built the village of Charkay, which originally was Chirkab [Dirty Water], and settled there. Emir Timur crossed the Quy-su via the passage of Ikat and then laid siege to the town of Ghadar, which was a big city with 7 or 8,000 families. He besieged it, but its conquest was difficult due to its inaccessibility. Eventually, peace was concluded and with the pretext of sending goods in boxes as a reward for the soldiers, he sent armed men inside them into the city. They invaded it from inside and outside and occupied the city and destroyed it. Now the town of Ghadar is a village of about 400 households in the land of the Shamkhal. Meanwhile an emir [78] from the lineage of the former emirs of Qomuq named Gobden, who was blind in one eye, was sitting on a cow and thus came into the presence of Timur and told him: "I the blind one have a question for you the lame one: who are we that a king mighty like you comes to make war on us; what do we have that you want to take from us?" Emir Timur liked his naiveté and he returned all his property to him, which is now the village of Gobden. He with all his tribe came down from the mountains and built a village under his name and stayed there. His lineage and his tribe are known as Qarachi Peykan [the Peykan Gypsies]. Some of them later on settled in the village of Qarabodagh-kend and many other places, and the most famous of the remains of this great king in this place is a hill that is known as Bakhsaq

Timur Bey Uri, [i.e. the Hill of Timur Leng]. This hill begins near Darband in the Turkman district, then becomes a group of hills that reaches until the Utemish Plains; it then becomes like a wall under Buynaq and Tarkhu [Tarkhi], and it reaches until Timur-Quye [Timur's Well], after passing the river Sulaq, below Enderey, between Machgach and the land of Naseran, and Qarachay to the location of Timur-quye and the Qobbeh stream and, according to some, extends until the Black Sea. The reason for the construction of this impressive landmark is not known other than that it projects power and might.

In short, Emir Timur after accomplishing his affairs as much as possible went from abovementioned Buynaq; this place of his encampment has become famous, and entered Darband in the spring of the year 798/1396 and from there he went to Armenia. When he reached the banks of the river Kur, the ruler of Shirvan, who was accompanying him on that campaign, for a few days made a big feast. He gave precious gifts and was favored by Emir Timur and was dismissed and Emir Timur then came to Qarabagh. In the place of Aghtam [now Aqdam] he gave his son Miranshah the provinces from Darband to Baghdad and from Hamadan until the borders of Rum and then he went to Soltaniyeh and from there to Samarqand and then he went to India in the year 801/1399. He fought a major battle in Delhi with the kings of that land, he won and having reached his goal returned to Samarqand. At the beginning of the year 802/1400, he again turned to Iran and in 803/1401 he put to flight Malek Farraj the ruler of Syria and took possession of all of Syria. From there he went to punish Soltan Ahmad Jalayer who previously had abandoned Baghdad to Timur's army and had fled to Rum and had come back and retaken it and thus Timur went after him. Soltan Ahmad fled and again he went and took refuge with Bayazid, the Soltan of Rum. Timur after besieging Baghdad for a while and by storming it conquered and destroyed it and massacred its people. He wrote a hostile letter to the Soltan of Rum and asked for the return of Soltan Ahmad and Qara Yusof Turkman. The refusal to give them back was the reason for the war with Rum. He returned and made his winter-quarters in Qarabagh. [79]

In the year 804/1402 he went to Rum and defeated Bayazid in battle and captured him and the realm of Rum came into the hands of this great king. In the year 806/1404 he returned to Georgia. After a few victories King Giorgi VII (1395-1405), the ruler of that kingdom, through the intercession of Emir Ebrahim, the ruler of Shirvan gave gifts and accepted to pay poll-tax and Emir Timur returned to Qarabagh and wintered there. Because Miranshah was feeble-minded he gave his lands to his son, Prince 'Omar. The princes who had the two Iraqs and Fars were forced to accept him. In the case of governance he gave good pieces of advice. Fifty thousand Turkic families from Rum and Sham [Syria] and some from the people of Rum, from where hails the tribe of Ayrum in the vicinity of Ganjeh, were moved. Most of them are of the same 200,000 families who had come with Hulagu Khan from Turkestan to Iran and gradually over time they had dispersed and he settled them in the lands of Ganjeh, Qarabagh and Erevan and most of the tribes of these regions are descended from these people. Timur built a strong wall around the city of Bileqan in Qarabagh that had been built by Qobad, son of Firuz the Sasanian.

Hulagu had besieged it for a while and stormed and destroyed it. Timur wanted to make it prosperous, but because of the numerous snakes it did not happen.

In the year 900/1495, Dowlatshah Samarqandi in the *Tadhkerat al-Shoʻara* says that Shahrokh, son of Emir Timur wanted to make this city prosperous. The wise men of the kingdom advised him not to do this, because this city had been damaged many times by earthquakes. However, he made the river Bileqan flow and mills operate there which still can be seen. The present author says: There were two magnificent domes above the tombs of the kings in the city. One of them is half in ruins and can be seen. It is because of this that the common people called them Bileqan Millar [towers]. Timur after having done this came to Ardabil and made a pilgrimage to the tomb of Sheikh Safi and bought many villages and fields and endowed them to the shrine. From there he returned to the capital Samarqand. After a few days, while it was very cold he went to China and became sick and in the town of Otrar he passed away in the year 807/1405. He was a great conqueror, wise and of good fortune. In spite of many great things that he had in mind he did not neglect the needs of the people of learning [80] and the instructions that he left for his descendents display the extent of his wisdom, statesmanship, his great resolve and conquering spirit.

At that time, the descendents of Timur, Khalil Soltan b. Miranshah, at the age of 20 acceded to the throne; he was negligent of the army and the country, because he left its control to his wife. Every day the foundation of the throne was diminished, the dynasty lost control of most of the provinces and its kingdom was limited to Transoxiania and Khorasan and later on they moved to India. It is written in the *Golshan-e Kholafa* [9] that, after the conquest of Anatolia (Rum) by Timur, Soltan Ahmad and Qara Yusof had gone to Egypt and the king of Egypt had taken them prisoner and wanted to send them to Emir Timur when the news of his death reached him. Soltan Ahmad came to Baghdad and expelled Abu Bakr Mirza, who was the grandson of Timur. Then he went to Azerbaijan in the company of Qara Yusof, son of Qara Mohammad to fight Miranshah and Prince ʻOmar. They were victorious and Miranshah was killed. Prince ʻOmar fled for his life and most of Iranian kingdom came again into the hands of Soltan Ahmad. Eventually enmity appeared between him and Qara Yusof. In the area of Azerbaijan, in the year 813/1411, Soltan Ahmad was defeated, captured and put to death in Tabriz by Esfandiyar, the son of Qara Yusof. The kingship passed from this dynasty to that of the Qara-Qoyunlu. In short, their history is as follows: Qara Yusof, son of Qara Mohammad, son of Beyram Khvajeh had been from father to son emirs of the great tribe of the Turkman Qara-Qoyunlu. Under the guidance of Soltan Ahmad Ilkhani he became a very powerful man and after him he became a well-known king. In the year 816/1414, when he was going to fight Shahrokh b. Timur with a large army, he suddenly died at Ujan. His son, Eskandar became king and he fought Shahrokh three times and was defeated. In a manuscript it is written that Eskandar in the year 828/1425 came to Shirvan and began killing and pillaging the people and destroyed Shamakhi. At this time, his brother, Mirza Jahanshah with some troops and Turkman emirs went to Shahrokh promising to withdraw to the provinces of Diyarbekr

---

9. This text is unknown to us and we have been unable to identify it.

and Azerbaijan if he would defeat his brother. Ultimately, Eskandar took refuge in the fort of Alanjaq in Nakhjevan. After a while his evil son Qobad, conspiring with a slave girl with whom he was in love, at the instigation of Jahanshah, suddenly killed him and, according [81] to the history of Nokhbeh,[10] Qobad was also killed by the treachery of Jahanshah and joined his father. For 22 years Jahanshah ruled Diyarbekr and Azerbaijan as deputy of Shahrokh and after the latter's death he ruled the whole of Iran, except for Khorasan. He was an enemy of Hasan Bey Bayandori Aq-Qoyunlu Turkman and he had continuous feuds, which was the cause of a battle between them. To gain time Hasan Bey moved to different areas until the armies of both sides scattered and the fight was postponed until the following year. When Jahanshah was 80 years old and with 500 or 600 people was drinking wine near a stream Hasan Bey took the opportunity and killed him in the year 872/1468. The kingship passed from this dynasty to the kings of the Aq-Qoyunlu. Their story is that the Qara-Qoyunlu and the Aq-Qoyunlu were two nomadic Turkman tribes, i.e. the Turkman who came in the time of Arghun Khan to Iran and the Qara-Qoyunlu settled in the region of Azerbaijan, Erzerum and Sivas. The Aq-Qoyunlu settled in Diyarbekr and every day they grew stronger and stronger. Qara 'Othman, the grandfather of Hasan Bey in the time of Emir Timur was the governor of some of the districts of Diyarbekr. After him his son 'Ali Bey and after him his son Hasan Bey, known as Uzun Hasan likewise were governors. After the killing of Jahanshah, his son Hasan 'Ali Mirza asked help from Soltan Abu Sa'id b. Mirza Mohammad b. Miranshah b. Emir Timur Guragan, who at that time was the king of Transoxiania and Khorasan. The aforementioned Soltan sent his emirs to occupy the provinces of Iraq and Fars and he himself with 27,000 men marched to Azerbaijan. Hasan Bey sent envoy after envoy professing obedience and of being content with having Azerbaijan and he did not stop the Soltan. Hasan Bey's mother who had gone there to intercede returned without success. The Soltan came to Soltaniyeh and Hasan Bey went to Qarabagh of Arran. After the king's retinue had arrived he went to Miyanaj [Miyaneh]. Hasan Bey sent his son, Yusof Bey, expressing his obedience and asked for time, so that after the winter he would abandon Azerbaijan. The Soltan did not accept this and in consultation with his emirs he assigned a place for winter quarters in Qarabagh for Hasan Bey. After arriving at that place at a distance of seven *farsakh* he went to Mahmudabad of Shirvan due to lack of provisions, for the grass in the plains underway was poisonous. [82] Many of his animals died and provisions also became scarce. Hasan Bey controlled the roads and did not allow anyone from Khorasan and Iraq to come to the camp of the Soltan. For a few days they would bring provisions from Shirvan by ship. Then the Shirvanshah because of Hasan Bey's threat opposed the Soltan. The animals of the Soltan's camp became weak and the Turkman army in that vicinity started to kill and pillage. Per force the Soltan returned to Ardabil and passed a muddy area with difficulty. Hasan Bey, while fighting, was following them. Every day 500 people of the Soltan's army would perish. The Soltan asked for peace and sent Sayyed Ghiyath al-Din Mohammad, who was the most revered emir of the Sari family, as an emissary and following that he sent

---

10. Bakikhanov refers to a manuscript entitled *Nokhbat al-Akhbar* by 'Abdol-Vahhab Shirazi (1841).

his mother with Sayyed Ebrahim of Qom. Hasan Bey honored them greatly and wanted to make peace, but the Lord of Ardabil, Sheikh Heydar Safavi, who had gone before as a messenger and had learnt about the disorder of the Soltan's camp opposed this. Hasan Bey returned the Soltan's mother without accepting her request and honored Sayyed Ghiyath al-Din and gave him the governorship of Sari. The Turkman army again attacked and some of the troops of Khorasan joined Hasan Bey's army and the Soltan was forced to flee. Yusof Bey, the son of Hasan Bey pursued him and at night he was captured and brought to his father. Lengthy negotiations occurred between Hasan Bey and the Soltan and at the advice of the Turkman emirs and the instigation of the judge of Shirvan, Soltan Abu Sa'id was put tot death in the year 873/1468.

Poem
Truly, how he is not going to be killed, when he had already "been killed"
Which is the date of the time of the killing of Soltan Abu Sa'id

الحق چه گونه کشته نگردد که کشته بود
تاریخ سال مقتل سلطان ابوسعید

Hasan Bey became the ruler of Iran and died in the year 882/1477. His son Khalil Mirza acceded to the throne and he died after one year of reign in the battle with Ya'qub Mirza his brother. Soltan Ya'qub, after having reigned for 13 years was unwittingly poisoned by his mother in a place Soltanbud in Qarabagh and she ate the same food and died with her son in the same place. One of the poems of this king is:

Quatrain
In this world that I see there is little stability
In every joy of it I see a hundred griefs [83]
It is a like an old caravanserai where from every side
There is a road to the desert of annihilation

دنیا که در آن ثبات کم می بینم
در هر فرحش هزار غم می بینم
چون کهنه رباطی است که از هر طرفش
راهی به بیابان عدم می بینم

The Turkman emirs were divided into two groups. One was in favor of the kingship of his brother Masih Mirza and the other of the kingship of his son Beysongor Mirza. Eventually they ended up fighting and Masih Mirza was killed and Beysongor became a king and imprisoned his cousin Rostam Mirza b. Maqsud b.Hasan Padshah in the fort of Alanjaq. However, Rostam Mirza with the help of Abiyeh Soltan was freed and defeated Beysongor and became king. Beysongor was forced to go via Qarachedagh and Ahar to the

Shirvanshah in Shirvan who was his uncle and his father-in-law. The Turkman emirs were united in the rule of Rostam Mirza, but the Shirvanshah to help Beysongor was mustering his forces. Rostam Mirza at the advice of the emirs had brought Soltan 'Ali b. Sheikh Heydar from the fort of Estakhr where he had been imprisoned and wanted to send him to fight the Shirvanshah, because whether he was defeated or victorious it would be to his benefit. At this time, Beysongor with the Shirvan army came to Azerbaijan. Rostam Mirza sent Soltan 'Ali with his followers and relatives and Abiyeh Soltan with some troops of the Turkman army to fight Beysongor and the Shirvanis. Around Ahar and Meshkin the two forces met, Beysongor was defeated and killed. In the sixth year of the reign of Rostam Mirza, Ahmad b. Hasan Padshah had gone to the Ottomans and had become the son-in-law of Soltan Bayazid II. He came to Azerbaijan and at the banks of the river Aras they fought and he was victorious. Rostam Mirza was taken by the emirs and given to him and he killed him. He himself after six months in the year 903/1498 was killed at the hands of Soltan Abiyeh Soltan. Morad b. Soltan Ya'qub was appointed his successor, but Mohammad Mirza, son of Yusof, son of Hasan Padshah defeated him and killed Abiyeh Soltan as well and took Azerbaijan. Soltan Morad went to Iraq. Alvand Mirza with his brother Mohammadi fought and took his kingdom. Mohammadi Mirza escaped to Isfahan. Soltan Morad came from Shiraz to Isfahan and in the year 904/1400 captured Mohammadi [84] and attacked Tabriz. Alvand Mirza wanted to fight, but through the intercession of well-wishers made peace. Diyarbakr and Azerbaijan went to Alvand Mirza and the two Iraqs and Fars to Soltan Morad.

Concerning the kingship and lineage of the Shirvanshahs

As to their circumstances, what is known is that their kingship was not independent and was mostly under the authority of powerful Persian, Arab and Turkish rulers and sometimes they were without income.[11] The [history of the] lineage before the great Khaqan Manuchehr is not very well known. In the time of the caliphate of 'Omar b. al-Khattab, a certain Shahriyar, from the line of the Shirvanshahs, on whom Anushirvan the Just had bestowed this title, was ruling in Shirvan. Seraqeh b. 'Amr and 'Abdol-Rahman b. Rabi'eh were the commanders of the Islamic army. After that Habib b. Salameh, Hodheyfeh b. al-Yaman, Mogheyreh b. Sho'beh, Ash'ath b. Qeys, 'Abdol-'Aziz Baheli, Abu 'Obeydeh Jarrah, Sa'id b. 'Amr Harshi and Maslameh b. 'Abdol-Malek the caliph ruled Shirvan. In the time of the caliphate of the 'Abbasids mostly the governors of Armenia and Azerbaijan were ruling Shirvan. At the beginning of the 2nd century/*hijri* Farrokhzad b. Akhshijan and after him Filanshah under the name of Akhsatan ruled on behalf of the caliphs.[12] In

---

11. For the history of Shirvan and the Shirvanshahs see Sara Ashurbeyli, *Gosudarstvo Shirvanshakhov* 2 vols. (vi-xvi vv.) (Baku, 1983); Rahim Rais-Niya, *Tarikh-e 'Omumi-ye Mantaqeh-ye Shirvan (dar 'ahd-e Shirvanshahan)* (Tehran, 1380/2001); and Bernhard Dorn, "Beiträge zur Geschichte der Kaukasischen Ländern und Völker, aus der Morgenländischen Quellen. I. Versuch einer Geschichte der Schirwanschahe," *Mémoires de l'Académie Impériale des Sciences de St. Petersburg* (St. Petersburg, 1845), pp. 523-602.
12. See also Minorsky, *The History of Sharvan*, pp. 135-38.

the beginning of the 4th century, Rabe'eh 'Ali b. Heysham and after him Mohammad b. Yazid from the lineage of Bahram Chubin, who ruled only for one month, were the rulers of Shirvan. After a while Soltan Fereydun ruled and after him the manner in which it was ruled is unknown. In the middle of the 6th century hijri Manuchehr, known as the Great Khan, was powerful and independent.[13] The well-known poet Khaqani of Shirvan was his contemporary. In an ode he describes his might and power. He gives a complete description of the manner in which his son's [85] hunt took place in Baku, between the sea and the burning oil wells, where during that time, because there were very few inhabitants, lions and other wild animals lived. The *Tadhkereh al-Sho'ara* says that Ebrahim b. 'Ali Khaqani, who was a man of leaning and status wanted to go on the *hajj*, because he wanted to retire from the world. The *Khaqan* did not agree, but he went anyway without his permission. The agents of the *Khaqan* caught him in the city of Beylaqan and sent him back. From this incident it becomes clear that Beylaqan was part of the province of Arran, which was under his authority. Qadi Beyzavi in the *Nezam al-Tavarikh*[14] says that the Shirvanshahs are of the lineage of Bahram Chubin and in several generations it reaches Ardashir Babakan. Qazi Ahmad Ghaffari[15] considers them to be from the lineage of Anushirvan, thus, Manuchehr b. Kisran b. Kavus b. Shariyar b. Gushtasb b. Fereydun b. Faramarz b. Salar b. Zeyd b. Jun b. Marzban b. Hormuz b. Anushirvan. Manuchehr, according to many historians, was a just king. He loved the sciences and the arts. All the time he endeavored to improve the welfare of his subjects. After him came his son Farrokhzad[16] and then his son Goshtasb,[17] who, according to some historians, was the builder of the town of Goshtasbi that is situated between two branches of the Kur and the sea. It is a big city, full of products. His son Faramarz and his son Farrokhzad and his son Key Qobad were known for their justice. His son Kavus was known for the improvement of the state of his subjects and he ruled for a long time and helped Jani Bey Khan enormously to expel Ashraf Chubani. He died in the year 774/1373 and his tomb is outside the city of Qobbeh, which is still in existence in our own time. His son Hushang ruled for 10 years in a just and cultured manner. After him, because of the looming threat of their enemies they lost their kingdom. A certain emir who was the ruler of Shirvan was a tyrant. The Shirvanis got together and killed him and enthroned Sheikh Ebrahim of Darband, son of Soltan Mohammad, son of Key Qobad Shirvanshah, who lived like a dervish in the city of Sheki, one of the dependencies of Shirvan, where he was engaged in farming. They found him sleeping under a tree and put him in a proper dress, put a royal turban on his head and put him on the throne.[18] As it was mentioned he was a contemporary of Emir Timur Guragan and some historians say that he conquered Tabriz. The following year he wanted to go further, but he

---

13. Abu Mozaffar Manuchehr II (r. ca. 1094 - 1155).
14. Naser al-Din 'Abdallah b. 'Omar Beyzavi, *Nezam al-Tavarikh* ed. Bahman Karimi (Tehran, 1313/1934).
15. Ahmad b. Mohammad Ghaffari, *Tarikh-e negarestan dar navader-e halat-e kholafa va moluk-e eslami*. Morteza Modarres Gilani ed. (Tehran, 1341/1962).
16. Farrokhzad (r. 1171 - 79), who was preceded by Akhsatan I (r. 1155 - 71).
17. Goshtasb (r. 1179 - 1204).
18. Sheikh Ebrahim Darbandi (r. 1382 - 1417).

[86] lost whatever he possessed. This event was at the time that Qara Yusof Turkman was busy fighting Soltan Ahmad Ilkani. The affairs of Azerbaijan were in disorder. It is known that Emir Qara Yusof after killing Soltan Ahmad in the year 813/1411 went to Tabriz. He took Tabriz from Emir Ebrahim and also ruled Shirvan, because in the city of Darband the gate called *Qiyamat* (Resurrection) was built by the order of his son, Emir Esfandiyar, in the year 814/1412 and his name is written there. To verify this statement Hajji Zeyn al-'Abedin Shirvani in the *Riyaz al-Siyaha* says that Qara Yusof came with a large army to Shirvan and destroyed many places and he captured Emir Ebrahim and took much property from him, but returned the governorship to him. In the year 820/1418 Emir Ebrahim died. His son Emir Khalil, whose name corresponds to the chronogram of the date of his accession, acceded to the throne. He built some of the caravanserais on the road to Baku, Qobbeh and Saliyan as well as the wall and the fort of Darband and many of the towers and mosques in Baku. His name is still on them. He had a beautiful palace in Baku and its ruins still show its splendor and glory. In the *Riyaz al-Siyaha* it is mentioned that Eskander, son of Qara Yusof with a huge army came to Shirvan. Soltan Khalil fled and the Turkman caused much damage to the city. It was with the help of Shahrokh Mirza the Timurid that their evil was driven away. After having reigned for 53 years Soltan Khalil passed away.[19] His son Farrokh Yasar, the chronogram of the date of his accession is Shirvanshah, took his father's place. He was killed in the year 906/1501 in the battle with Shah Esma'il Safavid. After that Bahram Bey and Qazi Bey, the sons of Farrokh Yasar each ruled for nearly one year. They were just and caring for their subjects. After their deaths Ebrahim known as Sheikhshah, son of Farrokh Yasar came to the throne. After a while he made peace with Shah Esma'il and Shah Tahmasp. He ruled for 22 years and then he passed away. Then his son Soltan Khalil II ruled and he was honored by being the son-in-law of Shah Tahmasp. In the year 942/1536 he died. After him with the agreement of the emirs Shahrokh b. Soltan Farrokh b. Sheikhshah became ruler. Since he was a child his affairs were not in order. [87]

In the year 945/1539 the province of Shirvan came into the possession of the king of Iran, Shah Tahmasp I Safavid, who gave its government to his brother Elqas Mirza. After his revolt in the year 954/1547, he sent his own son Esma'il Mirza to that province. In the year 955/1548 a certain Borhan Mirza took the opportunity and ruled for a short while and then he died. After that the province of Shirvan came to 'Abdollah Khan Ostajalu, his aunt's son and his son-in-law and after 17 years he died. Aras Khan Rumlu ruled for 13 years and in the year 986/1578 at the instigation of Abu Bakr Mirza, son of Borhan Mirza, the Ottoman Laleh Pasha 'Askar came and occupied Shirvan. He appointed 'Othman Pasha as the governor and returned. The Ottoman and the Persian army fought for a while and then the grand vizier Mirza Salman came and defeated 'Othman Pasha. He went to Darband and Mohammad Qoli Khalifeh Dhu'l-Qadr became the governor of the province of Shirvan, but he was killed in the Ottoman and Tatar battles and Shirvan again came into the possession of 'Othman Pasha. Mirza Salman came back again and 'Othman Pasha went to Darband. Peykar Khan Qajar was appointed as governor of Darband and

---

19. Khalil Allah I (r. 1417 - 1465).

after his death Khalifeh-ye Ansar-e Qaradaghi became the governor, but neither of them could do anything and both of them died very soon. 'Othman Pasha and after him Hasan Pasha and after him Mahmud Pasha and then Ahmad Pasha governed in Shirvan until in the year 1016/1607 Shah 'Abbas I conquered it. Dhu'l-Feqar Qaramanlu for two years, Yusof Khan for 18 years, 'Arab Khan for 8 years, Faraj Khan for 3 years, 'Arab Khan for 11 years, Khosrow Khan for 8 years, Manuchehr Khan for 6 years, Hajji Khan for 3 years, Mohammadi Khan for 2 years, Najaf Qoli Khan for 7 years, Mehr 'Ali Khan for 3 years, Mokri Qoli Khan for 2 years, Sayyed Khan for 7 years, 'Ali Qoli Khan for 6 years, Musa Khan and Hasan 'Ali Khan for 20 years, Hoseyn Khan for 2 years ruled as governor-general of Shirvan.[20]

In the year 1124/1712 Hajji Davud Moskuri with the help of the Usmi and Sorkhay killed the ruler of Qobbeh and took over Shamakhi and ruled there. From the year 1138/1725 until the coming of Nader Shah the authority was in the hands of Sorkhay Khan for a period of 9 years. After the conquest of Shirvan, Mohammad Qoli Khan Sa'idlu and 'Ali Qoli Khan were appointed to the province. After the crowning of that king his brother Ebrahim Khan [88] was the governor for three years from Qaplan Kuh [Qaflan Kuh] until the outer limits of Daghestan. Mehdi Khan Khorasani was *emir al-omara* in Shirvan for one year. After the killing of Mehdi Khan, Sardar Khan Qereqlu for five years and Heydar Khan Afshar for one year were governors. In the year 1155/1743 Sam Mirza and Mohammad Khan, son of Sorkhay Khan for a short while ruled Shirvan and destroyed the peace of the people. Although Ashur Khan, general (*sardar*) of Azerbaijan, and Fath 'Ali Khan Afshar expelled them, the affairs of Shirvan were in disorder and the affairs of the government not properly managed, because the end of Nader's reign was a time of general disturbance. After Nader Shah's death each of the five provinces that is Shirvan, Sheki, Baku, Qobbeh and Darband, had an independent emir, who had nothing to do with the others. However, the land of Darband soon went to the Khan of Qobbeh. The [four remaining regions of this] province passed from the rule of four khans into the possession of the Russian state in different periods.

---

20. The list of governors given by Bakikhanov is not entirely correct. For an annotated list of the governors of Shirvan during the Safavid period see Willem Floor's commentary to Mirza Naqi Nasiri, *Alqab va Mavajeb-e Salatin-e Safaviyeh* ed. Yusof Rahimlu (Mashhad, 1992) translated into English with commentary by Willem Floor as *Titles & Emoluments in Safavid Iran. A Third Manual of Safavid Administration* (Washington D.C, 2008).

The fort at Shush, from: Basile Vereschaguine, *Voyage dans les provinces du Caucase*

CHAPTER FOUR

From the Rise of the Safavids until the Death of Nader Shah

According to the *'Alamara*[1] and the *Habib al-Siyar*[2] and many other histories, the Safavid kings are called Safavids, because they are the offspring of Sheikh Safi al-Din Eshaq. Sheikh Safi al-Din, whose splendid shrine in Ardabil is still a popular place of pilgrimage, was from a long line of noble sayyeds and sheykhs and in 21 generations his ancestry reaches the seventh Imam Musa al-Kazem. After him, his son Sadr-al Musa, and after him, his son Khvajeh 'Ali, and then his son Ebrahim, known as Sheikhshah, and after him, his son Sheikh Joneyd.[3] They combined in themselves the spiritual and secular realms and many disciples from all parts sought their guidance. As day by day Sheikh Joneyd's means of glory and splendor as well as the number of disciples was increasing the Turkman Jahanshah Qara-Qoyunlu, who was then ruler of both Iraqs and Azerbaijan, fearing the fall of his kingdom was having evil thoughts about Sheikh Joneyd, but fearing a bad reputation could not reveal his enmity. Eventually, directly and indirectly he asked him to go elsewhere. Sheikh Joneyd accompanied by many of his followers went to Diyarbekr. The Turkman Hasan Bey Aq-Qoyunlu who was the governor of half of that province [**89**] did not obey Jahanshah, and gave his sister Khadijeh Beygom in marriage to him.[4] After some time Sheikh Joneyd returned to Ardabil and at that time Jahanshah thought of eliminating him. Meanwhile, Sheykh Joneyd had increased the number of his followers and claimed kingship and with 10,000 men he marched to Shirvan intending to make holy war on the

---

1. Eskander Bey Monshi, *Tarikh-e 'Alamara-ye 'Abbasi*. Iraj Afshar ed. 2 vols. (Tehran, 1350/1971), translated into English by R.M. Savory as *History of Shah 'Abbas the Great* 2 vols. (Boulder, 1978).
2. Khvandamir. *Habib al-Seyar*, 4 vols. ed. Mohammad Dabir-Siyaqi. (Tehran, 1362/1983 [3rd. ed.])
3. On the Safavid order and its leaders see, for example, Michel Mazzaoui, *The Origins of the Safawids* (Wiesbaden, 1972) and *CHI* vol. 6.
4. On the Aq-Qoyunlu and Uzun Hasan see John E Woods, *The Aqquyunlu. Clan, Federation, Empire* (Minneapolis 1976).

Cherkes. It is mentioned in the *Fotuhat-e Amini* that he had gone to conquer Shirvan.[5] At any rate, Soltan Khalil Shirvanshah prevented him from going towards the Cherkes at the urging of the people of Tabarsaran. He therefore gathered troops and went to fight him. Sheikh Joneyd was killed in battle and some of the people of Tabarsaran who were sympathizers of the Safavids took his body from the battle field, which is situated on the left bank of the Samur river close to the village of Qebchah, where the place of his death can still be seen, and took his body and carried it to the village of Quriyan, belonging to the districts of Qobbeh and Qolhan, which is now called Hazreh and buried him there. This event took place in the year 851 (1447). After 100 years Shah Tahmasp I erected a large shrine over his tomb, whose remains are still to be seen and is the place of pilgrimage of the people of that area.

Sheikh Heydar, the son of Joneyd, who was Hasan Bey's sister's son, took his father's place. After Hasan Bey became king he gave his daughter Halimeh Beygom in marriage to Sheikh Heydar, increasing his importance and authority. From that moment Sheikh Heydar, instead of the Turkman headgear that was customary in those days, put a *taj* on his head made of red shawl with 12 folds indicating the 12 Imams, claiming that in a dream he had been ordered to do so. The disciples followed his example and distinguished themselves from others by this hat, hence they were known as *Qezelbash* (Red Hats).[6] After the death of king Hasan, his son Khalil, and after him Soltan Ya'qub came to the throne,[7] but Sheikh Heydar did not find his cousin's behavior well-intentioned. In the year 893 (1488), he wanted to fight the Cherkes and went via Sheki to Darband. The people there began to oppose his troops, and therefore he decided to conquer Darband. The situation of the besieged in the fort became desperate. Farrokh Yasar Shirvanshah, who did not have the means of opposing Sheikh Heydar sent envoys to Soltan Ya'qub who was Heydar's son-in-law and asked for help and submitted that if Sheikh Heydar conquered Shirvan then the Torkman state also might fall. Soltan Ya'qub chose 4,000 troops under the command of Soleyman Bey Bijan-oghli and sent him to help the Shirvanshah. The latter gathered his own troops and sent them after Sheikh Heydar. While the fall of the fort of Darband was imminent the news of their arrival was reported to Sheikh Heydar. He hurried from the fort to meet them and near Tabarsaran the two sides faced one another and a fierce battle ensued and from both sides many fell and perished and Sheik Heydar himself was killed by an arrow. [90] According to the *Fotuhat-e Amini*, the tales of this battle were gathered from the people present at the scene such as Hasan Bey Laleh and Farrokh Aqa at the order of Shah Esma'il, the son of Sheikh Heydar. The followers buried Sheikh Heydar's body in Tabarsaran in the year 915 (1510) and the second time that Shah Esma'il came to Shirvan 22 years had passed and he had his father's body exhumed and transferred to Ardabil. The present author says that in the districts adjacent to Tabarsaran, which are

---

5. Amir Sadr al-Din Ebrahim Amini Heravi, *Fotuhat-e Shahi*. Mohammad Reza Nasiri ed. (Tehran 1383/ 2004).
6. On the *taj* and the *Qezelbash* see Willem Floor, *The Persian Textile Industry in Historical perspective 1500-1925* (Paris 1999) and Ibid., *Safavid Government Institutions* (Costa Mesa, 2001).
7. Uzun Hasan (r. 1453-1478); Soltan Khalil (r. 1487-81); and Soltan Ya'qub (r. 1481-1490).

on the left bank of the Rubas River there is a place commemorating the site where he was killed and in the village of Tenit, at a distance of one *farsakh*, there is a dome indicating his place of burial, which still is a place of pilgrimage for the people of those parts.[8]

After the incident of Sheykh Heydar his son Soltan 'Ali succeeded him as spiritual guide (*morshed*); he prepared himself for leadership, and the followers renewed their allegiance to him. Soltan Ya'qub sent him, his brothers and mother, who was his sister, to the fort of Estakhr in Fars where they were imprisoned. Four and a half years they were there, until Rostam Mirza, because of the conditions prevailing at that time, brought them to Tabriz and after the killing of Beysangor Mirza, Soltan 'Ali was sent with great pomp to Ardabil. After some time, because of the gathering of the Safavid groups and the increase in the number of Soltan 'Ali's followers he had regrets and returned them to Tabriz and kept them under surveillance. As the coming and going of the followers continued Rostam Mirza thought of eliminating him and Soltan 'Ali with his brothers and 700 of his followers went to Ardabil. Abiyeh Soltan with 4,000 soldiers was ordered to follow him and reached him north of Ardabil; a battle ensued and Soltan 'Ali was killed. The elders of the Sufis took his brother Esma'il Mirza, who was only 6 years old (the date of his birth is the chronogram of the beginning of the *Qezelbash* state) together with Ebrahim Mirza and brought them secretly to Ardabil and after 40 days took them to Gilan, which events took place in the year 898 (1493). Mirza 'Ali Karkiya showed much kindness to them until there was conflict amongst the Torkmans and their unity was broken.[9]

In 906 (1501) Esma'il Mirza rose up with 1,500 followers and Sufis from Rum (Anatolia) and Syria and came to Ardabil, but having few followers he did not think it appropriate to fight and went to Talesh. After spending the winter there he came to Ardabil, then went to Qarabagh, and from there with many troops that had gathered around him and with royal pomp he marched to Shirvan. Farrokh Yasar with 20,000 cavalry and several thousand footmen [**91**] met him in the winter quarters of Jilani near the Golestan fort that is situated on the way to Shamakhi on top of a mountain, whose ruins can still be seen and are known as Qiz Qal'asi. There he was defeated and killed with many of his commanders. Ebrahim Sheykh Shah, the eldest son of Shirvanshah took a boat and went to Gilan. From here the fame of Esma'il's kingship spread everywhere. He spent the winter in Mahmudabad in Shirvan and took forts and buildings in Shirvan with the treasuries therein, although the people in some of them resisted. Shah Esma'il, after some resistance and besieging, first took the citadel of Baku, which on one side had a very deep moat and on three sides was surrounded by sea and it was very strong and it was said that Anushirvan had built it and the kings of Shirvan had improved it. Then he besieged Fort Golestan, which was one of the famous forts, and some of the emirs and people of Shirvan had taken refuge there. At this time, news came that prince Alvand with the Turkman troops had come to Nakhjevan and had been put in battle formation to attack him from two sides. From there Shah Esma'il went to Azerbaijan and prince Alvand sent Amir Othman Mowsellu with many troops after him and Shah Esma'il from his side sent troops to oppose

---

8. On these events see Mazzaoui, *Origins* and *CHI*, vol. 6.
9. For more details on these events see *CHI* vol. 6.

him. After a fierce battle the Torkman army was defeated and Amir Othman and a number of commanders was captured and killed. Prince Alvand himself with 30,000 troops hurried to oppose Esma'il and at Sharur in Nakhjavan in the year 907 (1502) Shah Esma'il with 7,000 troops defeated him and many soldiers and commanders were killed and he collected an enormous booty. Prince Alvand fled to Erzenjan and Shah Esma'il went to Tabriz and acceded to the throne. He proclaimed Twelver Shi'ism as the official religion, which had been secret until then. Near Hamadan he defeated Soltan Morad, who after the defeat stayed for some time in Baghdad and from there asked for assistance from 'Ala al-Dowleh Dhu'l-Qadr, who was his son-in-law and his protector. In the year 912 (1507) he came with the Dhu'l-Qadr army and took some of the forts and buildings of Diyarbekr and the next year Shah Esma'il went to wage battle; the flames of the battle burnt for two days. On the third day Soltan Morad fled and again went to 'Ala al-Dowleh, and Esma'il through consecutive victories conquered Diyarbekr, both Iraqs, Fars, Khorasan and [92] some part of Mesopotamia and returned to Tabriz. At that time news arrived that Sheikhshah had taken the province of Shirvan claiming independence and refusing to pay tribute. This caused the flame of the king's anger to burn in the midst of the cold winter of 915 (1510) and he went to Shirvan. Sheikhshah could not resist and escaped to Fort Bighord, whose ruins are still to be seen to the north of Shamakhi at a distance of three *farsakh* in an inaccessible place in a village that is still know by the same name.

Shah Esma'il's army came to Shirvan and he appointed Laleh Bey as the governor of Shirvan province [with his residence] in Shamakhi and he busied himself with the taking of the forts and buildings of that province. The castellans of the forts of Baku and Shaberan came to him and the Darbandis resisted for a few days and then surrendered. Shah Esma'il gave orders to move some of the Bayat Turks from Iraq to Darband and Shaberan to serve the governors of those places. In the same winter Esma'il came to Qarabagh and in the spring he came to Soltaniyeh. Soltan Selim came to wage war on Iran and defeated Shah Esma'il in the plains of Chalderan in 920 (1514) and after occupying Tabriz for nine days he returned to Turkey. He ordered Farhad Pasha to punish 'Ala al-Dowleh who out of arrogance did not take notice of any kings. 'Ala al-Dowleh with many of his tribe was killed and the rest of his troops were dispersed over Anatolia and some, with his grandson, known as Dhu'l-Qadr-oghlu, came to Azerbaijan. The district of Shams al-Dinlu belongs to them and many of them are dispersed in the region of Jar, Talej and in the neighborhood of Daghestan. The Lezgis of these parts changing 'z' to 'th' called them Bulghadar. This tribe is of those Torkman that Hulagu Khan had brought from Turkestan and they had been settled in Shiraz and then they went to Diyarbekr and Mosul, and then in the desire of glory and power were invading neighboring provinces. Ten of them for a period of 138 years ruled that province. The power of the last of them, 'Ala al-Dowleh reached such a degree that when the rulers of Egypt and Syria were fighting they were asking for his help. He used to say: "I have two fowls; one lays golden and the other silver eggs." In the year 929 (1523), when Shah Esma'il was in Azerbaijan, Sheikhshah the governor of Shirvan came to his court in obedience and presented whatever he had as a gift, and his daughter entered the royal harem of [93] Shah Esma'il. Due to these good services the governorship of Shirvan was again bestowed upon him and the following year at the end of summer of the year 930 (1524) Shah Esma'il died. He was a glorious, fire-tempered, heroic king who was irreconcilable with his enemies. In spite of his great royal preoccupations he sought the companionship of learned people and composed poetry. His excellent Turkish poems under the name of Shah Khata'i are still popular among people.[10] This single couplet in Persian is from him:

My lamentation moved Bisetun Mountain from its place,
Claiming that another Farhad has appeared

بیستون ناله زارم چو شنید از جا شد
کرد فریاد که فرهاد دگر پیدا شد

After him his son Shah Tahmasp ascended the throne and soon thereafter Sheikh Shah also died. His son Soltan Khalil II became independent governor of Shirvan and the son-in-law of Shah Tahmasp. In the year 940 (1533) Soltan Soleyman, son of Soltan Selim Khondegar, at the instigation of Olameh Soltan Tekkelu, who had revolted against his king and was the driving force in the war with Iran, came with a large army to Azerbaijan. Shah Tahmasp thought it wise not to face the enemy, but to have him battle with the cold of winter, lack of provisions and fodder. Soltan Soleyman marched with great difficulty to Soltaniyeh and then to Baghdad. After the conquest of that city he came the following year to Azerbaijan and took Tabriz. Because of rebellion and disorder in the army he was forced to return to Anatolia (Rum). 'Abdol Fattah Fumeni, the author of the *History of Gilan*,[11] writes that Amir Dubbaj known as Mozaffar Soltan, who was the son-in-law of Shah Tahmasp and governor of Gilan, went to the presence of the Soltan in Khoy and Salmas with 8,000 troops. When he returned Amir Hatam, governor of Kohdom, who was a protégé of his attacked him and put him to flight and plundered his army camp. After that the people of Gilan turned away from him and he took ship and went to Shirvan. After entering Shamakhi it became evident that another Mozaffar Soltan, who was the governor of Darband and the son-in-law of the shah had died and his wife had become a widow. He went to the house of the late governor hoping to take this sister of Shah Tahmasp in the place of the other sister, who was his wife and had died previously, and then to capture the strong fort of Darband. After some time he expressed his intention with emphasis and repetition. In secret, the princess sent a message to her brother, who was in Tabriz, [94] and explained the situation. In accordance with the royal order that was issued, Bayazid Soltan Shamlu, governor of Moghan and Arasbar went speedily to Mozaffar Soltan and took him to Tabriz in chains under humiliating and degrading conditions with a restraining yoke (*takhteh-kolah*). Then they dressed him with a gun-

---

10. For the text of these poems see Tourkhan Gandjei, *Il Canzoniere di Shah Isma`il Khata'i* (Naples, 1959); Vladimir Minorsky, "The Poetry of Shah Isma`il," *BSOAS* 10 (1939 - 42), pp. 1006-53.

11. `Abd al-Fattah Fumeni, *Tarikh-e Gilan dar vaqaye`-ye salha 923-1038 hejri qamari*, ed. Manuchehr Setudeh (Tehran 1349/1970).

powder laden vest and put him in a tight iron cage that was hung from the *Rashidiyeh* tower and in the year 943 (1537) they sprayed bullets at him.

After the death of Soltan Khalil, since he had no offspring, the leaders of Shirvan made his nephew Shahrokh, son of Soltan Farrokh, son of Sheikh Shah, who was just a child, king. The rule of this dynasty lost its prosperity and disorder prevailed because of stubbornness of the emirs. At this moment, a dervish claiming that he was Soltan Mohammad, son of Sheikh Shah gathered a large army and seized Saliyan. The companions of Shahrokh, on account of the disorder of the leaders and lack of union of the army, could not oppose him and they escaped to the fort of Bighord. The dervish came to Shamakhi, which was the capital of Shirvan. Because the followers of the dervish consisted of rabble, who were without competent leaders, and because of lack of direction and incompetence they left Shamakhi and returned to Saliyan. The leaders of Shirvan who were in the fort of Bighord received news about his departure and accompanied by the retinue of Shahrokh Mirza they hastened after him. The dervish was defeated and was caught by the Shirvanis. Sheikh Paydar killed him, but the emirs of Shirvan became more and more rebellious and injustice began; they misused people's property and honor. Because he was not of age Shahrokh Mirza could not stop them. The *qurchi-bashi-ye padar*,[12] part of the army and the subjects took their case to Shah Tahmasp and complained of the injustice of the emirs. In the year 945 (1538) he sent his brother Elqas Mirza, accompanied by Mantasha Soltan and some of the Qajar emirs and people from Tavalesh in Qarabagh, to Shirvan. The Shirvanis rebelled and forty-five forts of that region were defended by capable men. The Qezelbash army first took the fort of Sorkhab and then the fort of Qabaleh. The prince ordered an army group to capture the fort of Golestan, which was the strongest fort of Shirvan and he himself came to the fort of Bighord where Shahrokh Mirza was residing. Hoseyn Bey, the regent of Shahrokh Mirza, with a brave army came to oppose him and in the valley of Bighord the fire of battle raged. Hoseyn Bey was put to flight and returned to the fort and started preparing for the siege. The siege had lasted four months when Mohammad Khan, the governor of Sheki, came to the assistance of the Shirvanis; he, intending to make a night attack, came close to the camp of the Qezelbash. He beat the drums and whistled; but some of the royal household troops came to oppose him and defeated him. The governor of Sheki, Dervish Mohammad Khan suffered many casualties and without having achieved anything returned. Since there was no support for the Shirvanis they gave up [95] defending the fort as well as their opposition and sent a message saying that if the king came himself they would surrender and hand the fort over to him. The emirs apprised Shah Tahmasp of the situation, who then came from Marand to the fort. The next day Hoseyn Bey, the regent, with the leaders and dignitaries of Shirvan brought Shahrokh Mirza to him and gave him the key of the fort and the treasures. The castellan of Fort Golestan also came to his presence and surrendered. Hoseyn Bey and most of the leaders were executed and after one year Shahrokh Mirza also died. The government of Shirvan

---

12. This refers to the chief of that section of the royal household guards or *qurchi*s that were drawn from Azerbaijan's Padar nomadic tribe. There is also a village of Padar in the Oghuz district, located on south slopes of the Greater Caucasus in the Sheki-Zagatala zone, but it is unlikely that this is referred to here.

was given to Elqas Mirza, who governed Shirvan for nine year independently and finally, because of an excess of power, wealth, and troops he became arrogant and rebelled against his king and elder brother. Disobedience to the rights of his king afflicted him with eternal despair.

The summary of the events is as follows: Elqas Mirza out of stubbornness committed every day more and more acts contrary to his brother's wishes and became more rebellious. Eventually Shah Tahmasp to oppose his rebellion turned his attention to Shirvan. Elqas Mirza awakened a little bit from his sleep of neglect and expressed repentance about what had passed and sent the mother of his son Ahmad Mirza to intercede with the royal court and tried to apologize. With strong vows he pledged his sincerity and obedience. The king himself went to Georgia and ordered him to make holy war with the Cherkes. But since he had struck coins in his name and had put his name in the *khotbah* in Shirvan, Shah Tahmasp, after returning from Georgia, while Elqas Mirza was in the land of the Cherkes, sent Ebrahim Khan Dhu'l-Qadr, Gukcheh Soltan Qajar and Shahverdi Khan Ziyad-oghlu with part of the army to march speedily there. Mehtar Dowlatyar who was the confidante and the commander of Elqas Mirza's army camp took his family and goods and sought refuge in Fort Golestan. The emirs took Shirvan and laid siege to Fort Golestan. Elqas Mirza hearing this news returned to Darband; he twice sent an army against the emirs, but it was defeated. Shah Tahmasp sent another army to the emirs, and he himself followed and attacked Elqas Mirza, who became worried because of the royal army and fled to Khenaleq and his men dispersed gradually. The emirs reached him near the Samur River and with great difficulty with forty or fifty people he managed to get to Daghestan to the Krim-Shamkhal and from there he went to Kafeh and then to Istanbul. For a while, the forts of Darband and Golestan were in the possession of his appointees. After their occupation, Mehtar Dowlatyar, with some other people, was executed. Shah Tahmasp gave Shirvan to his son Esma'il Mirza and put Gukcheh Soltan Qajar in his service [**96**] and he himself returned.

Meanwhile, a certain Borhan Mirza from the line of the kings of Shirvan whose seal is on the decrees as Borhan 'Ali, son of Key Qobad, son of Ababakr, son of Amir Eshaq, son of Sheikh Ebrahim, who had been living among the people of Qeytaq, in the year 945 (1547) came to Shirvan and took up residence in the fort of Qolhan. He gathered some troops around him, who trained for war in the forest and bushes. Esma'il Mirza and Gukcheh Soltan went to oppose them with a large army. The skirmishers fought fiercely with the people of Borhan Mirza. After the arrival of the prince's retinue, the army of Shirvan was put to flight and many were killed, while Borhan Mirza fled to Daghestan.

After Elqas Mirza had gone to Turkey (Rum) he encouraged Soltan Soleyman to invade Iran and he for the third time in the year 955 (1548) with a countless army and innumerable cannons and much war equipment marched to Iran. Shah Tahmasp also fully equipped hurried to oppose him and Esma'il Mirza and Gukcheh Soltan with the Shirvan army also accompanied him. In short, after much fighting Soleyman returned to Turkey. Elqas Mirza went to Persian Iraq and Fars and caused much turmoil there and from there he went to Baghdad. Eventually he was captured and became a prisoner for a long time in the fort of Qahqaheh and at the end of his life he went to Mashhad and died there. He had a talent for poetry.

Quatrain

Like ferocious lions we are hunting

In support of each we are all together

When the curtain is dropped

It will be revealed what we all were doing

چون شیر درنده در شکاریم همه

دائم به هوای خویش بیاریم همه

چون پرده ز روی کار ها بر خیزد

معلوم شود که در چه کاریم همه

But in the absence of Esma'il Mirza and Gukcheh Soltan, Borhan Mirza found Shirvan undefended and he came to Shamakhi and for a few days claimed rulership and then he died. In the year 956 (1549), the governorship of Shirvan passed to 'Abdollah Khan Ostajalu, son of Khan Mohammad who was the sister's son and the son-in-law of Shah Esma'il. [97] The Shirvanis, because they had been obedient for a short period to Borhan Mirza became afraid of 'Abdollah Khan and came together in a place and appointed a relative of Borhan Mirza called Mehrab to the throne. 'Abdollah Khan put down the rebellion and many Shirvanis were killed. Mehrab Mirza fled and his fate is unknown. The Shirvanis revolted a second time and appointed a certain Qorban 'Ali, one of Mehrab Mirza's relatives and they took refuge on one of the islands of the Caspian Sea. In spite of the fact that 'Abdollah Khan sent letters of appeasement it was no use. Eventually he went to fight them and the Qezelbash army fought in the midst of water and fire. They took the island and put Qorban 'Ali and many others to the sword and they collected much booty. After this event peace reigned for a few years.

One of the conquests of Shah Tahmasp in this area was that of Sheki. The details of the story are as follows. For generations, Hoseyn Bey's family belonged to one of the branches of the Shirvan dynasty. Due to marauding and attacks by the Georgians in the time of Shah Esma'il he had taken refuge with him, who had always received them with kindness. In the year of Shah Esma'il's death, Lavand Khan, the ruler of Kakht came to Sheki and Hoseyn Bey was killed in battle. The leaders of Sheki chose his son Dervish Mohammad Khan as the governor of Sheki. He, contrary to his father, opposed the government of Iran and as has been mentioned earlier he made a night attack on the Qezelbash in the battle with Shahrokh Mirza. Therefore, Shah Tahmasp himself came to conquer Sheki in 958 (1551). The Georgian Lavand Khan, king of Kakht, came to offer his services in the town of Arash where he was received royally and an order pertaining to appease Dervish Mohammad Khan was issued. Because he relied on the inaccessibility of his position, he rebelled and some of the leaders of Sheki took refuge in the fort of Kish and Dervish Mohammad Khan himself in the fort of Gelesen Goresen [meaning: Come and see for yourself], another group went to the slopes of the Elburz, where they made the place that they occupied into a retrenchment in preparation for battle. Sevendok Bey, *qurchi-bashi* and Badr Khan Shah Qoli Khan Ostajalu with an army group went to conquer Fort Kish. Lavand Khan, ruler of Kakht, and 'Abdollah Khan the governor of Shirvan went to fort Gelesen Goresen and Shah Qoli Khalifeh, the seal bearer, with another regiment went [98] to seize the retrenchment. The emirs were laying siege to it and with the firing of guns and cannons they wanted to make a breach and the castellan of the Kish fort came out with a sword and a shroud to the king's court and surrendered the keys of the fort and was received with kindness. At the order of the king the fort, the towers and walls were destroyed and leveled. Then the royal entourage moved to the retrenchment and its people became frightened by the king's majesty and beged for forgiveness and were forgiven. Dervish Mohammad Khan repented of his doings and one night fled from fort Gelesen Goresen, but he was unlucky in that he passed Lavand Khan's and 'Abdollah Khan's camps. A group of soldiers followed him; they fought and killed him with 400 of his companions. Dervish Mohammad Khan fought with somebody called Pir Qoli Khan Kuseh [the beardless] who was an attendant of Charandab Soltan Shamlu. He cut off his head, which was puffed up with the desire of lordship and threw it down under the hoof of his own king's horse. The country of Sheki came under the mighty rule of the leaders of the powerful kingdom.

In the year 961 (1554), Soltan Soleyman came to Azerbaijan for a fourth time and he sent a certain Qasem Mirza, who was of the lineage of the rulers of Shirvan. He had taken refuge at the Porte via Kafeh in the Crimea and was sent to Shirvan. When Qasem Mirza passed through Darband the Shirvanis once again turned away from 'Abdollah Khan and gathered around the former. 'Abdollah Khan with the Qezelbash army hurried to oppose him. In a narrow and inaccessible pass, a fierce battle occurred. 'Abdollah Khan returned to Shamakhi, while Qasem Mirza came to Fort Bighord to prepare for battle. He attacked 'Abdollah Khan with 10,000 Turks and Shirvanis. The elders of the Qezelbash, because of their small number and the size of the opposing army hesitated and faltered before the battle. 'Abdollah Khan, with the 10,000 men that he had, gave it his best and near Fort Golestan they engaged in battle and for one whole day the fire of battle burnt. In the evening the army of Shirvan was put to flight and many of them were killed and the remaining ones fled to Tabarsaran; the fate of Qasem Mirza was unknown. 'Abdollah Khan extended his power over that area more than before and punished the rebels and took care of the subjects with kindness and nobody [99] could oppose him. Apart from the affairs of the country he paid special attention to the development of trade. The English Company trading house, which was called factory, was in Shamakhi under his protection in the year 969 (1561), when Jenkinson returned to England from this country. He sent an envoy with him to discuss some affairs with the king of Russia, Ivan Vasilivich [the

Terrible].¹³ After having ruled for 17 years he died in the year 973 (1566) and the country of Shirvan was given to Aras Khan Rumlu and it remained for a long time in his hands.

In the year 984 (1576) Shah Tahmasp died after 54 years of reign. He was a powerful and just king, although his early life he had spent in playing and in forbidden things, but he never failed dealing with the affairs of the subjects and soldiers. He had a good poetic talent; as to his repentance, its chronogram is *towbatan va nosuhan*.

Quatrain
For a while we went after crushed emerald [i.e. opium]
For a while we were immersed in fresh ruby [i.e. wine]
In whatever color it was it was stained
We washed ourselves with tears and became purified

یک چند پی زمرد سوده شدیم
یک چند بیاقوت تر آلوده شدیم
آلودگی بود بهر رنگ که بود
شستیم به آب دیده آسوده شدیم

And he described the characteristics of several cities in poetry.

Couplet
The dog of Kashan is better than the notables of Qom
And a dog is better than someone from Kashan

سگ کاشی به از اکابر قم
با وجود اینکه سگ به از کاشی است

Of the Tabrizis you see nothing but impertinence
Therefore it is better that you never see Tabrizis [100]

ز تبریزی بجز حیزی نه بینی
همان بهتر که تبریزی نبینی

Isfahan is a paradise full of bounty
Except that there should be no Isfahanis in it

اصفهان جنتی است پر نعمت
اصفهانی در آن نمی باید

---

13. See E. Delmar Morgan and C.H. Coote eds., Early Voyages and Travels to Russia and Persia by Anthoney Jenkinson and other Englishmen (New York, 1971).

After him his son Esma'il II was king for nearly one year and unlike the reigns of his father and grandfather he gave the affairs of the people to unworthy people. With the excuse that the names of the holy ones should not be in everybody's hands he changed the phrase [which was on the coinage] of "There is no God but God and Mohammad is his prophet and 'Ali is his regent" to the following couplet:

From East to West if there is an Imam
Ali and his family are enough for us

ز مشرق تا بمغرب گر امام است
علی و آل او ما را تمام است

In this manner, which is neither approval nor denial of the three [first] caliphs, he aimed to eliminate the discord between Sunnis and Shi'ites [in Iran], which was then at its height. The same thing has been said by Mohammad b. Idris Shafi'i.[14]

Couplet
I do not say bad things about 'Adi va Tayyem[15]
But I am an admirer of the Hashemis

عدی و تیم لا اوحاول ذکرهم یسوء
و لـــكنی مـــحب لهـا شـمی

But because of too much bloodshed and lack of clemency he did not benefit of state and life, for he was poisoned. This couplet is from him [101]

Your eyelashes target me and I am happy
That while aiming them at me your eyes beckon me

شادم به خدنگ تو که ناوک فکنان را
سوی هدف خویش نهانی نظری هست

---

14. Copy T has the following paragraph in the margin, probably because it has [in Iran] in the text: in accordance with the tradition of the ancestors they had various ways to experience Sunni Islam, but his essential aim was this that this word is heresy that from the time of the prophet of God until the day of corruption and calumny this word [probably *vali ollah* or 'the beloved of God'] was not heard of. And the reason for the conflict among the community is exactly this, because believing that Ali, may God be satisfied with him, has been explictly declared [to be the heir] of necessity leads to the ruination of the majority of Moslems and is the cause of corruption of the Truth. Believing that those whom God refers to in the Koran as 'the best of the people' are the worst of people, because of heretical beliefs negates '[God's] justice.' Thus, by omitting this word from the call to prayer and prayer …
15. The epynomous ancestor of the clans of the Bani Tayyim of Abu Bakr (the first of calpih) and the Bani Adi (the clan of the second caliph, Omar). The Bani Hashem was a clan of the Qoreysh tribe to which the first Shi`ite Imam, `Ali belonged.

After him his older brother Soltan Mohammad Khodabandeh acceded to the throne. Aras Khan as before remained in the province of Shirvan and he bestowed also a district in Shirvan on Ordughdi Khalifeh Tekellu as well as on a group of the Shamlu and other emirs. 'Isa Khan Gorji, son of Lavand Khan, ruler [of Kakht], who had been honored to marry the daughter of Sam Mirza, son of Shah Esma'il, he appointed to the governorship of Sheki. During the reign of Soltan Mohammad Khodabandeh, who was a God-fearing man and foreign to the ways of the world, the affairs and integrity of the kingdom became corrupted due to his weakness and the fact that the treasury was emptied through excessive stipends as well as by interference of women in matters of state and differences and lack of cooperation between the emirs and the tribes. The result was that friends became idle and enemies ready to fight. Among these the province of Shirvan became rebellious. The enemies called upon Abu Bakr Mirza, son of Borhan Mirza, who was mentioned above, and who had been wandering aimlessly in the lands of the Cherkes and Daghestan, and 2-3,000 of the Lezgi and Qaraburak tribe, who formed the remainder of Shirvan army gathered around him and started a rebellion. The aforesaid person sent an envoy to the Ottoman Soltan and said that he wanted to be part of his Empire and asked for help to capture the province of Shirvan. A group of Shirvanis went to Istanbul and expressed their agreement with the [Sunni] religion of the Soltan and complained about the oppression and occupation by the Qezelbash. Soltan Morad Khan decided to conquer the provinces of Shirvan and Azerbaijan. In the year 986/1578, he sent Mostafa Pasha, who was known as Laleh Pasha, with an army of more than 100,000 to conquer those lands. In the area of Akhsaqeh, he defeated the *Beyler-bey*s of Erevan and Qarabagh, who had gone to oppose him. He then came to Georgia and conquered the fort of Tiflis and then he went to Shirvan. 'Isa Khan could not stay in Sheki; he withdrew to a corner. Laleh Pasha without any opposition came to Shirvan and the emirs of Daghestan and the Lezgi tribes helped him and the subjects of Shirvan also [**102**] obeyed him. Aras Khan, *Beyler-bey* of Shirvan who was an able and wise man could not stay in the fort and went out with his family and troops to the bank of the Kur where he camped. Laleh Pasha made Othman Pasha *Beyler-bey* of Shirvan. He left Qeytamas Pasha in Arash and appointed in each district a governor and strengthened the forts of Shamakhi, Arash, and Baku. He left Abu Bakr Mirza in Shirvan to help the Turks and promised him the governorship of Shirvan on behalf of the Soltan and he himself, while fighting, returned to Erzerum via Georgia.

On the side of Iran it was the advice of the emirs of the state that Hamzeh Mirza, the oldest son and heir apparent of Soltan Mohammad Khodabandeh, should go to Azerbaijan and Shirvan. When the prince arrived at Qarabagh, Aras Khan and the emirs of Shirvan who were staying on the banks of the Kur on the Moghan side, considered it important that before the prince's arrival they would go to Shamakhi to fight the Turks and perhaps without the help of others they might take Shirvan. With this intention and resolution they marched with the troops that they had with them and arrived at Shamakhi. When Laleh Pasha was appointed to this campaign there was a request that Mohammad Geray Khan, governor of the Crimea, who was a descendent of Juji, son of Chengiz, to come with the Tatar army to Shirvan. Therefore, his brother, 'Adel Geray Soltan, was sent with an army of 20,000 Tatars to that region. Othman Pasha who knew the date of their arrival came outside the city and readied himself for battle. Aras Khan and other emirs put themselves in battle formation, when the vanguard of the Tatars arrived, which covered the mountain. The Qezelbash army seeing the situation thus were worried and wanted to retreat fighting. But the troops of Turks, Tatars, Lezgis, Qaraburaqs, and Shirvanis surrounded them. Aras Khan with most of his emirs was killed and the remainder of the army barely escaped and fled until they crossed the Kur. After this event Othman Pasha came to Shamakhi, while 'Adel Geray Soltan and Abu Bakr Mirza intended to plunder the army camp of Aras Khan and went to the banks of the Kur. When this news reached Hamzeh Mirza orders had already been given that the emirs of Talesh and the area around it had to go and protect the camp of Aras Khan. The officials, who were in charge of guarding the bridge to allow the wounded of the Qezelbash to cross, cut it. Some of them jumped into the water anyway and reached land. A fierce battle ensued. It became apparent that a number of Tatars and Lezgis [103] had crossed the river from another place with the guidance of the Shirvanis and appeared at the back of the Qezelbash army and pursued it. Therefore, the Iranian army was routed and each one sought to save himself. The army of Tatars and Lezgis reached the army camp that was on the move. The people ran away, women and children with lots of property, which had been gathered for many years, fell into their hands. That same day they went to Shirvan, but at this time Salman the vizier, who had come in haste with the emirs and soldiers from Qara Qepek in Qarabagh, which is also called Takht-e Tavus, had crossed Quyun Ulami and was besieging the citadel of Shamakhi; he left some people at the citadel and went himself to welcome them, when he heard of the return of the Tartar and Lezgi troops. 'Adel Geray Soltan, in spite of knowing the situation, but because of having become emboldened by the war with the Qezelbash, of whose prowess he had a low opinion, marched to Shamakhi to help Othman Pasha and at the banks of the Aq Su Yurt he met Molla Hasan and the two sides fought. The 12,000 Tatars, Lezgis and Qaraburaks that he had with him put themselves in battle formation. Amir Hamzeh Khan Ostajalu who was the chief skirmisher of the Qezelbash army went ahead with a regiment and engaged them in battle. The troops that had been left in Shamakhi to serve as the rearguard preferred to fight the Tatars and without the permission of the emirs engaged them in battle. The Tatar army in spite of frequent attacks from the Qezelbash resisted from morning till evening and showed great bravery. Finally, 'Adel Geray Soltan sensing the weakness in his army entered himself into battle to encourage them. While fighting with Baba Khalifeh he was thrown down by the thrust of his spear, but he made himself known and was taken prisoner. After this event the Tatar army fled, many were killed and the remainder of the army fled into the forests and mountains. The property and the captives of the camp of Aras Khan and the strings of his camels fell into Persian hands unscathed. Othman Pasha despaired of help and saw no alternative but to leave the citadel of Shamakhi and hurried to Darband. The troops that were sent after him went up to Shabaran, captured part of his artillery and returned. Othman Pasha relying on the help of the people of Daghestan came to Darband, while leaving Mirza Salman and some other emirs to hold Shirvan. At first, 'Adel Geray Soltan was kept with much honor in the royal palace, but eventually due to unruliness of the emirs it was proposed to send him to one of the forts. He did not agree and was killed in the [ensuing] dispute. After the news of the good treatment of [104] 'Adel Geray Soltan reached his mother in the Crimea many gifts were sent to Iran by the khan. The news of the killing of her son reached her in the village of Kafer-Qomuq in the land of the Shamkhal. Because of the wealth that she had with her the people harassed and plundered her. That woman called them Qomuq heretics and ever since they are thus called. She died there and her tomb, known as Tatar Sin [i.e., the Tatar Tomb], is situated on a hill next to the village.

The province of Shirvan was given to Mohammad Qoli Khalifeh Dhu'l-Qadr by the royal court; and [within that province] some emirs also received a district. Since the people of Sheki and Shabaran had gathered around Abu Bakr Mirza and were supporting Othman Pasha and the governor of Daghestan they did not give the Qezelbash any rest in Shirvan. On the other hand, Laleh Pasha in Erzerum was preparing for next year's campaign. Therefore, the royal army was transferred from the capital Qazvin to Tabriz. Meanwhile, a letter from Mohammad Qoli Khalifeh reached the capital reporting that Ghazi Geray Soltan and Safi Geray Soltan, the brothers of 'Adel Geray Soltan were coming to Darband with the Tatar army, either at the order of the Ottoman Soltan or to revenge their brother. It was decided that Mirza Salman with the emirs and the generals of the army should go to Shirvan. They had not yet reached Qarabagh when Ghazi Geray Soltan had arrived at Shirvan with a huge army. Mohammad Qoli Khalifeh opposed him on the banks of the Samur river, where they fought a fierce battle. Mohammad Qoli with many men was killed and the rest fled from Shirvan and their possessions and family fell into the hands of the Tatars. The Tatars would not rest for one moment from killing and plundering. A number of the Tatar army that was heavily loaded with booty after hearing the news of the coming of the Qezelbash army returned home. Ghazi Geray and Safi Geray remained in Daghestan to help Othman Pasha. Of the people of Shirvan who had suffered because of the events some returned to Othman Pasha and some gathered around Abu Bakr Mirza in Khachmaz. Mirza Salman with the emirs and the troops that had come to Shirvan could not do much and the people that he had sent against Abu Bakr Mirza at Khachmaz came back.

In short, the destruction of the country, the scarcity of wheat, due to the drought that had struck Qarabagh, Azerbaijan and both Gilans that year, and the lack of order and union among the emirs were the main reasons that they left Shirvan and returned to Tabriz. They therefore sent orders to everyone to prepare for the journey. The summer quarters for the royal retinue were fixed at Ashkanbar and Kalanbar and the winter-quarters in the region of Qarabagh. Salman Khan was sent to the province of Shirvan [105] as well as some of the Ostajalu emirs to govern the districts there. He traveled via Arasbar and along the Kur river. Due to the warm weather they stayed at the location of Hameh Sahreh, which is at a distance of 2 *farsakh* from the sea at the location of an old city, which is called in Ferdowsi's *Shahnameh* Abarshahreh and there they were busy mobilizing an army and the requirements for campaigning. Ghazi Geray and Safi Geray Soltan quickly came with a big army to Shirvan and asked about the situation of the Qezelbash army and without hesitation and with the guidance of the Shirvanis they crossed the Kur river. At that time because of too much rain and mud the Qezelbash army had no knowledge about the other and the Tatar army attacked them. They did not give much time [to the Qezelbash army to prepare itself] for battle and killed many of them and plundered and looted their camp. The same day they returned to Shirvan. In total disarray, the Qezelbash army stayed in the area of Qezel Aghaj. Othman Pasha came to Shamakhi and sent some Turkish troops to the citadel of Baku and fortified it. When the news of the arrival of Mirza Salman and the emirs reached the Turkish and Tatar army they came to oppose them and in Yurt Molla Hasan the skirmishers fought with each other. Considering the strength and the size of the Qezelbash army Othman Pasha could not confront it and returned to Darband and the Tartar Soltans to Daghestan. Meanwhile, Salman Khan *Beyler-bey* with the emirs attached to Shirvan crossed the Kur to take revenge for the defeats that they had suffered at the hands of the Tatars and decided to take the citadel of Baku. Amir Khan with an army that had gone to Shabaran came to the citadel of Baku. The siege lasted 18 days and achieved nothing. Due to the shortage of food and fodder staying there became difficult. In the beginning one Tabrizi *man* of barley flour was sold for silver coins weighing 6 *methqals*. At the end there was nothing left and the army was forced to leave Shirvan and go to Qarabagh. The emirs and the grandees decided that it was in the interest of the state that the defense of Shirvan would be entrusted to the Qajar tribe, the Utuz-iki clans and many other people who were in Qarabagh. The command of this force was given to Emam Qoli Khan Ziyad-oghlu Qajar *Beyler-bey* of Qarabagh. Although he did not accept it, they made him. They made Peykar Soltan Ziyad-oghlu Qajar *Beyler-bey* of Shirvan with the title of Khan. Some other Qajar emirs were given districts in that province and they were sent with him to Shamakhi.

Ghazi Geray Soltan came with a large army of Tatars and Turks to Shirvan. Peykar Khan who had received much help from Emam Qoli Khan hurried with the Qajar, Chakerlu, Qaramanlu and other tribesmen to oppose him. Between Shamakhi and Shabaran a battle took place. Ghazi Geray Soltan who had become emboldened in the war with the Qezelbash did not took notice of them and rode his steed of bravery [**106**] into the battlefield. During the fighting he fell into the midst of a group of Qajars and he was taken prisoner. His army with Safi Geray Soltan fled. Ghazi Geray Soltan after having been taken to the royal camp was sent to Fort Alamut, which is one of the famous forts located between Qazvin and Gilan. He stayed there a while and after having been released he went to Turkey and in the year 997/1589 with the help of the Ottoman Soltan received the kingship of the Crimea and the steppes. They say that he was a brave emir, with a Sufi inclination, and a lover of poetry and music.

In the year 991/1583, a group of Qezelbash was assigned to a fort, which had been built by Ebrahim Pasha. The said Ebrahim Pasha was defeated and fled and the fort was occupied and destroyed. Another army group went to Qabaleh and did not spare anybody from plunder and killing. At this moment Peykar Khan died of illness. Again the Ottomans invaded and the Shirvanis revolted. The royal court assigned his province to Khalifeh-ye Ansar-e Qaradaghlu. He punished the Shirvanis and destroyed and burnt the houses of the people of Qabaleh who intended to revolt and plundered them and before long he hurried to the next world.

Othman Pasha, in the company of Ja'far Pasha, Heydar Pasha, Shamsi Bey and Piyaleh Bey, when he had reached Darband with the new Ottoman army, attacked the Qezelbash at Palaseh near the Samur River where a battle took place. A number of Qezelbash, including Emam Qoli Khan and some [other] emirs were killed; the remainder returned to Iran. After these events and also because of the return of the royal army to Persian Iraq, which took place in the following year, the affairs of Shirvan got into such a disorder that none of the Qezelbash emirs could stay there. Othman Pasha came from Darband to Shamakhi, reinforced the fort and became independent [governor] in that province.

In the year 993/1585, Ja'far Pasha moved from Darband and captured Fort Kur whose people were rebellious and he destroyed and plundered it. In the year 996/1588, when Soltan Mohammad went from Ganjeh in Qarabagh to Persian Iraq his eldest son and heir-apparent Hamzeh Mirza was killed by his barber, whose name was Khodaverdi, in a place called Abu Shahmeh. After this event Farhad Pasha *sar 'askar* went from Erzerum with the permission of Simun Khan, the king of Kartli, who did not have the power [**107**] to oppose him and together they went to Qarabagh and built the fort of Ganjeh. At the same time they captured Tabriz and most of the cities of Azerbaijan. At this time [only] Ardabil was in the hands of the Qezelbash and the Ottomans for 20 years without fighting and contestation were ruling in all these [other] provinces. In that year Soltan Mohammad Khodabandeh became a recluse and gave his kingdom to his son Shah 'Abbas, who spent a few years preparing the army and the government and looking after the subjects and eliminated the attitude of disobedience of the emirs and the tribes. At this time, when the affairs of Shirvan and Daghestan were in extreme disarray,[16] Khan Ahmad Khan, the nephew of Mirza 'Ali Kar-kiya, the governor of Lahejan, who ruled over all of Gilan from the year 975/1568 and who had been imprisoned in the forts of Qahqaheh and Estakhr for a period of 12 years and in the reign of Soltan Mohammad Khodabandeh had been appointed to the same governorship, revolted. After the arrival of the Qezelbash army in the year 1000/1592 he took ship and escaped to Shirvan with Ahmad Amin Khan, the son

---

16. In manuscript B, from up to 3,000 soldiers, pp. 108-110 the following text has been written in a different handwriting in the margin. It was under the dominance and occupation of the Ottomans. Khan Ahmad Khan, the governor of Lahejan, who was ruler of all of Gilan from the year 975 was imprisoned for 12 years in the fort of Estakhr and in the time of Soltan Mohammad Khodabandeh, when he had been again appointed as governor, he started a rebellion. On learning that the Qezelbash troops were coming he, in the year 1000, out of necessity, boarded a ship and fled to Shirvan with Mohammad Amin Khan, son of Jamshid Khan, the governor of Gilan. He sent his vizier to the High Porte asking for help. From there an order was issued summoning him to Constantinople and Hasan Padshah, governor of Shirvan was appointed as his host. Mohammad Amin Khan died in Ganjeh and Khan Ahmad Khan went to Turkey and his fate is unknown. The following year Amir Hamzeh Khan Talesh, the governor of Astara, who had opposed the government of Iran became desperate because of the siege. He asked for amnesty and was allowed to go to Shirvan. For a while he was showered with favors by the Ottoman government until two ungrateful companions killed him during a hunting event. His family then returned home. In the year 1003/1594, Fyodor, son of Ivan, the king of Russia sent 3,000 troops. [B]

of the Shamshir Khan, the governor of Gilan. He also sent his vizier asking for the help of the Ottoman Soltan. From the Porte an order was issued summoning them to Constantinople. Hasan Pasha the governor of Shirvan became his host. Mohammad Amin Khan died in Ganjeh and Khan Ahmad Khan wrote an elegy for him:

Quatrain

From the turning of the world and tyranny of time

Our heart is bereaved our soul afflicted

Instead of tears our eyes shed blood

We buried a wondrous treasure in the land of Ganjeh [**108**]

از گردش روزگار و جور افلاک   ما راست دل حزین و جان غمناک

خون ریز به جای اشک ای دیده که ما   گنج عجبی به گنجه کردیم به خاک

Khan Ahmad Khan himself went to Turkey and eventually died in Najaf. The following year Amir Hamzeh Khan Talesh, the governor of Astara, who was opposing the government of Iran lost heart because of the tightness of the siege and asked for amnesty and was granted permission to go to Shirvan. For a while there he was ingratiating himself with the Ottoman government until two of his ungrateful companions killed him during the hunt and his family returned home. After some time Abu Bakr Mirza, son of Borhan Mirza, who had turned away from the Ottomans, and was fomenting rebellion [against them] because he wanted to conquer the province of Shirvan, sent the son of Borhan 'Ali Mirza to the royal court to ask for Iranian protection. In the year 1010/1602, he, together with Shah Mir Khan of Sheki, marched via the Kur, Tabarsaran and the other mountains, gathered an army and destroyed Akhti and Meskenjeh and in Palaseh near Aghbil he gave battle to Ahmad Pasha, who was the governor of Shirvan at that time and was defeated. The Ottomans killed a number of people and plundered the area of Qobbeh and Moskur and build a fort in the village of Qosar and placed guards there. Shah Mir Khan could not stay in Sheki and went to Iran, but the fate of Abu Bakr Mirza is unknown. The disorder of the affairs of Daghestan was such that when Chuban Shamkhal, who was ruler over the Qeytaq, Kur, Avar, and the Cherkes until the Terek River and the sea, died in Buynaq in the year 982/1574 [his kingdom was divided among] his sons, Eldar in Buynaq and Tarkhu [Tarki], Mohammad in Qezanesh, Andiya in Kafer-Qomuq and Geray in Heli. After that the Shamkhals came from these four families, according to age and competence and ruled all these lands. Since the year 1187/1773, the position of Shamkhal remained in the family of the Emir of Buynaq. In short, these four persons, who were born to the daughter of Soltan Ahmad Usmi, considered their own brother Soltan Bud, who was born to the daughter of Uzun Cherkes, not of noble birth (*jankeh*), and gave him no share of the land. He came to Chelyurt, an old city of the Ahran with three murderers from Andab, who were living there and went to the Cherkes. He brought a large army and the brothers were forced to come to an agreement with him. All the lands between Sulaq and Terek as well as lower Machgach and the district of Sala-Tav until Mount Kerkhi, which is the border of Gonbet, was given as his share. He gathered the Qomuq tribe around him [109] and settled them in Chelyurt.

Soltan Ahmad Usmi, son of Hasan 'Ali Usmi, who was an intelligent, courageous, and powerful emir gave the governorship of the Qeytaq to his son Khan Mohammad Usmi in the year 996/1588 and died. Four major works that he had accomplished became his legacy. One, he founded the village of Majales, in an empty space that was used for gatherings. Two, he established the difference between a '*bey*' and '*jankeh*', which is still the rule in Daghestan, meaning that if a son of an emir (*amirzadeh*) is not born from a princess he cannot rule. Three, he wrote the law governing property of which the judge of the district of Hapshi [Qeytaq] still has a copy and people use it. Four, he developed the lands of the Turkman, because they were vacant and belonged to the people of Urjamil and Bashli, who, when they cultivated it, gave very little to the Usmi. When the son of the Usmi had gone there to gather taxes (*kharaj*), the people of Urjamil humiliated him. Apparently he had gone without the permission of his father and gathered an army of the Shamkhal, who was his sister's son and killed some of the notables of that place. After a while, the Usmi himself gathered the remaining notables on the pretext that they wanted to rebel and killed them. He had brought a number of Shirvan Turkman, who were looking for a safe haven, because of the unsettled times, and he founded the villages of the Turkman area and made them subjects of his family.

While these disturbances were going on in the affairs of Daghestan, Fyodor, son of Ivan, king of Russia, in the year 1002/1594 sent an army of some 3,000 men and built a town on the banks of the Sulaq River called Quy-su. He intended to build another town near Tarkhu, which the sons of the Chuban Shamkhal stopped, who had gathered the tribes of the Cherkes and Qomuq of Daghestan. To establish his dominion over Daghestan, Boris, son of Fyodor Godonov, when he became king of Russia built three forts in Tarkhu [Tarki], Enderey and at a third place that is not known and garrisoned them and [*voyvode*] Yuvareh Buturlin was its commander.[17] After a while, in the year 1012/1604, Soltan Bud brought thirteen thousand troops [110] and with the help of his brother Geray Khan Shamkhal and the support of the Crimean Tartars attacked all three forts. After much fighting, the garrisons saw no other means than to come to an agreement with the enemy and to return to their country. But because they wanted to make them prisoner, which was contrary to the agreement, the Russians started to fight and they were all killed. The garrison of Quy-su set fire to the town and went home. Soltan Bud then came with his tribe and settled in Enderey. All the Qomuq emirs are from the line of his sons Aytmut and Qazanalp. The Qomuq tribe, through intermarriage with other people, who are now living in Enderey, Yakhsay, Kostak, Ghazi Yurt and other villages, number about five thousand families and are still related to them. The ancient tribe of the Tumanler also lived on the right side of the Quy-su between the Turkhaleh and Teymur-Quyi tribes and owned streams and pastures. After the fall of their own special princely family the chieftainship belonged to that of the sons of Qazanalp, son of Soltan Bud. Now it is a quarter of Enderey, and two people from Qonbud and Arghunay who claim to be descended from

---

17. On this episode see Karamzin, *Istoria*, vol. 11, chapter 3, p. 37.

the khan of the Avars were killed there. After much fighting, while negotiating a peace, part of lower Machgach, which includes Chechen-Tala, Qermunchuk-Shali and Ataqah were given as blood-money to their heir, a person known as Terlav. He brought people from Nashaq and made that place prosperous. This land takes its name from the river Mecheq, and Mecheqich or Andar means "inside the river." It is divided into three parts, mountain, wilderness, and forest. Tav-Machgach, which is a mountain, was always independent, Aghaj-Machgach and Tuz-Machgach, which are forested and wild were until our days tributary to the sons of Terlav. The Terlav-oghli emirs in their old land of Kunbet and Arghunay also owned other mountainous lands and a village with peasants and every year they received taxes. Also, the villages of Avoq and Bayan that have oil wells and the Sala-Tav district that has 12 villages and 12,000 people gave taxes and services to the Enderey emirs.

On the other hand Shah 'Abbas after the conquest of Azerbaijan took his winter quarters [**111**] in Tabriz in the year 1014/1606. To Konstandil [Constantine] Mirza, son of Alexander Mirza of Georgia, who came with his family and retinue, he gave the title of khan and of the [function of] *amir al-omara* of Shirvan and some other persons were also given the dignity of emir and assigned a district. Alexander Khan, who was given a special turban (*taj*), an aigrette, a studded belt, and other honors, went to Georgia with his son Konstadil Mirza, his emirs and army so that they would go from there to take Shirvan. The emirs who accompanied him and who held districts in Shirvan were as follows: First, Shah Mir Khan, who was of the family of the former governors of Sheki had served for a time at court. He was given the governorship of Sheki. Second, Shamshi Khan Qazzaqlar. Third, 'Ali Khan Movafeq from the Shamlu tribe. Fourth, Begtash Soltan, son of Mohammad Khan Mowselli Turkman, who is related to Konstandil Khan. Fifth, Tizru Soltan Moqaddam. Sixth, Akhi Soltan Chakerlu. Seventh, 'Ali Khan Shams al-Dinlu. Eighth, 'Ali Soltan Arshi with a group of royal musketeers. When Alexander Khan with his son and emirs came to Georgia he was dilatory in preparing for the campaign to Shirvan, because his elder son and crown prince, Gorgin Khan, was creating problems. Eventually a conflict arose between the father and sons, which ended in fighting. Kostandil Khan, who was a Moslem, killed his father and brother with the help of the Qezelbash emirs and army there and then he became the independent king of Georgia. He prepared for the campaign in early 1015/1607 and departed with 2,500 Qezelbash troops and Georgians. As he arrived in the province of Shirvan most people and dignitaries accepted his governorship. Shah Mir Khan, governor of Sheki, with some of the emirs who formed the vanguard of the army fought in the vicinity of Qabaleh with Mohammad Pasha, the governor of that place and defeated him. Mohammad Amin Pasha with a group of Ottomans was killed. The rest of the army took refuge in the fortress of Qabaleh. The besiegers were preparing the siege works when Mahmud Pasha Jeghal-oghli *Beyler-bey* of Shirvan gathered the Ottoman army from different places in the city of Shamakhi and with artillery went to confront them. Konstandil Khan put some people in the fortress of Qabaleh and with the rest of the army he went to oppose him. On the banks of the river Aq Su the fire of battle raged. In the beginning, the Ottomans launched the skirmishers [**112**] of the right and the left to reach the center of the army. It was almost turning out to be a major defeat for the Qezelbash, but Kostandil Khan with an army unit went forward and attacked. The emirs and soldiers of both right and left [wings], who were intending to flee, returned and the Ottomans were defeated and put to flight. Many of them were killed and taken prisoner. Kostandil Khan followed Mahmud Pasha and intuitively knew that he was going to kill him, but suddenly an arrow struck him and prevented him from doing so. Two thousand Ottomans were killed and Mahmud Pasha with the rest came to the city of Shamakhi. The army group that was besieging the fortress of Qabaleh did not stay, for during the retreat of the Ottomans it came to the battleground. The garrison of the fort of Qabaleh on hearing about the defeat fled. The ruins of the fort, which was founded by Qobad, son of Firuz, still exist. The wonderful remains of the gate of the fort and of the extremely deep moat can still be seen. The castellans of other forts also gathered at Shamakhi; except for the forts of Baku and Darband nothing remained in the hands of the Ottomans. Konstandil Khan, according to the agreement that was made in the presence of the king, gave districts to the emirs and sent the heads of the killed with some persons, who were alive and 12 banners to Shah 'Abbas in Tabriz. In return for this service a special turban (*taj*), belt, jewel-studded dagger, sword and other honors were sent to him. After a few days when his wound was somewhat healed he started the siege of Shamakhi and siege equipment, like artillery and arms, was sent from the royal court. The time of the siege lasted long. Kostandil Khan who had become arrogant was not paying attention to the emirs and the Georgians became disaffected with him for two reasons. First, the difference in religion. Second, unlike his father Alexander Khan, who, whenever a Georgian emir went to him, treated him very kindly, he, however, assumed a royal air and would not give a public audience but once in ten days. They agreed to take the grandson of Alexander Khan, who was there, to Georgia to disobey him. Although one of his well-wishers informed him of this, he out of pride did not pay attention. Ziya al-Din Kashi, who was his and his father's vizier, prevented him from punishing them and with kind advice aimed to restore [**113**] the loyalty of the Georgians. Outwardly they expressed their friendship and said we have no complaint, but that we are tired of the long duration and time of campaigning and we cannot remain in Shirvan. The vizier ensured them that they would be dismissed after one month and that the means of their return would be prepared. The anxiety of the khan was thus relieved. The Georgian lords, who were keeping guard, revolted one night and surrounded the tent of the khan. A certain Qarapiri, who was one of the royal attendants, informed him and he tore the back of the tent and fled to the house of 'Ali Khan Movafeq. The Georgians lords killed some servants thinking that one of them was the khan and they took the grandson of Alexander Khan and returned to their own army group. In the house of 'Ali Khan, the shawm [a big horn] was sounded and the Qezelbash army gathered. From the gathering of the army the Georgians realized that Kostandil Khan was alive, so they took the prince and all of them went to Georgia. In the morning, the khan and some of his troops caught up with them. The Georgians prepared for battle and they were saying openly: "You are a Moslem and we need to have a Christian ruler." Then the khan decided that it was not wise to fight and returned. Out of fear he did not go to the fort and did not stay anywhere until he came to Ardabil. The entire army camp with whatever was there fell into the hands of the Ottomans. Kostandil Khan related the event to the king who was at the foot of the fort of Maku and asked for help. Although he was promised help by the royal court, he, without permission, willy-nilly gathered some money from the merchants and accompanied by his emirs went to Georgia. A large army of Lezgis, Shirvanis and rebels of the Utuz-iki tribe were with him. Shah Mir Khan came from Sheki and joined him. When the Georgians became aware of the royal dissatisfaction they became emboldened and assembled at the river Qanoq and opposed and fought him. Kostandil Khan was defeated and killed.

Couplet

The killer of the father is not worthy of kingship
Even if he were he would not last more than six months

پدرکش پادشاهی را نشاید   اگر شاید بجز شش مه نپاید

His army set itself in motion with many difficulties; some went to Azerbayjan and some to Sheki with Shah Mir Khan. [114] H.M. Shah 'Abbas, after conquering the forts of Ganjeh, Tiflis and Tumanes intending to conquer Shirvan moved from Bargoshat in Qarabagh early in the winter of 1015/1607. He sent Mohammad Bey, who was one of his confidantes and an intelligent man, with letters of good advice to Shamakhi to Ahmad Pasha *Beyler-bey* and the leaders of the Ottomans. H.M. himself came to Arasbar. Meanwhile at the advice of Shams al-Din Pasha, one of the princes of Shirvan and confidante of the Ottomans, who wanted to prevent the shah to march by misleading him with different stratagems, replied to Mohammad Bey: "however special Shirvan was to Iran, we cannot move during winter; there should be a postponement of three or four months. Then we ourselves will vacate the province." But some adherents of the shah (Shahsevans) in Shamakhi secretly told Mohammad Bey that the Ottomans were preparing to abandon Shamakhi and stay in Darband, which had a strong fort, with the help of Daghestan. But Shams al-Din Pasha who had gone to Istanbul and was nearby had brought orders from the Ottoman government addressed to the Ottomans and notables of Shirvan. They spread rumors that a few thousand janissaries had come to Kaffa and that Ghazi Geray Khan ruler of the Crimea also had been sent with a Tatar army to Shirvan. Thus, in the beginning of spring an innumerable Ottoman army would come from two sides and apart from this he pretended that he had a revelation that the Sufi saints and spiritual poles had told him that no harm could come to Shamakhi at the hands of the Qezelbash army. The general public believed him and became more determined to stay there. In short, the royal army moved from Khan Arkhi Arasbar and came to the Javad Gorge. Because the Ottomans had cut the bridge, the army crossed the Kur with boats that had been joined together and pitched camp at Qara Su. From there the army went to Shamakhi. The transportation and the moving of the army camp across the Kur took 10 days. Many drudges and pack animals drowned, died and suffered many difficulties due to the ice and cold. The royal train with proper ceremonies came to Yasamal from behind. At the western side of the town they pitched camp in an appropriate place between two mountains most distant from the fort. That place is still called Shah-yurti [the king's camp] and the stream there is still called Shah Bulaghi [the king's stream].

The Ottomans had closed the gates; they numbered 4,000 men and made preparations to defend the fortress. The fortress of Shamakhi is situated in the middle of the valley; the length of city and the fortress is at the widest part of the valley. The heart of the town, where the houses of the people are, is situated at the southern slope of the mountain. The houses of the governor and past rulers are situated towards the northern part of the mountain, which is higher. The Ottomans each had made a fort and had interconnected them, and at the northern fort they had made high towers, [115] and all with a strong foundation. The Shah after looking at this place designated the sites for the entrenchments on the northern side where it was very difficult to make entrenchments. One entrenchment for Allahverdi Khan and on the western side another five entrenchments, which were assigned to each of the commanders. The digging of the entrenchments began from a distance and every few feet they made a tower-like construction and as necessary put guards there. Due to the heavy rains that lasted for three months and the abundance of mud they reached a stage where going and coming was difficult. Due to shortage of fodder and pack-animals they sent the troops to lower pastures. Therefore the Ottoman cavalry sallied from the fort occasionally and carried out raids. Some wealthy people to punish them brought their horses and did not allow the horsemen to leave the fort. The besieged invaded the entrenchments several times and they could not do much. The Shah issued orders to bring cannons to take the fort. To maintain order in the kingdom's affairs and of the subjects Dhu'l-Feqar Khan Qaramanlu was appointed as *amir al-omara* of Shirvan. Meanwhile, the conquest of the fort of Baku and Darband took place.

The details of the events are as follows. Since the Ottomans had spent much effort, whatever they had in their power, to keep Shamaki, they had not paid enough attention to Darband and Baku and their guards were not more than 100 or 300 and most of them were local and were paid to perform this service. After some time the people expressed their devotion to the shah. Since the castellan wanted to punish some of them they attacked the Ottomans. Some they killed, some they took prisoner, and they sent their heads and those who were alive to the shah. As recompense for this service they received the plunder of the Ottomans, many tax exempt land assignments, and stipends. A castellan and guards were appointed for that strong fort. The people of Darband who had mostly joined the Ottoman cause wanted to follow the example of the people of Baku. In particular, the son of Khvajeh Mohammad Darbandi who had done good services in the time of Shah Tahmasp had received royal favors. He sent somebody to Rostam, son of Mohammad Usmi of the Qeytaq, who out of loyalty for the royal cause had gone into the presence of the king during the campaign in Georgia and returned from the Alkit River with the appointment order to the governorship of Darband. He brought 2 to 300 people to the city, who expressed their devotion to the shah. Gazar Hasan, the castellan of the fort with 60 to 70 Ottomans hurriedly took refuge in the keep of the fort. The son of Khvajeh Mohammad with some of the notables of Darband and the retainers of Usmi Khan came into the shah's presence and were honored with royal favors. The taxes [116] of his properties were granted to him as a tax exemption (*soyurghal*) and the people of Darband were exempted from government imposts and orders showing royal favor were given to the Usmi and Manuchehr Bey, the special servant, who was known for competence, as well as some Chaghatay, Khorasani, Iraqi, and other musketeers were appointed as castellans of the fort and as guardians of the roads. Some emirs and soldiers like Shah Nazar Bey Tekkelu Chaghatay, Shah Qoli Bayat, Emir Ne'matollah Soltan and others were sent on their way to help them. Together with Rostam Khan Usmi they tunneled under the towers and walls. Life was made difficult for the defenders. Gazar Hasan sent somebody to the emirs to ask for amnesty, because he with his friends wanted to take service with the king. His request was granted and he became one of the attendants of the royal court. The king decided to fortify Darband and sent Qanbar Bey Guzi Beylu, the head of the arsenal (*selahdar-bashi*) to repair the towers and reinforce the walls and gave orders to build a tower into sea whose walls had to be joined with the defenses of fort as much as possible, so that when the water level went down passage would not be possible. It is interesting to remark that when the tower was being built in the sea the remains of an old fort with stone and iron bars appeared. The foundation of the new tower was laid upon it. It is known among the people that this is the same as Alexander's wall, which is mentioned in the Koran. This is the same wall as the Gate of Gates, which was built to constitute a defense against the Gog and Magog-like people of the steppes. It was extended from the sea until the Elburz Mountain. During that time a man called Hajji Beyram, accompanied by Taleb Bey, who formerly had gone as ambassador to Ghazi Geray, came with a friendly letter that expressed friendship and sincerity. This event caused much disturbance among the besieged of the forts of Shamakhi. Dedeh Fal, the mother of Tamurath Khan, the governor of Georgia came with 1,000 people and with the emirs of Daghestan, the princes of the Cherkes, the brothers of Rostam Khan, the Usmi of the Qeytaq, 'Ali Bey Zakhuri and Ma'sum Khan the governor of Tabarsaran who also came to the royal court. Because the people of Daghestan are wild by nature Ma'sum Khan without reason became frightened and without permission from the royal camp returned to Tabarsaran. The Shah sent a robe of honor after him and tried to set his mind at ease. It so happened that on the day of the festival of Abraham's Sacrifice (*'id al-adhha*) a feast was laid out in a portico made of wood and pillars of reed next to the government house there and the high dignitaries, the knowledgeable olama, the emirs and the grandees were waiting there for the king. Suddenly the portico collapsed; the princes of Daghestan who were on one side went out quickly, but some of the olama and grandees were killed or wounded. They say that at the time that the king had to come an unexpected sleep overtook him and made him come late.

In short, Hoseyn Qoli Bey Qajar, the brother of Emir Guneh Khan, who was responsible for bringing big cannons from Ganjeh, carried them safely to the army camp. They installed one of them in the retrenchment of Allahverdi Khan and the other one in the retrenchment of Qarachay Bey. Because of the damage done by the 30 *mann*-cannons and the tunnels that had passed the moat [117] and had come as far as under the wall, day by day the weakness of the fort and the besieged was increasing. The besiegers prepared to attack waiting for the order. But the king did not want to take the city by force and to shed blood and plunder the innocent and guilty equally. Eventually, several of the *qurchi*s (royal household troops) in Qarachay Bey's retrenchment found a way to go up via a tower that had been damaged by cannon fire. The soldiers took this as the order to invade and attacked via the same route. Since stopping Qarachay Bey would be useless and cause the death of many soldiers he had no choice but to give the order of attack. In Dhu'l-Feqar Khan's retrenchment, without the help of cannon fire, part of the old tower had collapsed and two of the besieged came and told them that the tower was undefended, [saying:] "If you want you can come in." The soldiers did not loose the opportunity and nearly 150 people went up. Dhu'l-Feqar Khan thus seeing the situation came to the top of the tower and ordered the kettle-drum and the trumpets to be played and the attack began. The whole army attacked the city. In a short time the fort, the city and the lower fort were taken. Nearly 2 or 3,000 of the besieged were killed, but from the royal army only 3 or 4 people were killed. The Ottomans fled into the upper fort and started to defend themselves. The soldiers who had come into the city from house to house opened the way and tunneled under the towers of the upper fort and the space in between the two forts and destroyed it. From the other side, the royal household troops of the retrenchment went into the moat and from there via a secret way reached the upper fort, attacked and seized it. Then the Ottomans fought from house to house, and when there was no other possibility, Ahmad Pasha with some of his confidantes came to the roof of a mansion that in the past had been the palace of the kings of Shirvan and defended himself. Eventually through intercession of Allahverdi Khan he asked for one night reprieve so that he might surrender the fort the following day. The king accepted his request. The guards were put so that nobody could leave the fort. In the morning when the siege had lasted almost six months a royal banquet was given. The king performed prayers and sat on the throne and the kettledrums of joy were sounded. Qarachay Bey with his *qurchi*s and musketeers was ordered to secure the fort and gates. Hoseyn Bey Dhu'l-Qadr, the chief herald (*jarchi-bashi*) was sent to call Ahmad Pasha, Shamsh ol-Din Pasha, his brother, his son, Kuchek Hasan and some others. Ahmad Pasha who was a wise and eloquent man received amnesty, Shamsh ol-Din Pasha who had claimed the revelation that the Qezelbash could not take the fort had his beard plucked, because he had a long beard, at the king's order and then he was killed together with his brother, son and some others after much torture. The Ottoman army, after taking their property, was allowed [**118**] to go wherever it wanted. Much property was taken from the wealthy and the notables of the city. Rewards and stipends were given to whoever of the people of Shirvan deserving it. The governor gradually expelled those people whom he feared might revolt. The Shirvanis showed their loyalty to the Qezelbash by killing the Ottomans with whom they were acquainted or related. Dhu'l-Feqar Khan who had been appointed governor of Shirvan committed a very heinous act and was censured by the king and the army. The details are as follows. The sister and two daughters of his brother had fallen into the hands of the Ottomans in Shirvan, because of the affairs of Ahmad Khan Gilani. Some of the Ottoman dignitaries out of humanity and respect for their honor had married them and they had given birth to children. In one night, the ruthless Dhu'l-Feqar Khan denied any relationship with them and killed all of them, male and female, altogether 32 people. He did not benefit from life and prosperity. As we will see shortly the governorship of Darband and Shabaran was given to Cheragh Soltan Ostajalu and Shah Nazar Tekellu became his deputy. Dhu'l-Feqar Khan came to Shamakhi and busied himself with developing its affairs and buildings. The king because of the heat had gone to the winter quarters of Shamakhi and was amusing himself and had entertained the chiefs of Daghestan and Circassia, i.e. those who were in his presence or who had sent emissaries to show their obedience and who were shown royal favors. For Rostam Khan Usmi appropriate presents were sent and to set Ma'sum Khan's mind at ease, who was afraid, the king sent gifts and presents through Mohammad Saleh Bey, the vizier of Shirvan. He in his turn to show his gratitude sent one of the ladies of his harem to the royal harem and considered himself loyal to the royal court.

After having dealt with the affairs of Shirvan and Daghestan, 'Ali Bey Javanshir was appointed to build the bridge in the Javad Gorge, and the royal train went to Ardabil. Because during the turmoil in Shirvan, the Ottomans had taken possession of one of the districts of Shabaran, which is adjacent to Tabarsaran, they, because of their need of the help of the people of Tabarsaran, did not claim it. At that time the Tabarsaranis would not leave it in the hands of the governor Shabaran as they should have. The government officials could not freely come and go there out of fear for them. Therefore, the king's order was issued in the name of Dhu'l-Feqar Khan *Beyler-bey* of Shirvan instructing him to build a strong fort there as well as to make available provisions and guards, so that the road would be safe from the attacks of the rebellious mountain people. Dhu'l-Feqar Khan came there with an army and explained the situation to the governor of Tabarsaran, but he did not agree to this. At the time of deciding on the site of the fort he [**119**] attacked with a few thousand of infantry and cavalry. Dhu'l-Feqar Khan by sending numerous messages asked him to turn away from this path, but it was of no avail. The troops were put in battle formation and in the first attack the Tabarsaranis were defeated and up to 1,000 of them were killed. Dhu'l-Feqar Khan in a short time accomplished his mission and reported about it to the royal court. However, since HM the king favored Ma'sum Khan and some of his relatives were in the royal harem this event did not sit right with the king. He then ordered Dhu'l-Feqar Khan to send a confidante and make peace with Ma'sum Khan. The governor regretted what he had done. Because of the function and arrogance of Dhu'l-Feqar Khan and the construction of the fort the governors of Daghestan and the wild-natured Tabarsaranis were afraid of their own downfall and did not have peace of mind, therefore in the year 1018/1609 the king of Iran, when he was wintering in Qarabagh, sent a confidante of the court, Qarachay Bey, with some royal slaves and troops, accompanied by Dhu'l-Feqar Khan and the emirs of Shirvan to Shabaran to assure the governors of Daghestan with kind letters, give consideration to the ones who were obedient and ask that some of their relatives and children be sent to perform services at the royal court and to punish the rebellious ones.

The aforementioned after his arrival at Shabaran by pretending that a secret letter has come from the king secluded himself with Dhu'l-Feqar Khan in his tent. Some [of his] slaves entered and killed the khan. In accordance with the royal order, the governorship of Shirvan was given to Yusof Khan, the Master of the Hunt (*mir-shekar*), who was the governor of Astarabad. Some of the Qaramanlu clans became royal guards and the rest were ordered to enter into the service of Yusof Khan. The governor of Daghestan, who was afraid of Dhu'l-Feqar Khan without fear returned to Qarachay Bey and expressed his devotion and with worthy presents was sent to the royal court.

In the year 1024/1615, when the news of the coming of the Ottoman army spread, turmoil arose in the border areas and this led to a rebellion in Georgia. In Shirvan those who were known as sympathizers of the Ottomans and had been exiled were given the opportunity [to rebel], in particular an old prince who was the head of the Turkman of Qabestan, known as Dalv Malek. He gathered a group of rebels from Shirvan and Daghestan, and started to plunder the kingdom. Therefore the province of Shirvan was in a topsy-turvy situation. He sent someone to Tahmurath Khan, governor of Kakht, who had rebelled and with the men that he had [**120**] he went to Mohammad Hoseyn Soltan, who was the grandson of 'Emad al-Din Bey of Shirvan and the daughter's son of Shah Qoli Bey Dhu'l-Qadr Mohrdar who was the governor of Arash. When the Soltan came to welcome the baggage train he was pulled aside and attacked. With the few people that he had with him he did his utmost to oppose them, but they all were killed. The Soltan's retainers closed the gate of the fort. They thought that with the passage of time they would find relief. Dalv [sic, Deli] Malek with his retinue stayed in front of fort Arash. On hearing the news of the coming of the Qezelbash army, which had arrived to put down the rebellion of Georgia and Shirvan, Dalv Malek's men scattered. He himself became a wanderer in Georgia and Daghestan, in the land of misery and obscurity. In the year 1025/1616, when Shah 'Abbas himself went to punish Georgia, Yusof Khan with the army of Shirvan via Zagam had come down near the river. The Christians of Zagam gathered and attacked the Shirvanis. There was a fierce battle and the people of Zagam were defeated and lots of them killed and many fled. The Shirvanis destroyed Zagam completely. Rostam Khan, the Usmi of the Qeytaq, who had come from the river Alkit to express his allegiance to the king, returned with proper ceremony and the royal order appointing him to the governorship of Darband.[18] The other governors of Daghestan and Tabarsaran who had sent their people with worthy gifts were honored with good robes of honor and much royal favor. The affairs of that place were settled accordingly as desired. The king ordered the city of Ganjeh to be removed from its old place to one *farsakh* higher in the place where it is now. The square, mosque, and caravanserai are of the build and design of the great Sheikh Baha'i al-Din 'Ameli who in scholarship and accomplishments truly was a perfect man.

After these events the province of Shirvan until the downfall of the Safavid dynasty remained in the hands of its emirs and *Beyler-beys*. Shah 'Abbas was famous throughout the world for embellishing the country and maintaining the comfort of the people. Many of his laws of governance and military regulations have become the manual for Iranian kings. In European histories where the worthiness of kings is valued by special standards especially this king, who loved knowledge and industry, is described as great and

---

18. Rostam Khan is further known as the recorder of the customs of the Qeytaq. The Arabic text was translated into Russian in 1868 (*Sbornik Svedenii o Kavkazskikh Gortsakh* (Tiflis, 1868).

he is known for his justice among high and low. [121] In building and constructing public buildings during the Islamic period in Iran there is no equal to him. He built mosques, madrasas, subterraneous water channels, and caravanserais in remote places all over Iran, including in Shirvan. His work can be seen in the province of Shirvan and because of his encouragement many scholars in the sciences became unique in the world and famous all over. In spite of being so busy and solving problems he was inclined to talk with the people of accomplishment and his sharp talent was inclined to poetry.

Couplet

Everyone for himself has taken the tresses of a beloved
They are chains, but in short supply as mad lovers abound

هرکس برای خود سر زلفی گرفته است
زنجیر از آن کم است که دیوانه پرشده

Couplet

Two groups in the world follow no one
The Sunnis of Balkh and the Shi'as of Kashmir

دو گروه اند در جهان بی پیر
سنی بلخ و شیعه کشمیر

In the year of 1038/1629, Shah 'Abbas's life, when he was 54 years, came to an end in the town of Ashraf in Mazandaran that he himself had built and where he had moved many Georgians whom he had settled there. After him Sam Mirza, son of Safi Mirza, son of Shah 'Abbas, had been named heir-apparent after the death of his [grand]-father. At the age of eighteen he became the king under the name of Shah Safi. He fought many successful battles against the Ottomans and he captured the citadel of Erevan that Soltan Morad Khan had conquered after several months in the year 1048/1639. In spite of the fact that the Ottoman ruler had incited Rostam Khan the Usmi to wage war against Iran Shah Safi strengthened Amir Qomuq Surkhay Mirza, son of Eldar Khan, son of Surkhay Shamkhal and made him the Shamkhal. In the previous year, Mikael, son of Fyodor the Russian tsar also had confirmed him in the position of Shamkhal. He died in Qomuq in 1049 (1640), which date cannot be found on his gravestone there. It is clear that in Qomuq, the former capital of the Shamkhals and their heir-apparents, nobody had replaced him, [122] because the Ghazi-Qomuqis through the intermediary of the deputy for a while paid the fixed Shamkhal's tribute and eventually started to rebel. Elqas Mirza, the brother of Surkhay Mirza, who had been sent as hostage, as is the custom, to Shah Safi received the title of Safi Qoli Khan when he was governor of Shirvan and Erevan. Shah Safi died in the year 1052/1642. His son, Shah 'Abbas II, was only 10 years old when he acceded to the throne. He campaigned in Georgia and plundered and killed many rebels. In spite of the splendor, royal trappings and magnificence his talent was for writing poetry as well. This is by him.

Couplet

Remembering your stature I wept hard at the foot of the cypress

With the blood of my eyelashes I stained its leaves one by one

بیاد قامتی در پای سروی گریه سر کردم
چو مژگان برگ برکش را بخون دیده تر کردم

He died after 24 years and his son acceded to the throne of Iran as Shah Safi and after a while he became known as Shah Soleyman. From the contents and dates of the decrees in the name of 'Omma Khan, the children of Eldar Khan, Geray Khan and the son of Sorkhay-ye Shamkhal it becomes evident that this king and his father, apart from cash amounts, entrusted several villages in the province of Shirvan to the emirs of Daghestan. They more than ever frequented the court and became devout servants and served them well. In that time the Usmi family had two branches; one resided in Majales and the other in Yeki kend, and whoever of these two branches became Usmi in his turn would go and reside in Bashli. A conflict arose [between the two branches]. The Yenki kend branch defeated the Majales branch, which was bigger, and killed them all except for a young boy named Hoseyn Khan. Eydeh Bey, one of the trusted servants of this branch took him and fled to the Shamkhal. After some time when he had become an adolescent [123] and excelled in the arts he went to Iran and for a while he was a guest of the qadi of Rudbar-e Saliyan and he married his daughter. After going to Isfahan he could not find the means to gain access to the royal court and he therefore became involved in merry-making and sold all the goods and arms of his retinue. During this time a girl called Zohreh Khanom of the family of the Qajar emirs became enamored of him and his beautiful face, which was very tender, and she became his lover and helped him in every way. This poem, which is very well-known in this country, is about Hoseyn Khan by that girl.

Ghazal

Drawing the veil on her face that rebel wants to take my life

When she puts a headband on her head she plunders the Darband of my heart

The brand of Daghestan like the brand of infidel cannot be contained in his chest

Black-clad people of Qomuq they have covered the Qebchaq plain

Can all flowers by God be so fragrant in this abode

As if he has found a paradisiacal rose-garden in this land of Qobbeh

The sugar-infusing lips when talking or smiling

You imagine it evokes tulip petals fluttering in the breeze

I know the tears of my eyes eventually destroy my heart

Of course, it will destroy every abode where happens to be a water dripping place

چکیب رخساره یاپونچی اندر جان قصدین اول یاغی
کؤنول در بــند ینی چاپدی قویانده باشه قیطاغی
داغستان داغنی گؤر گؤر صیغینماز داغی کؤ کسونه
قرا گیمش قموق خلقی دوتوبدر دشت قبچاقی
بوتون هرگل اولور خوشبو تعالی الله بو منزلده
گلستان ارم بــولمش مگر بو قبــــــه توپراغی
لب لعــل شکــر بارین تکــلمدن تــبسـمدن
صــناسین بــاغ آرا دترر صبادن لاله بایراغی
گوزوم یاشینی من بیللم ییخار کونلوم ایوین آخر
اولور البته ویران اولسه هر منزل صو اویناغی

    In short, he married that girl. Because of his outstanding services he became known for his valor and skills to the shah and [therefore] the country of Qobbeh and Saliyan was given to him. From this union his son Ahmad Khan was born and therefore Aqa Mohammad Shah [Qajar] acknowledged Sheikh 'Ali Khan as his kin and in the same manner the mother of Fath 'Ali Shah [Qajar] carried on a friendly correspondence with Khadijeh Bey, the mother of Mirza Mohammad Khan II. From the daughter of the judge of Rudbar in the Saliyan [district] a daughter was born and the emirs of that area are descended from her. Hoseyn Khan built Fort Khodad in Qobbeh and made it his seat of government. A garden that still exists there has been designed in Persian fashion [124] and the Shi'a faith, which he had adopted in Iran continued to be adhered to in his family. In the year 1100/1689, he came to Bashli and took back his hereditary governorship from 'Ali Usmi. 'Ali Soltan gathered an army of 30,000 men from the neighboring tribes and he again regained the governorship of the Qeytaq. Hoseyn Khan returned to Qobbeh and died.

    All historians agree that Shah Soleyman was a just ruler, skilled in the art of statesmanship, lover of sciences, promoter of the faith, and merciful to his subjects. He maintained good relations with other kings. At the end of his life he suffered from foot pain for seven years and was bedridden. In the year 1105/1694, he died and his son Shah Soltan Hoseyn acceded to the throne. He was a religious man, humane, and was always in discussion with the olama. At night he would perform non-obligatory prayers and his underlings would plunder the caravans during the day. They ruined the country and cracks appeared in the foundation of kingship. In the last years of this unfortunate king, when the affairs of state were in disorder and corrupt officials were enjoying themselves, the provinces of Shirvan and Daghestan became the scene of turmoil and chaos. 'Ali Soltan Usmi died and Amir Hamzeh took his place in 1107/ 1696 and he was confirmed by the king. He was Usmi for more than 10 years. Ahmad, son of Hoseyn Khan, with much help from the Qeytaq people took Bashli. Amir Hamzeh fled to the upper districts and after a few years he died. Two years after his death Ahmad Khan, son of Ulu Bey Usmi, son of Rostam Khan came to oppose him and after a few months he governed in Bashli and Ahmad Khan, son of Hoseyn Khan in Majales. Finally, at the instigation of Ahmad Khan, son of Ulu Bey one of the retainers of Ahmad Khan, son of Hoseyn Khan Usmi killed him in his house in Majales, which is still in existence. Ahmad Khan, son of Ulu Bey became Usmi. At that time [125] he blinded Soltan Hoseyn Fath 'Ali Khan, son of Safi Qoli Khan, son of Eldar Khan Shamkhal who had ruled independently as vizier from the year 1120/1708 for 12 years and kept him away from matters of government, and in spite of him the affairs of Daghestan that until that time had been under the Shamkhal changed. According to the order from the year 1123/1710, Ahmad Khan Usmi was put in charge of the land of the Qeytaq. His pension was 100 *tuman*s per year and he fixed it at 200 *tuman*s. Day by day he increased his power and he came with a big army to Tabarsaran. Mohammad Ma'sum with his retainers offered peace and Rostam and 'Ali Bey with their troops rose up to fight. After the plundering and burning of some of their villages, they by giving hostages, asked for amnesty. Thereafter the Usmi by contriving different means and sending letters was inciting the people of Shirvan to rebel and oppose the Qezelbash. During that time the people of Jar and Taleh together with the people of Zakhur, who live in the province of Sheki, started to rebel. They killed Hasan 'Ali Khan, *beyler-bey* of Shirvan, who had come to punish them, in the districts of Sheki and plundered his army camp. After plundering the city of Shamakhi they returned to their homes. After that Hajji Davud, who was a well-known scholar and had a school, went as representative of the community of Moskur to the Usmi and settled the dispute in an amiable fashion. The Usmi had sent troops under the command of Morteza 'Ali, son of Amir Hamzeh Usmi and the Sunnis of those parts also gathered and together they attacked Shabaran. After heavy fighting they captured and destroyed it and burnt it down. According to the manuscript belonging to the family of the Usmi, which discusses these affairs, they killed the children in their cradles and the remains of this famous city on the right bank of the river Shabaran shows that it used to be a great and prosperous city. When the news of this conquest reached Ahmad [126] Khan Usmi he sent a person named 'Ali Jeruq with another army to help the rebels of Qobbeh and the conquest of the Khodad fort so that they might rise up against their emir Soltan Ahmad, son of Ahmad Khan, son of Hoseyn Khan. His father-in-law Hajji Ghayeb Alpani and Nadhir his sister's son Hajji Davud Moskuri were in revolt. After a short siege the Khodad fort was taken and Soltan Ahmad Khan while fleeing was caught and killed with his retinue. Some of his supporters had secretly taken his baby son, Hoseyn 'Ali Khan, to the village of Akhti and kept him there. At the time when Peter the emperor of Russia came, in accordance with his order, his hereditary lands were returned to him. In the time of Nader Shah by expressing loyalty and performing services he was shown favor by that king who gave him Saliyan as in former times.

In short, after the conquest of Khodad, the Usmi by spending money bought the loyalty of his army, the emirs of Qomuq, the chiefs of Aqusheh and others. Together with Kuklovchi[19] Ghazi-Qomuq Sorkhay Khan, son of Geray, son of 'Ali Bey he came to Moskur. From there he marched with Hajji Davud and the people of Qobbeh with an army of about 30,000 and besieged the city of Shamakhi. Without gaining any result they returned [after a while.] The people of Shamakhi fortified the surrounding area of their town and started to plunder those of Moskur. Ahmad Khan Usmi sent Khass Fulad, son

---

19. This term is a title to denote a leader or commander.

of Amir Hamzeh Usmi to protect Moskur and after spending the winter in the Kaferi plain of Darband, he with Sorkhay and others intended to capture Shamakhi. Geray Khan Shamkhal came to oppose them and sent a message stating, "I am the servant of the government of Iran. If you go to Shamakhi I will take your country." Therefore, Ahmad Khan remained to protect his own lands and Sorkhay and Hajji Davud with a contingent of troops of the Usmi marched and after 15 days of siege with the help of the Sunnis of the city they captured the city in the year 1124/1712. They went out of their way to plunder and kill the Shi'is of the city. Hoseyn Khan [127] the new *beyler-bey* of Shirvan was killed and more than 300 Russian merchants, who had 400,000 *tuman*s in property, were killed and their goods confiscated. After a while Sorkhay and Hajji Davud sent a letter to the Porte and paved the way to be attached to that high government. The edict of the governorship of Shirvan was issued in the name of Davud Bey and Saru Mostafa Pasha was appointed to help him with an army. Because they had closed Sorkhay's path to advancement a fight broke out among them. Sorkhay, who had many of the districts of Sheki under his control, departed to take Ganjeh, but returned without getting any result. After that order from the Ottoman government 'Ali Soltan Zakhuri received the title of Pasha and became *beylerbey* of the province of Sheki including the district (*sanjaq*) of Zakhur.

Gradually the provinces of Erevan, Ganjeh, Georgia and most of the districts of Shirvan came under the rule of the Ottomans. Ahmad Khan the Usmi under the pretext of opposing Hajji Davud's rebellion and to make war on the Ottomans came to Shirvan. As is clear from Tahmasp II's royal order, he was expressing his loyalty to the government of Iran. On learning the news that Peter, emperor of Russia, was coming he returned to his land. Golikov in the history of the deeds of Peter[20] states that after observing the affairs of the kingdom of Iran and the killing and plundering of the Russian merchants in Shirvan the emperor of Russia, Peter, son of Aleksi, son of Michael, on the 15th of June in the year 1134/1722 arrived at Astrakhan and wrote a circular letter to the provinces of Iran with this message that Davud Bey, the Lezgi emir and Sorkhay Amir of Ghazi-Qomuq had rebelled against their king in 1712 of the Christian era. They had stormed and conquered the city of Shamakhi, killed and plundered the Russian merchants and up till now nothing had been done about that although the *beyler-bey* of Astrakhan had sent somebody to them, while we also had sent an envoy to the king. The king of Iran does not have the power to stop these evil-doers so therefore we are coming this way to punish and take revenge. Whoever sits quiet in his place will not suffer from our army. Those who help the evil-doers or who want to escape [128] will feel the brunt of royal wrath."[21] During that time Emir Mahmud Afghan was holding Soltan Hoseyn in Isfahan under siege and Tahmasp Mirza his son, heir-apparent and regent had come to Qazvin to prepare an army and free his father, but due to weakness and incompetence he could not do anything. Peter sent

---

20. Ivan Ivanovich Golikov, *Dieianiia Petra Velikago*, 12 vols. (Moscow, 1788 - 89).
21. The text of this circular letter was published as an 8-page pamphlet in German (and clearly also in other languages) for distribution in Persia with the title: *Manifest welches Ihro Russisch Kayserl. Majestät in Persien austheilen lassen* (Astrakhan, 15 June 1722). The text further mentions that no harm would befall Ottoman merchants, who were present in these lands. For an English version of the text see Julius H. Klaproth, *Travels in the Caucasus and Georgia* (London, 1814), pp. 194-96.

an order to his consul, i.e., his representative Avramov,[22] who resided in Gilan, to obtain a signed agreement from the king or any of his grandees who are available with the promise of protection and of the suppression of the rebellion in exchange for the transfer of in particular the border provinces to the Russian government. After that 9,000 dragoons, 20,000 Cossacks, 30,000 Tatars, 20,000 Qalmuq, which adds up to 79,000 horsemen marched overland and in July 1720 ships and boats, which carried 22,000 infantry and 5,000 hired men, went by sea. In a place called Chahar Tappeh the letter of 'Adel Shamkhal Khan indicating his submission and expressing his assistance reached him. Therefore on the 24th of that month from the island of Chechen, he sent Lieutenant Lopukhin[23] with 30 fast couriers to the Shamkhal to distribute the circular letter in the provinces of Shirvan and Daghestan. Then he came himself ashore and assigned the landing place and the troops arrived on the 28th of that month from the mouth of the Agher Akhan. At a distance of three miles from Sulaqchay the emperor pitched camp and fortified its surroundings with entrenchments. The emperor was spending the night on the ships with the grandees. After a few days of waiting for the army's horses, which were coming with the cavalry overland, it was necessary to remain at that place. The reason for the delay was the difficulty of the road, scarcity of water and fodder, and the fighting with the people of the village of Enderey. Therefore, four dragoon regiments under the command of brigadier Witrani were ordered to capture that village.[24] In case of opposition they had to conquer the village, destroy it and punish that valiant tribe, for, in spite of being in alliance with the Shamkhal, they were an impediment in the road and plundered the surrounding areas and had to be made into an example of punishment for others. In a gorge near [**129**] the village, 5,000 of the people of Enderey attacked on the 23rd of the said month and killed 70 dragoons and wounded a number of them. Finally, Colonel Naumov withdrew the army from that place after some fighting; the village was destroyed and burnt down and 300 people were killed and the rest fled. After the cavalry and the pack-animals joined the big army Peter left 200 soldiers and 1,000 Cossacks with the sick in the Agher Akhan redoubt. Boats were left on its banks. The ships destined for Darband were sent under the command Soymonov[25] and he left. On the 7th of August the passage from Sulaqh took place with difficulty. Soltan Mahmud Emir of Yakhsay together with the envoy of the Shamkhal came there and gave as gift (*pishkesh*) 850 cows and 9 good horses and they expressed their obedience. They received gracious favors as well as the confirmation of their rights from that famous king. Everywhere the emperor was marching in front with the vanguard. In spite of the fact that by the order of the Shamkhal many wells were dug on the route they suffered from shortage of water in some stages. On the 12th of that month 'Adel Geray Khan Shamkhal came

---

22. Semen Avramov, first Russian consul in Iran (Isfahan) in 1720, who had moved to Rasht when the siege of Isfahan began in March 1722.

23. Perhaps a member of the Boyar family of the Lopukhins, and thus a relative of Peter's wife Yevdokiya Lopukina.

24. On this and subsequent events see the account by a participant in this campaign, Peter Henry Bruce, *Memoirs of ... in the services of Prussia, Russia & Great Britain, containing An Account of his Travels in Germany, Russia, Tartary, The West Indies, &c.* (London, 1782 [1970]), pp. 306ff. Witrani is called general Waterang by Bruce.

25. Fedor Ivanovich Soymonov is the maker of the first Russian map of the Caspian Sea.

to welcome him outside the town of Tarkhu [Tarki], where they pitched their tents. During three days they waited for all troops to gather. The following day the Shamkhal invited the emperor to a feast after a tour of the town and its environs; they talked about everything at the table. The Shamkhal requested to be part of this campaign by offering an army, but he did not accept it. After the return to the army camp the representatives of Darband on behalf of their deputy-governor Emam Qoli Bey, who was a hundred-man (*yuz-bashi*) of the royal household troops, were received in audience and they expressed their loyalty and their pleasure about the promise of protection. Colonel Naumov with another officer and 12 Cossacks was sent to Darband to prepare the means and necessities for the entrance of the emperor. At the advice of the deputy-governor they put Russian guards that had come from the ships, which had arrived that day at the two northern gates, one upper and the other towards the sea. Soltan, the castellan of Darband, had previously gone to the court of Iran and the deputy, who was always chosen from among the natives, [130] was in charge. The Russian emperor on the 16th of that month moved from Tarkhu [Tarki] and on the 18th entered the land of the Utemish and sent an officer with three Cossacks to Soltan Mahmud the governor of that place who was under the authority of the Usmi of the Qeytaqs, to ask for his submission. Soltan Mahmud killed the envoys and with 16,000 of his own men the Usmi and others attacked the army camp, but he was defeated and the Russian cavalry pursued them for three miles until the town of Utemish and killed many of them. That town which had 500 families and 6 villages was plundered and burnt down. They took 15,000 cattle and arrested a few people and at the order of the emperor they were put to the sword. On the 21st of the abovementioned month, which was the day of entry into Darband, because of the scarcity of water, the excessive heat and the dusty winds, the army suffered greatly. Outside Darband, Emam Qoli Bey, the deputy-governor with a group of olama and other classes of people, put the silver key of the city on a tray and came to welcome him and expressed praise and satisfaction. Peter with pomp and military music entered the fort and 23 cannons were acquired. The infantry along the seashore and the cavalry consisting of dragoons, Cossacks and others were stationed at the river Mollakendi, and the ships, because of the situation of Darband, were anchored at the mouth of the river. With great haste two forts, one on the banks of Mollakendi and the other on the banks of the Urta Bugham River, were built for the fortification of Darband on two sides. Emam Qoli Bey, the deputy-governor was honored with the rank of general-major and the title of Khan, the government of Darband and the command of the local army. Lieutenant Lunin with some men was sent to Baku by sea to ensure by sending the new circular letter the governors and the people of that region would be willing to submit. In those days the environs of Darband and Moskur, which are situated between the rivers Yalamah and Belbeleh, were occupied by the Russian army. All the villages of Moskur, because of the rebellion and disturbances by the people, were in ruins. The same was true in the village of Dahdahlu, [131] where the house of Hajji Davud had a stone rampart, where the guards lived. Luni came from Baku and said that the people did not allow him into the city saying, "We we have kept ourselves from the corruption of the evil-doers without the help of others for a few years and now we do not see ourselves in need of Russian protection." Peter became angry, and wanted to subdue them by force, but because of impediments that required his return this matter was postponed till the following year.

Darband has two outer walls stretching from the mountains to the sea; on the inside it is divided into four parts with interconnecting walls. The first one is the keep of the citadel (*Narin-Qal'eh*), which is higher and smaller than all. The Russian army took that first and expelled all the people from there, where the emperor took up residence. In the two middle parts, there are the houses of the deputy-governor, the merchants, the guilds and the caravanserais. In the fourth part, known as *Du Baru* (Two Towers), there was a caravanserai, which was turned into two barracks (*qazarmeh*) and a warehouse for provisions, which was repaired when the emperor was there. While they were taking provisions from the ships a strong storm raged and caused cracks in the ships in such a way that the leakage could not be stopped. Eventually, the anchors were cut and the ships fell on their sides and were shipwrecked. With 30 ships that were coming from Astrakhan to the port of Agher Akhan the same happened. Of the provisions of whatever nature little was left. Because of the unrest in the neighboring areas getting provisions was not possible. Therefore, the return of the army to Russia was deemed necessary. It was very bad for the Russian emperor to return without having to show anything for his effort. In particular, he would have liked to take Baku and at the mouth of the Kur River to have built a great city for trade and to go from the same river upwards and to set the affairs of Georgia in order. Besides, from Astarabad he would not have minded to arrange trade with India. In short, he left troops to guard the fort of Darband and in early September he returned without much incident and arrived at the Agher Akhan redoubt. A town called the Fort of the Cross was built at the junction of the Agher Akhan River and the Sulaq because of its favorable location concerning water, fodder, and forests. He had built it to break [132] the power of the Daghestanis and to open the road to Darband, which was a necessity. To facilitate the movement of ships, he dammed the Sulaq River with big wooden pillars and beams so that the water would reach the river of Agher Akhan and some of these wooden pillars can still be seen in the water. The hetman of the Don Cossacks, Krasnoshtekov with 1,000 Cossacks and 40,000 newly arrived Qalmuqs went to Malek Hamri and killed many and plundered much and 350 men were taken prisoner and 11,000 head of cattle were taken. The emperor sent an envoy and letters to Georgia and to the Catholicus of the Armenians and while showing them kindness he assured them that he would return. After having appointed guards in the fort of the [Holy] Cross he sent all the cavalry by land and fortified the port of Agher Akhan even more and he himself on the 16th of that month boarded a ship and hurriedly went to Astrakhan. The infantry, under general-admiral Count Apraksin,[26] which was transported in ships after him, suffered much due to a storm en route. The 4th day of October when Peter had arrived at Astrakhan a request arrived from the governor of Gilan asking for protection. In five days ships and equipment were readied for travel on the 10th of that same month Colonel Shibov [sic; Shipov?] and Soymanov and two battalions of soldiers went to Gilan. Having arrived at the port of Peri

---

26. Admiral Count Fyodor Matveyevich Apraksin, commander of the Russian navy and in charge of the Russian fleet transporting troops from Astrakhan to the Caucaus. His elder brother Peter Apraksin was governor of Astrakhan at that time.

Bazar, Yazikov was sent to Rasht to look for transportation. Then an envoy appointed by Tahmasp Mirza came to the court of the emperor. He was Esma'il Bey, the adjunct of the grand vizier, who, while he was traveling in the Talesh Mountains, saw the Russian armada at sea and had returned to Gilan and was in Rasht.

The people there after consultation at the house of the vizier of Gilan replied that without the permission of the king of Persia they could not allow the Russian army into their land and they proposed that they would stay in their ships. The Russians took Peri Bazar and the vizier of Gilan after meeting with Colonel Shibov and getting assurances that they had come at the orders of the emperor [133] to provide protection, took him with a part of the army to a caravanserai outside the town to serve as their place of residence. Because of lack of Russian interest to make peace the envoy was prevented from returning with all kinds of excuses.

As on the 15th of the month of November 1722, Mir Mahmud had conquered Isfahan and Shah Tahmasp had acceded to the throne in Qazvin. The vizier wrote a letter to H.M. stating that no envoy had been sent and that he was waiting for his answer. The Russians got wind of this action and, with all kinds of pretexts and civilities, they took the envoy to the ship and kept him there. When a courier came from the king, Consul Avramov secretly went to welcome him and with tricks and bribes found out about the royal order, which was about not sending the envoy. He delayed him so much that Soymonov sent him away in the beginning of December, at mid-night with two ships under the pretext that it was an auspicious time, . The vizier of Gilan, after receiving the royal order and on learning that the envoy had departed, was saddened and in agreement with the governors and people of that place started preparing for battle and gathered an army. Colonel Shibov gradually brought military equipment and provisions from Peri Bazar and was readying himself. In the month of March, when Soymonov, in accordance with his mission's objectives, had gone with some ships and troops to the mouth of the Kur to select a site to build a city, the Gilanis took steps to propose the Russians to withdraw. The Colonel replied: "first, we do not have ships that allow us to return; second, this proposal should come from the king of Iran." Eventually a battle took place. The Gilanis had four cannons and all day were shelling the caravanserai. The Colonel did not do anything during the day and at night sent 1,000 soldiers and attacked the city from two sides in such a way that the Gilanis were not able to defend themselves. Many were killed and the rest fled. A new army under the command of general-major Levashev[27] arrived and took the city. Because the Russians had built a fort on the west side of the road to Qazvin, and from the east-side, where they had strengthened the caravanserai to make it into a fort, the city was between these two. In the same year, on the 6th of the month of July, general-major Matushkin with 9 ships, which contained four regiments, at that time a regiment was 1,000 men strong, anchored in the port of Baku. Esma'il Bey's letter addressed to Shah Tahmasp proposing to entrust the fort to the Russians was sent.

---

27. Vasilii Iakovlevich Levashev (1667-1751), commander of the Russian occupation forces and governor of the Caspian provinces (Astarabad, Baku, Darband, Gilan, and Mazandaran) from September 1723 until 1735 (Treaty of Ganjeh).

The ruler and notables of Baku did not allow the emissaries into the city [134] and replied: "for some time we have kept the city safe from evil-doers, so we will continue to keep it and we are not in need of any protection. We do not consider Esma'il Bey as plenipotentiary and do not consider the letter that is written in Russian valid." On the 21st day of the month, the general sent the army ashore and many horsemen came out of the city and fought and returned defeated. The Russians made entrenchments and seven ships came forward and silenced the cannons of the citadel. The fire of the mortars fell onto the city and caused a major fire that destroyed the wall. The night of the 26th was the day fixed for the attack, but as a result of a big storm the ships were scattered and the attack did not take place. The general discussed the terms of surrender and the city was taken as well as 72 cannons and much gun-powder, bullets and equipment. The guards of the fort, who numbered 700, with the commander Dargah Qoli Bey, entered into Russian service and the government as before was given to Dargah Qoli Bey. Soltan the castellan of the citadel, who was known to be the friend of Davud Bey was imprisoned and sent to Russia. Colonel Dargah Qoli Bey eventually, because of suspicion of treason, was dismissed and Russian castellans were appointed.*28 According to documents and information from Dargah Qoli Bey, [135] son of Heybat Bey, whose ancestors were from the family of the emirs of Nur-e Kojur of Mazandaran and from the ancient lineage of Espahbadan of Tabarestan, and who were in the vanguard of the army of Ahmad Khan Gilani in the year 1000/1592, came to Shirvan and in Baku where they had property and where they had become head of the hundred-men; the ruins of their buildings and forts are still in existence in the village of Ramaneh. In the sayings of the common people, the proverb is known: "Bolboleh, Emir Hajan, and Ramaneh are the Khan's villages." In the past, he had killed the Soltan of Baku and assumed the title of Khan and by hook and by crook and the support of the people he had been confirmed by the royal court. The new soltan was content with being the castellan of Baku. At a distance of half a *farsakh* on a hill, which from that time onwards is called the 'Bloody Hill', he crushed an army of Lezgis. His brother, Hoseyn Khan Bey was killed in that battle. Afterwards he began plundering the districts of Shabaran and Qobestan and every day his fame increased. When the Russians came he surrendered the city and

---

28. From this point* until "his government" has been omitted and instead the following has been added in the margin in a different handwriting: For some time he was plundering in the governate of Baku with some of his followers in the environs of Baku and after that he went to Iran and was given the title of khan and became one of the commanders of the army. In the year 1151/1738 when Ebrahim Khan, the brother of Nader Shah, was killed he was wounded in Jar and died. His son Mohammad Khan I who was at the court of that Nader Shah as one of his confidential emirs, after his death became independent governor of Baku and a hereditary governorship, which was in his family, lasted until 1231/1806. After him his son Hajji Malek Mohammad Khan and after him Mirza Mohammad Khan II; during the reign of Mohammad Khan II the former fought one year with him. The districts of Baku were under the rule of Mirza Mohammad Khan and the city of Baku was in the possession of Mohammad Qoli Khan son of Mirza Mohammad Khan I. One year after the death of Mohammad Qoli Khan, son of Mirza Mohammad Khan I, Hoseyn Qoli Khan, son of `Ali Qoli Aqa, son of Mirza Mohammad Khan I became the governor of Baku. All the time between him and Mohammad Khan II there was war. Hoseyn `Ali Khan because of cousinship, being his brother-in-law and son-in-law turned traitor in the battle, so that in the year 1221/1806 the governate of Baku was occupied by the Russians. Hoseyn Qoli Khan fled to Iran. Mirza Mohammad Khan II came to Qobbeh and resided there. [B]

was appointed to his previous government. His seat of government was in Mashqata'. The khan's garden, building and water reservoir still exist there and his courage and prowess are still remembered among the people. From the dates of his orders concerning the appointment of 'Abdollah Bey, son of Hajji Salim Bey to the governorship of the districts of Baku and his other government posts he was still governor of Baku in the year 1143/1731. It is not known in which year he turned away from the Russians and with a group of his followers started plundering the environs of Baku and Shirvan; thereafter he went to Iran and became one of the emirs of the army of Iran. In the year 1151/1738 when the brother of Nader Shah, Ebrahim Khan, was killed in Jar he was wounded and died in Zanjan.

In September of this year, after much discussion in the capital Petersburg, Esma'il Bey, on behalf of Shah Tahmasp, signed a treaty with the Russian authorities to the effect that all the border provinces from Astarabad to Darband became part of the Russian state. The Russian emperor committed himself to support and restore the government of Shah Tahmasp. The Ottoman government, which wanted the provinces of Shirvan and Azerbaijan, by declaring war, intended to dissuade the Russians from taking the border provinces. The grand vizier Ebrahim Pasha who was desirous of friendship with the Russians was not favoring war. Therefore, he sent an envoy to request the Russian government [136] that it would not occupy Iranian territory and consider Hajji Davud Bey as governor of Shirvan. Peter returned the envoy with a friendly reply. When the occupation of Gilan reached the ears of the Ottoman government the grand vizier once again sent an envoy and asked for the reason of this deed. The emperor again said that he had no intention to get into a conflict with the Ottoman government. "I have sent an army not to occupy Iran, but rather to punish the rebels and support the innocent king." But in secret he gave orders to the governor of the Ukraine to have 70-80,000 troops ready at the Ottoman and Crimean border and the Ottomans from their side annexed Armenia, Georgia and most of Shirvan. Eventually it was decided that both governments would keep the territorial gains of the ownerless Iranian lands. Through the good services of the Russian minister residing at the Porte, Nepluyev[29] and the intermediacy of the French minister Bonnac, and the good offices of the grand vizier Ebrahim Pasha a peace treaty was signed between the Russian and Ottoman governments in Constantinople on the 27th of June in the year 1137/1725. The provinces of Astarabad, Gilan, Baku, Saliyan and Darband were assigned to the Russian government. The remainder of Shirvan, Armenia and Georgia became Ottoman territory. The border was established between Shamakhi and Baku and the brother's son of Bonnac, who had come with the news of this peace treaty to Peter's court, was showered with royal favors. Rumiantsev[30] on behalf of the emperor was appointed to determine the border between the three countries. He went to Iran and Turkey and secretly observed the roads to Georgia, the situation of the Kur River, the military strength of Armenians and Georgians and the possibility to obtain provisions and fodder en route as well as gathered information about the distances and conditions in Georgia from the side of Quban. He

---

29. I. I. Nepluyev was Russian consul at Istanbul from 1721 until 1734.
30. Alexander Ivanovich Rumiantsev (1680 - 1749), was a member of Peter the Great's staff during the Persian campaign and was sent to Constantinople to ratify the 1724 Treaty with the Ottomans.

was supposed to encourage the Armenians to settle in Gilan in inhabited places and the homes of Moslems. Meanwhile, when the Fort of the Cross was nearing completion and the waters of the Sulaq were being diverted to Agher Akhan, Peter wrote and ordered General-Major Kropotov[31] to move to Shahr-e Turk and to destroy the entrenchments of Agher Akhan. The Shamkhal became afraid of the construction of the Fort of the Cross [137] and also due the incitement of the Ottomans who had made an agreement with him and had given him promises, he came with 30,000 troops and surrounded the fort of the Cross. He was defeated and returned. Kropotov destroyed all his lands and his seat of government. After this event, Peter abolished the function of Shamkhal and transferred his government to the general who would be governing in Shirvan. 'Adel Geray Khan Shamkhal himself, who had come to the Russian camp, was arrested and sent to Russia and died there.

On the 9th of November 1138/1725, general-lieutenant Matushkin the commander of these regions, who had gone to Russia, returned to Baku. It was known that Lt. Colonel Zimbulatov with his battalion had gone to the banks of the Kur and pitched his camp opposite the house of the princess there, Qabuli Khan, the wife of the Soltan of Saliyan, Hasan Bey, which site had been designated as the location for the new town. The princess expressed her friendship and devotion and invited him with all the officers to a party, and while they were eating armed men entered and killed all of them. The soldiers seeing this deed, with one sick officer who had remained in the camp, returned to their ships and sailed to Baku. It is strange that Peter prior to that event had written to general Matushkin to make him aware that the princess of Saliyan was a great thief and that he had to be on his guard, so that something bad would not happen.[32] General Matushkin with 300 people had gone to the mouth of the Kur River and had looked at the site of the city and then sailed to Gilan. General-Major Levashef had there six battalions of soldiers, 500 dragoons and some units of Armenians, Georgians and Don Cossacks. The vizier of Gaskar with 20,000 troops was facing them ready for battle. General Matushkin sent an envoy to Shah Tahmasp in Ardabil referring to the contents of the peace treaty of Esma'il Bey to prevent the vizier from making war. There was no reply, because the king's emirs did not trust this peace treaty and accused Esma'il Bey of treason; he himself stayed under the protection of the Russians and remained in the province of Gilan. The Persians attacked the caravanserai and one battalion of soldiers and three units of dragoons defeated and pursued them and most of them were killed. Afterwards the vizier of Astara and others came to help them; for two months every few days they battled and they were defeated and returned. [138] Eventually, they were so afraid that they did not come at all to give battle. It is a strange situation that a regiment of soldiers defeated 20,000 Persians who were armed with artillery and guns. These are the same Persians, whose famed bravery and conquest of countries in the time of Key Khosrow and soon after this in the days of Nader Shah was well-known. It is clear that all these changes depend on the ability of one

---

31. In 1730, Major-General Kropotov was commander of the Holy Cross Fort.
32. Bérézine, *Voyage*, pp. 352-53 discusses the various reports on this incident, some of which refer to the princess as "Khapulbi Khanoum."

person, viz. people like Key Khosrow and Nader made their country famous and their army victorious and people like Tahmasp made it a humiliated country without honor, which caused him to lose his authority among the tribes. In the history books such occurrences can be seen many times.

At this time the Russians moved from Baku and also conquered Saliyan and built there a small fort. Hasan Bey fled and joined with the Daghestani rebels. In those days Sorkhay Bey Ghazi-Qomuqi was higher placed as to authority and dignity than Hajji Davud Bey and he was grieving because of his government in Shirvan. With wiles and tricks he obtained from the Ottoman government an edict appointing him as the governor of Shirvan. He received the title of Khan and raised the banner of governorship. Saru Mostafa Pasha was appointed to Ganjeh and Hajji Davud Bey was summoned to the Ottoman court and died there on the 28th of December in the year 1138/1725.

Peter passed away in his 57th year. He was a decisive king, competent in administration and unique in conquering lands, and through many travels in Europe and by gaining knowledge he added to his native genius. He issued new property laws and army regulations, and by providing the advantages of war and peace he strengthened the power of Russia. He surpassed the fame of king Ashut[33] and built the capital Petersburg that became a wonder for the people of the world. Because of the great works that he accomplished the name Great was given to him.

Ustrialov[34] in his history writes that Catherine I, the wife of Peter, who acceded to the throne after him [139] followed the rules and decisions of her husband in every affair concerning the four provinces of Iran. She appointed a commission consisting of six Russian grandees to manage the affairs of the country. The Ottoman and Persian kings renewed their treaties and some of the abovementioned provinces came under Russian occupation. After her death on the 6th of May in the year 1140/1727, Peter II, son of Alexei, son of the Peter the Great, who was 12 years old, acceded to the throne. The same commission of counselors was taking care of the affairs of the country. He passed away on the 18th of January 1143/1730. Anna, daughter of Ivan, brother of Peter the Great, who was a widow, acceded to the throne. To establish Russian control over the border provinces of Iran troops, supplies, and money were being wasted uselessly for which there a great need [in Russia]. Because a capable emir and powerful conqueror, Nader, whose name equals its meaning [i.e., rarity] had appeared in Iran and after entering the service of Shah Tahmasp, who was wandering without throne and fortune in Azerbaijan and Mazandaran, the affairs of the kingdom found a new course and the army a new organization and prosperity was increasing day by day in the country. He defeated the large Ottoman army at Baghdad in such a way that rioting and disturbances broke out in Constantinople, so that Soltan Ahmad Khan despaired of his crown and Soltan Mahmud Khan

---

33. Ashot I Bagratuni (r. 885 - 890) was an Armenian prince who received the title 'prince of princes' from the Abbasid caliph and later received the crown from the Arabs and Byzantium to start a revival of the Armenian kingdom. It also could be Ashot II the Iron (914 - 929).

34. Nikolai Gerasimovich Ustrialov, *Istoria tsarstvovaniia Petra Velikago* (St. Petersburg, 1858 - 63).

took his place. At that time, the people of the border provinces rebelled and attacked the Russians. Because of the forethought of General-major Levashev, Russia was saved from this danger and the said general requested powerful help from the capital, but the empress, through Baron Shafirov, who was one of the grandees of Russia, sued for peace.[35] After discussions with the Persian representative in Rasht in the year 1145/1732 a peace treaty was signed stipulating that the Russians immediately would return the provinces of Gilan and Mazandaran to Persia and would leave the provinces of Shirvan and Daghestan as soon as the Persian and Ottoman wars, which were fiercely continued, came to an end. With this treaty the Russian government only aimed to bring about friendly relations with Iran and the withdrawal of the Ottomans from those parts.

The Story of Nader[36]

The story of Nader is that of a certain Emam Qoli Qereqluy Afshar of the Turkman who had come during the conquest of the Mongols from Turkestan to Azerbaijan, and who, after the rise of Shah Esma'il had migrated to Abivard and were living at the head wells of the Kurekan. On the 28th of Moharram [140] of the year 1101/1689 a boy named Nader Qoli was born who, by marrying two daughters of Baba 'Ali Bey Kuseh Ahmadlu, one after the other, had become famous among his peers and was known as Nader Qoli Bey for his valor and courage. After the death of Baba 'Ali Bey, he became an attendant to Malek Mahmud Seystani and subsequently he fled from him and took possession of Abivard. This was in the time of upheaval when the Afghans had taken the Persian capital as well as Persian Iraq, Fars and Khorasan. The Ottomans held half of Azerbaijan, Armenia and Georgia and Russia had occupied the Caspian provinces and the Lezgis in Shirvan were disturbing every day life and security on the roads. Moreover, in every shrine a dervish was claiming that he was one of the children of Soltan Hoseyn and in every corner claimants were plundering the country. Nader Qoli Bey, with the help of the Jalayer tribe, which had nearly 400 families, began to make a name for himself. He took control over the Afshars, Kurds and the tribes of Abivard and the forts of Daragez and Kalat with its environs and after fighting with Malek Mahmud and others he became famous. He became close to Shah Tahmasp and became known as Tahmasp Qoli Khan; first he became *qurchibashi* [chief of the royal household troops] and then the powerful general of Persia and the regent of all of Persia. He deposed Shah Tahmasp in the year 1145/1732 and struck coins in the name of his baby-son Shah 'Abbas III and he himself independently ruled the country. After having dealt a devastating defeat to the Ottoman army he, through the intermediary of Ahmad Pasha, the governor of Baghdad, in the year 1146/1733 made a truce with

---

35. Baron Peter Pavlovich Shafirov (1669 - 1739), senator and vice-president of the department of Foreign Affairs and one of Russia's leading diplomats. He fell from power and was banished to Siberia in 1723, but he was recalled after Peter the Great's death.

36. For a recent biography see Axworthy, Michael. *Sword of Persia: Nader Shah, from Tribal Warrior to Conquering Tyrant* (London, 2006). Also, still of great interest is Laurence Lockhart, *Nadir Shah* (Cambridge, 1938). Both books provide more information and clarification on the events reported by Bakikhanov.

the Ottoman government and royal edicts were signed agreeing that the pashas would vacate the occupied lands. Then Nader came to Ardabil and one of the royal edicts, which was addressed to Sorkhay Khan, the occupier of Shirvan, was sent with Musa Khan, the governor of Astara, and his people to Sorkhay Khan. He killed the bringer of the royal edict and wrote nonsensical words to Musa Khan: "I have occupied Shirvan by force of the sword of the Lezgi lions. How dare Ahmad-e Baghdadi and others to say such words." Therefore, H.E. Nader deemed the punishment of that arrogant man more necessary than the conquest of Shirvan as the key for the conquering of other forts. When he arrived near the Kur River, Sorkhay Khan had abandoned Shamakhi and had gone to Daghestan. [141]

Nader's army entered Shamakhi on August 17, 1146/1734 and he appointed Mohammad Qoli Khan Sa'idlu, the governor of Ardabil as the governor of Shirvan. Since it was learnt that a group of Lezgis and rebels had gathered in a place called Miji, at a distance of three *farsakh* from Shamakhi, and in a very impassable place, with the intention to make trouble, troops were sent to put them down and 500 heads and prisoners were taken. Order was given to free the prisoners and the *beyler-bey* of Shirvan sent them back to their lords. At this time news came that Sorkhay Khan with a large group of Lezgis and others was preparing for war in Qabaleh. Nader left his equipment and heavy baggage and left with his son Reza Qoli Mirza and the vanguard of the artillery and 12,000 cavalry to the fort of Shamakhi, with the intention of conquering a Ghazi-Qomuq, which is situated at a distance of 10 stages from Shamakhi, and within Daghestan it was the place of refuge of Sorkhay Khan. He went there on the 6th of September and ordered Tahmasp Qoli Khan, the general of Fars that he had to come three days after him with 12,000 troops to Qabaleh with the intention of punishing Sorkhay Khan. At one stage from Qabrak, one of the districts of Kur, the news reached him that the Lezgis of Jar and Teleh, Mostafa Pasha, Nur Pasha and Fath Geray Soltan with 8,000 Ottoman troops and Tatars had come to help him at the order of 'Ali Pasha, the governor of Ganjeh, who previously had been in Qabaleh. In total they had gathered 20,000 men. Before the arrival of Tahmasp Qoli Khan in a place called Deveh-batan, between Qabaleh and Shamakhi, one side of which is mountainous and the other forested, they had placed their musketeers at the beginning of the road, who, at the same time, were supported by other troops. The vanguard of Nader's army encountered the first of the opponent's troops and since it was a forest they did not know the extent of the number of the enemy and imagining that Qarat Gholam was Sorkhay Khan they came forward and courageously attacked and vanquished them and then they engaged with other troops who were coming from the back. The Lezgis supposing that this was Nader's army which therefore had attacked them with such boldness became disheartened and fled. Due to the flight of these troops, the center of the army of Sorkhay Khan and the Pashas collapsed and their order was disrupted. Many of them were killed, the Ottomans fled to Ganjeh and Sorkhay Khan to Ghazi-Qomuq and all the equipment of their army fell into the hands of the general. Another army unit plundered and set fire to the fort of Khachmaz, which had been founded by Sorkhay Khan and was a very prosperous place, [142] but now it had become a heap of ashes. H.E. Nader receiving this news sent troops to intercept the fugitives, but Sorkhay Khan got news of this and did not stop in any place. Traveling day and night, he passed via a short-cut above Khosrek and the troops that had been sent arrived there in the morning. They encountered a group of Lezgis and Tatars and killed or captured some 300 of them. They took possession of all the cattle and sheep, which were scattered in the mountains en route.

In short, Nader's army marched in 10 days over a long and difficult distance with the artillery and at most places they carried the guns on their shoulders and reached the village of Khosrek at one stage from Ghazi-Qomuq. On the way, Sorkhay Khan's petition, begging for forgiveness and pardon, was received. Nader did not consider his words trustworthy and tried to conquer Ghazi-Qomuq and went there that morning. Sorkhay Khan with a large group of Daghestanis had made entrenchments on the banks of the river at one *farsakh* distance from the town and had destroyed the bridge that was the only passageway and started to defend it himself. When the battle raged with the firing of muskets and camel-swivels, Ghani Khan of the Abdali Afghans with his troops was sent to secure a passageway. With much effort they found a narrow way to cross and like the blink of the eye in one moment they crossed the river. Sorkhay Khan and the Lezgis seeing this fled. Nader's army following the passage of the Abdalis, crossed and reached the mountains before the Lezgi troops. Although some of them were killed, Sorkhay Khan with only a few people and his family escaped and became a wanderer in the land of the Avars. The town of Ghazi-Qomuq was taken and all the treasures of Sorkhay Khan and the people of that place, that were hidden or known, fell into their hands.

At this time, Khass Fulad, son of 'Adelgeray Khan, son of Morteza 'Ali, who was the great Shamkhal of Daghestan, came to the presence of Nader and was confirmed as Shamkhal of Daghestan with robes of honor and he promised to serve and begged for forgiveness for the people. Since the cold season was close and capturing Sorkhay Khan was difficult in the near future, one week after the property of that place had been seized, all the captured Lezgis, men and women, were given to the Shamkhal and Nader returned. After entering the stage of Akhtipareh, it was known that the Lezgis had destroyed the bridge over the Samur River, [143] which was the passageway for the army and they were waiting on top of the mountain, in the fort of Shahbani that they had reinforced. Nader's army alighted at that side of the river and orders were given to gather bridge building materials and by nightfall they had built a strong bridge, so that at the time of dinner the entire army had passed and had taken their positions on the slope of the mountain. Troops were assigned to attack from the mountain side, where the baggage and family of that tribe had taken refuge. They went there, but the Lezgis could not hold out any longer and fled. Nader himself with some troops pursued the fugitives from morning till evening from valley to valley and killed and captured many. He sent equipment and provisions by way of Maskanjeh and Shahdagheh to Qabaleh and the following day he went himself by the way of Khachmaz, which was a difficult and impassable road. In some places on the mountain side, Sorkhay had made a road from rocks, bricks and mortar so that pedestrians, one by one, could pass over it in fear and danger.

In short, on the 3rd of November of the said year Nader's army reached the village of Qutqashin in one of the districts of Qabaleh. After three days, via Shahdaghi, the heavy equipment and provisions reached the camp and the big army from Shamakhi. On the 15th of that month, intending to conquer Ganjeh, it crossed a bridge, which had been built facing Arash. On the 13th of November Nader's army camped at Kalisa-kandeh in Ganjeh. The Ottomans and the Tatars vacated the city and took refuge in the citadel. From the other side the means of capturing the fort were prepared and entrenchments and redoubts were made. Seven tunnels were dug under the citadel, but the Ottomans got news of this and they neutralized them. In six other tunnels, 3,500 *man* of gun-powder that had been amassed there was slowly ignited and 700 of the guards and Omar son of 'Ali Pasha, the governor of Ganjeh were killed. The Ottomans also tunneled to the redoubts, of which the besiegers destroyed one and due to fire from another tunnel 40 men of the musketeers (*jazayer*) were killed. Several times the tunnels of each side reached each other and the tunnel diggers then fought with each other. One day the Ottomans emerged with hand grenades and threw them to the people in the redoubts. They attacked with sword and guns and forced the people of the redoubts to run to the end of the battle field. The besiegers pressed onwards and expelled the besieged from the redoubts and forced them back into the fort. Four months it continued this way and nothing was accomplished. After that [**144**] Nader's army constructed a strong dam and led the water of the river to the fort. The wall of Shir-Hajji with the citadel and towers at the south-east were destroyed and half of the citadel was ruined by the weight of water and the poundings of the Ottoman cannons and the water disappeared. Its course can still be seen until half of a *farsakh* to the north. At that time a number of Lezgi chiefs came to Jar and Teleh. They promised in 20 days to send troops to accompany Nader's army. Because they did not fulfill the promise, a number of khans and troops, who were around Aghdash, as well as troops from the camp, were appointed to punish those people and the Georgians of Kakheti led by 'Ali Mirza, son of Emam Qoli Khan were appointed to carry out this order. The Lezgis, who had abandoned their houses and had taken refuge in a high fort in the Elburz Mountain, suddenly attacked the troops that had been sent, and killed a number of them and some of them were also killed and they returned.

After this event, their fortification, which was in a place that was extremely inaccessible and the road to it was only a passage-way made of strong wooden beams, which was covered with ice. The Turkish Khans decided to return and killed 150 of these people, whom they had captured, and, after plundering whatever they could, they returned. During these events, H.E. Nader, in accordance with the treaty, which was signed by the Russian envoy, who was most of the time with Nader, asked for the return of all the forts of Baku and Darband. On the day of *Nowruz* of the year 1147/1735, the treaty with Russia was concluded and order was given to the governors of Saliyan, Baku and Darband to receive the prisoners who were in Russian hands and to escort the Russian troops and their belongings without any hindrance until the river of Sulaq, which was determined to be the border between the two countries.

Since the city and the fort of Shamakhi was in an unsuitable place and in a location vulnerable to the enemy, in the month May of the year 1148/1735, at the distance of 4 *farsakh* of a place called Aq Su, which had a suitable location, a site for the city was selected and in a short time the construction of the towers and citadel were completed. The people and the inhabitants of the old city came to the new one and it became the governor's seat of Shirvan. Since the siege of Ganjeh lasted a long time the besieged, with the support of 'Abdollah Pasha *sar-'askar*, were bolstered in their resistance. All affairs depended on the *sar-'askar*, but he was not moving from Qars. Therefore Nader assigned troops to the siege of Ganjeh and ordered a regiment to stay in [145] in Aghdash, so that if the Lezgis of Jar and Teleh or Daghestan began to instigate trouble the *beyler-bey* of Shirvan and the governor of that place would punish them. Nader himself, via Luri in Georgia, with 15,000 men went to fight the *sar-'askar* in Qars. Since the *sar-'askar* refused to oppose him and had taken refuge in the city of Qars Nader's army one night in a hurried manner left the environs of the city and turned towards Iran. Because of this the *sar-'askar* became brave and with around 100,000 men pursued him. As a result, near Erevan a big battle took place and the *sar-'askar* was defeated and was killed with many of the pashas. After this great victory the Ottomans of Ganjeh and Erevan asked for amnesty and surrendered the forts with artillery and prisoners and fled.

After these events, some of the Lezgis of Daghestan with the intention to rebel joined with some rebels of Qobbeh. They besieged the governor of that place, Hoseyn 'Ali Khan, son of Soltan Ahmad Khan, in the citadel of Qobbeh; its ruins and gardens can still be seen at a distance of three *farsakh* from Qobbeh. Khass Fulad Khan and the governor of Darband with a full complement of troops came to defend him. They killed or captured 300 people and the remainder fled. At that time, the Shamkhal had come and was in Darband. 'Omma Khan, the Usmi of the Avars had come to the border of the country of the Shamkhal and near the village of Paraval fought with him. The Usmi himself and some people were killed and the rest saved themselves by flight.

In the same summer of the year 1148/1735, Nader dismissed the Russian envoy at the summer-quarters of Erevan and appointed Mirza Kafi Nasiri as ambassador to Russia and sent him on his way with one string of elephants and some suitable presents. He himself had come to Tiflis to put the affairs of Georgia in order, when [the news of] the arrival of the governor of the Crimea reached him. Nader who knew of this beforehand had appointed 'Ali Qoli Khan, *beyler-bey* of Shirvan to go to Darband. If the Khan of the Crimea would come to those parts they would avoid confronting him and prepare for defense. The Ottoman Soltan, after the defeat and killing of 'Abdollah Pasha *sar-'askar*, had appointed the former governor of Ganjeh, 'Ali Pasha in his place to define the border between [146] the two countries. He issued a royal edict to the Khan of the Crimea and sent Eslam Geray Soltan, who was the brother's son of the aforementioned Khan and who was at the Ottoman court, as an emissary to Iran. At the time that the news of the coming of the aforementioned khan to the Sulaq area arrived, Eslam Geray Soltan also arrived. Nader did not allow the abovementioned Soltan to return. 'Abdol-Baqi Khan Zanganeh had orders to remain at Tiflis and to take 'Ali Pasha, who had come for peace negotiations, to Ganjeh to wait there for new orders. On the 22nd of October, Nader himself went to Daghestan and he left a big army on the banks of the river Qaneq. With troops he went to punish those of Jar and Teleh, but they had already fled and had settled on the top of a mountain, which was very inaccessible and which they had fortified. Riflemen and musketeers attacked from one side and took fortification. The Lezgis took refuge in the peaks and ridges of the mountains and they became wanderers in the land of the Avars. A large number of them were killed or captured and their property and homes were plundered and burnt. Nader's army went to Shamakhi via Sheki and Arash. There the news reached them that the Khan of the Crimea, after having entered the outskirts of Darband, had made Eldar, son of Morteza 'Ali, Shamkhal of Daghestan and had given Shirvan province to Sorkhay Khan and the government of Darband to Ahmad Khan Usmi. He had given 2,500 *tuman*s cash with some treasures and precious gifts to Sorkhay Khan. The latter had assigned his own son with 500 Lezgis to be in the presence of the abovementioned khan. It was at this time that the Khan of the Crimea learnt of the coming of Nader's army and hurriedly returned to the Crimea. In spite of the fact that it was a very cold winter and the roads were covered with ice and snow, Nader decided that his main objective would putting down the rebellion of Daghestan. He went via Alti Aghach and after entering Derehkend he issued an order to the general of Daghestan that after Darband he had to come to the valley of Tabarsaran to collect wheat. At the same time, he sent his equipment and heavy baggage with his own son, Reza Qoli Mirza via Shabaran and he himself went to punish the rebels of Boduq and Khenaleq. He also sent 6,000 men to Doquzpareh and Akhtipareh. He also sent some troops from the side of the cemetery to close off the road and stop the fugitives. After the killing and plundering of those people [147] he turned round via the stage of Kelyar-e Qobbeh and joined his army.

On the 11th of November, he pitched his tents on the northern side of the citadel of Darband. At this place it became evident that Eldar Khan, the new Shamkhal, the Usmi and Sorkhay had gathered in Ghazanesh with the intention to attack Khass Fulad Khan, the Shamkhal. Therefore, they made a night-attack, so that first they went to Majales where they collected Khan Mohammad, the son of the Usmi, who was there with the Lezgi troops. They began fighting and some were killed and captured, while the remainder took to flight. All the districts were destroyed and many treasures and property were seized. The next day Nader's army moved from there and stage by stage it plundered and killed and then it entered the village of Kubdan, which belonged to Khass Fulad Khan, the Shamkhal. Sorkhay, the Usmi and Eldar each fled to a different direction and Khass Fulad Khad with his followers came to court. From there Nader's army intending to punish Sorkhay Khan went to Ghazi-Qomuq and on the 20th of December it entered Sharrat at a distance of 3 *farsakh* from Ghazi-Qomuq. Sorkhay Khan had gathered a large number of troops; he had made the tops of the mountains his refuge and he occupied the valley, which was the passage way of the troops. Nader ordered to attack from four sides. The first group, the Afghan troops, attained the summit of the mountain and the fire of battle raged fiercely. While the other troops were busy climbing the mountains, the Lezgis started fleeing. Some were killed, some captured. Due to lack of time, Nader alighted at that same place and ordered the musketeers to guard the summit of the mountain. Eldar, who had come with some Lezgis of Daghestan and Avars, to help Sorkhay Khan, who had taken the musketeers, went among them and killed and captured some. Because advancing was difficult, Nader was satisfied when a few people from Qomuq asked for amnesty. The following day he departed from there to punish the Usmi and went to Fort Qoreysh. While he had gone to Ghazi-Qomuq, the Qazi of Aqusheh with the people of that place had come to beg for amnesty, but after that they had sent a group of people secretly to help Sorkhay. Therefore, they had to be punished. Nader assigned a number of people for this task and the qadi with his people fought and then fled. A large number of them were killed, defeated and captured. The next day the qadi came to apologize at Nader's court; he was pardoned and the captives of Aqusheh were freed. When Nader's army reached Fort Qoreysh, the Usmi sent his daughter to serve in the Harem and some of the grandees asked for pardon and they were given amnesty. Nader gave that daughter in marriage to Hoseyn 'Ali Khan, son of Soltan Ahmad Khan of Qobbeh. After a while the latter was overcame by madness and he went from Qobbeh to Bashli to the house of Amir Hamzeh Usmi. The Lezgis of Doquzpareh also gave him 1,000 horses as a gift and hostages from families of notables. The *kadkhodas* [148] of Tabarsaran sent notable families who had been ordered to go Darband in the company of the tax collectors. They professed their obedience. In this way the affairs of Daghestan were settled. Khass Fulad Khan and the other chiefs of that region were permitted to return with favors. Nader then went to the Moghan steppe. After he had entered Hasan-Qal'eh in Qobbeh, he, with a number of special troops, proceeded and traversed six stages of difficult road in one day and night and entered the fort of Aq Su. From there he entered the army camp in the Moghan steppe on the 13th of January. Since previously orders had been sent to all parts of the country, to the governors, noblemen, olama, and leaders of every province to gather on the 15th March in the Moghan steppe, while it also had been ordered that near the passage of Javad, which is a joining place of the Kur and Arash rivers, 12,000 houses, caravanserais, mosques, public baths and good buildings had to be built of wood and reeds, the number of people coming from the provinces had to be nearly 100,000. As a result of the discussions and consultations that lasted more than one month, Nader on the 26th of March in the year 1148/1736 acceded to the throne of Iran. The date of the enthronement was *al-kheyr fi ma vaqa'* or 'Whatever has happened is the best.'[37]

In public, with all the olama of Iran, it was decided that certain affairs had to be changed and favorable conditions be established, so that the differences between the two sects of the Sunnis and Shi'as might be resolved and the animosity among the followers of Islam be lifted. Although he had sent this declaration several times to the Ottoman court, it was not accepted.[38] Then Nader made some new appointments to government positions and he gave his brother Ebrahim Khan the governorship from Kaflan Kuh till Arpa Chay

---

37. On these events, see, e.g., Abraham of Erevan, *History of the wars: 1721-1736*, annotated translation with introduction and commentary by George A. Bournoutian (Costa Mesa, 1999).

38. On these religious unification efforts see Ernest S. Tucker, *Nadir Shah's Quest for Legitimacy in Post- Safavid Iran* (Gainesville, Fl, 2006), pp. 45ff.

and the borders of Daghestan and Georgia and he ordered that all the emirs and the governors of these regions be under his command. Mehdi Bey of Khorasan, the hundred-man (*yuz-bazhi*) of the camel-gunners, received the title of khan and was given the rank of *amir al-omara* of Shirvan.

In the year 1149/1737, Mehdi Bey, the *beyler-bey* of Shirvan had gone to set aright the affairs of Darband. Morad 'Ali Soltan Ostajalu, the governor of Darband, because of the animosity that he had with Mehdi Khan, incited the people of that city [against him] and killed him. Some of the killers went to take refuge with Ahmad Khan Usmi and some others took refuge in the citadel of Darband. The rest of the people of Darband, who had not participated, [149] attacked and killed those in the Narin-Qal'eh and put Morad 'Ali Soltan in chains and sent him to the royal court, where he was executed as soon as he arrived.

The king appointed Sardar Bey Qereqlu with the title of Khan to the governorship of Shirvan and Najaf Soltan Qarachurlu was appointed to the government of Darband. They went to their assignments with a group of musketeers to put the affairs of Darband in order. An edict was issued in the name of Ahmad Khan Usmi to seize the people from Darband who had taken refuge with him and to send them in chains to Sardar Khan. The Usmi acted accordingly and that entire group, together with some [other] rebels, was killed. Sardar Khan forced some people of Darband to emigrate to the new city of Aq Su. He resettled the Sursur tribe from Shirvan in the fort of Darband in their place. In the year 1151/1739, while Nader Shah was invading India, the Lezgis of Jar and Teleh, certain that the inaccessibility of the place would be on their side, revolted. Zahir al-Dowleh Ebrahim Khan went to punish him; initially he defeated and killed many of them, but he himself was killed by a rifle bullet. When this news reached Nader in Peshavar he sent Amir Aslan Khan Qereqlu to Azerbaijan and Safi Khan Baghayeri, who was the general of Georgia, as general to Azerbaijan to punish those people as much as possible with the troops of that region as well as to keep control over those regions and to wait for his return. After conquering India, he came to Afghanistan in the year 1152/1740 from Naderabad-e Afghan. Ghani Khan Abdali excused himself and his tribe from going to Turkestan and was sent to Shirvan, so that in the winter season when the roads of the Elburz Mountain are blocked, he would punish the people of Jar and Teleh. He assigned Fath 'Ali Khan Quseh Ahmadlu and Mohammad 'Ali Khan Qereqlu, who was the new general of Azerbaijan, with some governors and 15,000 troops from Khorasan to this task. He also sent the governors of Georgia with them. On the 23rd of February of the year 1153/1741, these troops reached the river Qaneq and the Lezgis had fortified three positions, viz., Jar, Kadekh [Kavekh], and Aghzibar. They started fighting in Jar, which was the first redoubt, but they were unable to defend it and retreated to Kadekh to oppose them. [150] After several days of non-stop fighting the Lezgis retreated to the third redoubt and continued fighting. That place was a woody and forested area on top of the mountain and there was only one road. The courageous Abdalis volunteered to attack and the battle lasted the whole day until dusk and many on both sides were killed. They started climbing the mountain at midnight, in spite of the fact that the Lezgis were rolling rocks and firing at them. It was of no use, [although] one hundred Abdalis were killed, [for] the redoubt was captured. Because the road on the northern side was closed as an escape route for the Lezgis a number of them jumped in desperation from the mountain and died. The remainder was either killed or captured. Some of them managed to escape. All the dwellings and houses of that tribe were destroyed and the remainder of them, with their families and cattle, fled to the ridges and the peaks of the mountain. The Abdalis pursued them until the river Samur to the place called Kesrokhi. Some of them were killed, and their wives and children were captured. In that area nothing was left standing and everything was destroyed. Returning from the mountains there was a big storm and 200 of the troops were killed.

In the spring of 1154/1742, Nader's army, after conquering Bokhara and Khvarezm, went to Daghestan and in Savadkuh in Mazandaran near Fort Owlad he was shot at from behind a tree. His left hand was wounded and, according to Mirza 'Abdol-Karim Monshi in the *Zobdat al-Tavarikh*,[39] after an investigation it became evident that his eldest son Reza Qoli Mirza, who was his heir-apparent while he was invading India, had been tempted to send Mirza Mohammad Hoseyn Qajar to kill the abdicated Shah Tahmasp in Sabzavar. For this reason he was criticized and was kept away from important affairs. So due to youthful pride and evil intention, which was part of his nature, he had sent a slave called Nik Qadam Tayemini[40] to do this. Nader Shah, ignoring paternal affection, blinded the prince and extinguished the light of his fortune. Thereafter, he became suspicious of everyone and changed the way in which he governed the country. In the early summer, via Qarajehdagh and Barda', he entered Qabaleh and from there via Shahdaghi went to Ghazi-Qomuq. En route, all the chiefs and leaders of the Lezgi tribes of those parts came to him and showed obedience and provided what was needed for the troops. On the 2nd of July, he entered Ghazi-Qomuq and stayed there for one month. [151] Khass Fulad Khan, Sorkhay Khan, Ahmad Khan Usmi and some of the grandees and people of Daghestan came to his presence and were honored with robes of honor, horses, and golden accessories. In the early month of August he went to punish the Avar rebels whose habitation is one of the most difficult places in one of the most remote mountains of Daghestan and in the region of Andallal near the village of Jukh there was a fierce battle. He could not achieve much and a large number of people were killed. Since the season of fall had arrived and traveling was difficult in the mountains he went to Darband and took Sorkhay Khan with all his family and cattle with him. When Nader was departing from Ghazi-Qomuq, he had sent Ahmad Khan Usmi with a number of troops so that he could bring the appointed families and retainers of the Qara-Qeytaq to Darband. Near Cheragh news arrived that in Hapqay, two *farsakh* above Bashli, the people of Qeytaq incited by the Usmi had attacked the troops and killed many of them and that they had plundered their equipment and horses. Therefore Nader wanted to punish the rebels and put the affairs of Daghestan in order and assigned tax collectors from Tiflis to Tabriz and Ardabil to collect supplies of wheat and transport these to the army camp.

---

39. Mohammad Mohsen, *Zobdat al-Tavarikh* ed. Behruz Gudarzi (Tehran, 1375/1996).
40. The Tayeminis are a tribal group from Herat.

On the first day of October Nader entered Darband and on the 9th day of that month he went to the country of the Qara-Qeytaq. From Darband to the borders of the land of the Shamkhal, Nader built strong forts over a distance of 2-3 *farsakh* and appointed some people there, so that they would not allow anyone from the Qeytaq-Lezgis to come there. The 4th day of November, to the north of Darband, at a distance of 3 *farsakh*, he found a pasture with many streams and chose it as his winter quarters. The harem, equipment and heavy baggage was brought there from Darband and houses were built of wood and reed. From that time onwards this was place was called 'Ruined Iran' (*Iran-e Kharab*), because the Iranian troops suffered many difficulties and shortages in this place. The Lezgis of that area, perhaps the Qara-Qeytaq, were busy plundering in and outside of the army camp. They would stop the transportation and collection of life necessities. In the spring, on May 17th, the king first went to punish the people of Tabarsaran and he did not spare anything or anyone; he plundered, captured, burnt houses and destroyed the sown fields. After that, in the other parts of Daghestan, he conquered fortified buildings and his troops were like wolves among the cattle and like flood among the houses. Most of the time, the Shamkhal and Sorkhay Khan were in his presence in Fort Qoreysh, which is situated on a mountain and surrounded by forest and has only one narrow and difficult access road. The Usmi had taken refuge in this fort. [152] Nader's army went there and after fierce attacks and hard fights that lasted three days and nights the Usmi became a wanderer in the land of the Avars and the people of the Qara-Qeytaq came to apologize and asked for pardon. That strong castle which was built of stone and mortar was totally destroyed and Mohammad 'Ali Khan Qereqlu was appointed governor of Darband and a number of troops was given to him.

On the 28th of January 1155/1743, Nader went to the Moghan. Snow, rain fall, a surfeit of mud, in addition to scarcity of pack animals and much disorder made that it took 40 days to get from Darband until the Kur. He gave Heydar Bey Afshar the title of khan and the governorship of Shirvan and he himself went to the border with Turkey. At this time, there was a person of unknown origin in Azerbaijan, whose name was Sam, who claimed to be the son of Soltan Hoseyn. Ebrahim Khan who was the governor of Azerbaijan cut his nose and let him go. He went to Daghestan. Mohammad, the son of Sorkhay Khan, who had rebelled and was wandering among the Avars made Sam the Cutnose an excuse for rebellion and gathered a number of people around him and incited the people of Darband and Tabarsaran. They started corresponding with the people of Shirvan. Mohammad 'Ali Khan sent a report to Nader's court. Heydar Khan was sent to help him. The rebellion of the people of Daghestan and Darband spread to Shirvan. Heydar Khan was captured between Shabaran and Shamakhi and was made prisoner. After a few days he was killed and his property was plundered. Mohammad Khan, son of Sorkhay Khan with Sam Mirza, in reaction to his invitation, came and took the fort of Shabaran, which is on the left side of the river; its remains can still be seen. They laid siege to it and because of the tunnels, part of which can still be seen, the fort was destroyed and conquered. Abdal Ostajalu and his retinue who were there were captured and killed. Mohammad Khan married the daughter of Abdal Khan and Sorkhay Khan II was born from her. From there they went to Aq Su, which was the capital of the province of Shirvan, which they captured. The people of Shabaran and Tabarsaran per force submitted themselves. [153] The group of Moghanis and others who had been assigned to Fort Qabr, one of the dependencies of Darband, killed a group of Afshars who had been with them. They gave Fort Qabr into the hands of the Lezgis, who joined Mohammad and Sam. After this event, Mohammad 'Ali Khan killed some of the chiefs and rebels of Darband and the Moghani retainers who were suspected of sedition. Some he blinded and sent them to Moghan and he himself fortified the citadel and towers of Darband. Ashur Khan Afshar, the general (*sardar*) of Azerbaijan, who was in Erevan when he heard this news, went with his army to Shirvan and started making a bridge on the banks of the Kur with Hajji Khan Jemeshgezek, *beylerbey* of Ganjeh. Karim Khan Afshar was appointed by Nader Shah to the Moghan region. Troops were assigned to support Ashur Khan, while Prince Nasrollah Mirza with Fath 'Ali Khan Afshar and 15,000 royal troops were sent to Shirvan. In accordance with the royal order, Fath 'Ali Khan was sent ahead to join Ashur Khan. On 24 December of the year 1155/1743, Mohammad and Sam and a large group of Lezgis and Shirvanis came down from the top of a mountain, which is above Mount Shah (Dagh-e Shah), ready to fight. Fath 'Ali Khan and Ashur Khan engaged them and won. One thousand men were killed and captured, while flags and kettle-drums were seized. Mohammad, son of Sorkhay Khan was wounded and with the remainder of the army fled. Sam with a few fled to Georgia. The khans laid siege to the citadel of Aq Su and within a few days they took it. Many Lezgis who were defending the citadel were captured and the city was plundered. This incident still is known as *allahdad*, i.e. free-for-all.

Soon thereafter Nader's army returned from the Ottoman border and in the neighborhood of Barda', in a place where from the point of view of water and grass was plentiful, he took up his winter quarters. After a few days, in spite of the fact that the winter was very severe, on the 11th of January, he with a group of soldiers went to Daghestan and crossed the Javad bridge and during the entire journey he covered two stages [154] in one day. On the 24th of January Nader left Darband and divided his army into four groups. He plundered all those people that were residing with confidence in those places, because they had not expected Nader to come under such circumstances and he seized cattle and so many animals that there were too many to count. After he had been plundering in that area for three to four days the chiefs and leaders of Daghestan came to the royal presence and were shows kindness and generosity. On the day of the Feast of Sacrifice, he returned to Darband and after he had put the affairs of that place in order he entered the royal camp via Tabarsaran on 5th of February. Nader stayed there for 20 days and because of the scarcity of water and grass he went to the north of the Kur and pitched his tents at Arash. From there, in the spring of the year 1157/1745, Nader went to the summer quarters of Sheki, where he stayed for a while in the fortifications of Gelesen Goresen. Here a group of the people of Sheki together with Hajji Chelebi, son of Qorban had killed their king and had taken refuge and he fought them. Because of the inaccessibility of the place Nader could not achieve much. At the end of Gemini (*Jowzeh* = May), at the beginning of June, via Khachin-Qarabagh and Miyankuh, he went to Gokcheh-yeylaq and from there the battle against the Ottomans started. After the battles and victories a truce was concluded. In that year in Shirvan an order for a free-for-all was given, i.e., the hooligans and cutthroats took the property and life of the weak and the governors did not have the force to prevent them from doing so. At that time, the Ottoman Soltan made use of the sectarian differences and incited the people of Daghestan against the rule of Iran. According to his orders, he gave the title of vizier to Ahmad Khan Usmi, and that of Pasha to his son Khan Mohammad, to Ahmad Khan Bey Jangta'i, the title of Salahshuri and Shamkhal and twenty purses of cash, and to each of the chiefs of Tabarsaran, who are the rulers (entitled Ma'sum and Qadi), two banners and 200 *tumans* cash, to Mohammad Bey Zaghuri two banners, the governorship of Zaghur and some cash with the intention of creating disturbances and riots in those parts. In short, as the authors of the *Nader-nameh*[41] and the *Zobdat al-Tavarikh*[42] and others are writing and making clear the events bear out that this great king whose genius was known to all the world and in fact was unique in his time, after returning from the campaign in Khvarezm, due to various temptations and suspicions and also owing to selfishness and greed of conquest that dominated his mind, forsook good governance and practiced injustice and oppression; [155] he blinded his own son Reza Qoli Mirza and he made the dear ones of the court live in misery. He punished many devoted emirs and khans without reason and submitted them to the sword of ruthless executioners and many of them were dying under the bastinado of the tax collectors, so that the affairs of the country were totally in disorder and the weak subjects were trodden under the hoofs of tyranny and the signs of upheaval were apparent in every region, and in every place disorder appeared to the liking of the evil-wishers. The country of Iran which had prospered under his justice, fell into ruin under his injustice. Ultimately, in the night of 9 May 1160/1747, in the way station called Fathabad in Khorasan, at two *farsakh* from Khabushan, several of his emirs and intimates at the instigation of his disgraced brother's son killed him. Because of this event rioting spread to all provinces of Iran and the country of Shirvan more than anywhere else became the scene of disturbances and in each country an emir claimed independence.

---

41. Mohammad Kazem Mervi, *'Alamara-ye Naderi*. 3 vols. ed. Mohammad Amin Riyahi (Tehran, 1364/1985). The title of *Nadernameh* is a generic one as Bakikhanov may not have had access to other manuscripts dealing with Nader Shah's life.

42. Mohammad Mohsen Mostowfi, *Zobdat al-Tavarikh* ed. Behruz Gudarzi (Tehran, 1375/1996).

CHAPTER FIVE

From the death of Nader until the treaty of the government of Russia and Iran in the village of Golestan[1]

When the news of the death of Nader Shah spread among the army, the Afghans and the Uzbegs, led by Ahmad Khan Abdali, who later on became the king of Afghanistan, made war with the Afshars, who were the killers of the king, and they were victorious and plundered the army and returned to their homes. 'Ali Qoli Khan, the son of Ebrahim Khan, the brother of Nader Shah came from Herat to the holy city of Mashhad and sent his slave called Sohrab and suddenly conquered the fort of Herat, which was one of the wonders of world and killed Reza Qoli Mirza with 15 of his relatives, big and small. Nasrollah Mirza and Emam Qoli Mirza, the sons of Nader Shah and Shahrokh Mirza, the son of Reza Qoli Mirza, who was born of the daughter of Shah Soltan Hoseyn, were brought to Mashhad and he killed those two brothers and Shahrokh Mirza, who was fourteen, was secretly imprisoned in the citadel of the fort and he spread the news of his death. If the Persians would not agree with his accession he would have the prince in his hands, who was worthy [to the succession] from two sides. He himself acceded to the throne as 'Ali Shah and brought all the treasures of Nader from Kalat, which, apart from jewels and precious stones, consisted of 15 *korur*[2] of cash and brought it from Kalat to Mashhad and started to waste it. His brother Ebrahim Khan who was holding Isfahan rebelled. 'Ali Shah who had stayed in Mazandaran for seven months marched to Isfahan to punish his brother. Between Zanjan and Soltaniyeh battle took place and 'Ali Shah was defeated and fled to Tehran [**156**] and was arrested at his brother's order and blinded. Ebrahim Khan hoping to get Shahrokh Mirza and the treasures of Nader sent his brother Hoseyn Bey with some emirs to Khorasan with the message that it was his intention to bring H.H. Shahrokh to the rightful throne and suggested that the prince should come and

---

1. On the events during this period see, for example, John R. Perry, *Karim Khan Zand: a history of Iran, 1747-1779* (Chicago, 1979); Hormoz Ebrahimnejad, *Pouvoir et succession en Iran: les premiers Qajar, 1726-1834* (Paris, 1999); and Christoph Werner, *An Iranian town in transition: a social and economic history of the elites of Tabriz, 1747-1848* (Wiesbaden, 2000).
2. One *korur* is 500,000.

ascend the throne in Persian Iraq. But the Kurds of Khorasan and the chiefs of Khorasan did not think it wise that the prince should go and, in spite of his unwillingness, on the 17th August in the year 1161/1748, he acceded the throne and the date is (indicated by the chronogrdm) *Soltan-e A'zam*.

On the 24th of November of the same year, in Tabriz, Ebrahim Khan also acceded to the throne and had coins struck and the *khutbeh* read in his name. He gave every beggar a governorship and the title of khan and called this action 'gaining the hearts'. From Azerbaijan he marched to Khorasan and sent his equipment and baggage with the blinded 'Ali Shah, who was accompanying him in chains, to Qom. When he arrived at the stage of Surkheh-ye Semnan his army started to disperse. Therefore, out of necessity he went to Qom with the Afghans, who supported him, but the gate keepers of that city closed the gates to him. Using force he made his way into the city and plundered it and then took refuge in the fort of Qalapur. The people of the fort put him in chains and reported the situation to Shahrokh's court. The order was issued to send him and 'Ali Shah, but he was killed en route and 'Ali Shah in holy Mashhad. Some time later, Shahrokh Mirza at the advice of the noblemen was also blinded and deprived of his rule. Mirza Sayyed Mohammad Sadr, the custodian of holy Mashhad, who was the son of a daughter of Shah Soltan Hoseyn acceded the throne as Shah Soleyman II, but after a while he was also blinded and deposed. Shahrokh Mirza was again put on the throne. Fortune did not smile on Azad Khan the Afghan, although he was making waves for a while in Khorasan. Mohammad Hasan Khan Qajar dominated Persian Iraq, Tabarestan and Azerbaijan and struck coins and had the *khutbeh* read in his name. At this time 'Ali Mardan Khan Bakhtiyari with Karim Khan Zand went to Isfahan and fought with Abu'l-Fath Khan, its governor. He was defeated and returned to the city. Then they signed a treaty and all three agreed to make Abu Turab, the son of one of the daughters of Shah Soltan Hoseyn, king under the name of Esma'il III. 'Ali Mardan Khan became regent, Abu'l-Fath Khan governor of Isfahan and Karim Khan became the general of the realm. When Karim Khan left Isfahan, 'Ali Mardan Khan killed Abu'l-Fath Khan and took with him the nominal and powerless king and went to Shiraz and took the province of Fars. Karim Khan, who, after the murder of Abu'l-Fath Khan, was afraid, went to [157] Mohammad 'Ali Khan, the general of the realm of Shahrokh Mirza and defeated him and he took his camel artillery and baggage and went to Kurdestan. After conquering Kurdestan he went back to conquer Isfahan. 'Ali Mardan Khan came to oppose him from Shiraz, but he was defeated and killed and in his place Karim Khan became the regent. After going there and conquering the regions of Astarabad, he was defeated by the Qajars and returned to Isfahan. At this time an unknown person claiming to be a son of Tahmasp, under the name of Soltan Hoseyn II, with the help of Mostafa Khan Beydeli, came to Persian Iraq. Karim Khan intending to oppose him went to Kermanshah and was victorious. The unknown king was killed in battle.

After that Azad Khan came from Urmiyeh to Persian Iraq. Karim Khan was defeated in battle and returned to Isfahan. Azad Khan besieged Fort Pari and succeeded in getting it peacefully. He sent the relatives, the wife and mother of Karim Khan, who were there, to Urmiyeh with 1,000 cavalry. At one of the stages, the Zand women broke the chains of their male relatives and put the guards to flight and joined Karim Khan. After Azad Khan's army entered Isfahan, Karim Khan fled to Kazerun and then he went to Shiraz and conquered that city and returned again to Isfahan. At this time Mohammad Hasan Khan Qajar defeated Karim Khan, who returned to Shiraz. Mohammad Hasan Khan besieged Shiraz. At this time because of the return of the Afghans he had to go back to Mazandaran, but he was killed at the hands of his servants.[3] Karim Khan came back and captured Isfahan, Yazd and Tehran and then marched to Azerbaijan.

Now, let us see how the state of Shirvan and Daghestan [158] was. As soon as Nader Shah died the army of Iran left this country and in every corner a powerful man

---

3. Fath 'Ali Khan Afshar, the governor Urmiyeh, who was claiming kingship, and who, besides Azerbaijan, had gained control over Erevan, Qarabagh, and Sheki. Hoseyn Bey, son of Hasan Aqa, son of Hajji Chelebi, in whose family the governorship of Sheki was hereditary until the year 1221/1806, had given him the title of khan and rose to fight [him]. Panah Khan Javanshir, the governor of Qarabagh, who at first was the herald of Nader Shah, while at the end of the reign of Nader Shah he had taken refuge in Qabaleh and Qarabagh. After Nader's death, in many fights, he had taken the province of Qarabagh and had built the city of Shushi. His son was Ebrahim Aqa, who was hostage in the hands of Fath 'Ali Khan. He went to see Karim Khan and helped him in taking Urmiyeh and killing Fath 'Ali Khan and he freed his son. Karim Khan sent the son Ebrahim Aqa with the title of Khan to Qarabagh. He kept Panah Khan all the time at his court until he died in Shiraz. Karim Khan had started to have friendly relations with Fath 'Ali Khan of Qobbeh, and his sister, Fatemeh Khanom, who was eventually given to Mohammad Reza Khan Shirvani, and asked her hand for his son Abu'l-Fath Khan. When he had conquered all of Azerbaijan the claim by Zaki Khan to the throne and his coming [158] to Isfahan at the instigation of the Bakhtiyari tribe became known. Karim Khan with the emirs and the army marched to Isfahan. Zaki Khan taking the notables with him went to Sardasht. Nazar 'Ali Khan Zand was sent by Karim Khan and he defeated him and then pursued him to the utmost regions of Lorestan. Zaki Khan to save his life took asylum in Karim Khan's stable and was given amnesty. A defeated and arrested Azad Khan from Georgia went to Bey for mercy to the court of Karim Khan and was forgiven. Mohammad Hasan Khan also in the year 1172 was killed by his servants and thus the kingdom of Iran fell to Karim Khan without any opposition. Eventually, the Arabs of the environs of Basra rebelled and they killed Mohammad Khan, his sister's son with a number of other people. This disastrous news had a great impact on him and resulted in a fatal disease. On the 13th of Safar in the year 1193/1779 he died. This just and art-loving king reigned nearly 30 years and always was thinking of the welfare of the subjects and the development of his country. Because of his humaneness and his respect for the dignity of kingship, and in spite of the power that he had all over Iran he called himself *vakil* (regent). Because of quarrels between the Zand emirs his corpse was not buried for three days. Eventually Zaki Khan overcame his rivals and took the body and buried it and made his son Abu'l-Fath Khan the king and imprisoned Sadeq Khan, Karim Khan's brother and other relatives and he ruled himself. 'Ali Morad Khan Zand also revolted and after a nine-month siege he took the citadel and killed him and furthermore he blinded Abu'l-Fath Khan and other progeny of Karim Khan, and imprisoned all of them. He himself after 3.5 years of reign in the year 1198/1784 died. Ja'far Khan, the son of Sadeq Khan in Isfahan acceded to the throne in his stead. But, after a while, he was defeated in a battle with Aqa Mohammad Khan Qajar and went to Shiraz. While he was sick his relatives who were imprisoned took the opportunity in the year 1203/1789 and killed him. His son Lotf 'Ali Khan fled to Bushire. From there he returned to Shiraz and bravely fought several battles with Aqa Mohammad Khan, but eventually he was captured and killed. It was thus that the rule of Iran went to the Qajar dynasty and it still is in their hands. The Qajar tribe is descended from the Jalayer Turks and they were among the 200,000 families that Hulagu Khan brought from Turkestan [159]. [B]

claimed independence and imposed obedience on others. Hoseyn 'Ali, son of Soltan Ahmad Khan, the governor of Qobbeh and Saliyan, moved to Fort Khodad and repaired the fort of Qodyal, which is the modern-day Qobbeh and he subjugated most of the parts of the country that had become independent during the time of lawlessness. The people of Darband choose Mohammad Hasan Bey Qurchi, son of Emam Qoli Khan mentioned above, as khan. Mirza Mohammad Khan, son of Dargah Khan aforementioned of Baku, who was one of the officials of Nader's court, independently occupied Baku. The people of Shamakhi appointed as governor the receiver of supplies Hajji Mohammad 'Ali, son of Sufi Nabi Zarnava'i. Then the sons of 'Askar Bey, the son of Allahverdi Bey, chief of the Khan Chupani tribe, raised the flag of despotism among the tribes of Shirvan. Hajji Chelebi, son of Qorban Nakhavi, who in the time of Nader Shah was in charge of collecting the tax remittances (*havalajat*) in Sheki, became the representative of the people, but at the end he fled and during three years [159] he was in the stronghold of Gelesen Goresen. He claimed independence and subjugated the provinces of Sheki, Arash and Qabaleh. Panah Bey, son of Ebrahim Khan of Javanshir, who had fled in the time of Nader and was living in Sheki and Shirvan engaged in a series of continuous battles in Qarabagh and claimed governorship. He was elevated to the title of khan. He first built Fort Bayat and then Fort Tarnavat. The remains of its shops and walls still can be seen in the place called Shah Bulaghi, which were the winter quarters of Shah 'Abbas. After a while, at the request of Malekshah Nazar-Verandeh, the other Armenian *maleks* who had animosity with him, he built the Fort Panahabad near Shushi [Panahabad] and subjugated the Armenian *maleks*. Day by day he became stronger and he conquered a territory from the Khoda-Afarin bridge until the Karak River and Bargoshat and also the districts of Meqri and Guney, which belonged to Qaradagh, Tatif and Sisan, which belonged to Nakhjevan and Tatar, Terterkulani, which belonged to Erevan, and Zang-Zur and Qapan, which belonged to Tabriz. Sometimes he would rule over neighboring provinces such as Ardabil and others. Shahverdi Khan Ziyad-oghlu took possession of Ganjeh, and Sorkhay Khan Ghazi-Qomuqi had left his lands to his son Mohammad Khan in the last part of the Nader's reign and had retired to the village of Qatrukh, which is 10 *farsakh* from Ghazi-Qomuq. Ahmad Khan Usmi died soon thereafter and his grandson, Amir Hamzeh, son of Khan Mohammad, had taken his place and had become known for his bravery, and Khass Fulad Khan Shamkhal in his own province was powerful and Nowsal Khan, son of Ibn 'Omma Khan, in the country of the Avars became governor and, besides these, other great emirs in the same manner, such as Mehdi Bey, son of Ahmad Khan Bey Jangkuta'i, from the line of the Avar kings, and, according to some other sources, he was from the Mongol and Tatar people, became governor of Mahdevali and Hoseyn Khan Bey in the region of Zakhur and Ilisu[4], was an emir and descendent of the soltan and governed in Enderey and Yakhsay and the heirs of Terlav governed in Machgach, and Morteza 'Ali, son of Mohammad Ma'sum, became the Ma'sum and Morteza 'Ali, son of Rostam, became the Qadi of Tabarsaran.

---

4. Ilisu is located at the foot of the Caucasus Mountains, under Mt. Ahvay, not far from Daghestan.

In those days the Emir of Buynaq, Mehdi, son of Morteza 'Ali, who Nader Shah had exiled to Astarabad, because of his bad and quarrelsome behavior towards Khass Fulad Khan, came to the Qebchaq plains after Nader Shah's death and from there he went with an army of Qalmuq in the vicinity of Ghazanesh in between two rivers; there was a fierce battle and he was victorious. Finally, he reached a truce with Khass Fulad Khan and, as before, became the governor of Buynaq. In the year 1162/1749, Ahmad Khan Shahsevan came to the old city of Shamakhi, which was the seat of the Al-e Sarkar. Aqa Razi Bey, son of 'Askar Bey faced him in battle and killed his brother Mohammad Reza Khan. Ahmad Khan himself took part in the battle to take revenge and was severely wounded by Aqa Razi Bey and was defeated and after half a *farsakh* he died.

Meanwhile, [160] Erekle Khan, the *vali* of Georgia under the pretext of giving advice concerning the defense against Hajji Chelebi, met with Shahverdi Khan of Ganjeh, Panah 'Ali Khan of Qarabagh, Kazem Khan of Qaradagh, Hoseyn 'Ali Khan of Erevan and Heydar Qoli Khan of Nakhjevan and arrested all of them in one place. On learning of this event, Hajji Chelebi together with Aqa Razi Bey, who because of his bravery had become the head of the Al-e Sarkar, went very fast to the *vali* and in the place called Qezel-qayeh (Red Rock), at half a *farsakh* from Ganjeh, defeated him and freed all these khans and sent them away and they pursued the *vali* and occupied the districts of Qazzaq[5] and Buzchalu (see map). His son, Aqa Keshi Bey, plundered those places for nearly two years. His fortified place in Baydar, at four *farsakh* from Tiflis, can still be seen. Finally, the *vali* asked for help from the Cherkes and others and gathered people around him. Aqa Keshi Bey was returning to Sheki. After a while Erekle Khan with lots of equipment went to bring about the return of Yengolu tribe, who the people of Jar had taken from Georgia. Hajji Chelebi came to help the Jar people near to the left bank of the river Qaneq; a fierce battle took place and the *vali* was defeated even worse than the first time and returned.

In the year 1168/1755, Hajji Chelebi came to conquer Shirvan with a huge army and began the siege of the city of Aq Su. Hajji Mohammad 'Ali Khan asked for help from Hoseyn 'Ali Khan of Qobbeh. He, with 3,000 troops, the army from Qobbeh, along with Amir Hamzeh Usmi, who had 500 troops with him, interceded between the warring parties. A certain Hajji Piri, who had come from Hajji Chelebi as a messenger, uttered threats and asked him to return. Eventually a battle took place and the numerous army of Sheki facing this small group of ruffians was defeated and many people were killed and captured. Hoseyn 'Ali Khan after three days of feasting returned to his seat of government.

In the year 1169/ 1756, he had sent his son Fath 'Ali Khan with an army to get the hereditary district of Saliyan from his relative Ebrahim Khan Rudbari, who at the time of the rebellion had occupied it and he got it back. In the year 1171/1758, Hoseyn 'Ali Khan, the valorous emir died, who always had tried to provide for the welfare of the people. Aqa Razi Bey, son of 'Askar Bey immediately went and plundered the Barmak area of Qobbeh and forced 200 families to migrate and brought them with him. Fath 'Ali Khan, son of Hoseyn 'Ali Khan, wanted to take revenge and 'Ali Razi Bey went to oppose him and outside the old city he was defeated and killed. Fath 'Ali Khan after a siege of a few months

---

5. The name of this district is also written as Kazakh.

and after killing and plundering returned again with his tribe. In the year 1172/1759, with the encouragement of the Darbandis, who were suffering from the ill-treatment of Taher Bey, the brother of Mohammad Hoseyn Khan, he went to Darband and after a short siege conquered it. [**161**] Mohammad Hoseyn Khan, because of his responsibilities took his residence in Baku and Hajji Chelebi who was known for his perseverance, love of art and good governance died after that defeat. His courageous and honorable son, Aqa Keshi Bey was governing when Mohammad Khan Ghazi-Qomuqi, at the instigation of Malek 'Ali Arashi, came to the district of Arash and asked him for advice and when he met him he killed him and occupied the country of Sheki. He gave his daughter, who was the wife of Aqa Kishi Bey, to Belghas Bey Ilisu'i. Ahmad Khan Soltan was borne to her. Mohammad Khan governed Sheki for 40 days and possessed the treasures of Hajji Chelebi and committed many atrocities. Until Hoseyn Aqa, son of Hasan Aqa, son of Hajji Chelebi, who after the murder of Aqa Kishi Bey had gone to Darband to Fath 'Ali Khan via Qobbeh with the help of the army of Qobbeh and together with the notables of Sheki expelled Mohammad Khan and retook his own country. After three years from this event in the year 1175/1762, Fath 'Ali Khan Afshar, one of the leading emirs of Nader, who, after conquering Azerbaijan, was claiming kingships went to Ganjeh and Qarabagh. Panah Khan pretended to obey him and gave his son Ebrahim Khan as a hostage and when Malek 'Ali Arashi had gone to see him asking for the governorship of Sheki, Hoseyn Aqa with Kalb 'Ali Soltan Qutqashini and others of his followers entered, were favored with the title of khan and returned and killed Malek 'Ali.

In the year 1176/1763, a great plague struck Shirvan, especially the city of Aq Su and many people died. During that time, Karim Khan *vakil* came with the intention of conquering Azerbaijan. Panah Khan Qarabaghi to save his son joined him and in conquering Urmiyeh and killing Fath 'Ali Khan was of great help. The *vakil* honored his son Ebrahim Khalil Aqa with the title of khan and gave the governorship of Qarabagh to him. He had him [i.e. Panah Khan] all the time in his presence. At any rate he died in Shiraz and his body was taken to Qarabagh. They say he was a brave emir, simple and pleasantly-mannered.[6]

In short, after conquering Azerbayjan, when the claim to kingship by Zaki Khan Zand and his coming to Isfahan at the instigation of the Bakhtiyari tribe, became known, the *vakil* with all his emirs and troops went to defeat him. Zaki Khan forced the notables of Isfahan to move to Sardasht and Nazar 'Ali Khan Zand at the order of the *vakil* went and defeated him and pursued him to Lorestan. Zaki Khan per force took refuge in the stable of the *vakil* and received amnesty. Azad Khan Afghan, who had been defeated and captured, came from Georgia and was given clemency. In this way the entire country of Iran without other claimants belonged to Karim Khan.

In the year 1178/1765, [**162**] Mohammad Sa'id Khan and Aghasi Khan who had received the title of khan from Karim Khan captured the city of Aq Su and killed Hajji

---

6. On the events in Qarabagh see George A. Bournoutian, translator and annotator, *Two chronicles on the history of Karabagh: Mirza Jamal Javanshir's Tarikh-e Karabagh and Mirza Adigo zal Bey's Karabagh-name* (Costa Mesa, 2004).

Mohammad 'Ali Khan, who was a luxury-loving and tolerant man. At that time Fath 'Ali Khan had married the sister of Amir Hamzeh Usmi, who was called Tuti Begeh and the Usmi had asked for the hand of the sister of Fath 'Ali Khan, Khadijeh Begeh, who had been borne to the daughter of Hoseyn Khan Rudbari. As Fath 'Ali Khan had given this sister to Malek Mohammad Khan Baku'i, whose father Mirza Mohammad Khan I had made him governor during his lifetime, there was animosity between Amir Hamzeh Usmi and Fath 'Ali Khan. After a while, the Usmi, under the pretext of visiting his sister, had come to Darband and captured the citadel (*Qal'eh-ye Narin*). Fath 'Ali Khan then entered [the city] with the army of Qobbeh and the Usmi defended it with guns and rifles for three days. Eventually he could not stay and via the Herald's Gate (*Jarchi Qapu*) he returned to his lands. After that he bore even lasting hatred for Fath 'Ali Khan and was intent on taking revenge.

Furthermore, Eldar Bey who had turned away from his uncle Mohammad Khan Ghazi-Qomuqi and was trusted by Fath 'Ali Khan and was the deputy of Darband was increasing the animosity of the Usmi with unworthy talk and behavior. The latter under different pretexts also had resorted to hostilities. His sister's son, Rostam b. Morteza 'Ali b. Rostam, Qadi of Tabarsaran supported him. Sheikh 'Ali Bey b. Mirza at that time had killed Morteza 'Ali Ma'sum b. Mohammad Ma'sum and he himself became the Ma'sum. However, his affairs did not have the desired result, because, at instigation of the Usmi and the Qadi, the people revolted and expelled him. He came to Fath 'Ali Khan and Nowruz Bey, son of Morteza 'Ali became the Ma'sum. But since he was a mute, his mother, the daughter of Qara Khan from the lineage of the Ma'suman, was ruling like a man. In the year 1181/1767, Fath 'Ali Khan with Hoseyn Khan of Sheki came from two sides and laid siege to the old city of Shamakhi that had been rebuilt by Mohammad Sa'id Khan and Aghasi Khan. Per force, Mohammad Sa'id Khan went to Fath 'Ali Khan and Aghasi Khan went to Hoseyn Khan. Hoseyn Khan blinded him and Fath 'Ali Khan captured Mohammad Sa'id Khan and sent him to Darband and moved the [people of the] city to Aq Su. He appointed two deputies from the two sides and divided the country into two. The district of Qasani went to Hoseyn Khan and the remainder of Shirvan went to Fath 'Ali Khan. After a while Fath 'Ali Khan occupied of all Shirvan and rebuilt the old city of Shamakhi.[7]

The blind Aghasi Khan lived in Kutvan on the banks of the Kur[8] and was trying to get his land back. He went and tried to get Hoseyn Khan's help and he gathered an army of Avars under the command of the nobles (*khanzadegan*) of that place, [named] Bolach and Mohammad Mirza, who came to Shirvan to fight Fath 'Ali Khan. When the two armies faced each other and discussed peace arrangements suddenly, because of a fight between some people of both sides, there was a fierce battle. Bolach [**163**] and Mohammad Mirza were killed and Hoseyn Khan was defeated and he went to Sheki and Aghasi Khan returned to Kotvan.

---

7. Gmelin, *Travels*, pp. 36-39.
8. In the Baku edition the text is not legible and we have guessed the meaning of the words (on the banks of Kur).

In the year 1187/1773, Khass Fulad Khan Shamkhal died; he had appointed his sister's son[9] the Amir of Buynaq, Morteza 'Ali b. Mehdi b. Morteza 'Ali in his place. Khass Fulad Khan, who was a generous, courageous and stern emir, was treating his relatives badly. His brother's son, Amir Khan Ghazanesh Mohammad the Toothless who was known for his great courage and wisdom opposed him. With the help of the emirs of Enderey, Nowsal Khan b. 'Omma Khan of Avar and Amir Hamzeh Usmi he came and expelled him from Tarkhu [Tarki] and Buynaq and he himself became Shamkhal. Morteza 'Ali Shamkhal with the support of Fath 'Ali Khan and the help of the people of Quy-suybuy and the Aqusheh districts, who in most important activities were supporting and helping the Shamkhal, [while] in the appointment of the new Shamkhal their presence was desired, after one month took control of the country. The toothless Shamkhal and after him his son Khass Fulad were satisfied with the governorship of Ghazanesh.

In the year 1188/1774, Aghasi Khan had come to Qarabagh and had joined with Nowsal Khan of Avar, who was the mortal foe of Fath 'Ali Khan, and captured the city of Shamakhi. Fath 'Ali Khan with many of his troops and from Daghestan along with Malek Mohammad Khan Baku'i came and was victorious in the battle and Aghasi Khan fled and Nowsal Khan took refuge in an inaccessible place above the city. Eventually Fath 'Ali Khan gave amnesty to Nowsal Khan who then came to him. When the three khans were seated in a place, the Aqusheh army gathered and demanded Fath 'Ali Khan's presence and because of the enmity that they bore Nowsal Khan they asked for his death. Then Fath 'Ali Khan per force ordered to tear the back of the tent and drag out Malek Mohammad Khan and killed Nowsal Khan with his retainers. Amir Hamzeh Usmi took the opportunity with Mohammad Khan, the Toothless Shamkhal and his son-in-law Mohammad Khan Ghazi-Qomuqi to make war on Fath 'Ali Khan. After this they came to Qobbeh and Aghasi Khan took Shirvan. There was a fierce war in Palaseh Gavdushan and the allied forces were about to be defeated when 'Ali Bey, the son of Usmi, with some courageous soldiers attacked the center of the army and victory was gained as a result of his bravery. Mohammad, the Toothless Shamkhal and Eldar Bey, the brother's son of Mohammad Khan, and Sheikh 'Ali Ma'sum were killed on both sides. Fath 'Ali Khan was defeated and did not think it wise to stay in Qobbeh and went to Saliyan and the Usmi took the body of the Shamkhal and from nearby Darband sent the news of Fath 'Ali Khan's death to Tuti Begeh and asked for the surrender of the fort. [Tuti] Begeh did not believe this and day and night she was attending to the defense of the fort. **[164]** Mohammad Khan took Qobbeh and the Usmi went to Baku. Since conquering the fort was not possible he plundered the herd of Malek Mohammad Khan and his properties and villages and returned. Fath 'Ali Khan sent Mirza Bey Bayat of Darband to the court of the empress Catherine II of Russia asking for protection. He himself secretly came from Shabaran and Moskur to Darband and after a while his supporters began gathering and after some time he left Qobbeh and returned to his land. The following year 1189/1775, some Russians led by general-major Medem came to help him and to punish Amir Hamzeh Usmi. Previously he had impris-

---

9. Bakikhanov mistakenly calls him the sister's son as he was his brother's son, while Amir Khan Ghazanesh was his sister's son, see Willem Floor, "Who were the Shamkhal and the Usmi." (forthcoming).

oned the famous Russian traveler Gmelin, caused his death and Medem was ordered to punish him.[10] The Usmi with some troops faced the Russian army at one *farsakh* from Bashli, but he was defeated and most of his men were killed. Fath 'Ali Khan's army burnt and plundered the villages of the Turkman and returned to Darband. Afterwards he put to flight the huge army of Mohammad Khan in the region of Kur and after skirmishing and subduing upper Tabarsaran he went to Qaluq. The inhabitants of that place being in forests and mountains prepared to fight and after having been defeated they came to obey him. The Russian army returned in that year to Kizliar. This help was the reason of the stability of Fath 'Ali Khan's authority and dominance. The Al-e Sarkar expressed friendship and became his supporters. Mohammad Sa'id Khan, who had been imprisoned in Darband for seven years, was freed and he, in the city of Aq Su, and Aghasi Khan, in Elvand, became the governors of Shirvan. At this time, Amir Hamzeh Usmi with 3,000 brave soldiers passed Darband, Qobbeh and Shirvan and went to Ardabil. After plundering throughout Qarabagh he came to Ganjeh and started plundering in a manner worse than at Ardabil and via Sheki, Akhti and Kur he returned to his land with much booty. The emirs of the God-protected lands did not dare to oppose him and by sending some presents they wanted to get rid of him. Fath 'Ali Khan brought Mohammad Khan Bey, the brother's son of the abovementioned Usmi, to his side, who was known for his valor and took 100 families from Qobbeh and constructed a fort at three *farsakh* from Darband. He tried to thwart the activities of the Usmi by different means. Besides, although in the interests of the emirs and notables of Daghestan, everyday he was becoming more inclined to Fath 'Ali Khan and the Usmi could not undertake any major activity. Therefore, out of necessity, he came asking for peace and truce. Shah Mardan Bey, because of enmity that he had for his brother Sorkhay, who had been born to another mother and who also was at odds with his father, expressed loyalty and devotion to Fath 'Ali Khan, who gave him the governorship of the lower part of Kur, which belongs to the village of Qaberek, the other side belongs to Darband and the district of Guney which belongs to Qobbeh. The Qorah district was a separate community that he held himself. **[165]** Because Mohammad Khan did not have the power to oppose this he went along with it.

The Amireh of Tabarsaran had died. 'Ali Qoli b. Sayel b. Mirza pretending friendship with the mute Ma'sum and with the help of Rostam Qadi killed him and his sons and became Ma'sum himself. Mohammad Hoseyn Bey, Sohrab Bey, Chamghal Bey and Mostafa Bey, sons of Sheikh 'Ali Ma'sum his brother, who was killed in the battle of Gavdushan in the service of Fath 'Ali Khan, went to Qobbeh. Fath 'Ali Khan, after a while, called 'Ali Qoli Ma'sum to Darband and imprisoned him and sent him to Saliyan. He himself came with the army and made Mohammad Hoseyn Bey b. Sheikh 'Ali the Ma'sum in Cheragh, which was the seat of the previous Ma'sums. After him, his brother Sohrab Ma'sum, Shamkhal Ma'sum, and his son Qerkhlar Qoli Ma'sum successively became Ma'sums. Hoseyn Khan who had become independent governor of Sheki because of the trouble that had arisen with his uncle Ja'far Aqa killed him. He thus created enmity within his family. Hajji 'Abdol-Qader son of Hajji Chelebi with his followers turned away from

---

10. For the detailed events, see Gmelin, *Travels*, pp. xxiii-xxv, 301-03.

him and he settled in the place called Dorduqaz, adjacent to the river Kur, with the help of Ebrahim Khan. Hoseyn Khan went to fight him several times, but he returned without success. Then Soltan Qutqasheni, Hajji Aqa Qeshlaqi, and Hajji Rasul Bey, son of Hajji Sheikh 'Ali, who were followers of Hajji 'Abdol-Qader, imprisoned them. After a while Hajji Rasul fled and those two people were killed.

In this year of 1193/1778, the just emir and lover of arts Karim Khan *vakil*, who had tried his best to make his country prosper, had ruled Iran for 30 years and out of his humanity and consideration for the dignity of kingship he had been content with the title of *vakil*, went to the other world. Because of differences between the emirs, the Zand dynasty very soon was on the road of decline. The next year of 1194/1779, Hajji Abdol-Qader with the help of Rasul Bey, son of Hajji Sheikh 'Ali, and the son of his uncle Hajji Chelebi together with the landed gentry (*malek-zadegan*) of Arash and the notables of Sheki suddenly attacked the fort of Nokhuy, entered it and killed Hoseyn Khan, who had ruled for 22 years. Hoseyn Khan, in spite of being a virtuous, courageous, and good administrator and somebody who persevered, by nature was impatient and ruthless. Because of the dominance of Mohammad Hasan Khan Qajar in the Caspian provinces, Hedayatollah Khan of Gilan had been defeated and a plea for help came to Baku and then to Qobbeh. Fath 'Ali Khan sent 9,000 soldiers under the command of Mirza Bey Bayat via Saliyan [166] and Talesh and established him in his previous seat of governorship in Rasht. In the year 1196/1781, Hajji Malek Mohammad Khan, son of Hajji Mir Mohammad Khan of Baku, who was a religious emir, appointed his 11-year old son, Mirza Mohammad Khan II, governor of Baku under the tutelage of his maternal uncle Fath 'Ali Khan. While he was on pilgrimage at the holy sites of Iraq, he died in Najaf. At this time, Mohammad Sa'id Khan asked for the hand of Fatemeh, the sister of Fath 'Ali Khan, who had been betrothed to Abo'l-Fath Khan, the son of Karim Khan. His brother Aghasi Khan who considered Fath 'Ali Khan a claimant to the governorship of Shirvan was not happy with this wrote this line of Fozuli and sent it to him.

The mountain carver has carved his image on the mountain and deceived Shirin
See how ignorant he is that he makes a rival for himself out of stone

کوهکن شیرینه اوز نقشین چکوب ویرمیش فریب
گور نه جاهل در یونار طاشدان اوزیچون بیر رقیب

Mohammad Sa'id Khan wrote in answer:

The mountain carver with one thousand chisels has carved the mountain
I have torn away one thousand mountains with one finger

کوهکن کند ایلمش مین تیشه نی بیر داغله
بن قوپاروب اتمیشم مین داغی بیر طرناغله

In short, because of marrying the sister of Fath 'Ali Khan, animosity and dissent came about between the brothers and in the year 1198/1784 Fath 'Ali Khan fought with Ebrahim Khan who was helping Aghasi Khan and destroyed Aqtam and plundered the lower district of Qarabagh. Hajji 'Abdol-Qader Khan also was with the army of Sheki. Therefore, Ebrahim Khan released Mohammad Hasan Aqa b. Hoseyn Khan, who, when his father was killed, had escaped to Qarabagh and had been imprisoned in secret, and sent him to Jar. With the help of the Lezgis of that place he came to Sheki; the first time he was defeated and the second time he was victorious. Hajji 'Abdol-Qader Khan fled to Alvand to Aghasi Khan, and Aghasi Khan seized him and gave him to Mohammad Hasan Khan, who was in pursuit and asking for him, and who killed him with his seven sons. They say that he was a brave emir, but concerning the poll-tax he was oppressive. [**167**]

In the year 1199/1785, Fath 'Ali Khan had gone to Shirvan to fight Aghasi Khan and his ally Mohammad Hasan Khan. Mehr 'Ali Bey had turned away from Ebrahim Khan of Qarabagh and when he was staying with Fath 'Ali Khan one night on the way to Shirvan he happened to meet Ahmad Bey, the elder son of Aghasi Khan and they fought. Mehr 'Ali Bey was killed. Fath 'Ali Khan sent his body with great respect to Qarabagh, and because of this Ebrahim Khan became a friend of Fath 'Ali Khan. From both sides troops were mobilized and Aghasi Khan was forced to go to Fath 'Ali Khan with his sons and they were imprisoned and sent to Qobbeh. After that Fath 'Ali Khan went to Sheki. Mohammad Hasan Khan who had been defeated in battle gave his sister to Fath 'Ali Khan and made peace. Fath 'Ali Khan also in order to strengthen his alliance gave his sister Huri Peykar Khanom in marriage to him. In this year Morteza 'Ali Shamkhal died, who was a courageous and well-mannered emir, but without dignity and a detestable hatemonger. His brother Mohammad became Shamkhal.

In the year 1201/1787, Fath 'Ali Khan asked for the hand of Keychi Begeh, daughter of Mohammad Shamkhal for his son Ahmad Aqa, who was born to the sister of the Usmi and with much pomp, ceremony, dowry and festivities they brought her to Darband. It was in that year that Amir Hamzeh Usmi died and his brother Ustar Khan took his place. Mohammad Sa'id Khan was afraid, because of the capture of his brother and in secret was trying to restore what had been lost. Fath 'Ali Khan pretending as he if would give the governorship to Aghasi Khan and two of his elder sons, Ahmad Bey and Mohammad Bey, brought them to the village of Qunaq kend in Qobbeh. Mohammad Sa'id Khan went to Qasani and from there to Qobbeh. Mohammad Reza Bey, who was the brother-in-law of Fath 'Ali Khan, rushed to welcome him. Fath 'Ali Khan sent Aghasi Khan and his sons to Baku and he himself came to the city of Aq Su. Nominally he gave the governorship to Mohammad Reza Khan, but he himself remained in control. He sent someone to Mohammad Hasan Khan asking for Mohammad Sa'id Khan with his sons and Mostafa Bey, son of Aghasi Khan. Since Mohammad Sa'id Khan found the situation contrary to his liking, he, perforce, came to Fath 'Ali Khan, who sent him with two of his sons, Mahmud Bey and Eskandar Bey, to Saliyan, and Mohammad Reza Khan to Qobbeh, where they were imprisoned. 'Askar Bey and Qasem Bey, sons of Mohammad Sa'id Khan and Mostafa Bey, son of Aghasi Khan, had fled to Qarabagh because of this event. Shehab al-Din Soltan, brother's son of 'Ali Arashi at the order of Mohammad Hasan Khan misled and seized them. Mohammad Hasan Khan sent them shackled with the envoy [168] of Fath 'Ali Khan, Mohammad Karim Bey b. Hajji Safar 'Ali Bey and with Hajji Sayyed Bey his own confidante to Shirvan. It so happened on the banks of the Gokchay at the border of Sheki and Shirvan that one of the followers of the Al-e Sarkar disclosed the false news that Fath 'Ali Khan had crucified and imprisoned the merchants of Sheki and that he was preparing for war. Hajji Sayyed Bey released the princes of Shirvan and put Mohammad Karim Bey in chains and returned. These three fled to Jar and from there to Avar and brought 'Omma Khan, the brother's son and son-in-law of Nowsal Khan to Shirvan asking him to revenge their uncles. Fath 'Ali Khan who had not mobilized his army was besieged for nine months in Aq Su. Eventually Fath 'Ali Khan gave his daughter Pari Jahan Khanom as well as the district of Saliyan as blood-money for the uncles to 'Omma Khan and made peace.

'Omma Khan went to Avar and the nobles (*khanzadegan*) of Shirvan to Qarabagh and from there they went to Akhalkalak in the Ottoman lands. At that time Morteza Qoli Khan Qajar turned away from his brother Aqa Mohammad Khan and came to Baku, and he had come two months prior to the siege of Shirvan. In the defense of the fort he gave Fath 'Ali Khan much help and, after the siege had ended, he went to the court of the empress of Russia to ask for help. In the year 1202/1788, the prisoners of the Al-e Sarkar were killed, viz. Mohammad Sa'id Khan, who was an emir pure of heart and mercurial, with two sons in Saliyan and Aghasi Khan, who was brave but not trustworthy, with two sons in Baku, and Mohammad Reza Khan in Qobbeh. Two or three of the sons of Aghasi Khan were blinded. Mohammad Hasan Khan, because of the event with 'Omma Khan and at the instigation of the Shirvanis became emboldened and together with 'Ali Soltan Bey b. Mehdi Bey Jangutay suddenly went to the city of Aq Su. He was on the point of winning the war and some of his soldiers had even entered the city when Fath 'Ali Khan with his army invaded Qobbeh and Darband. From the other side, the Lezgis led by Mehdi Bey b. Mohammad Shamkhal, who were first hesitant, rushed to fight. Mohammad Hasan Khan was defeated and fled to Sheki. Through intercession of the aforementioned Mehdi Bey 'Ali Soltan Bey with his defeated army was allowed to return home via Qobbeh and Darband.

In this year Fath 'Ali Khan conquered Ardabil. The emirs of the Shahsevan and Hasan Khan Moghani submitted to him. Mir Mostafa Khan b. Qara Khan, first imprisoned in Qobbeh and after that under his protection governed in Talesh as well as Hedayat Khan who governed in Gilan. Only Ebrahim Khan of Qarabagh, because of the inaccessibility of the place, was persisting in his enmity, but the lower districts were never at rest from his plundering and the Shamkhal, the Usmi and Ghazi Khan Qomuq were expressing devotion to him and the Khan of the Avars and Emir Mehdi Vali out of necessity [169] were getting along with him. The Ma'sum and the Qadi of Tabarsaran were obedient to him and most of the emirs, judges and the notables of Daghestan were in his service and apart from his private lands, including Qobbeh, Darband, and Saliyan, he had complete possession of the province of Shirvan and the under-age Khan of Baku was also under his tutelage. Because of the upheaval of Iran, most of the emirs of Azerbaijan, such as those of Qaradagh, Tabriz and others were hostile to Aqa Mohammad Khan Qajar and hoping to get protection became close to him.[11] Finally, Fath 'Ali Khan, who had the means of prosperity and independence, to set the affairs of the Azerbaijan, and perhaps of all of Iran, in order began discussions and consulations with Erekle Khan, the ruler of Georgia. Mohammad Hasan Khan regretting his actions sent his wife, who was Fath 'Ali Khan's sister, to get amnesty and forgiveness and he himself went to see Fath 'Ali Khan. The latter with much pomp and ceremony went to stay for a few days in the town of Nakhoy for relaxation. He spent a few days in festivities and then went to Ganjeh. Javad Khan, son of Shahverdi Khan Ziyad-oghlu Qajar, with a number of notables of the country came to welcome him at the banks of the river Kur and opened the doors of the fort to him. Fath 'Ali Khan took back the Shams al-Dinlu district, which Javad Khan had lost, from the ruler of Georgia and returned it to him. In short, the two great rulers met each other near Shamgir and hoping to get the support of the government of Russia exchanged ideas. While returning Fath 'Ali Khan was struck by a chronic fever, which increased day by day and therefore with great haste he went to Shirvan and from there to Baku to his sister. On the 22nd of March of the year 1203/1789, when he was 54 years old, he died. The signs of his wisdom and his stable governance were apparent in him. In gaining the hearts of people and deceiving the enemies he was very skillful.

Mohammad Khan Ghazi-Qomuqi who was a skillful emir, but short-tempered also died in this year. He was succeeded by his son Sorkhay Khan II. Ahmad Khan, the eldest son of Fath 'Ali Khan, came to power; he was young, full of pride and negligent of the affairs of the country, but one year later, Mohammad Hasan Khan, out of all the hatred that he felt, began confronting the people of Shirvan and he called to him 'Askar Bey, Qasem Bey and Mostafa Bey, who had come from the Ottoman lands, and they came with Manaf Bey, son of Haji Mohammad 'Ali Khan to fight Shirvan. [170] Ahmad Khan did not consider it opportune to oppose them and went to Qobbeh. He appointed the Al-e Sarkar among the tribes and Manaf Khan to the governorship of the city of Aq Su and after getting much money from merchants and the like, after a stay of a few days, he returned to Sheki. After one week the Al-e Sarkar came and took the city and Manaf Khan who was weak and without wisdom was killed. 'Askar Khan, son of Mohammad Sa'id Khan, who was older than the others was appointed as governor. Mostafa Bey went to Alvand and took position in the retrenchment of Qatran.

In the year 1205/1791, there was resentment between Ahmad Khan and Mirza Mohammad Khan II of Baku. Ahmad Khan instigated by Mohammad Qoli Aqa, son of Mirza Mohammad Khan I, who promised him the collection of the taxes (*kharaj*), under the pretext of going to Saliyan went with an army to Baku and Mohammad Qoli Aqa came in secret and with the help of his followers after a short fight seized the town and sent Mirza Mohammad Khan to Qobbeh. Mohammad Qoli Khan became independent ruler and did not pay taxes to Ahmad Khan, who regretted what he had done and sent an

---

11. The editor of the Tehran edition has read the word *khosusiyat* as *khosumiyat*, which does not make sense, as the term already occurs earlier in the same sentence and is not in harmony with the purport of this paragraph.

army to Baku to help Mirza Mohammad Khan. Mohammad Qoli Khan out of necessity ordered the people to plunder the properties that had been gathered in the house of Mirza Mohammad Khan during the time of Nader Shah. In this way most of the people became frightened of Mirza Mohammad Khan and became followers of Mohammad Qoli Khan. Mirza Mohammad Khan out of necessity after laying siege and many fights returned to Qobbeh. Mohammad Hasan Khan, who, because of the killing of Manaf Khan, was against the Al-e Sarkar sent a messenger to Ahmad Khan and apologized and promised that he would help to conquer Shirvan. Ahmad Khan and Mohammad Hasan Khan from two sides came with their army as well as with the Lezgis of Daghestan. They surrounded the city of Aq Su. The siege lasted long and the weather was very hot. 'Askar Khan in secret sent 5,000 *tuman*s in cash and in kind to the Lezgis in the army camp of Mohammad Hasan Khan. Therefore, there was a conflict within the army and soon thereafter Ahmad Khan died and his 13-year old brother, Sheikh 'Ali Aqa, who was the deputy governor of Saliyan, came to Qobbeh to take over the governorship and sent his seven-year old brother, Hasan Aqa as the deputy-governor of Saliyan. Six months had passed of the governorship of 'Askar Khan, when, because of his weakness, the notables of Shirvan turned away from him and gathered around his brother Qasem Bey. 'Askar Khan was imprisoned for a while and then he fled to Sheki. Qasem Khan attacked the redoubt of Mostafa Bey at Alvand, but he was defeated and returned. Since he was very particular about details and would not make any difference between the poor and rich the Shirvanis became displeased with him and he considered them to be against him. By sending some presents to Shahbaz Bey, son of Mohammad Shamkhal, he brought him with some Lezgis and put him in charge of the people imagining that this would bring stability and prosperity to the government. Until the year 1206/1792, at the request of the people of Shirvan, especially by Yuzbashi Bey Howzi and 'Omar Soltan Sa'dari, Mostafa Bey [171] came from Alvand and raised his standard over the city, and Qasem Khan with a group of his followers went to Qabaleh and Qobbeh. In that year Ustar Khan Usmi died, 'Ali Bey b. Amir Hamzeh Usmi became the Usmi. Mohammad Hasan Khan Baku'i who was a cruel and stone-hearted emir also died. His brother's son, Hoseyn Qoli Aqa, son of Hajji 'Ali Qoli Aqa with the help of some of the Beys such as his cousin and son-in-law Qasem Bey b. Mansur Khan Bey and other followers became governor. Mirza Mohammad Khan with an army came to Qobbeh; with the army of Qobbeh he again came to Baku. Hoseyn Qoli Khan in the city and Mirza Mohammad Khan in the villages were sometimes at war and some times at peace. They were divided the country and the mines [between them]. At this time Mostafa Khan came to the banks of the Gok Chay and Sorkhay Khan came to Ghachmaz and caused turmoil in the three districts of Qabaleh. Shehab al-Din Soltan Arashi also brought an army of Qarabaghis and he started scheming against Mohammad Hasan Khan. But the aforementioned Khan due to a courageous defense slowly forced Sorkhay Khan, Mostafa Khan and the Qarabaghis to return. With wise counsels he tried to make the country peaceful. The same Shehab al-Din Soltan, because of the strength of the fort and the help of the neighboring emirs, persisted in his opposition and would not leave the districts of Arash and Aghtash at peace. Mohammad Hasan Khan invaded many times but did not succeed. Finally, the aforementioned soltan showing his obedience and asking permission to go on the *hajj* came to Mohammad Hasan Khan, but he was killed with many of his sons. In the year 1208/1794, Mohammad Hasan Khan and Sheikh 'Ali Khan with a view to help Qasem Khan came to Aq Su. After laying siege for a few months, on a certain day, when, because of the heavy rain and the floods the situation of the army was very perturbed, the besieged led by 'Omar Soltan Sardari attacked and broke the siege. Sheikh 'Ali Khan and Mohammad Hasan Khan returned to their lands. Qasem Khan in the mountains of Qaraborqa between Qobbeh and Sheki made a place of residence for himself there. In the year 1209/1795, the brave and noble emir 'Ali Bey died and Rostam Khan known as Mamay b. Soltan b. Khan Mohammad b. Ahmad Khan Usmi became the emir. Because Mirza Mohammad Khan II was a sufi-type and ease-seeking emir and mostly neglectful of the affairs of the country. Hoseyn Qoli Khan came one night with the help of the Shirvani army and took the fort of Ba'lkhani, where there is an oil well, which the old writers called 'Ameliyan. At that time it was the center of government of Mohammad Khan. He went again to Qobbeh.

At that time when the southern Caucasus was the scene of disturbances and revolts the rule of Iran had come into the hands of the great Qajar dynasty. Aqa Mohammad Khan marched to conquer these regions. Briefly, the tribe of the Qajars comes from the Jalayer Turks who were brought by Hulagu Khan to Turkestan. 'Abdol-Razzaq Bey in the *Ma'ather-e Soltaniyeh*[12][**172**] says that a certain Sartaq, one of the leaders of this tribe, at the order of Aqaba Khan, became the Atabeyk of Argun Khan and he was the *amir al-omara* in Khorasan and in Tabarestan. He had a son whose name was Qajar and most of the people from this tribe are from his lineage. Many of them had gone to Anatolia and Syria over time. Mir Timur moved 50,000 families of them to the regions of Erevan, Ganjeh and Qarabagh. Gradually their number and power increased. Many of the Qajar emirs in the time of the Safavids were important officials and in Armenia and Shirvan they were powerful. The governors of Erevan were of this lineage; the governors of Ganjeh and Qarabagh were known as the Ziyad-oghlu Qajars; who were governing regions from the Khoda-Afarin bridge until the village of Sholaver in Georgia above the Sunaq bridge. Since they did not vote in the big assembly in Moghan for the rule of Nader Shah, because they wanted to re-establish the Safavid government, Nader Shah after gaining the throne tried to break their power and authority and he moved most of the people of Qarabagh to Khorasan and he took away the districts of Bargoshad and Khamseh and entrusted them to the governor of Azerbaijan. The [inhabitants] of the Qazzaq districts, who Hulagu Khan had taken from Turkestan, and the [inhabitants] of the district of Buzchalu, who Shah 'Abbas I had taken from Buzjalu in Persian Iraq, had been forced to settle at the border of Georgia and Nader had put them under the authority of the *vali* of Georgia. Therefore the aforementioned khans had become very weak and their authority was limited to the governorship of Ganjeh.

In the year 1218/1804, the Russian general Prince Tsitsianov attacked Ganjeh and conquered it. Javad Khan b. Shahverdi Khan Ziyad-oghlu with most of the inhabitants of

---

12. 'Abdol-Razzaq Maftun Donboli, *Ma'ather al-Soltaniyeh* ed. Gholam Hoseyn Sadri Afshar (Tehran, 1351/1972).

Ganjeh were killed. Today a few of his lineage are still in Ganjeh; the remaining ones are in Iran. Many of the people and the *mirs* of Erevan, Ganjeh and Qarabagh are from the Qajar lineage and most of the time they were living pleasantly in the country of Shirvan and governing it. The people of Daghestan even now call the people of this place Qajars. Shah ʿAbbas I moved 30,000 Qajar families from these parts and moved them to the region of Marv in Khorasan and Fort Mobarakabad in Astarabad. The present dynasty of Iran is from the lineage of the Astarabad Qajars. Although the author of the *Maʾather-e Soltaniyeh* considers this lineage to be of the old Qajar inhabitants of Astarabad, however, [173] the presence of their ancestors is known among the people of Shamgir in Ganjeh and on the left bank of the river below the ruins of the city of Shamgir the place of their *yurt* as well as of their houses, platforms, and plane trees still can be seen, and it is known as Mehdi Beylu.

In the court of Shah Tahmasp II, Fath ʿAli Khan of this lineage was so powerful and influential that Nader Shah after becoming close to the king turned the king away from him so that in the year 1139/1726 he was done away with. He had two sons, one Mohammad Hasan Khan, who in the time of Nader Shah rebelled in the region of Astarabad and was defeated and lived in the Turkman steppe. After the murder of Nader Shah he occupied Tabarestan, Persian Iraq and Azerbaijan and he received the title of *sardar*. He struck coins and the *khotbeh* was read in his name. He fought many battles with Azad Khan and Karim Khan *vakil*. Eventually, in the year 1172/1759, he was killed by one of his servants. His younger brother Mohammad Hoseyn Khan had two sons. One, Aqa Mohammad Khan and the other, Hoseyn Qoli Khan, who were both kept by Karim Khan at his court as hostages. After the death of the great emir, Aqa Mohammad Khan went to Astarabad and he gradually increased in power and royal authority. He conquered the Zands and gradually the provinces of Persian Iraq, Fars, Tabarestan, Gilan and Azerbaijan. In the year 1209/1795 he went to take Qarabagh. He repaired the Khoda-Afarin bridge, which had been destroyed by Ebrahim Khan of Qarabagh to prevent the passage of the Iranian army and went to the Panabad castle, which is known as Shushi. He dismounted at the stage of Tupkhaneh and laid siege to the castle. After almost one month he went to Georgia and after killing, plundering and destroying Tiflis he returned and in a place called Chehel Nam in the Moghan made his winter quarters. The governors of Shirvan, Baku, Sheki, Qobbeh and Darband by sending letters and gifts expressed their obedience. Mohammad Hasan Khan b. Hoseyn Khan, the governor of Sheki, on account of bad-mouthing Mostafa Khan b. Aghasi Khan sent his confidante Hajji Sayyed Bey to Aqa Mohammad Khan. But this person, bad-mouthed Mohammad Hasan Khan himself and he sent Mostafa Khan Develu Qajar, who was the general, to punish [174] Mostafa Khan. Mohammad Hasan Khan with the army of Sheki outwardly supported him. Mostafa Khan of Shirvan gathered the tribe of Khan Chubani and gave orders to move [the people of] the town Aq Su to Mount Fet.[13] The people there, due to scarcity of life necessities and the severe cold, died and perished and some went to live in Fet and some of them went to Qobbeh and Darband. The *sardar* came and whatever was left in

---

13. Mount Fet is situated near the village of Lagich.

the city he plundered. From there he went to Aghdash and from there to the district of Ghachmaz. He was in the village of Terkesh where 8 months earlier Salim Aqa, the elder brother of Mohammad Hasan Aqa had fled and from there to Jar and he, with the inhabitants of that place and with the army of the Avars, led by 'Ali Eskander, father of Hamzeh Bey of Hezati, came to conquer Sheki and defeated Mohammad Hasan Khan and moved the town to Gelesen Goresen. He killed the seven sons of Mohammad Hasan Khan; one of them was the sister's son of Fath 'Ali Khan, who were in Qobbeh. He gave his sister to Ebrahim Khan of Qarabagh and took his daughter in marriage. Mohammad Hasan Khan hoping for help came to the *sardar*. But contrary to his expectations, in accordance with an order that had been issued earlier by Aqa Mohammad Khan, as a result of complaints by the people of Sheki and bad-mouthing by Hajji Sayyed Bey concerning the blinding of Mohammad Hasan, he took out his eyes and sent him as a prisoner to Tabriz. To find out more about this matter Aqa Mohammad Khan summoned him. He with 200 to 300 people was on his way to the royal camp when a number of Shirvanis encountered them and killed him. At this moment the news of the arrival of the Russian army came. The governor of Qobbeh, Darband and Saliyan, Sheikh 'Ali Khan sent Khedhr Bey, son of Hajji Bey Qurchi of Darband and asked for help from Aqa Mohammad Khan. But his army suffered from a shortage of provisions, a scarcity of horses and the severity of the winter and was in great distress and he did not consider it wise to fight the Russians. To conquer Khorasan he went to Tehran. The Russian army entered Shirvan.

The details of these events are that after the signing of the treaty of peace with Nader Shah the rules of friendship between Russia and Iran had always been respected. The Empress Anna, daughter of Ivan died on October 1152/1740 [**175**] and the two-month's old baby Ivan III,[14] the son of the daughter of the brother of Peter the Great, became emperor. His mother Anna became the regent. After seven months, Elisabeth, daughter of Peter, rebelled against them and with the help of special regiments acceded to the throne and imprisoned Anna with her son and husband. She ruled the country for more than 20 years with a view to develop the country and people's prosperity. On 25th of November 1174/1761 she died. Her heir Peter III, son of Anna, daughter of Peter the

---

14. At this time Fath 'Ali Khan, son of Hoseyn 'Ali Khan, the governor of Qobbeh, Darband and Saliyan was defeated by Amir Hamzeh Khan Mohammad b. Ahmad Khan Usmi of the Qeytaq in the year 1188/1774 and also by Mohammad Khan b. Sorkhay, governor of Kur and Qazi-Qomuq. He therefore sent Mirza bey Bayat of Darband with a sincere petition to the court of the empress and asked for help. In 1775 a Russian army led by general-major de Medem came to help him and punish the Usmi who had imprisoned the famous traveler Gmelin in the year 1188/1774 and had made him despair of his life. The Usmi with others attacked the Russian army at one *farsakh* from Bashli. The Usmi was defeated and many of his troops were killed and he himself fled. Fath 'Ali Khan's army pillaged and burnt the Turkman villages and returned to Darband and after that they went to Mohammad Khan in the land of Kureh and they defeated him and killed many of fhis troops. From there to subdue the people of Tabarsaran they went to a place that is known as Qaluq. Because of the forest and mountains they were emboldened and wanted to fight. But after having been put to flight they came to Fath 'Ali Khan and Beyed for amnesty. In that year the Russian army returned to Kizliar and this help was the main reason for the establishment of the government of Fath 'Ali Khan and twenty years had passed from this incident that the empress … [B]

Great acceded to the throne. After six months, his wife Catherine II acceded to the throne and ruled the country wisely and by preparing for peace and war she increased the power of her government.[15]

After the death of Fath 'Ali Khan, who had kept the southern Caucasus at peace, the signs of revolt and disturbances appeared everywhere. Aqa Mohammad Khan Qajar who had become powerful in Iran intended to come and capture this land. He came to Georgia and started to kill and plunder. The empress, in the year 1210/1796, wanted to make war on Iran and a well-equipped army was sent under the leadership of Count Zubov.[16] General-major [176] Sobolev, who was obediently accompanied by Mohammad Khan Shamkhal, Rostam Khan Usmi and Rostam Qadi of Tabarsaran arrived at 8 *farsakh* from Darband and asked Sheikh 'Ali Khan, the governor of Qobbeh and Darband, who the previous year had indicated that he wanted to renew the special ties with Russia, to submit himself. He, contrary to expectations, expressed his opposition and the abovementioned general on the day of 11 February of this year reached the outskirts of Darband and started the siege from the northern side. This lasted some time. Sheikh 'Ali Khan and Sorkhay Khan, governor of Kur and Qazi-Qomuq with 20,000 soldiers, both horse and foot, wanted to attack the Russian army. The general considered the siege useless and withdrew on the second night of April and he struck camp at the mouth of the river Darvaq. At the end of April, Count Zubov, the Russian general camped at the bank of the Darvaq River with a large army. The next day he arrived at Darband and the cavalry of Qobbeh and Darband at the distance of one *farsakh* fought with the Cossacks and were defeated. They closed the gates and prepared for the defense. Major-General Bulgakov was assisted by Rostam Qadi of Tabarsaran to pass with 10,000 troops via a difficult road, full of trees and valleys between Darvaq and Tabarsaran. He arrived on the 3rd of May at the southern side of Darband. From the north, a big tower was attacked and conquered, which Sheikh 'Ali Khan had built. Many Darbandis were killed and the rest fled. The following day a bombardment of projectiles from guns, cannons and mortars was raining down on the city from two sides. The Darbandis could not stand this and Khedhr Bey b. Hajji Bey Qurchi was sent as an envoy asking for clemency from the general. He accepted and Sheikh 'Ali Khan and the notables of Darband were summoned and with some other people were imprisoned in the camp. After six days Pari Jahan Khanom, the daughter of Fath 'Ali Khan was appointed as caretaker of Darband and Qobbeh. Ten of the people of Darband at the instigation of Khedhr [177] Bey were sent to Astrakhan. General-major Sobolev was charged with the protection of Darband and went to Qobbeh where he stayed

---

15. On the various Russian campaigns leading to the conquest of the Caucasus see, inter alia, John F. Baddeley, *Russian Conquest of the Caucasus* (Mansfield Centre, CT, 2006); George A. Bournoutian (translator and annotator), *Russia and the Armenians of Transcaucasia, 1797-1889: a documentary record* (Costa Mesa, 1998); Ibid., *Armenians and Russia, 1626-1796 : a documentary record* (Costa Mesa, 2001); Ibid., *Two chronicles on the history of Karabagh : Mirza Jamal Javanshir's Tarikh-e Karabagh and Mirza Adigo zal Bey's Karabagh-name* (Costa Mesa, 2004), and Anonymous, *The Dynasty of the Kajars* (New York, 1973).

16. Count Valerian Zubov was in charge of the Russian campaign against Persia during 1796-97; he was 24 years of age at that time and owed his appointment to that fact that his brother Count Platon Zubov was Catherine II's favorite.

for three days in Tepeh Lar at half a *farsakh* of Qobbeh and then came to Shabaran. One day, during the march in the Perreh-ye Khalil plain Sheikh 'Ali Khan under the pretext of horse racing fled from the army. Because of this incident the city of Qobbeh started to revolt. His court, equipment and family joined him in the district of Boduq. Count Zubov sent general Bulgakov with 5,000 soldiers to pacify the people of Qobbeh and the people returned to their city and their villages. Sheikh 'Ali Khan went to Qariz and from there via Qabaleh to Akhti and Maskanjeh. The Russian general went to Baku and Hoseyn Qoli Khan, the governor of that place rushed to welcome him and was well received. A group of soldiers were appointed to guard the city. When the general wanted to go to Shirvan Mostafa Khan, the governor of that place rebelled and moved the [people of the] town of Aq Su to Mount Fet. Since the previous governor of Shirvan, Qasem Khan, came down from the mountain of Qara Burqa with the help of Yuzbashi, son Safar 'Ali Bey Howzi, Mostafa Khan fled and went to Qarabagh. Although Ebrahim Khan was not happy about this, his son Mohammad Hasan Khan protected him. Qasem Khan gathered the notables of the province and came to the banks of the Kur River to submit to the Russian general. In exchange for this service he became governor of Shirvan. Pari Jahan Khanom, at the order of the general, took her elder brother Hasan Aqa, who had gone to his mother's people at Ilisu, to Qobbeh and sent him with the notables of Darband to the general. At the orders of the empress the studded aigrette and the governorship of Qobbeh was given to him and he returned. At this time Sheikh 'Ali Khan with the help of Sorkhay Khan with 10,000 soldiers had come to the village of Alpan, which is at half a *farsakh* from the city of Qobbeh. Bulgakov sent 1,000 soldiers and several cannons and there was a fierce battle and many people on both sides were killed, because of the difficulty of the terrain and the Russians returned and the following day they went with a larger group, destroyed Alpan and returned. General Bulgakov, accompanied by Hasan Khan from Qobbeh and Sobolev [178] together with Rostam Khan the Usmi and Mehdi Khan, son of Mohammad the Shamkhal and Rostam Qadi from Darband intending to punish Sorkhay Khan, came to the river Samur. Sorkhay Khan had no choice, but to ask for amnesty and swore that he would sincerely obey the Russian government. Count Zubov chose his winter quarters on the banks of the Kur. He sent a regiment to Ganjeh and the governor there, Javad Khan Ziyad-oghlu, came in obedience and surrendered the fort. Ebrahim Khan of Qarabagh and Salim Khan of Sheki sent letters expressing their sincere devotion. On the day of the 9th of November of this year the empress Catherine II died and her son Paul I, son of Peter II acceded to the throne. To settle the affairs of the country and bring about changes in foreign and domestic policies he stopped the war with Iran and ordered his army to return.

In the spring of the year 1211/1797, the dismissed general Count Zubov, who was accompanied by Morteza Qoli Khan Qajar, who had fled from his brother Aqa Mohammad Khan and first had gone to Fath 'Ali Khan in Qobbeh and after his death, in the year 1203/1788, had taken refuge with the government of Russia, and had joined this campaign to make a bid for the kingship of Iran, from Baku went by ship to Astrakhan and general Bulgakov with his entire army went via Daghestan to Kizliar. Pari Jahan Khanom chose Mehdi Bey, son of Mohammad Shamkhal, who had become Shamkhal after his father, as her husband. He took with him all the properties and treasures of the family of Fath 'Ali Khan, which had been collected during many centuries. He deprived the other heirs of them. He gave his sister Chamnaz Khanom in marriage to 'Abdollah, son of Rostam Bey Qadi without permission of Sheikh 'Ali Khan. Hasan Khan went to Qeytaq, Rostam Khan the Usmi married his mother, Hurizad Khanom, who was from the family of the emirs of Ilisu. The Russian army was in the Kaferi plain when Sheikh 'Ali Khan of Qazi-Qomuq entered Darband. Because Javad Khan of Ganjeh in spite of his many virtues and good characteristics was a ruthless emir and a dare-devil the people of country were dissatisfied with him and the neighboring emirs wanted to get rid of him. The Russians, when they were leaving, gave the lands of Ganjeh to Erekle Khan, *vali* of Georgia. Ebrahim Khan of Qarabagh and [179] Selim Khan of Sheki came with an army before the city of Ganjeh. They appointed as regent, on behalf of the *vali*, 'Ali Soltan Shamsh al-Dinlu. Javad Khan had no choice but to flee, but his wife Shekufeh Khanom sent some people to 'Ali Soltan as a welcoming gesture and reminded him that previously she had freed him from the Javad Khan's prison and torture of 'Ali Soltan out of loyalty and humanity that was part of his nature came to Javad Khan and with sincerity and respect gave him the key of the fort and was at his service. Because of this event, the people of Ganjeh showed their previous obedience and these khans returned to their lands.

From the other side Aqa Mohammad Khan, after entering Tehran in the year 1210/1796, crowned himself and then went to Khorasan. He easily conquered the city of Mashhad and Shahrokh Mirza, after having given Nader's treasures, went to the next world. His son Nader Mirza fled to Qandahar and took refuge with the sons of Timur Shah of the Afghans. The following year the royal army intended to conquer the fort of Shushi and Shirvan province and with 100,000 troops it left immediately after crossing the river Aras. Ebrahim Khan fled to the region of Jar; the fort of Shushi was conquered without resistance and problems. He submitted to 'Ali Qoli Khan, the general who was appointed to Shirvan. Qasem Khan, although he showed outward obedience, but since Mostafa Khan had gone to the shah from the redoubt of Qatran, where he had come from Qarabagh after the retreat of the Russians, fled in panic to Sheki and abandoned Shirvan. Javad Khan of Ganjeh and Hoseyn Qoli, Khan of Baku also came to the royal presence and they were rebuked. The end of the affair of each of the three persons is unknown. On the 12th of June of the year 1211/1797 at sun rise two or three servants who were afraid of the cruelty and bloodshed of the king killed him. Several of the emirs on guard-duty and others took whatever they could in jewelry and valuables and fled to Tehran. The big army camp further down gathered around Sadeq Khan Shaqqaqi who was one of the most trusted court emirs and to whom the murderers had taken the sword, dagger, arm-bands and the treasury-box of the king. After the conquest of Azerbaijan he turned to Qazvin, but he could not get into the city and in the battle with [180] Fath 'Ali Shah b. Hoseyn Qoli Khan, heir-apparent and brother's son of the murdered king, he was defeated and returned to Sarab. Fath 'Ali Shah came to Zanjan. He sent Hajji Ebrahim Khan Shirazi to Sadeq Khan asking for his submission and the surrender of the royal insignia. He returned all of them with a letter of apology and was forgiven and became the governor of Sarab and Garmrud.

After the murder of Aqa Mohammad Shah, Mohammad Bey b. Mehr 'Ali Bey b. Panah Khan for a few days claimed kingship, but as soon as Ebrahim Khan fled to Sheki Mohammad Hasan Khan, the governor of Sheki imprisoned him and sent him to Mostafa Khan of Shirvan. He killed him to revenge his father and brothers whom he had killed in Baku at the order of Fath 'Ali Khan of Qobbeh. Ebrahim Khan sent the body of the king accompanied by olama and proper ceremonies with a letter expressing devotion to the new king, which was gracefully accepted. He sent his son Abu'l-Fath Aqa to attend to the king. When he was returning from Shushi to Shirvan, Mostafa Khan took the blinded Mohammad Hasan Khan, whom the king had brought from Tabriz and who was in the Moghan steppe, with him, conquered Shirvan and from there he went to Sheki. Salim Khan fled to Qarabagh and Mohammad Hasan Khan again became governor. Mirza Mohammad Khan, as soon as the news of the killing of the king arrived, marched from Qobbeh to conquer Baku. Hoseyn Qoli Khan who had arrived before him prepared the fort for defense. Eventually peace was restored in the kingdom and again they divided the land between them. Hoseyn Qoli Khan remained in the city, Mirza Mohammad Khan in the village of Mashqata'. They repaired the fort and governed. After some time Ja'far Qoli Khan Donboli, one of the confidantes of the king, who was honored with the governorship of Khoy and Tabriz, because of old hatred that he had for Sadeq Khan destroyed Sarab on a pretext and he made it like a mirage. Sadeq Khan fled via Moghan to Shirvan to Mostafa Khan. After some time, when Ja'far Qoli Khan rebelled, Sadeq Khan returned from Shirvan to Sarab and in his company were several other emirs who started to rebel. As soon as Ja'far Qoli Khan was shown to be an absolute traitor he came to the royal court. He was kept in a bare room and because of hunger he despaired of his life. Ja'far Qoli Khan went to Khoy and his brother Hoseyn Khan slammed the door in his face. For a while he was wandering about. After the death of his brother he took Khoy and after a while 'Abbas Mirza, the dearest of the shah's sons, who was sent to put the affairs of Azerbaijan in order, defeated him and he went to Maku and from there [181] to Chamlibel[17] of Koroghli on the borders of Turkey and he settled there. Because after the arrival of Hasan Khan in Qobbeh, during the Russian campaign, Mohammad Khan, the brother's son of Ebrahim Khan of Rudbar, had taken Saliyan and expelled Mir Qobad Soltan b. Mir Kalb'Ali Soltan the deputy in the year 1213/1799, the same year that there was a plague in the land of Shirvan and especially in the city of Aq Su many people had perished, the army of Qobbeh with Russian boats had gone to Saliyan and captured it. Sheikh 'Ali Khan went there with 4,000 Lezgis and in the month of Ramazan behaved very cruelly and committed sins at the instigation of his confidantes. After his return, Mostafa Khan of Shirvan with the help of the emirs of Rudbar and at the suggestion of the people of Saliyan went and took that place and moved the town four *farsakh* higher in a place that still exists and built a [new] town. He gave the governorship to 'Ali Khan b. Ebrahim Khan. After a while, in the spirit of equal partnership he left it to 'Ali Khan and his cousin Mohammad Khan. But 'Ali Khan very soon

---

17. The name of this mountain is also written Chanlibel, meaning 'misty mountain'.

imprisoned Mohammad Khan and tried to get help from Mostafa Khan of Talesh. From the other side Sheikh 'Ali Khan after returning from Saliyan became very sick in Darband. Sorkhay Khan Ghazi-Qomuqi one night in secret sent his own son Nuh Bey under the name of Hasan Khan to the fort of Qobbeh and seized it and he himself camped in the village of Qollar of Qobbeh and acted there as governor for one and a half month. Sheikh 'Ali Khan brought an army of 10,000 men from the Shamkhal and the Aqusheh Quy-suy-buy districts. After the expulsion of Sorkhay Khan from Qobbeh, he went to Kureh and a big battle took place and Sorkhay Khan was defeated. That whole region was plundered until the village of Cheragh. From there he returned and he gave the Lezgis six months of festivities in Qobbeh. He committed many evil deeds by his demands, even going so far as demanding rent for the teeth of the people of Qobbeh and Sheikh 'Ali Khan paid the fixed pensions of 8,000 people from the taxes of Qobbeh. He brought 2,000 Lezgis to Darband whom he also paid from the revenues there. These two days that the festivities were given at the expense of Darband led to a general uprising. People were dissatisfied with Sheikh 'Ali Khan, who, because of his hedonism, did not know what to do. Mirza Mohammad Khan II of Baku who had come to see Sheikh 'Ali Khan at that time went to the gathering of the Darbandis quieted them with the promise of expelling the Lezgis. Sheikh 'Ali Khan bore a grudge and went to Qobbeh. In the beginning of the year 1214/1800, the scarcity of wheat in Darband was very severe; 400 carts were sent from the land of the Shamkhal to transport wheat to Qobbeh. The Darbandis, by the use of force stopped them. This deed was against [182] the liking of Sheikh 'Ali Khan and it made him more depressed than before. The Darbandis instigated by Soltan Bey Bayat rioted and expelled Mohammad Hasan Bey, son of Ahmad Bey Bayat, who was deputy governor of Darband. Sheikh 'Ali Khan came to Darband and found Soltan Bey with a large group of supporters. He had no choice but to make Khan Begeh Khanom, his sister and the wife of Mirza Mohammad Khan II, the governor of Darband and made Soltan Bey her caretaker.

Soon after the return of Sheikh 'Ali Khan to Qobbeh, Sorkhay Khan II had brought Hasan Khan b. Fath 'Ali Khan by different means from Qeytaq to himself. After the agreement with the Darbandis, who had many differences among themselves, in the month of May of this year he was made the governor of Darband. One night Soltan Bey Bayat with Khedhr Bey Qurchi fought in the Khan's palace and a number of people were killed on both sides. Khedhr Bey was killed and Soltan Bey was wounded and fled. The following day at the order of the khan and in agreement with the general opinion of the Darbandis he was punished. After this event Sheikh 'Ali Khan asked for help from the khans of Shirvan, Sheki, Baku, Shamkhal and the people of Aqusheh. From both sides they laid siege to Darband. The Qadi of Tabarsaran was taking the side of the Darbandis. After a siege of 12 days Sheikh 'Ali Khan without succeeding in his purpose returned to Qobbeh. He fell ill and the news of his death was spread. Sorkhay Khan with an army came to the village of 'Aniq and defeated the army of Qobbeh that had come to oppose him. After having learnt Sheikh 'Ali Khan's fate he returned home. Afterwards he encouraged Hasan Khan to take the governorship of Qobbeh and suddenly with a huge army they came to the village of Zizik at one *farsakh* from the city of Qobbeh. Sheikh 'Ali Khan, although he had recovered somewhat, had not made any preparation for defense. His wife, Zeyb al-Nisa Begom, the daughter of Hajji Malek Mohammad, Khan of Baku, who at the time of the fleeing of the Russians had exchanged vows with Sorkhay Khan to be [respectively] like daughter and father [to each other], by preparing festivities and sending of messages of friendship induced Sorkhay Khan to return and Hasan Khan per force went to Darband. After a while, although Sheikh 'Ali Khan had recovered somewhat, he had no means of defense and, except for the city of Darband, Hasan Khan had control over no other place. At the end of this year Gorgin Khan, the *vali* of Georgia died. The notables of that country to be free from internal disturbances and also from foreign intervention sent representatives to the court of the emperor Paul I, son of Peter III of Russia and asked to join the Russian empire. The imperial edict indicating acceptance of this request was issued on the 18th of January of the year 1215/1801 and lieutenant-general [**183**] Knorring[18] was appointed governor of Georgia and a separate edict dated 23rd of that month was issued in his name to that effect. It stated that 'he should not be concerned with other conquests, unless people themselves ask for help, because having harmonious co-signers is better than having disrespectful subjects.' After that, on the 12th of March, emperor Paul suddenly died. His son Alexander I acceded to the throne and the affairs of the Caucasus continued to be managed in the same way.

As in the previous year, from the side of Hasan Khan of Darband, Hajji Taqi, and from the side of Sheikh 'Ali Khan of Qobbeh, 'Askar and from the side of Hoseyn Qoli Khan of Baku, Mirza Hadi Bey together with the envoys of Mostafa Khan Talesh and the emirs of Daghestan such as Mehdi Khan Shamkhal, Rostam Khan Usmi, 'Omma Khan Avari and Rostam Qadi of Tabarsaran went as envoys to the court of the emperor of Russia asking for help. The imperial edict was issued on 28th of August in the name of each of these emirs, stating that they should work together peacefully, and that Qobbeh belonged Sheikh 'Ali Khan and Darband to Hasan Khan in accordance with the division that they had made. Therefore, those two brothers met each other on the banks of the river Samur and renewed their ties of friendship and brotherhood. After two years of Alexander's reign had passed in this way the incorporation of Georgia into Russia became too expensive. Because the *vali* of Bash Achoq and the emirs of Mingrelia, from the time of Aleksei, son of Michael, the king of Russia, had been trying to open the door of friendship, requested this government's help, the Shamkhal of Tarku and the khans of Baku and Darband in the time of Peter the Great had been obedient to him and the khans of Shirvan, Sheki, Qarabagh and Ganjeh, in the time when Count Zubov had come, had asked for help. Again, by sending envoys, most of them were asking to become part of Russia. Emperor Alexander eventually entrusted this important task to General-in-chief Prince Tsitsianov,[19] who

---

18. Lieutenant-General Karl Fedorovich Knorring was appointed commander of the Caucasian Line in March 1799 and after the annexation of Georgia was appointed commander-in-chief. He was removed in 1802 after complaints from the Georgian royal family.

19. Prince and General Paul Dmitrievich Tsitsianov (1754 - 1806) was a member of the Russified-Georgian noble family Tsitshishvili. He served under Zubov, subsequently was retired under Paul I, but was reinstated by Alexander I who appointed him commander-in-chief in September 1802. He was extremely harsh in his treatment of peasants and

was originally Georgian, but who lived in Russia. This general made much effort to put the internal affairs in order, exercise justice, make foreign acquisitions and defeat the enemies. [184] In the year 1217/1803 Hasan Khan almost died of small-pox. The people of Darband appealed to Zeyb al-Nisa, the wife of Sheikh 'Ali Khan, who had come to see him and she gave them assurances on behalf of her husband. She sent a courier to Qobbeh to inform how matters stood. As soon as Hasan Khan died Sheikh 'Ali Khan came and after performing the mourning ceremony he left Emam Qoli Bey as deputy in Darband and returned to Qobbeh. At this time Hoseyn Qoli Khan of Baku with the help of Mostafa Khan of Shirvan took the fort of Mashqata' and Mirza Mohammad Khan fled to Qobbeh and by different means wanted to get his lands back. In that year 'Omma Khan Avari whose natural talent made him well-known during the last years of Fath 'Ali Khan began plundering neighboring parts, and several times he came to Georgia and conquered and plundered Kumesh-khaneh and went to Akhsaqeh and from there returned to Belkan and plundered places around Ganjeh. With the help of his son-in-law Ebrahim Khan of Qarabagh he captured Nakhjevan, but he was quickly put to flight and came to Qarabagh. Erekle Khan, *vali* of Georgia to keep his neighboring lands every year gave him 5,000 *manat* as a pension and wanted to get along with him. After his submission to the Russians in the previous year he was given 5,000 *manat* as a salary. He died in the region of Jar. Since he did not have a son or heir, his not noble-born (*jankeh*) brother Kebek asked for the governorship. He wanted to marry his wife, Kehli, daughter of Nowsal Khan. But she, in secret, conspired with Soltan Ahmad Bey, son of 'Ali Soltan Bey Jangutahi, the sister's son of 'Omma Khan who had married Pakhu Begeh, his daughter from another wife and one evening she deceived and killed Kebek and married Soltan Ahmad, who was the Khan of the Avars. Her elder brother Hasan Khan remained governor of Mehvali, his ancestral lands. The following year Tsitsianov had come to conquer Ganjeh, because Javad Khan, son of Shahverdi Khan Ziyadoghli, who was the worst enemy of Georgia, first had outwardly submitted himself to Russia and then to Iran, but then had plundered the merchants of Tiflis. Nasib Soltan Shamsh al-Dinlu, brother's son of 'Ali Soltan abovementioned, joined forces with him and Javad Khan gave battle outside the city. He was defeated and took refuge in the fort. In the morning of the Ramazan Festival, the 3rd of December, the end of the year 1218, they attacked the fort and Javad [185] Khan with a number of sons and many others were killed and Ganjeh was renamed Elisabethpol.

The Russian commander sent general-major Guliakov[20] to the Jar region. He was attacked by the enemy in difficult terrain, was defeated and killed. But the Lezgis of those parts had become so afraid that they immediately sent representatives to Tiflis and apologized and expressed their sincere friendship. The Emirs of Mingrelia and Abkhazia [also] came to submit themselves. Soleyman Khan, the *vali* of Bash Achoq came to submit him-

---

Moslems and was treacherously killed on 8 February 1806, under the walls of Baku. The rank general-in-chief, from the French *général en chef* and in Russian *генерáл-аншéф*, was the second in the military hierarchy and second in the grade in the so-called table of ranks.

20. Major-General Guliakov, commander of a brigade in the Caucasus under Tsitsianov, who sent him to conquer Jaro-Belakan in 1803.

self. The government of Iran became worried about these conquests. Alexander Mirza, the son of Erekle Khan, in the hope of getting the governorship of Georgia had gone to the government of Iran to create disturbances among the emirs and the people of Georgia and to reinforce his operation and the protection of Erevan and Qarabagh it entrusted him to 'Abbas Mirza. Mohammad Khan Qajar, the governor of Erevan who in secret had turned away from Iran sent most of the tribes of Erevan to Ottoman lands and took refuge with some of his people in the fort and asked Russia for help. Prince Tsitsianov left to conquer Erevan and near Uch Kelisa in a place call Qorkh Bulagh faced the army of 'Abbas Mirza that was four times bigger than the Russian army and defeated it. At this time, Mirza Shafi', the grand vizier went to the fort of Erevan and with various arguments brought Mohammad Khan back into the fold of Iran. The Russian general laid siege to the fort. The shah who himself had come to join the war returned without having achieved his goal. Because the siege lasted long and attacking the fort would achieve nothing as well as the scarcity of provisions and the high prevalence of deadly diseases all added to the difficulty. Out of necessity the Russian general returned to Georgia on the third of September of the year 1219/1805.

After this event, the Lezgis, the Ossetians and the Qabartis revolted and attacked Georgia at the instigation of Alexander Mirza. The road to Russia became blocked. Prince Tsitsianov with great bravery pacified them and opened the road to Russia. In that year the Russians came by sea to Rasht and without having achieved anything they returned to Baku and began to bombard it from two sides. Eventually the Russians landed and surrounded the city. A number of Iranian troops and Sheikh 'Ali Khan of Qobbeh and Nuh Bey, son of Sorkhay Khan II Ghazi-Qomuqi with their own people came to the assistance of Hoseyn Qoli Khan. The Russian army boarded the ships and went to Talesh. In this year Rostam [186] Khan the Usmi died. 'Ali Khan, son of Ustar Khan became Usmi which gave cause to resentment. Mostafa Khan brought Salim Khan from Qarabagh and went to Sheki. Mohammad Hasan Khan went to oppose them. Since he saw that the situation was not favorable to him he released his army and he himself came to Mostafa Khan and brought both brothers to Shirvan. He appointed his uncle' son, Sheikh 'Ali Bey as deputy-governor, but the people of that place revolted and Fath 'Ali Aqa, who was blinded by his brother Mohammad Hasan Khan early in his governorship, was made khan. After three months Mostafa Khan per force sent Salim Khan as governor to Sheki and took his daughter as wife. Mohammad Hasan Khan went to Qobbeh and Darband. From there he went to Jar and eventually he went to the Russians in Astrakhan. He was art-loving, caring for people, but zealous and bloodthirsty.

In the year 1220/1805, 'Abbas Mirza, the heir-apparent of the shah, was given the title of Na'eb al-Saltaneh (viceroy) and the governorship of Azerbaijan. He created a new army of soldiers and artillery and forts based on the European model. The Russian general on the banks of the river Korak met with Ebrahim Khalil Khan of Qarabagh. According to the treaty, he accepted to give every year 10,000 *ashrafi*s as tax as well as to incorporate his country into Russia and he took 500 soldiers for his protection into the Shushi fort. From the imperial Russian government he received the rank of lt. general and his sons Mohammad Hasan Aqa and Mehdi Qoli Aqa that of general-major, and Khanlar Aqa that of colonel. On the other hand, Nayeb al-Saltaneh intending to conquer Qarabagh sent Esma'il Bey Damghani and 'Ali Qoli Khan Shahsevan with 10,000 soldiers from the side of the Khoda-Afarin bridge. Mohammad Hasan Aqa with the Russian army opposed him and in the gardens of Jebra'illu fought with him. He returned to Shushi and the king himself came to the place called Takht-e Tavus of Qarabagh. Nayeb al-Saltaneh via Aq Ughlan and Chenaqchi came to the lower part 'Askaran. He fought with colonel Karakin [Koliagin] and others who were coming from Ganjeh to go to Shushi. The colonel returned to Fort Tarnavat at Shah Bulaghi. From there at the river Tartar he joined Prince Tsitsianov who with 2,000 soldiers was going to fight the shah.

Because of the news of the shah's return, the Russian general came to the fort of Shushi. Nayeb al-Saltaneh went to Ganjeh and the Russians of that place with some Armenians took refuge in the fort and he, in accordance with the request of the people of Ganjeh, moved them to Qazzaq via Hasan Suyi and he himself went to Tabriz. He stayed for a few days in the place called Akhstafeh. He wanted to induce the districts of Qazzaq, Buzjalu and Georgia to join him, but he did not succeed and returned to Erevan. The people of Qazzaq [Kazakh] [187] on the plain of Dilejan opposed him and started killing and plundering. Prince Tsitsianov came to Shirvan and after Mostafa Khan apparently submitted to him he went to Baku. The Russians from Sari joined him via the sea. 'Abdol-Rahim Aqa, brother of Mirza Mohammad Khan II, who had come from Qobbeh to Shirvan came to the general and was appointed to some post, although he said that Hoseyn Qoli Khan's sincerity and allegiance was to the Iranian government the general attributed his words to ill-intentions and did not accept them. Eventually, on the 2nd day of February 1220/1806, when outside the fort, conversing with Hoseyn Qoli Khan about his submission, in spite of the promise of non-violence, he was killed by Ebrahim Bey, son of 'Ali Bey Aqa, son of Mohammad Hoseyn Khan, son of Emam Qoli Khan Darbandi either at the instigation of the Persians or at the orders of Hoseyn Qoli Khan himself, who was the son of his aunt. His head was sent to the father of the killer and then was sent to the shah. The Russians boarded the ships and went to Sari. Because of his murder all the khans except for the Shamkhal of Tarkhu [Tarki] revolted. Mir Mostafa Khan of Talesh who was always afraid of the Iranians and wanted Russian protection after meeting with Mirza Bozorg Qa'em-Maqam received assurances and became an opponent of Russia. Mostafa Khan of Shirvan fought with Salim Khan who was leaning towards the Russians. In response to the request of Salim Khan some of the Russians of Ganjeh went to Sheki and Mostafa Khan wanted to oppose them, but he was defeated and returned. The *vali* of Bash Achoq himself opened the door of friendship to the opponents of this government [i.e. Russian]. The Iranians again crossed the river Aras and the Ottomans, because of the annulment of the truce between the two governments, decided to go to Georgia. General-in-chief Count Gudovich[21] became the commander. Ebrahim Khan of Qarabagh by send-

---

21. Count and General Field Marshal Ivan Vasil'evich Gudovich (1741 - 1820). He was commander of the Caucasian Line in 1791 until he was replaced by Zubov in 1796. He was reinstated in 1797 and replaced by Knorring in 1799. After the death of Tsitsianov he was appointed administrator of the Caucasus. He was replaced by Tormasov in 1809.

ing many letters was expressing his sincerity towards the government of Iran. According to his request, his son Abu'l-Fath Khan came to the fort of Shushi with a regiment [188] via Qapan. The Nayeb al-Saltaneh himself had crossed the Khoda-Afarin bridge. It was at this time that major Lisanevich, the commander of the Russian army in Shushi, at midnight of the 2nd of June in the year 1221/1806, attacked Ebrahim Khan, who was staying outside the fort with his equipment and his family and killed him with his wife, who was a sister of Salim Khan of Sheki and the daughters and the sons of many notables and the servants. He was an able and just emir, but stern and hard of heart and casual of manners. The same day Abu'l-Fath Khan returned; Ja'far Qoli Aqa b. Mohammad Hasan Aqa b. Ebrahim Khan followed him until the vicinity of Ordubad and he plundered and killed many. Mehdi Qoli Aqa was appointed instead of his father to the governorship of Qarabagh. After a while, Abu'l-Fath Khan with the help of 'Ata Ollah Khan Shahsevan moved the tribe of Jebra'illu and the other tribes of Qarabagh to the Qapan district, when the Russians and Ja'far Qoli Aqa arrived and the Jabre'illu revolted and in forested places they fought the Iranians who were defeated, killed and captured. The tribes returned to their own places. Meanwhile, Nayeb al-Saltaneh went to Shirvan via Aslanduz and Qarabagh. The people who had been gathered by Mostafa Khan on the banks of the river Kur with a view to impede the Iranian army from crossing were scattered and he moved the tribes of Shariyan, Morad Khani and others who numbered around 6,000 families to the Moghan steppe. They camped outside Aq Su and Mostafa Khan moved the [population of the] town to the inaccessible Mount Fet to seek refuge. Sheikh 'Ali Khan took some of the cavalry of the prince's army under the command of Pir Qoli Khan Qajar with him to Qobbeh. He returned in the company of Mohammad Qoli Khan Baku'i. After a while, when the request of the Nayeb al-Saltaneh was not fulfilled, Salim Khan sent the governor of Sheki, who was afraid of the Iranians, to Mirza Abu'l-Qasem, the son of Qa'em-Maqam to intercede and he called Pir Qoli Khan from Qobbeh and ordered him to stay in the Moghan and he himself returned to Azerbaijan.

Count Gudovich in many campaigns in the Caucasus had pacified the Lezgis, the Ossetians, Machqach, and from Qezlar he ordered general Glasenap[22] to take Darband, Qobbeh and Baku. After having arrived at Buynaq, Mehdi Khan Shamkhal, who submitted and accompanied him, the Darbandis gathered [189] under 'Ali Panah Bey b. Ahmad Bey b. Mirza Bey Bayat and they expelled Sheikh 'Ali Khan about whose behavior they were dissatisfied and they sent representatives to welcome the Russians and they submitted themselves. On the 21st of June in the year 1221/1806 Darband was taken by the Russians. The Ulus districts were given to Lt. General Mehdi Khan Shamkhal in reward of his sincere services with the title of Khan of Darband and the deputy-governorship of the town was given to Major 'Ali Panah Bey. In one month's period, General-in-Chief Bulgakov[23] had come at the head of an army and went to Qobbeh. He was accompanied by Mirza Mohammad Khan II who was vexed, because of Sheikh 'Ali Khan's agreement with

---

22. General Gregory Ivanovich Glazenap (1751 - 1819) was commander of the Caucasian Line (1805-06). See Baddeley, *Russian Conquest*, pp. 74-75 as to how he won the Shamkhal's support.
23. He replaced Glazenap in 1806.

Hoseyn Qoli Khan. He went there and after his arrival at six *farsakh* from the city of Baku Hoseyn Qoli Khan who was valiant, but weak and pure-hearted fled to Iran with all his people and the people of Baku expressed their obedience and Bulgakov took Baku in the name of Russia. When he returned to Qobbeh he met Sheikh 'Ali Khan who was apparently expressing his obedience and took hostages. Messengers from Sorkhay Khan arrived expressing submission. Qerkhlar Qoli the Ma'sum and Mohammad Qadi of Tabarsaran, 'Ali Khan the Usmi of the Qeytaq were expressing their obedience. Then a Russian regiment from Ganjeh came to Shirvan. Mostafa Khan per force accepted them. He wanted to return his tribe from the Moghan steppe with their help and he went to Pir 'Ali Khan Qajar who was taking the tribes to Talesh. He fought with him, but was defeated and returned. Then he sent his people with the Russians to Saliyan. Mir Baqer Bey, the brother of Mostafa Khan of Talesh, who was there with 300 people, without knowing that a number of people from Saliyan felt enmity towards 'Ali Khan, the governor of that place, and that he had secret relations with Mostafa Khan Shirvani, he started fighting and killing and the people of Saliyan returned and 'Ali Khan fled and was captured by the Talesh people. At this time, Salim Khan of Sheki in revenge of the killing of his sister, the wife of Ebrahim Khan, began to oppose the Russian government. He killed a few Russians who had come to help him from Ganjeh some time ago and the rest returned to Ganjeh.

After this event, General Nebol'sin,[24] at the orders of the commander Gudovich, went from Ganjeh to Sheki. Salim Khan, who had taken prior to that time a large amount from the Nayeb [**190**] al-Saltaneh, brought the Lezgis of Jar and the Avars and thinking that the inaccessibility of the place would be helpful to him properly readied himself for battle. During the battle the Lezgis fled with his family and relatives and he left his country and went to Iran. He was well-behaved, but a pleasure-loving and cruel emir.

In the year 1221/1806 the province of Sheki was conquered by the Russians. Lt. General Ja'far Qoli Khan Donboli, who in the previous year had taken refuge with the Russian government in Chamlibel of Koroghli, was appointed to that governorship. Count Gudovich on the 18th June trounced Yusof Pasha Sar 'Askar on the banks of the Arpa Chay. In the year 1223/1808, he intended to conquer Erevan and he sent some troops via Qarabagh to Nakhjevan and the Nayeb al-Saltaneh also came and there were continuous fights in those places, but eventually winter time arrived and because of the severity of the cold the Russian army returned without success. It was in this year that 'Ali Khan Usmi who was a brave and stern emir died. His brother 'Adel Khan was appointed in his place. Sheikh 'Ali Khan in revenge of what had happened to him one year earlier had plundered the herds of Barmak and then had gone to Shirvan and after putting up some resistance and plundering he returned. Because of the enmity that Mostafa Khan bore the family of Fath 'Ali Khan he came to Qobbeh in the company of Colonel Tikhonovski, the Russian resident commander in Shirvan, and after a few fights Malek Bey b. Hajji Bey of the lineage of Malek Adi of Boduqi and most of the Beys and the people turned away from

---

24. Peter Fedorovich Nebol'sin (d. 1820) rose through the ranks and was promoted to major-general in 1804 and was one of the Russian generals commanding troops during the first Russo-Persian war.

Sheikh 'Ali Khan and submitted to the Russian government. Sheikh 'Ali Khan who, in spite of his hedonism and negligence of the country's affairs, was known for his bravery, generosity and high-ambition, with many people from among the Beys and other followers came to the region of Tabarsaran to the house of his son-in-law [191] and from there accompanied by him he went to Aqusheh, where most of its people were devoted and loyal to his house. Within the passage of 40 days he came with an army of 5,000 to Qobbeh and he conquered all the land except for the fort. Near the fort of Shabaran he fought with a number of Russians, who had come from Baku to Qobbeh to help, but Sheikh 'Ali Khan could not do much and general-major Gur'yev with an army arrived from Baku and in the village of Charkhi put him to flight. He again went to Tabarsaran and the region of Qobbeh was permanently occupied by the Russians. Its governorship was given to Mirza Mohammad Khan II of Baku who had rendered great services in the conquest of Baku and Qobbeh. Sheikh 'Ali Khan again went to Tabarsaran and resided in the village of Yersi. 'Abdollah Bey was joined by the other children of Rostam Qadi and his paternal uncle Mirza Qadi. They were fighting and plundering in the region of Darband and Qobbeh and the Russian army in the company of some of the emirs of Tabarsaran and also the army of Darband went to the village of Mahraqeh. Sheikh 'Ali Khan and the sons of Rostam Qadi came to help Mirza Qadi, but were defeated and returned. The Russians destroyed that village and returned.

In the year 1224/1809, General-in-Chief Tormasov[25] replaced Gudovich as the commander [of the Russian army]. He was in the process of pacifying Bash Achoq and Abkhazia when Mohammad 'Ali Mirza, the son of the Persian shah and governor of Kermanshah, came to campaign in Georgia. The Nayeb al-Saltaneh was sent to Kukjeh Yeylaq in Erevan to help him. Farajollah Khan Nasaqchi-bashi became the border governor of the Moghan district. He sent Mohammad 'Ali Mirza Esma'il Bey of Damghan with some troops to fight the Russians at Hamamlu and Bey-kendi. A few fights took place and the former tribes of Erevan, who lived in Pambak and Shuragel and especially Naqi Bey, who had done some services for the Iranian government and following Mohammad 'Ali Mirza, came and after plundering Buzjalu, because of 'Abbas Mirza's desire to create problems for him, in secret went from Qars to Erevan and from there to Kermanshah. Farajollah Khan Nasaqchi-bashi after entering Ardabil asked 'Ali Khan Shahsevan to gather troops for him and because of the relationship that he had with Emir [192] Mostafa Khan Talesh he refrained from doing so. Mir Mostafa Khan moved a number of notables and troops of Talesh to a place called Gamishvan, which is surrounded by the sea and marshland and is only connected with Langarkonan from one corner. He brought some Russians to help and sent his son Mir Hedayat Bey to Mostafa Khan Shirvani asking for help. In the case of Mostafa Khan, in spite that some time before 'Omar Soltan Sa'dari, who was one of the notables of Shirvan, in order to improve the relations between the two Mostafa Khans and for the moving the tribes to Shirvan had been suddenly killed in a fight by Mir Hoseyn Bey, son of Mir Mostafa Khan, a group of infantry from Shirvan went to Gamishvan and

---

25. Count and General Alexander Petrovich Tormasov (1752 - 1818) was administrator-in-chief of the Caucasus from 1808-11.

Amir Hasan Bey with a regiment suddenly came down to Hoseyn Qoli Khan Baku'i and Hashem Khan the fugitive Mostafa Khan of Shirvan, 'Ali Khan Rudbari and Mohammad Khan Beydeli who were all staying in the neighborhood of Jarud. He suddenly attacked them; 'Ali Khan and Mohammad Khan were captured and the rest fled. By that time Nasaqchi-bashi imprisoned Nazar 'Ali Khan and Farajollah Khan Shahsevan with the authority that he had acquired on that occasion. He burnt the city of Lenkoran and then besieged Gamishvan, but he could not do anything. Eventually they agreed to make peace. Mirza Bozorg Qa'em-Maqam came from the shah and met with Mir Mostafa Khan and signed a treaty of friendship.

In the year 1225/1810, Sheikh 'Ali Khan, who had stayed for more than one and a half year in Tabarsaran, with the encouragement of Khan Butay Bey b. Hajji Sharif Bey Hazreh, whose ancestors from the time of the Safavids had been custodians of the shrine of Sheikh Joneyd, had obtained the support of most of the people of Qobbeh and spent four months to [try and] take the land and laid siege to the fort. He moved some of the people to the village of Qriz and they made a plan for a new city and it was at this time that Colonel Lisanevich[26] came with the Russian army and cavalry of Sheki and Shirvan and defeated Sheikh 'Ali Khan near the village of Chechi and expelled him from the country. Sheikh 'Ali Khan again went to Aqusheh and his son-in-law 'Abdollah Bey could not stay in Tabarsaran and joined him. After a while Sheikh 'Ali Khan with an army of 3,000 composed of people of Aqusheh and its neighboring parts without any resistance passed through the land of the Usmi and came to Tabarsaran. Colonel Mohammad Qadi who had become governor after his brother Rostam [193] Qadi came at half a *farsakh* from the village Khucheni. In a place where Enhesar Bey had passed he made trenches and started to defend it. The Lezgis hesitated to attack it. Sheikh 'Ali Khan with his people attacked him and took the trenches. Mohammad Qadi fled and 'Abdollah Bey was appointed in his place in Khucheni. Two months after the return of Sheikh 'Ali Khan Mohammad Qadi came back. 'Abdollah Bey expelled him and he took his place. In short, for a while the borders between Russia, the Ottoman Empire and Iran were the place of fighting and especially the country of Qarabagh was in particular the scene of the passage of armies and tribes, until Tormasov, in the year 1226/1811, was called to Russia to fight the French. Lt. General Marquis Paulucci replaced him.[27] Sheikh 'Ali with the help of Aba Bakr Qazi of Aqusheh, because of the money that was sent to him from Iran, again instigated the people of Aqusheh to fight. With an army of 8,000 he came from Aqusheh, Mehdivali, Tabarsaran and Ghazi-Qomuq together with Nuh Bey b. Sorkhay Khan II to Qobbeh. The Lezgis returned their horses from Maharam-kendi, which was near the Samur River, to Tabarsaran and came on foot to the village of Jibir. General-major Gur'yev attacked them the next day and he took the western road, which was good and was shown to him by the Beys of

---

26. General Dimitrii Tikhonovich Lisanevich (1780 - 1825) participated in the Russian campaign against Persia in 1796, was promoted by Tsitsianov, and appointed commandant of Shushi in 1807. He left the Caucasus in 1812 to participate in the Napoleonic War.
27. Marquis and General Philipp Osipovich Paulucci (1779 - 1849) was an Italian in Russian service since 1807. In 1810 he was appointed as chief-quartermaster of the Caucasian Line. From 1811-12 he was Administrator-in-chief of Georgia and the Caucasus.

Qobbeh and he then attacked from the eastern road, but, because of the inaccessibility of the place, he was defeated and put to flight and returned to Zeykhur. Sheikh 'Ali Khan went to the village of Rostov[28] and again submitted the country to him. The fort of Qobbeh and the village of Zeykhur, which were left in the hands of the Russians after nearly two months general-major Khatuntsev with a new army arrived and put Sheikh 'Ali Khan to flight in the village of Rostov and expelled him from the country. Many Lezgis with Abu Bakr Qazi of Aqusheh were [194] killed in this battle. General Khatuntsev came to Kur to punish Sorkhay Khan. His brother's son, Aslan Aqa b. Shahmardan, who previously had fled from his uncle to the Ottoman lands, had come the previous year to Tiflis and from there to the Qeytaq to the Usmi where he was staying. The general sent for him and attacked Sorkhay Khan who was entrenched in Sheikhi-kand. Sorkhay Khan was defeated and went to Ghazi-Qomuq and the region of Kur was occupied by the Russians. Aslan Aqa with the title of khan and the rank of colonel became the governor. To support him one battalion of soldiers stayed in Qorah. He was an able, stern, but drunken and bad-mannered emir and Sheikh 'Ali Khan after fleeing from Qobbeh stayed for a while in the village of Sombat and his relatives were staying in the village of Jomjuqat. With the help of Bahan b. Abi Bakr Qazi and by other means he returned to Aqusheh and resided there.

At the end of this year, because of the suspicion of being loyal to Iran, Colonel Ja'far Qoli Aqa b. Mohammad Hasan Aqa b. Ebrahim Khan was imprisoned and was sent with a group of Russian infantry and some Cossacks to Tiflis. When he was crossing the river Tatar he snatched the rope of his horse from the hand of the soldier and threw the other soldier who was seated on the horse with him into the river and fled to the tribe of Jebra'illu. On learning this news the Nayeb al-Saltaneh marched to Qarabagh. He sent some troops under the command of Amir Khan Qajar together with Ja'far Qoli Aqa to move the Jebra'illu tribe and the other tribes of Qarabagh and he himself with the artillery and infantry came to the redoubt of Soltanbud. The Russian battalion, which was there with Mehdi Qoli Khan of Qarabagh, was put to flight. Many people were killed and the rest were captured. Mehdi Qoli Khan saved himself by fleeing. Amir Khan and Ja'far Qoli Aqa moved from every side about 5 or 6,000 families and crossed the river Aras and joined Nayeb al-Saltaneh. The latter pacified the tribes of Qarabagh one by one, and gave the governorship of Qarabagh with the title of Khan to Ja'far Qoli Khan and returned to Tabriz. At this time Sorkhay Khan Ghazi-Qomuqi came to Kur and defeated Aslan Khan who had gone with the Russian battalion to the village of Kerkhen at three *farsakh* from Qorah. Sorkhay Khan left his son Morteza Qoli Aqa, who was born of the mother of Aslan Khan,

---

28. B. After the defeat he once again went to Tabarsaran and in the village of Yersi stayed with his son-in-law, 'Abdollah Bey b. Rostam Qadi and whenever he went to Darband he was plundering and fighting and by any means he was trying to regain his country. He went asking for help from the people of Aqusheh and they out of hospitality and because of the devotion that they had towards his father, Fath 'Ali Khan, came with him as well as with Nuh bey b. Sorkhay Khan Ghazi-Qomuqi to Qobbeh. General-major Gur'yev opposed them and in the village of Jabr [Jibir] a fierce battle took place. Because of the inaccessibility of the place the general was defeated and returned and Sheikh 'Ali Khan took the whole country except the fort. At this time general-major Khatuntsev came with a new army and defeated him in the village of Rostam and many of the Lezgis and Abu Bakr qadi of Aqusheh .... [B].

as governor of Ghazi-Qomuq and he himself went to Iran. Aslan Khan due to his close relationship with his mother's brother stayed with him. Sorkhay Khan in the following year came from Iran [**195**] and took Mortaza 'Ali Khan, brother of Aslan Khan, under the pretext that they were going to fight and killed him on the way and joined his father. Aslan Khan returned to Kureh and Sorkhay Khan again occupied Ghazi-Qomuq. He was an emir who looked after his subjects, but was short-tempered and cruel. Marquis Paulucci after learning of the coming of Nayeb al-Saltaneh in great haste came from Qobbeh to Qarabagh and left General Kotliarevskii[29] to guard there. He himself to put the affairs of Georgia in order, where there was a rebellion because of famine and disturbances, went to Tiflis, but he was dismissed and returned to Russia. In his place General-in-Chief Rtishchev[30] became the commander.

In the spring of 1227/1812, Nayeb al-Saltaneh with much equipment and staff, which the shah had sent to him entered Meshkin. Amir Khan Qajar with infantry and artillery from one side and others under his command from the direction of Arkavan, Zovand and Astara were charged to punish Mir Mostafa Khan Talesh who once again had turned away from the government of Iran and had asked for assistance from Russia. On the fourth day of August the officials entered Lenkoran and the Russian troops and Mir Mostafa Khan after fighting took refuge in Gavmishvan. The Iranians built redoubts and towers opposite them and for two months fire was exchanged from land and sea. Eventually, because the conquest of Gamishvan was not possible at the orders of Nayeb al-Saltaneh three forts in Lenkoran, Arkavan and Astara were built and they were equipped with guards, artillery and provisions. The remainder of the army returned. At this time, through intercession by the British envoy Sir Gore Ousely, peace negotiations started.[31] The Russian commander started negotiations with Nayeb al-Saltaneh on the banks of the river Aras, but they were not successful. The aforementioned commander Kotliarevskii left 2,000 soldiers and six cannons on the left bank of the Aras and he himself returned to Tiflis. From Soltan Hesan, Nayeb al-Saltaneh sent Pir Qoli Khan, Mirza Mohammad Khan Qajar and 'Ali Mardan Khan Khamseh'i with cavalry to Sheki and he himself with soldiers and artillery came to Aslanduz. He sent Sadeq Khan Qajar and Ja'far Qoli Aqa to move the tribes to Qarabagh.

General Kotliarevskii who was staying in Aq-Ughlan one night secretly crossed the river Aras and in the morning attacked the Persian army camp, which was several times the size of his army and defeated it. Some of them fled in absolute terror and Nayeb al-Saltaneh and the remainder of the army was fighting, but the general on the 10th of October attacked and destroyed them completely and returned with much plunder. The

---

29. Lieutenant-General Peter Semenovich Kotliarevskii (1782 - 1852) joined the army at 14 and participated in the 1796 campaign against Persia. He became an officer at 17 and rose through the ranks during the Caucasian campaigns, in particular at Aslanduz and Lenkoran. He retired in 1813 due to his serious wounds received at the latter town.
30. General Nicholas Fedorovich Rtishchev (1754 - 1835) was appointed administrator-in-chief of the Caucasus from 1812 - 1816. He signed the Treaty of Golestan on behalf of Russia and retired in 1816.
31. See Peter Avery, "Sir Gore Ouseley," *Encyclopedia Iranica* and [http://en.wikipedia.org/wiki/Gore_Ouseley]

soldiers who had been sent to Sheki and Qarabagh on hearing this news returned to Nayeb al-Saltaneh. [196] Hurriedly they returned to Meshkin and from there to Tabriz. General Kotliarevskii went to the Moghan steppe and moved the Qarabaghi tribes from there and conquered the fort of Arkavan and went to Lenkoran and laid siege to its fort. In the night of 'Ashura, the first of December of the year 1228/1813 he attacked and both sides gave a good and brave accounting of themselves. Finally, because of the fearless nature of the Russian general the fort was conquered and Sadeq Khan and Mohammad Bey, the Qajar colonel, who were the commanders of the garrison with many Russians and Moslems were killed. Kotliarevskii himself had three dangerous wounds.

In the spring of this year the Iranian government had given up hope of getting back the occupied lands from the Russians and the truce with the Ottomans and the disturbances in the affairs of Khorasan were added to this and the Shah therefore expressed the desire to make peace. Mirza Abu'l-Hasan Khan Shirazi from his side was sent as envoy and general Rtishchev came to the place called Golestan in Qarabagh. On the 12th day of October the treaty between the governments of Russia and Iran was signed. The government of Iran yielded the lands and the khanates of Ganjeh, Qarabagh, Talesh, Sheki, Shirvan, Baku, Qobbeh and Darband, all of Daghestan and Georgia and the tribes neighboring to Russia and confirmed that it did not have any claim on them. The Russian Emperor undertook to help and establish [on the throne], whoever from among his sons the shah made his crown prince.

The house where Peter the Great stayed when he visited Darband in 1722.
From: A. V. Williams Jackson, *From Constantinople to the Home of Omar Khayyam.*

CONCLUSION

On the lives of the people of the province of Shirvan and its neighboring regions who are authors or who have other accomplishments that are worthy to record.

The extent of the accomplishments, the good standing, and the characteristics of every people can be observed from their monuments and writings. The ruins of the cities and the multitude of tombs and holy shrines, among them the shrine of St. Sham'un in the city of Arran, and the three holy *emamzadeh*s in the city of Shamakhi as well as in the ancient cities of Ganjeh and Barda' and another *emamzadeh* in the village of Balbaleh, the shrine of Bibi Heybat in Baku, whose blessed name is Halimeh Khatun, daughter of Emam Musa Kazem, the shrine of Sufi Hamid [197] in Qabestan [now Qobestan] of Shirvan and the holy shrines of great sayyeds, sheikhs and respected scholars in most of the places indicate that these parts have always been favored by religion, and have been the dwelling place of scholars and Sufis regardless of other advantages, viz. that they are situated in one of the most temperate climates and that the characteristics of the weather, and other benefits of the earth exist in their mountains, plains, forests, and valleys. The inhabitants are a mixture of all human groups and the characteristics and the behavior of all of them can be seen in them. Therefore, by their perfect internal and external virtues they are capable of every possible art. According to European scholars, the people of Sam are distinguished by the beauty of their complexion and the built of their body, and by the extent of their knowledge and intelligence from the blacks and Turks, i.e., the descendants of Kham and Jafeth. They live in the western parts of India, Iran, Turkey (Rum), Arabia, and in the Greek and Slavic regions, Germany, France and other [countries] and they are related to the best race of the Caucasians. If the means of security and the advantages of education are properly added to the innate talents of these people what great progress might not come from them? In spite of misfortune, due to many changes and ruination because of continuous battles, most of them have gone to different parts of the world to learn sciences and different arts. They have been respected and honored in every age and they were trusted. But, unfortunately, from their writings nothing is known prior to the 6th century. In truth, the time of the reign of the great Khaqan Manuchehr and his descendents, which lasted for 400 years, is the greatest era of the Shirvanshahs and the time of prosperity of Shirvan. For a while, in the time of the Safavids the battles between the Ottomans and the Qezelbash were the reason for upheaval and disorder. After the appearance of the late Shah 'Abbas, by people's behavior and nature this land became more tolerant and prosperous. Learning prospered, but at the end of the reign of Shah Soltan Hoseyn, due to the dominance of evildoers and the passage of different armies and the campaigns of Nader Shah, conditions became absolutely chaotic and most of the places were ruined and the khans, who ruled separately over these parts, because of the continuous wars, were unable to encourage the development of [learning] and the betterment of their subjects. At any rate, the life of the scholars is discussed here, as much as possible, considering every era abovementioned, along with an account of the results of their thoughts.

Mention of Mowlana Sheikh 'Abdollah 'Ali b. Mohammad Baku'i

According to many historians, he was accomplished in esoteric and exoteric sciences. From early youth he sought out the companionship of great men and he met Sheikh 'Abdollah Khafif, Sheikh Abu'l-Qasem Qosheyri, and Sheikh Abu Sa'id Abu'l-Kheyr.[1] [198] Between him and Mowlana there were conversations and with Sheikh Abu'l-'Abbas Nehavandi he, for some time, was engaged in scholarly pursuit. The aforementioned sheikh praised him for his virtues. At the end of his life he retired to a cave near Shiraz. Most of the sheikhs of these parts and the leading scholars had discussions with him. His death occurred in the year 442/1051. He is buried in that pure land and regretfully nothing is known of his writings.

Mention of the learned lady Mahsati Ganjavi[2]

Mah is the abbreviated form of *māh* or 'great' and *sati*, or 'lady.' Adhar [Beygdeli] in *Ateshkadeh*[3] has related that she was of a noble family in Ganjeh and that she was a companion of Soltan Sanjar and that she was most honored. Here are some examples from her divan of poetry and her innate talent:

Quatrain

That beloved whose face is the envy of rose and jasmine

His coquettish glance is temptation to men and women

---

1. Sheikh Abu Sa'id Abu'l-Kheyr (967 - 1048 CE) was a famous Sufi and his quatrains are well-known.
2. For Mahsati Ganjavi, see, e.g., Mo'in al-Din Mehrabi, *Mahsati Ganjeh'i, bozorgtarin-e sha'er-e roba'sara* (Tehran, 1382/2003) and Fritz Meier, *Die schöne Mahsati; Ein Beitrag zur Geschichte des persischen Vierzeilers* (Wiesbaden, 1954).
3. Lotf 'Ali b. Aqa-Khan Adhzar Beygdeli, *Atashkadeh-ye Azar*. Ja'far Shahidi ed. (Tehran, 1337/1958).

I saw him on the road gracefully strolling like running water
From that running water my eyes are still tearful

آن بت که رخش رشک گل و یاسمن است
از غمزه شوخ فتنه مرد و زن است
دیدم برهش ز لطف چون آب روان
ز آن آب روان هنوز در چشم من است

Every night you torment me anew
Instead of sleep I see tears in my eyes
When my eyes close like your narcissus-like eyes
A dream more disheveled than your tresses enters my eyes

هر شب ز غمت تازه عذابی بینم
در دیده بجای خواب آبی بینم
و انگه که چو نرگس تو خوابم ببرد
آشفته تر از زلف تو خوابی بینم

An old companion cannot keep me in the house
A lonely house cannot keep me either
One whose tresses were like chains
Cannot be kept at home by chains

ما را بدم پیر نگه نتوان داشت
در خانه دلگیر نگه نتوان داشت
آن را که سر زلف چو زنجیر بود
در خانه بزنجیر نگه نتوان داشت

Alas, your rose-like face is surrounded by thorns
A crow came and plucked the tulip with this beak [199]
Your silvery chin is blackened by ink
The vermillion of your ruby lips is covered with rust

افسوس که اطراف گلت خار گرفت
زاغ آمد و لاله را بمنقار گرفت
سیماب زنخدان تو آورد مداد
شنجرف لب لعل تو زنگار گرفت

Mention of Hakim Ma'navi Sheikh Nezami Ganjavi[4]

His name was Abu Mohammad Nezam al-Din b. Yusof b. Mo'ayyed and his place of birth and burial was Ganjeh. To praise his virtues and greatness words fail. His poetic style is obvious from his words and everyone agrees that he had no peer in the manner of describing banqueting and all poets acknowledge his mastery.

---

4. Kamran Talattof and Jerome W. Clinton eds. *The poetry of Nizami Ganjavi: knowledge, love, and rhetoric* (New York, 2000).

This line is from him.

In this art do not seek to make a name
For Nezami has closed the door to fame

زین فن مطلب بلند نامی   کاین ختم شده است بر نظامی

During his youth he wrote the book *Vis and Ramin* and dedicated it to Soltan Mahmud Saljuqi. Although some attribute this book to Nezami-ye 'Aruzi, it does not fit the period of writing.[5] The Sheikh was one of the disciples of Akhi Farrokh Zanjani; at the end of his life he spent the rest of his life in seclusion and practiced the cleansing of his inner self, or, as he himself said.

A beautiful rose amidst the sad clover
Like me it has withdrawn into the bud

گل رعنا میان غنچه حزین   همچو من گشته اعتکاف گزین

In the *Tadhkereh al-Sho'ara*, Dowlatshah Samarqandi relates that Atabey Qezel-Arsalan Saljuqi went to see the Sheikh to test him. Because he looked at him with contempt he appeared to him for a moment from the unseen world; he saw him seated on a studded royal throne surrounded by a thousand servants and pages, who were beautifully dressed and the boon companions and chamberlains were standing at its feet. The Sheikh was seated on that throne with such authority and splendor that it was unimaginable. The Soltan was overcome by all this splendor and glory and wanted to humbly kiss the Sheikh's feet, because from the unseen world it had been made clear that this old man who was seated on a piece of felt in a cave and only had a Koran, a prayer rug, ink, pen and a walking staff in his hand. He kissed the Sheikh's hand with humility and his devotion to him increased manifold. The Sheikh sometimes paid attention to him and sometimes he would go to see him as he says: [200]

Couplet
I said I will kiss his foot as I kiss the earth
I suddenly saw heaven in front of me

بگفتم بوسمش همچون زمین پای
بدیدم کاسمان بر خاست از جای

---

5. *Vis and Ramin* was written by Fakhr al-Din Gorgani. For an English translation by Dick Davis see *Vis and Ramin* (Washington DC: Mage Publishers, 2008).

He wrote the story of *Khosrow and Shirin* at the request of the Soltan. He received four prosperous villages as a reward for it.

Couplet

He looked at my praise and loyalty
And gave Hamdaniyan [village] as my property

نظر بر حمد و بر اخلاص من کرد
ده همدانیان را خاص من کرد

The Sheikh's death was in the time of Toghrol, son of Arsalan in the year 576/1181 and a great tomb was built over his grave, which still exists in Ganjeh. Because it was becoming dilapidated, Mirza Adi Gural, of Cossack origin and living in Qarabagh, has repaired some of the buildings. Five versed stories that the Sheikh wrote: *Mazkhan ol-Asrar* [Treasury of Secrets], *Haft Paykar* [Seven Beauties], *Leyla va Majnun*, *Khosrow va Shirin* and *Eskandar-nameh* [Alexander's Tale] have been collected by scholars into one volume and it is called the *Khamseh* or Quintet.[6] Their poetic qualities are known all over the word and his poetic talent and strength is displayed in these works. His divan of poems apart from the Quintet has 20,000 couplets and it has many *ghazals*, which are full of poetic artifices and embellishment. This Persian *ghazal* is given as an example:

The world is wrapped in darkness and the road is hard, rein your steed
For a moment take your existence to the seclusion of the soul.
Drive away the crows of nature from the garden of intimacy
Bring the Homays of fortune into the snare of experience
When you become devoted to the soul of souls, abandon carnal form
In a moment quaff thousands of drinks of wisdom for free
When you are drunk with His wisdom break down the firmament
Shake the pillars of heaven; pull down the rope of heaven's pavilion
On His way go without feet; look at His beauty without eyes:
Tell His story without speech, taste His wine without mouth. [201]

---

6. See, e.g., *Mirror of the invisible world: tales from the Khamseh of Nizami* [adapted and translated by] Peter J. Chelkowski; with an essay by Priscilla P. Soucek (New York, 1975).

Nezami what are these poems that you have plucked from your mind?
No one reads your symbols, hold your peace, hold your peace.

جهان تیره است و ره مشکل جنیبت را عنان در کش

زمانی رخت هستی را بخلوتگاه جان در کش

کلاغان طبیعت را ز باغ انس بیرون کن

همایان سعادت را به دام امتحان در کش

چو خاص الخاص جان گشتی ز صورت پای بیرون نه

هزاران شربت معنی بیک دم رایگان در کش

چو مست حکمتش گشتی فلک را خیمه بر هم زن

ستون عرش در جنبان، طناب آسمان در کش

طریقش بی قدم میرو   جمالش بی بصر می بین

حدیثش بی زبان میگو شرابش بی دهان درکش

نظامی این چه اشعار است کز خاطر برون دادی؟

کسی رمزت نمی داند زبان در کش زبان درکش

Mention of the Master of Poets Abu'l-'Ala Ganjavi

From his life we know this much that in the time of the great Khaqan Manuchehr he was the poet laureate of Shirvan and he had great wealth and Khaqani and Falaki were his pupils. Hamdollah Mostowfi in his *Tarikh-e Gozideh* says that Abu'l-'Ala gave his daughter in marriage to Khaqani. Falaki who wanted to become his son-in-law was disappointed and wanted to travel. Abu'l-'Ala gave 20,000 *derham*s to him and said this is the price of 50 Turkish slave girls, each one of them is better than my daughter. Falaki was not content and when Khaqani became famous and found splendor, he became arrogant and hurt his master. Abu'l-'Ala writes about this:

Fragment
Oh Afzal al-Din, if you ask me truly
By your dear soul, I am not pleased with you
In Shirvan they called you the 'son of a carpenter'
I gave you the title of Khaqani [which means kingly]

For you I did many good deeds

I have trained and taught you

Enriched you and gave you my daughter as wife

Now, why don't you respect me

How often will you tell me that 'you have said such and such'

Because I cannot recall having spoken these words

I did not say that which you say I said, but I said that which you say I did not say

I gave you that which you say I did not, but I did not give what you said I did

تو ای افضل الدین اگر راست پرسی

بجان عزیزت که از تو نه شادم

دروگر پسر بود نامت بشیروان

به خاقانیت من لــقب بر نهادم

بجای تو بسیار کردم نکویــی

ترا هم پســر خوانده هم استادم

چرا حرمت من نداری که حالا

ترا دختر و مال و شهرت بدادم

بمن چند گویی که گفتی سخنها

کزینسان سخنها نباشد بیــادم

نگفتم بگفتم بگفتم نگفتم

بـدادم نـدادم ندادم بدادم

Mention of Hesan al-'Ajam Khaqani Shirvani

His name was Afzal al-Din b. Ebrahim b. 'Ali Najjar. He originated from the village of Malhamlu above Shamakhi and he was a master of sciences and of poetry and he was famous. [202] Scholars called him the Hesan of the Persians.[7] Rashid Vatvat, one of the great poets of Iran, praised him in this manner:

Poem

Afzal al-Din, Master of Virtues who is

A Philosopher, a stimulator of religion and a detractor of heresy

افضل الدین بوالفضایل آن که هست

فیلسوف دین فزا و کفــر کــــاه

At the beginning his *nom de plume* was Haqayeqi. From the great Khaqan he received the title of Khaqani. One of his *bon mots* that he sent to the Khaqan is this:

---

7. His namesake was the famous Arab poet Hisan b. Thabet, who was a contemporary of the prophet Mohammad, and who is said died between 674 and 682.

Strophe

Give me a mantle to embrace me

Or a fair young slave whom I may embrace

وشقی ده که در برم گیرد
یا وشاقی که در برش گیرم

Vashaq is a robe made of wool and *voshaq* is the face of the beloved. The Khaqan was furious and ordered Khaqani to be killed. As soon as he became aware of this he caught a fly and sent it to the king. The king expressed his anger [as follows], 'why has not he asked for both of them at the same time, it is as if he is negotiating [with me].' The sending of the fly was to show that due to it an extra dot [had been added] so that *ba voshaq* became *ya voshaq*.[8] Athir al-Din Akhsikati came from Turkestan to Shirvan to see Khaqani and have a poetic debate with him. On the way he was honored by Arsalan b. Toghrol and he challenged Khaqani and Khaqani wrote this *ghazal* and sent it to him:

Wisdom is the scriber of my pen

Speech is the groom to my imagination

By God, who makes the world turn around

This era is my era and time is my time

In the drought year of speech I am the Joseph of Time

As my tongue is the host for the famished of thought

I am not afaid of the vain words of any fool

Because one who is my peer has not come to this world yet

In revelation of thoughts I am the prophet of poets

Because to-day the miracle of speech is in my speech

خرد خریطه کش خامه بنان من است
سخن جنیبه بر خاطر بیان من است
بکردگار که دور زمـــــان پدید آورد
که دور دور منست و زمان زمان منست
منم که یوسف عهدم بقحط سال سخن
که میزبان گرسنه دلان زبان منست
ز ژاژخایی هر ابلهی نترسم از آنک
هنوز در عدم است آنکه همقران منست
منم بوحی معـــانی پیمبـــر شعــرا
که معجز سخن امروز در بیان منست

---

8. Khaqani sent a fly to the Khaqan and "said this is real criminal; I wrote *ba* [with], not *ya* [or], but this fly alighted on the single dot of the *b* while the ink was still wet and converted it into the two-dotted *y*." Browne, *History*, vo. 2, p. 394.

Eventually the desire for seclusion and purity of imagination came over him and he gave up the attendance at court. The Khaqan who was very much attached to his companionship was not allowing him to do so, so that when he fled from Shirvan the officials [203] of the Khaqan caught him in Beylaqan and sent him to the Khaqan. He was imprisoned in the fort of Shadravan [Shabaran] and other places. He wrote an ode full of long artifices about this. After the imprisonment he became a Sufi and left Shirvan in the company of Jamal al-Din Mowseli who was a world of generosity. They traveled to the Hejaz and he made the following praise to him:

Couplet

I can call him the Soltan of the Heart as well as the Caliph of Great Ideas
Because his father called him Soltan and his brother Caliph

سلطان دل و خلیفهٔ همم خوانمش از آنک
سلطان پــدر نوشت و خــلیفه برادرش

He wrote the *Tohfat al-'Iraqeyn* [The Gift of the two Iraqs][9] about this journey and he excelled in poetry and the divan of his poems is very well written and styled; a few lines are given from his famous and long poem:

Ode:

Oh heart, observer of examples, look through my eyes
And see the palace of Mada'en and the mirror reflecting the adversities of time
This is the same palace that from the tracing of people's faces
Its threshold was like a wall of the painter's workshop
It is the same gateway whose gatekeepers were kings
The king of Babel is the usher and the servant was the king of Turkestan
Imagine it is that age and through your mind's eye see
The chain of justice in the resplendent square
The earth is drunk for it has drunk instead of wine
In the skull of Hormuz the heart blood of Nushirvan
That wine yielded by the vine is the heart blood of Shirin
The farmer's vat is made of Parviz's elements
You laugh at my eyes, wondering why this weeping?
They laugh at the eyes not becoming tearful here. [204]
You know why you can compare Mada'en and Kufa
Turn your chest into a hearth and from your eyes bring forth a storm

---

9. Afzal al-Din Shirvani Khaqani, *Tohfat al-Iraqayn* ed. Iraj Afshar (Vienna/Tehran, 2006).

This is the sea of wisdom; don't pass it by without a drink
From such a river you cannot go away thirsty
Khaqani from this gate glean wisdom
So that the Khaqan will come begging to your door.
Friends when they return from journeys they bring presents
This poem is a gift for the heart of my friends

هان ای دل عبرت بین از دیده نظر کن هان
ایوان مداین را آیینهٔ عبرت دان
اینست همان ایوان کز نقش رخ مردم
خاک در او بودی دیوار نگارستان
اینست همان درگه کو را ز شهان بودی
دیلم ملک بابل هندو شه ترکستان
پندار همان عهد است از دیدهٔ فکرت بین
در سلسلهٔ درگه در کوکبهٔ میدان
مست است زمین زیرا خورده است بجای می
در کاس سر هرمز خون دل نوشیروان
خون دل شیرین است آن می که دهد رز بن
ز آب و گل پرویز است آن خم که نهد دهقان
بر دیدهٔ من خندی کاینجا ز چه می گرید
خندند بر آن دیده کاینجا نشود گریان
دانی چه مداین را با کوفه برابر نه
از سینه تنوری کن وز دیده طلب طوفان
این بحر بصیرت بین بی شربت از آن مگذر
کز شط چنین بحری لب تشنه شدن نتوان
خاقانی از این درگه در یوزه عبرت کن
تا از درگه تو زین پس دریوزه کند خاقان
اخوان که ز راه آیند آرند ره آوردی
این قطعه ره آورد است از بهر دل اخوان

People differ about the time of the death of Khaqani, whether it was in 590 (1194) or in five ninety five. He is buried in the poets' cemetery in Sorkhab in Tabriz.

Mention of Falaki Shirvani[10]

He was one of the famous scholars and eloquent poets. His name was Mohammad and his place of birth and burial was Shamakhi. In his early life he was in love with the son of an astronomer. For his sake he studied astronomy. Because of his talents he became accomplished in this science. He was eager to write poetry and therefore in his poetry he chose the *nom de plume* of Falaki [Astronomer]. This is a poem written by him in praise of the Shirvanshah.

---

10. See Hadi Hasan, *Falaki-i-Shirwani: his times, life, and works* (London: Journal of the Royal Asiatic Society, 1929).

Ode

You are the high firmament of nobility and the zenith of the world
You are the world of generosity and the meaning and the light of Mankind
You are the king of the fifth climate and the only one of the eighth star
The second Jamshid revered by the great Lords
Saturn in stature, Destiny in hand, Achiever of Goals and Heavenly temperament
Generous of nature, gentle in governance, with Jesus-like angelic lips
Wise like Arash, generous like Bahman
World-conquering like Rostam, art-showing like Neyram
Manuchehr of heavenly love whose sun-like face
Cleansed the smoke of tyranny from the face of the evil world

سپهر مجد معالی محیط نقطهٔ عالم
جهان جود و معانی چراغ دودهٔ آدم
خدیو کشور پنجم یگانهٔ هشتم انجم
جم دوم بتعظیم خدایگان معظم
زحل محل و قضا ید قدر مراد و فلک کین
شمال طبع و صبا فر مسیح لعل ملک دم
ستوده رای چو آرش سخا فزای چو بهمن
جهانگشای چو رستم هنر نمای چو نیرم
سپهر مهر منوچهر کو چو مهر بچهر
زدود دود مظالم ز روی عالم مظلم

Mention of 'Ezz al-Din Shirvani

In his own age he was one of the great scholars, encourager of scholars and teacher of sufis and a contemporary of Khaqani. From the collection of his poems the following is a sample: [205]

The musk scattering breeze of morning passed the meadows
I awoke by the scent of flowers in the morning.
In a corner of the meadow my beloved
Was passing with a thousand coquetries.
Her collar open like the breaking of the morning
That has left an indigo mark of drunkenness on her brow
Like a rose under the dew of morning
Her cheeks perspiring from the warmth of wine.
Her slender stature inclining because of wine
As the rose bush bends to the passing wind.
Her silvery sides are hurt by the shirt

Her tender lips apart because of hard breathing.
When smiling her ruby lips resemble
The heavenly signet ring of Jamshid
It is because of his justice that in their houses
The innocents lay down in peace.

صبا چو غالیه افشان گذشت از گلزار
شدم ببوی ریاحین ز خواب خوش بیدار
بگوشهٔ چمنی با پیالهٔ پـــر مــی
همی گذشت نگارم بصد هزار نـــگار
گشاده کوی گریبان چو صبح از سینه
کشیده داغ صبوحی ز نیل بر رخســار
عرق گرفته ورا عارض از حرارت می
چو زیر قطرهٔ شبنم صحیـــفهٔ گلنار
زیاده قامت زیبایش گشته میل پـذیر
چنانکه شاخ گل از عطف باد در گلزار
بر چو سیمش از آسیب پیرهن مجروح
لب لطیفش از آمد شد نفس افـــکار
ز شکل لعلش پیدا بــوقت خـــندیدن
مثال خــــاتم جمشید آسمان مقـدار
ز عدل اوست در خانه های مظلومان
نـهاده پشت فراغت ز امن بر دیــوار

Also by him:
Fallen into your path heaven saw me last night
You did not say who threw you into that plight
It is because of her two alluring eyes he said: Be aware
Drunks are out-of-their minds, go before they kill you

دوشم که فلک دید بکوی توفتاده
گفتا که بدین روزنگفتی که فکندت
گفتم که دو چشم خوش او گفت که هیهات
مستان خــرابند برو تا نــکشند ت

Mention of Mojir al-Din Beyleqani

In his youth he went to Shirvan and he found service with Khaqani and was occupied in writing his compositions. He fell in love with one of Khaqani's relatives. Because of opposition by Khaqani he was disappointed and dejected and he traveled and went to the court of Atabey Eldegoz, who had married the mother of Toghrol, son of Arsalan in the time of Soltan Mas'ud and for many years he was responsisble for the affairs of the Seljuqs and was one of the [206] art-loving and generous kings and Beyleqani was extremely close to him and was living in splendor and luxury. He would compose colorful panegyrics in the praise of Atabey Eldegoz [r. 1137 - 1175] and [his son] Qezel-Arsalan [r. 1186 - 1191].[11] When he was sent to Isfahan to collect government taxes, the scholars there did not pay proper attention to him and he wrote this poem:

Quatrain

I said from Isfahan help will come to my soul

Chivalry is a jewel that does not come from a mine

How would I know that the people of Isfahan are blind

Given that so much antimony[12] is coming from Isfahan

گفتم ز صفاهان مــدد جان خیزد
لعلی است مروت که نه از کان خیزد
کی دانستم کاهل صفـــاهان کورند
با این همه سرمه کز صفاهان خیزد

From his *divan* of poems:

Strophe

The scent of milk comes from the mouth of the lily

Because the teat of the breast of Saba is still in her mouth

She has ten tongues, yet she is silent

She has every right to be silent with such a short span of life.

بوی شیراز دهن سوسن از آن می آید
که هنوزش سر پستان صبا در دهن است
ده زبان دارد و خاموش بود حق با اوست
با چنین عمر که او راست چه جای سخن است

Also by him:

You have said take away your shadow from me

How can shadow be taken away from the earth?

You turned your eyes from me

Yet the noble Lord took me up

King Qezel Arsalan whose hand and heart

Took away from the world the names of "sea" and "mine."[13]

---

11. For more information on the Atabeys see [http://en.wikipedia.org/wiki/Atabegs_of_Azerbaijan] and *CHI*, vol. 5.

12. Antimony was an important ingredient of *kohl* or eyeshade and allegedly enhanced eyesight.

13. In Persian panegyric poetry often the hand is likened to the sea, i.e., being generous, and the heart to 'a mine', meaning ever producing.

گفته ای سایه از تو بر دارم
سایه از خاک چون توان بر داشت
تو فکندی مر از چشم ولی
کرم شاه کامران برداشت
شهٔ قزل ارسلان که دست و دل
از جهان نام بحر و کان بر داشت

Quatrain

Saki poured wine from the azure-colored goblet
The ministrel's bow poured down lustrous pearls
The blood-letter and physician came together
One taking the pulse and the other letting blood. [207]

ساقی که ز مینا می گلگون می ریخت
مطرب که ز زخمه دَرّ مکنون میریخت
فصاد و طبیب گشته بــودند بـــهم
این نبض همی گرفت و آن خون میریخت

Mention of the esteemed Sayyed Dhu'l-Feqar Shirvani

His name is Qavam al-Din Hoseyn, son of Sadr al-Din 'Ali. He was a great scholar and outstanding poet and he wrote long and well-styled odes in the praise of Sadr Sa'id al-Masteri, the vizier of Shirvan. He received seven *kharvar* of raw silk as a reward. He ended up in Iraq and became a companion to Soltan Mohammad Khvarezmshah. He wrote his letters and about the events of his kingship and he was honored and received rewards. In the time of the Mongols, Atabey Yusof, the vizier of Abaqa Khan, also displayed great munificence towards him. He died in the time of Abaqa Khan. He is buried in Sorkhab in Tabriz. A few lines of his odes are quoted:

O your praise, the ornament of the assemblies
A prayer for you is an embellishment of the gatherings
Your honor is proven with a hundred proofs
In generosity you are affirmed with a hundred affirmations
Your hand is supported by many hands
Your value is validated by many virtues
Your fortune is like that of Jamshid, and your justice
Emboldens the lost caravans to seek tribute from the highwayman

CONCLUSION

ای نسخه ثنایت پیرایه مجالس
وی خطبه دعایت آرایش محافل
اندر شرف مصدّر باش بصد براهین
و اندر کرم مسلم باش بصد دلایل
دست ترا ایادی قدر ترا معـــــالی
طبع ترا مکارم ذات ترا فضـــــایل
جمشید بخت ودولت کزیمن پاس عدلش
از دزد باج خواهد وامانده قوافل

Also by him:
Compared to ruby lips the cornelians of Badakhshan pale
The crescent-like black tresses adorn your moonlike face
Jamshid-like king Yusof, the master of the world
At his door the king of stars is Lord
O you for your well-wisher brings honor to honor
O that your ill-wisher brings shame to his name

ای ز یاقوت لبت لعل بدخشان بیرنگ
بر مه روی تو از زلف هلالی شبرنگ
شاه جم مرتبه دارای جهان یوسف شاه
که بود بردر او شاه کواکب ســـرهنگ
ایکه از رسم نکو خواه تو فخر آرد فخر
ایکه از نام بد اندیش تو ننگ آرد ننگ

Mention of Abu Saʻid Abdal Bakuʼi [208]

He was a dervish known for his miracles, a man of wealth and honored for his 'spiritual poverty' and outside the city of Baku he stayed in a monastery. He had a little for living, but he entertained visitors. According to the royal deeds, the Sheybani oil and farms were allocated for his expenses. Eventually, because of disturbances in the region his mosque and guest-house were ruined. His tomb and shrine have disappeared. A few houses in that place were known as Khalifeh Tamleri, [i.e. the Khalifeh houses]. In the year 1232/1817, Hajji Qasem Bey, son of Mansur Bey of Baku, built a shrine and a mosque. According to the evidence, the oil-well and the guest-house outside Baku, Abuʼl-Saʻid is the same dervish, whom Mohammad b. Mahmud Amoli mentions in his book *Nafaʼes al-Fonun*[14] when he talks about the characteristics of Soltan Oljeytu Mohammad Khodabandeh, when he says that one of his dervishes near Baku had dug an oil-well and would cover from it his own and the expenses of people coming and going from there. One day the Soltan came there and the dervish as was his custom rose to serve him. The Soltan

---

14. Shams al-Din Mohammad b. Mahmud Amoli, *Nafayis al-funun fi ʻarayish al-ʻuyun*. Mirza Abuʼl-Hasan Shaʻrani ed. (Tehran, 1377/1959).

wanted to give a gift to him, but the dervish refused. He said: "this suffices me and I do not need anymore." The Soltan liked what he said and made an investigation about his living, when he found out about how he lived he said: "what a wonderful kingdom you have." He gave the hand of brotherhood to him and said: "Do not forget me." That dervish out of consideration for him would send every year a gift to the Soltan. The Soltan would give that gift to Qara Mohammad, one of his notables, to sell it. He would keep this money for his shroud.

Mention of Mowlana Sayyed Yahya Baku'i

About the circumstances of his virtuous life this much is known that his name has been mentioned among the Sufi Saints of the mid-eighth century and his scholarly accomplishments and his virtuous manners were well-known and in the town of Baku a mosque was named after him, where his hermitage, school and tomb can be seen.

Mention of Mowlana Sheikh Molla Yusof Moskuri

His noble ancestors are from Qarabagh. After two generations they came to the region of Moskur of Qobbeh. He was born in the middle of the eighth century and after having completed his traditional training he received the Sufi mantle of guidance from Sayyed Yahya Baku'i. The gates of virtue and wisdom were opened to the seekers. His descendents were honored by kings and emirs and they received pensions. The village which is the burial place of the Sheikh is known as Sheikhlar and was their place of residence. From his writings nothing is known, except for the *Bayan al-Asrar* [Manifestation of Secrets], which is in Arabic and it is on the system of Knowledge, the celestial nature of things and the manner of Sufi customs. [209] In the introduction to 24 chapters of the book he summarizes the meanings in detail. He passed away at the end of the eighth century.

Mention of Abu Taher Shirvani

He was one of the wits of that place and known for his scholarship and accomplishments. Other things about him except for these two lines are not known:

Quatrain

I am amazed at old people
Why do they dye their hair
By dyeing no one is saved from dying
Why do they torment themselves?

عجب آید مرا ز مردم پیر
که چرا موی خود خضاب کنند
به خضاب از اجل چو کس نرهد
خویشتن را چرا عذاب کنند؟

Mention of Sayyed Hasan Shirvani

He was a preacher with great virtue and he wrote most styles of writing in the best manner and he was good in poetry, this is by him:

You have said you could reach that unkind beloved
If you sacrifice yourself you can reach God

گفتی توان به آن مه نامهربان رسید
گر بگذری از خود به خدا می توان رسید

Mention of Badr Saheb Qadr Shirvani

So much is known from his life that he had good taste and colorful poems. Many years he spent in eloquence and wit and seeking pleasure. This is the beginning of his collected works:

Drunkenly make a kebab from the bird of my poor heart
From my tearful eyes sprinkle brine onto it

مستانه زمرغ دل من ساز کبابی
وز دیده نمناک منش زن نمک آبی

Dowlatshah in the *Tadhkereh al-Sho'ara* says that Mowlana Katebi Torshizi in the time of Emir Ebrahim came to Shirvan and that there were many poetic competitions between him and Badr-e Shirvani. It is said that Emir Ebrahim cared very much for Katebi and as a reward he gave him 10,000 gold dinars. But he wasted it in one month in the caravanserai of Shamakhi and distributed it among poets, scholars and the needy. Some say it was stolen from him. One day he was in need of one *man* of flour [210] and he wrote this poem and sent it to the emir:

Quatrain

Yesterday I asked the cook to prepare a noodle soup
So that the food for us and our guests would be ready
He said: if I find the meat and fat, who will bring the flour?
I said: one that has made the mill of the turning heavens

مطبخی را دی طلب کردم که بغرایی پزد
تا شود ز آن آش کار ما و مهمان ساخته
گفت لحم و دنبه گر یابم که خواهد داد آرد؟
گفتم آن کو آسیای چرخ گردان ساخته

Mention of Mowlana 'Abol-Rashid b. Saleh Baku'i

He was a writer known for his virtues and his date of birth is 805/1403. He has written a book of geography in Arabic known as *Takhlis al-Athar va 'Ajayeb al-Malek al-Qahar* [Summary of the works and wonders of the omnipotent Lord]. It is about the Russians, the Slavs, the Varingians and the Pechenegh and he has interesting observations there and Academician Fraehn[15], who is one of the greatest scholars of Europe, has added many remarks to it and has printed it in his book known as Ibn Fazlan.[16]

Mention of Mowlana Kamal al-Din Mas'ud Shirvani

He was one of the greatest scholars of his time and in the time of Soltan Hoseyn Beyqara in Herat he was teaching in the mosque of Gowhad Shah Begom and also at the school of Emir 'Ali Shir. Many of the scholars of Khorasan acknowledged his scholarship. He has written a commentary on *Hikmat al-'Eyn*.[17] In the year 905/1500 he died.

Mention of Mowlana Mas'ud-e Shirvani

He was one of the poets of the time of Soltan Hoseyn [Beyqara]; his poetry is smooth.

By the burning hearts of the drunks and the smoothness of the pure wine
For my burning there is no cure but wine

بسوز سینه مستان برقت می ناب
که نیست سوز مرا سازگار غیر شراب

Mention of 'Abdi Shirvani

He was a witty and pure-minded man. He was a good calligrapher and he had poetic taste and he was also a good chess player. [211]

Strophe

Due to the burning of my heart my tongue became like fire in my mouth
Oh my adversary, don't do anything so that you might fall foul of my tongue

زبان از سوز دل شد همچو آتش در دهان من
مکن ای مدعی کاری که افتی بر زبان من

---

15. This refers to Christian Martin Fraehn's book, *Ibn Foszlan's und anderer Araber Berichte über die Russen älterer Zeit* (St. Petersburg, 1823).

16. For an English translation see Ahmad ibn Fazlan, *The Risalah of Ibn Fadlan: an annotated translation with introduction* by James E. McKeithen (Thesis Indiana University, 1979).

17. There are several works bearing this title. Perhaps it is the philosophical work by 'Ali b. Omar Qazvini or by Najm al-Din.

Mention of Mosaheb-e Ganjavi

His name is Kalb 'Ali Khan Ziyad-oghlu, *beyler-bey* of Ganjeh and Qarabagh. Because of his close companionship with rank and intimacy with Shah 'Abbas II [r. 1642-1666] he took the *nom de plume* of *mosaheb* (companion).[18] Apart from having great authority and political power he was accomplished in the arts of poetry and eloquency. Although the *divan* of his poems has not been collected here are some examples:

Oh Saki, go around and fill the cup and give it to us

For by going around and serving the wine our problems are solved

Gain purity of heart from the cup of wine, oh Saki

Because of the illumination of your heart the night of assemblies are lit like candles

الا یا ایها الساقی ادر کاساً و ناولها
که در دوران ساغر گشت بر ما حلّ مشکلها
صفا از باطن مینای می تحصیل کن ساقی
که از روشن دلی گردیده شبها شمع محفلها

And also by him:

My companion on the road to all-consuming love

Learn love from that child

When the mother fights with him

He even more clings to her lap

مصاحب در ره عشق جهان سوز
محبت را از آن کودک بیاموز
که چون مادر بجور او ستیزد
هم او در دامن مادر گریزد

Also by him:

Her two eyebrows are joined together as if

She has a wishbone and wager with me

دو ابرویش بهم پیوسته با من
جناقی دارد و دلخواه دارد

Mention of Mowlana Molla Mirza-ye Shirvani

In the arts of metaphysics he was unique in his time and he is still famous in Iran. In the time of Shah Soleyman he was teaching in Isfahan and he has left very valuable works. He had many debates with olama, which all indicate his great learning. For a while

---

18. Bakikhanov is mistaken, because Kalb 'Ali Khan was governor of Qarabagh in 1695 and thus he most likely was a companion of Shah Soltan Hoseyn (r. 1694-1722).

he chose seclusion in Karbala and Najaf. He died in the time of Shah Soltan Hoseyn. [212]

Mention of Molla Mohammad b. Najaf 'Ali Baku'i

He has works on the arts of sciences and regulations and he was distinguished in his time. There are many well-written letters by him. He was the teacher of Mirza Mohammad Khan II. At the request of Fath 'Ali Khan he translated *Kashkul* of Sheikh Mohammad Baha'i 'Ameli from Arabic into Persian and in a manner that is worthy of that famous book. He and 'Ali Hajji Mohammad Chelebi 'Aliji did research on the Sunni and Shi'a sects. 'Aliji wrote a very good tract in Arabic on the subject.

Mention of Hajj Mohammad Chelebi 'Aliji Qolhani

As to sciences he was among the famous people of his time, in particular in religious jurisprudence he was famous. Among his works there is one known as *Tadvin-e 'Aliji* (Exegesis of 'Aliji) and he explains the theological rules in a well-established manner. He is very well accepted among the scholars in this land. Seven times he went on the *hajj* and he died in the year 1223/1808. When the Russian army and Mostafa Khan of Shirvan were killing people in the city of Qodyal as well as the people of Qobbeh his body was brought to the cemetery of Baldeh and they called for prayers for the two sides to stop fighting and to pray together.

Mention of Mast 'Ali

Hajji Zeyn al-'Abedin Shirvani, who was very accomplished in sciences, was born in the middle of Sha'ban in the year 1194/1779 in the city of Shamakhi. After six months, his father Akhund Eskandar with his family left his country and went to live in Karbala. Zeyn al-'Abedin studied traditional sciences until the age of 17, when he lost interest in outward learning, because he was attracted by the inner self. He became the pupil of Ma'sum 'Ali Shah Hindi and after that in Baghdad he became a companion of Nur 'Ali Shah Esfahani and for a while he resided in Persian Iraq, Gilan, Shirvan, Moghan, Azerbaijan, and from there he traveled to Tabarestan, Khorasan, Qohestan, Zabulestan and Kabul. He benefited from interaction with leading olama and sheikhs. For a long time he was in the service of Hasan 'Ali Shah and after his death in the city of Peshavar in the year 1216/1802 he went to Panjab, Delhi, Oudh, Allahabad, Bengal, Gujarat and the Deccan. He became close to Jukiyan, Senasiyan, Birakiyan, Nanakshahiyan, idol worshippers and Zoroastrians. [213] He also had contacts with the Jalaliyan, Madariyan, Qaderiyan, Dahriyan, Holuliyan, and Mabahiyan. Furthermore, he also had relations with the sects of the Rayan, Rajgan, Brahmans and Ragiyan. He traveled to the islands of India, Sudan,[19] and Machin (Japan) and their ports. Eventually he came to the country of Sind and with difficulty he passed from Moltan to Kashmir. He also associated with the sects of the Five Saints, Siyah-Pushan, the Bi-navayan (Miserables), the Khaksars, and Nanakshahiyan. Via Mozaffarabad and Kabul he went to Tokharestan, Turkestan and the mountains of

---

19. The mention of Sudan here clearly does not fit and must be a mistake.

Badakhshan. He had contacts with Naqshbandis, Cheshtis, Sadi Jamegan, and also with Isma'ilis, Khota'iyan, Manaviyan as well as with Mazdakiyan, Khorramiyan and Ighuriyan. Via Khorasan and Persian Iraq he came to Fars and was in contact with the notables of that land and associated with Dhahabis, Nurbakhshis and other leading men. Then he wanted to go on the *hajj* and via Darab and Hormuz he went to Oman and Hazar Mowt[20] and then traveled to the ports of Yemen and Ethiopia and became familiar with the beliefs of Abakhiyan [sic; Abahiyan], Zeydiyan, Tabariyan, and Keysaniyan and after the performance of the rituals of the *hajj* and the pilgrimage of the shrine of our prophet Mohammad and of the Imams he had contacts with the Wahhabis and the people of the four Sunni schools. Then he went to Port Said and Egypt and learned about the ways of the Copts and Heretics. He met many of the sages and learned men of that place and then went to Syria and the Holy Land and met with saints. He worshipped in the Mosque of the Rock and he also went to Mount Sinai where he worshipped. He had contacts there with Ommayads, *Sheytan parastan* (devil worshippers), Jabriyan, Qaderiyan, Samariyan, Jews, and [Christian] monks. Then he went to Great Armenia, Rum, Qaraman, Greece, Constantinople, Aydin[21], Morroco, Algeria and the Barbary Coast. He had contacts with kings and the leaders of the Bektashis, Refa'is, 'Oshaqiyan, and Hamzadiyan. He also associated with Christians, Safiyan, Mowlaviyan, Khalvatiyan and Faramushiyan (Freemasons). He also had contacts with Europeans, Armenians, Georgians, and [with people] from Diyarbekr and Armenia Minor. He went to Azerbaijan and from there to Tehran. He met Hoseyn 'Ali Shah and Qowsar 'Ali Shah and, for a while, he was in the service of Majdhub 'Ali Shah of Hamadan and learnt many secrets and purified his soul and then he reached perfection with the Ne'matollahi order. Some orthodox people accused him of heresy and they incited the king of Iran against him. He went from [Tehran] to Shiraz and from there to Kerman. He suffered much at the hands of Ebrahim Khan, the governor of Kerman and came back to Shiraz. In the year 1236/1821 he married and some of the olama there and also some of the mojtaheds and their followers opposed or defended him. They wanted to hurt him to their own benefit. The governor-general of Fars, Hoseyn 'Ali Mirza, ordered him to be expelled. In the time of the plague, in the year 1237/1822, **[214]** he left with his wife for Isfahan. From there he went Qomishah, where he took up residence and wrote the *Riyaz-e Siyahah* (Garden of Travels). He described the state and wonders of each country along with the events and lives of the kings and outstanding scholars, the beliefs of people of different religions and many sects in a very detailed and accomplished manner.

Couplet

Whoever wants to be an arm-chair traveler

Let him study the *Riyaz al-Siyahah*

هر که خواهد سیاحت آسان

گو ریاض السیاحه را بر خوان

---

20. Area between Saudi Arabia and Yemen.
21. Aydin province in southwestern Turkey, located in the Aegean Region.

In truth, the aforementioned book is the source of much information and it is an indication of the author's vast knowledge of sciences and life experience. They have said that the author has opened up a place of guidance and he manifests many virtues and arts from his inner being.

Apart from the abovementioned persons who have distinguished themselves and whose existence stood out against the sun of truth, there are many other people of virtue, among them Abu 'Ali Rudbari, Sheikh Ya'qub Charkhi Shaberani, Sheikh 'Abdol-Karim Qabavi, Baba Rokn al-Din Shirvani, and among the class of the olama Sa'dollah Barda'i, Hanafi Qarabaghi, Ebrahim Arashi, Borhan al-Din Aghtashi, 'Abdol-Rahim Shakvi, Mohammad Amin, Hajj Ayub Efendi, Hajj Baba Efendi, Hajj Akhund Sharif Shirvani, Akhund Najaf 'Ali Baku'i, and Molla Aqa-ye Darbandi who are famous in sciences. Among the group of poets Neshat, Masih, Mirza 'Askar, Hajji Aqa-ye Zolali Shirvani, Yusof Kuseh, Aser Lanbarani, Molla Panah Vaqef, Mirza Moharram Mariz-e Qarabaghi, and Fath 'Ali Bey Hali Ziyad-oghlu Ganjavi were known for the purity of their poetic talent. In Daghestan there were also people who had excellent knowledge of Arabic and in different times they have become famous such as Mohammad Qadaghi, Hajj Ebrahim al-'Ordi, Fazel-e 'Eymaki, Yusof Zarir Qomuqi, Davud Osashi, and Sa'id Shenazi and others. Here this humble author himself, neither claiming fame nor virtue, but only because I am proud to belong to these parts, would like to submit a brief account of my own life.

Couplet

Though others are roses and jasmines, we are thorns
This much suffices that we are nurtured in the same garden [215]

دیگران گرچه گل و یاسمن و ما خاریم
این قدر هست که پرورده یک یک گلزاریم

The birth of this insignificant person 'Abbas Qoli Qodsi b. Mirza Mohammad Khan II was in the early hours of the day of Thursday, the 4th Dhu'l-Hejjeh, or the 10th of June in the year 1208/1794 in the village of Amir Hajan of Baku. At the age of seven, although they put me in the school, the disturbed situation and the wars did not allow me to study properly. During ten years, except for acquiring a rudimentary knowledge of Persian, I could not do much else. After that, in Qobbeh, I was studying Arabic and other subjects for ten years. In spite of the limited means available and other impediments I acquired some education, so that the commander of the armies of the Caucasus, General Yermelov in the year 1235/1820 summoned me and employed me in government service. I learnt to read and write Russian in Tiflis and I became acquainted with different kinds of learning and lives of different people, which had been translated into Russian. Due to the requirement of the service and being in the presence of the high officials of that government I traveled in most parts of Shirvan, Armenia, Daghestan, Cherkesia and Georgia. I also went to Anatolia and Azerbaijan and saw many of the notables and people of various walks of life. Concerning the war and peace with Iran and the Ottomans I was one of the confidantes of the great commander of the Russians, Paskevich.[22] In the year 1248/1833,

---

22. Count of Erevan, Prince of Warsaw, Field Marshall Ivan Fedorovich Paskevich (1782-1856). He participated in the Russian-Persian war (1806-12), was appointed

I went on mission and for nearly two years I was traveling through the steppes, the Tana district,[23] the Ukraine and the Russian lands, [as well as] Livonia,[24] Lithuania, and Poland, and I had contacts with the leading scholars of Europe. I saw many wondrous and strange things. In every land I gained some experience. Gradually my ignorance was reduced and the absurdity of what I had imagined became apparent. I saw that the high positions of the world are nothing but extremely low and great accomplishments [at the most] are nothing but to learn from experience. At any rate, because our wealth is subject to decline, our choice and power is subject to change, our skills are in need of different tools and corporal strength, nobility without pedigree is unknown abroad and disliked at home, and depending on them is like depending on [running] water, and the fortune that you can rely upon is science and culture. As 'Ali the Lord of the Believers has said:

> The ignorant and their deeds are many
>
> They are not equal to the people of science and literature
>
> If dogs are dressed in golden fabrics
>
> They are not like a lion that is devoid of gold [**216**]

الجاهلون و ان اعمالهم كثرت

لايستون لاهل العلم و الادب

ان الكلاب و ان البستها ذهباً

فليس كالسد العارى عن الذهب

This learning and culture does not consist of versified words and imaginary rules that people of outward learning boast of and brag about.

Couplet

> They say what cannot be contained in learning
>
> They seek what their senses comprehend

بگویند آنچه در دانش نگنجد

بجویند آنچه را محسوس دارند

Rather, it is an indication of their desires and deeds, which entails public weal and good organization, and through their remains they will be a lasting source of goodness for

---

administrator-in-chief of the Caucasus in 1827, and defeated the Persians and Turks resulting in the Treaties of Turkomanchay and Adrianople. In 1831 he crushed the rebellion in Poland, was vice-regent there (1832-52), then commanded the Russian army in the Crimea and retired in 1854 when he was wounded.

23. The term *molk-e Tana* refers to the area of what is now Rostov province, in southwestern Russia. It lies on the left bank of the Don River, 7 km east of the Sea of Azov. It was the site of Greek colony of Tanais, the first known major city in the region, which was founded there in the 6th century BC. It changed hands and was renamed several times over the ensuing centuries. It later became the Genoese colony of Tana (established 1316).

24. Livonia is situated east of the Gulf of Riga, and encompassed parts of Estonia and Latvia. For information about its history see [http://en.wikipedia.org/wiki/Livonia].

many centuries. Good deeds are rewarded by your Lord and are your best testimony in the world and there is no need to explain its virtue. Without that neither the manner of life will have support nor the work of Islamic law will have continuation.

Quatrain

If the wondrous writing pen

Does not reveal a new pattern from the old

Who else will give a sign of the past generation

And leave a gift for the generations to come

گر نکند کلک بدایع نگار
طرح نو از رسم کهن آشکار
کیست ز اسلاف نشانی دهد
تحفه به اخلاف نهد یادگار

According to the recollection of this humble author, he spent his spare time writing several works and I have written several texts in addition to monographs. Although nothing great has been achieved by them, at any rate so much suffices that I was working and was hoping that something good would come of it.

Couplet

Everyone will take his own goods to the bazaar

Whether it is a load of silk or a few strands

متاع خود برد هر کس به بازار
گر آن بار پرند این تار چند است

FIRST, the *Riyaz al-Qods* (Garden of Purity), which is in Azeri Turkish[25] and consists of 14 chapters. It describes in brief the lives of the 14 Pure Ones and details the incidents of the tragedy of the martyrdom of HH Hoseyn b. 'Ali. The reasons for its name and the date of its composition are as follows:

Poem

Because of the blood of the holy family the land of Karbala

Blossoms in autumn like the most graceful garden

Since it makes the events of Karbala apparent

Calling this book *Riyaz al-Qods* is suitable [217]

In truth, this garden, like *Riyaz al-Qods*

Is full of insights and is replete with truth

Another reason is its year of composition

---

25. The text has Tatar, which was the Russian term for, *inter alia*, both the Azeri language and those speaking it.

Its chronogram is equal to *Riyaz al-Qods*
Therefore, in conformity with this my pen name Qodsi
One by one adds up to the symbols[26]

زمین کرب بلا اهل قدس قانیندن
خزانده گللر آچوب الطف حدایقدر
ایدر وقایع کرب بلانی چون ظاهر
ریاض قدس دیمک بو کتابه لایقدر
ریاض قدس کیبی فی الحقیقه بو گلشن
لطایفیله دولو مظهر حقایقدر
دخی بو وجه سببدر که سال تاریخی
حسابده لریاض القدس مطابقدر
اولوب تناسب اوزیندن تخلصم قدسی
که جمعی بربره بو رمزلر موافقدر

SECOND, the *Qanun-e Qodsi* (Qodsi's Canon) is a Persian Grammar, which allows students to reach the stage of writing and speaking in three stages. The first stage is the explanation of the letters, which entails the distinguishing of letters and signs related to them, which again has three stages. The second stage is the explanation of words, which shows the derivations of Persian and Arabic words in two stages. The third stage is the explanation of sentences and it also involves the composition of words, which is explained in two stages. To facilitate comprehension and retention, I have versified most rules and examples. At the order of the emperor, I have translated it into Russian and it has been printed in both languages in Tiflis for the use in the imperial schools.

THIRD, the *Kashf al-Ghara'eb* [the Discovery of Wonders] in Persian; it is about how America, i.e., the New World, was discovered, which is the Western hemisphere of the world. It contains two sections.

FOURTH, the *Tahdhib al-Akhlaq* [the Purification of Manners], which is a detailed description of the usefulness of things and their use, according to the definition of the holy books and Islamic, Greek and Roman scholars and it has one introduction, twelve chapters and one conclusion.

FIFTH, the *'Eyn al-Mizan* [The Eye of the Scale], in Arabic, which has one introduction, two chapters and one conclusion. It is on words and the explanation and the origin and means of imagination and affirmation that constitute the science of logic along with the science of debate and its rules are explained.

SIXTH, the *Asrar al-Malakut* [Celestial Secrets], which is in Persian. It is on the science of astronomy and compares the ancient rules with new ones and applies logical reasons to ancient texts. It explains the situation of the globe and other heavenly bodies as much as possible and discusses the rules of their regularity. I have translated this book into Arabic as well.

SEVENTH, the *Joghrafiya* [Geography], which is in Persian and explains in detail in mathematical, natural, and political terms the situation of the world, of celestial bodies

---

26. This (*le'riyaz al-qods*) adds up to 1236/1820.

and the characteristics of elements, birth rates, boundaries of the continents, determination of the classes of people [218] and the manner of their livelihood in each country. The book has not been completed and this depends on the grace of God.

EIGHTH, *Mishkat al-Anwar* [Niche of Lights], in Persian, which explains different secret and good manners in anecdotes and poems. The book begins as follows:

Do not blame love oh people of purity

Because I do not see in asceticsm any sign of salvation

Who is bewildered by heresy and who by faith?

On whose disheveled musk-scented tresses the comb sits

To my soul the scent of the beloved reaches

It's like a fragrance reaches from the world of souls

I have attained a draught from a cup

And I have adorned this book with a name.

Because of the munificence of that great soul

As if the Sun arose from the black earth

Whatever I have said of his descriptions is not enough

For the knowledge of Man is equal to 'I do not know'

That sun of pleasure cast a ray onto me

And from every particle of me one hundred rays arose

My soul is the niche of his lights

And the store-house of the heart is treasury of his secrets

I want to write this book of his secrets

And could call it the niche of his lights (*Mishkat al-Anvar*)

لاتلوموا العشق یا اهل الصلاح

ما اری فی الزهد آثار الفــلاح

کفر و دین سر گشته و حیران کیست

شانه در گیسوی مشک افشان کیست

بر مشامم بوی جانان می رسد

نکهتی از عـــالم جان میرسد

جرعه حاصل ز جامی کرده ام

زیب این دفتر به نامی کرده ام

کز فیوض همت آن جان پاک

طالع آمد آفتاب از تیره خــاک

هرچه از اوصاف او گویم کم است

علم الانسان ما لــم یعلم اســت

پرتوی بر من زد آن مهر سرور

تافت از هر ذره ام صد شعله نور

جان من مشکوة انوار وی است

مخزن دل گنج اسرار وی است

خواهم این دفتر ز اسراش نوشت

می توان مشکوة انوارش نوشت

NINTH, *Majame'-ye Ash'ari* [Collected poems].[27] Poems that have been written in different ways and, because they are scattered, have not been made into a *divan*. Here are some examples:

In Arabic.

May God bless one whose name is Ahmad

Whose character is pure, and is exalted to high levels of Purity

He has heavenly virtue, is impeccable of character and God is witness to it,

He is the best of the believers who stand out among their good deeds

He is versed in learning and sincere in his message [219]

Swallower of ire and content with all miseries

More generous than the generous, pure and refined

Proof of God to the people, prayers be upon him

And upon his family; among his people he is peerless

Forgetting resurrection for them is the severest of neglect

For them God is everlasting and they do not doubt

Through them Qodsi asks for mercy on the Day of Judgment

Forgive us, have pity and accept our request

O most excellent and caretaker of needs

عافنا الله بمن احمد اسماً و صفات   الذی کان علیا بعلو الدرجات
عصمة الحق حسن الخلق و بالله شهید   انه زین عباد سبقوا بالحسنات
باقر العلم هو الصادق فی دعوته   کاظم الغیظ رضاء بجمیع البلوات
اجود کل جواد و نقی و ذکی   حجة الله علی الناس علیه الصلوات
و علی العترة فی الامه احدی الثقلین   عنهما الغفلة فی الحشر اشد الحسرات
بهما دام لنا الحق و لایفترقان   یسئل الرحمة قدسی بهما فی العرصات
فاعف عنا و ترحم و اجب دعوتنا   یا رفیع الدرجات و کفیل الحاجات

From the Ghazals.

O good heart, love whose love leads to passion

By itself it is Revelation, Gabriel, the Book and the Prophet

If the world condemns the lover as a heretic

This is the story of Salman and Abu Dhar[28]

---

27. Bakikhanov does not mention the *Ketab-e Asgariyeh* (The Book of Asgar), which was his first fiction book, written in Persian; a love story about two young people, persecuted by the fanatic society they lived in nor his *Ketab-e Nasihat* (The Book of Admonitions). The *Ketab-e Asgariyeh* has been published in Abbasqulu Ağa Bakixanov Qüdsi, Seçilmiş äsärläri ed. Mämädağa Sultanov (Baku, 2005).

28. Abu Dhar Ghifari and Salman-e Farsi are of the five companions, closest to the Prophet Mohammad. They allegedly added to the *shahadah*, i.e. the profession of faith, the

In the world of mystics there is no noble or commoner
Mercy is equal to tyranny and heresy equals faith
This point cannot be solved by logic, bring wine
So that I give that explanation if you believe me
Whoever does not see his own action is not a believer
The one who does not attribute it to God is an unbeliever
Without action nothing can come into existence in the world
For it is in our power to do all that which is destined
Qodsi, whatever comes from the friend is good
Hidden in every evil deed there is redemption

خود وحی و جبرئیل و کتاب و پیمبر است	ای خوشدلی که عشق به سودایش رهبر است
این ما جرا حکایت سلمان و بوذر است	عالم به کفر عاشق اگر حکم می کند
رحمت به جور و کفر به ایمان برابر است	در عالم سلوک خاص و عوام نیست
تا شرح آن دهم گرت از بنده باور است	این نکته حل نمی شود از عقل می بیار
وان هم که نسبتش نه به حق داد کافر است	هر کس عمل ز خویش نبیند نه مؤمن است
در اختیار ماست عمل هم مقدر است	بی قوه فعل را به جهان چون وجود نیست
در ضمن هر فساد صلاحی مقرر است	قدسی نکوست هر چه رسد از جانب دوست

Also,

I found my way to the curls of her tresses, finding the way to the heart is pleasant
On her face I saw that from everything beauty is better
The color and air of my beloved and her tresses
Have no need for beautifiers; a flower that grows by itself is beautiful [220]
Her stature has a different appeal in my eyes
I say truly, the straight cypress at the bank of a stream is beautiful
From your life-inspiring lips even bitter words are sweet
What grace is this, by God, whatever you say comes out beautifully
The disturbed mind of a crazed lover is calmed by a chain
That is why being entangled in the curls of the tresses is good
A beauty spot on the lip is like a shining star
It is as if a Hindu worshipper is prostrating towards the sun
The blessing of Qodsi of Tus[29] came from the blessed land [of Mashhad]
Whereas our Qodsi of Baku is delighted with the beauty of Baku

---

words 'Ali is the beloved of God.'

29. Hajji Mohammad Khan Qodsi of Mashhad was a Safavid poet, who traveled to India to join the court of Shah Jahan. He died in 1056/1646. Tus is often used instead of Mashhad-e Tus referring to the shrine of Imam Reza at Mashhad.

CONCLUSION خب 197

ره به تاب زلف او بردم که دلجویی خوش است
در رخش دیدم که از هر چیز نیکویی خوش است
آب و تاب روی و گیسوی دلارام مرا
حاجت مشاطه نبود گل به خود رویی خوش است
قامتش را جلوه ای دیگر بود در چشم من
راست گویم سرو رعنا بر لب جویی خوش است
از لب جان پرورت شیرین بود دشنام تلخ
این چه لطف است الله الله هرچه میگویی خوش است
خاطر دیوانه را زنجیر آرامی دهد
ز آن سبب شوریده دل در بند گیسویی خوش است
خال مشکین بر لب است و احتراق کوکب است
سجده یا بر آفتاب آورده هندویی خوش است
قدسی طوسی ز خاک پاک فیض قدس یافت
"قدسی با کویی" ما نیز با، کویی خوش است

From his fragments:

I am the one who every time in every breath sheds blood in the battle field

I have girded my belt to confront the enemy; my sword is lying in wait

By your soul, I mirror the enemy in this situation

If you are not content come and see this

منم که دم به دم از دم دم آورده به مصاف
میان به قصد عدو بسته در کمین غلاف
منم به مرگ تو آیینه دشمن این صورت
بیا معاینه کن بین گر نمی دهی انصاف

From the quatrains:

O my heart, you have no fear of burning

Don't you have the quality of a moth?

O bird of my soil, what stone has broken your wing

That you cannot extend your wings towards your nest

دلا از سوختن پروا نداری
مگر خاصیت پروانه داری
چه سنگ ای مرغ جان بال تو بشکست
که سوی آشیان پروا نداری

From the ghazals:

On the face of the sun, a moon arises or is it a crescent of the sun

Is this an eyebrow or simply is it the imagination of the lover?

In the mirror showing the world is it heaven that is reflected

Or is it your beauty spot or a sign of the star of my fortune?

Is it not strange that Moses is showing his magic hand

Now that it is the time of display of the flower blossom

The north wind scatters musk on the meadows

Or is it a gleaning of the garden of your beauty [221]

For a caged nightingale can there be

Yearning desire for singing and for flight

It is no wonder that my beloved does not hear my situation

Can she pay attention to a story of a frenzied heart

O Qodsi, my sallow face is crimsoned by bloodstained tears

The blossoming time of this garden is autumn

گون اوزره آی طلوعمی یا گون کمانیدر
یا قاشدور بو جمله سی عاشق گمانیدور
جام جهان نمایه دو شوب عکس آسمان
خالین سوادی اختر بختیم نشانیدر
گو سترسه یوخ عجب ید بیضا کلیم طبع
حالا که شاخ گلده تجلی زمانیدر
باد صبا عبیر فشان چمن میدر
یا بوستان حسن رخون بوستانیدر
شوق ترانه قوت پرواز اولورمی هیچ
اول عندلیب ایچون که قفس آشیانیدر
دلبر بیان حالم ایشستمزسه یوخ عجب
پروا قلورمی اهل جنون داستانیدر
قدسی عذار زردیمی اشک ایتدی لاله گون
بو گلشنین بهاری زمان خزانیدر

From the quatrains:

Is this a flower? No, flowers don't blossom in such a way

Is this a sun? No, a sun does not shine at night

I would say, neither king nor angel value love

Who is this that I cannot describe her?[30]

گل دور بو، دگیل، گل بیله خندان اولماز
گوندورمی، دگیل، گون گیجه رخشان اولماز
دیردیم ملک و ملک محبت بیلمز
کیمدر بو که تشبیهنه امکان اولماز

---

30. Herewith is completed the book *Golestan-e Eram*, one of the compositions of our great master 'Abbas Qoli Aqa Bakikhanov, may God increase his merit, in the hand of the humble servant of God 'Abdol-Rahim b. the late Molla Emam 'Ali of Baku on 22 Safar in the year 1260 *hijri* [13 March 1844]. In the margin it is written 'A. 'Alizadeh has written this. I wrote this for posterity. If I do not remain this writing will.
W. here was added: This book was completed on the first of the month of Shavval in the year 1283 *hijri* [6 February 1867] in the town of Qobbeh.
T. Here was added: I completed this on the 29th of Rabi'a al-Avval [18 April 1844] in the city of Tiflis with the great scholar Mofti of the People, Sheikh al-Eslam 'Othman Efendi al-Qazzaqi and the humble servant wasted by the calamities of time Karim al-Vardani al-Shakvi in the year 1260.

View of downtown Baku circa 1900

APPENDIX 1

Table 1: List of known governors of Darband

Date	Name
786-809	Hajji b. Hashem
869-884	Hashem b. Suraka b. Sadis b. Khaiiyn b. Hajji al-Sulami
884-885	'Omar b. Hashem
885-915	Mohammad b. Hashem
916	'Abdol-Malek b. Hashem
916	Abu Hajji b. Mohammad
916-939	'Abdol-Malek (second time)
939	Ahmad b. 'Abdol-Malek
939-941	Heysam b. Mohammad b. Yazid
941	Ahmad (second time)
941-942	Heysam (second time)
942	Ahmad b. Yazid
942-953	Ahmad b. 'Abdol-Malek (third time)
953-954	Hashram Ahmad b. Monabbih, king of the Lezgis
954-976	Ahmad b. 'Abdol-Malek (fourth time)
976-997	Maymun b. Ahmad b. 'Abdol-Malek
997	Mohammad b. Ahmad b. 'Abdol-Malek
998-1002	Lashkari b. Mayman
1003-1019	Mansur b. Maymun
1019-1021	Yazid b. Ahmad, Shirvanshah
1021-1023	Mansur (second time)
1023-1024	Yazid Shirvanshah (second time)
1024-1034	Mansur (third time)
1034	'Abdol-Malek b. Mansur
1035	Mansur b. Mosadded, vizier of the Shirvanshah
1035-1043	'Abdol-Malek b. Mansur (second time)
1043-10054	Mansur b. 'Abdol-Malek
1054-1055	Lashkari b. 'Abdol-Malek
1055-1065	Mansur b. 'Abdol-Malek (second time)
1065	'Abdol-Malek b. Lashkari
1065-1068	Aglab b. 'Alia, under Seljuq rule
1068	'Abdol-Malek b. Lashkri (second time)
1068-1071	Afreydun b. Shirvanshah Fariburz
1071-1075	'Abdol-Malek b. Lashkari (third time)
1075-1076	Mayman b. Mansur b. 'Abdol-Malek
ca. 1130-1150	Seyf al-Din Mohammad b. Khalif al-Sulami
1154	Abu'l-Mozaffar
ca. 1160-1164	Mozaffar b. Mohammad b. Khalif. *malek*
ca. 1170-1225	Bekbars b. Mozaffar, *malek*
ca. 1180-1225	'Abdol-Malek b. Beybars
1222	Rashid [?]
1227	al-Asad, regent
1301	Hajji Amir b. Hajji Tavakli, emir
1368-1369	Afriburuz b. Takhuyras
1411-1421	Esfandiyar, emir
1454	Mazid b. Amir al-Din
1509	Mansur Bey

until 1536	Mozaffar Soltan
1538-1542	Elqas-Mirza, brother of Shah Tahmasp I
From 996/1588 to 1015/1606	Ottoman governors
1580	'Othman Pasha
until 1606	Hazir Hasan
1606	Usmi Khan Qeytaq
1607	Qanbar Bey, *selahdar-bashi*
1607-1610	Cheragh Soltan Gerampa Ostajalu
1610	Jamshid Bey
1610	Mohammad Hoseyn Soltan brother of Shahqoli Soltan Kholafa-ye Rumlu
1614	Mohammad Hoseyn Soltan
1618-1621	Barkhordar Soltan
1623	Yutem Soltan
1626-1627	Qara Khan Bey Suvazly b. Pulad Bey
1627	Yutam Solta Gorji
1627-1631	Farrokh Soltan [Khan]
1632-1635	Siyavosh Bey [Soltan]
1635-1638	Shahverdi Bey [Soltan] Ostajalu
1638-1642	Bahram Beyh (Soltan) Ostajalu
1643	'Arab Bey [Khan] Aghzivar-oglu Shamlu
1653-1654	Bayazid Soltan b. Bahram Soltan
until 1672-1673	Urah Khan
1687	Eshaq Soltan
until 1721	Ahmad Khan Soltan
1722-1728	Emamqoli Bey, na'eb
1728-1735	Mohammad Hoseyn b. Emamqoli Bey na'eb; as of 1730 Khan
1735-1736/37	Morad 'Ali Soltan Ostajalu
ca. 1736-1737	Najaf Soltan Quchurlu
1741-1743	Mohammad 'Ali Khan Qereqlu
1743-1747	Hadi Khan
1747-1765	Mohammad Hoseyn Khan (second time)
1765-1789	Fath 'Ali Khan b. Hoseyn'Ali Khan
1781-1790	Ahmad Khan b. Fath 'Ali Khan
1790-1796	Sheykh 'Ali Khan b. Fath 'Ali Khan
1796	Pari Jahan Khanom d. Fath 'Ali Khan
1796-1797	Hasan 'Ali Khan b. Fath 'Ali Khan
1797-1800	Sheykh 'Ali Khan (second time)
1800-1803	Hasan 'Ali Khan (second time)
1803-1806	Sheykh 'Ali Khan (third time)

Source: L. I. Lavrov, *Epigraficheskie Pamiatniki Severnogo Kavkaza. Na Arabskom, Persidskom i Turetskom Yazikakh. Part 2, nadpisi XVIII-XX vv.* (Moscow, 1968), pp. 158-61; Willem Floor, *The Titles and Emoluments of Officials in Safavid Iran. A Third Manual of Safavid Administration* (Washington DC, 2008), pp. 200-04.

APPENDIX II

Table 2: List and dates of known Avars chiefs or Nowsals

Date	Legendary Nowsals/Name	Source
?	Abukhuarso	Istochnikovedenie 147
?	Avar Avaz	Istochnikovedenie 147
905	Bukht Yisho I	Istochnikovedenie 148
ca. 940-950	Filanshah	Istochnikovedenie 148
1025-1026	Bukht Yiso II	Istochnikovedenie 148
1065	T.qi b. F.rudzha (variant: Q.rudzh or Q.rukh)	Istochnikovedenie 148
?	Surakat (Suraqat b. Sirtan)	Istochnikovedenie 148
ca. 1090-1110	Bayar b. Surakata	Istochnikovedenie 149
early 12th century	Ma'sum	Istochnikovedenie 149
early 13th century	Amir Ahmad or Ma'sum Bey	Istochnikovedenie 149
mid 13th century	Amir Soltan b. Bayar 'Abbas b. Surakata	Istochnikovedenie 149-50
1318-139	Sirtan	Istochnikovedenie 150
	Historical Nowsals	
1485	Andunik I (Andunik-Nowsal aka Ebrahim)	Istochnikovedenie 150
1485	Bulach, brother's son previous one; perhaps = Mohammad Mirza Nowsal b. Durgi-Nowsal	Istochnikovedenie 150
1547/48-1554/54	Andunik II	Istochnikovedenie 150-51
1577-1578	Tuchalav [Borhan al-Din]	Istochnikovedenie 151
1590	Kan-Bulat	Istochnikovedenie 149
?	Mohammad I b. Barti b. Andunik I b. Mohammad	Istochnikovedenie 151
1595-1596	Shamkhal or Mohammad Shamkhal b. Tururava	Istochnikovedenie 151
1600-1601	Ebrahim	Istochnikovedenie 152
1614	Mehdi	Istochnikovedenie 152
1634-1635	Omma I b. Shamkhal Nowsal	Istochnikovedenie 152
1641-1645	Amir Hamzeh	Istochnikovedenie 152
1650	Muldar Mirza	Istochnikovedenie 152
1656/57 & 1667/68	Durgi I b. Mohammad Nowsal	Istochnikovedenie 152-53
1669/70-1687/88	Mohammad II b. Omma Nowsal	Istochnikovedenie 153
1687/88, 1690	Omma II b. Mohammad II	Istochnikovedenie 153
1699	Dugri II b. Omma Nowsal	Istochnikovedenie 153
1706-1070	Omma III	Istochnikovedenie 153
1708/08, 1721/22	Mohammad III	Istochnikovedenie 153
1727 or 1728	Omma IV	Istochnikovedenie 154
1730-1732	Mohammad IV b. Omma Nowsal	Istochnikovedenie 154-56
1761/62	Omma V b. Mohammad IV	Istochnikovedenie 156
1801	Gebek b. Mohammad IV	Istochnikovedenie 156
1802-1823	Soltan Ahmad	Istochnikovedenie 156-57
1823-1834	Abu Soltan b. Soltan Ahmad	Istochnikovedenie 157-58
1859	Ebrahim II b. Ahmad Khan Mehtulini	Istochnikovedenie 158

Source: "Materiali po khronologii i genealogii pravitelei Avarii (VIII-XIX vv.)" in *Istochnikovedenie* 1986; Lavrov, *Epigraficheskie* 2, 1968, p. 170-71.

INDEX

Ayn

'Abbas b. 'Abdol-Motalleb, 47, 54
'Abbas Mirza, ix, 155, 159, 163
'Abbas Qoli Aqa, vii, xiii
'Abbas Qoli Qodsi, 190
'Abdi Shirvani, 186
'Abdol-'Aziz Baheli, 42, 43, 77
'Abdol-Baqi Khan Zanganeh, 126
'Abdollah 'Ali b. Mohammad Baku'i, 170
'Abdollah Bey, 164, 165
'Abdollah Bey b. Rostam Qadi, 119, 163, 164
'Abdollah Bey, son of Hajji Salim Bey, 119
'Abdollah Khan Ostajalu, 79, 90
'Abdollah Pasha, 126
'Abdollah, son of Rostam Bey Qadi, 154
'Abdol-Malek, 8, 42, 44, 45, 46, 47, 52, 77, 200
'Abdol-Rahim Aqa, 160
'Abdol-Rahim Shakvi, 190
'Abdol-Rahman b. Rabi'eh, 41, 77
'Adel Geray Khan Shamkhal, 114, 120
'Adel Geray Soltan, 94, 95, 96
'Adel Khan, 162
'Adel Shamkhal Khan, 114
'Akari, 55
'Ala al-Dowleh Dhu'l-Qadr, 86
'Ali, 31
'Ali Arashi, 140, 146
'Ali Beg Zakhuri, 105
'Ali Bey, 75, 149
'Ali Bey Hali Ziyad-oghlu Ganjavi, 190
'Ali Bey Javanshir, 107
'Ali Bey, the son of Usmi, 142
'Ali Bey Zakhuri, 105
'Ali b. Heysham, 51, 78
'Ali Eskander, 151
'Ali Hajji Mohammad Chalabi 'Aliji, 188
'Ali Jeruq, 112
'Ali Khan b. Ebrahim Khan, 155
'Ali Khanlu, 12
'Ali Khan Movafeq, 101, 102
'Ali Khan Rudbari, 164
'Ali Khan Shams al-Dinlu, 101

'Ali Mardan Khan Bakhtiyari, 136
'Ali Mardan Khan Khamseh'i, 166
'Ali Mirza, 99, 125, 163, 189
'Ali Panah Bey b. Ahmad Bey, 161
'Ali Pasha, 123, 125, 126
'Ali Qoli b. Sayel b. Mirza, 143
'Ali Qoli Khan, 80, 126, 135, 154
'Ali Qoli Khan Shahsevan, 160
'Ali Qoli Ma'sum, 143
'Ali Razi Bey, 139
'Ali Shah, 135, 136, 154
'Ali Soltan, 154
'Ali Soltan Arshi, 101
'Ali Soltan Bey, 146, 158
'Ali Soltan Shamsh al-Dinlu, 154
'Ali Soltan Zakhuri, 113
'Ali, son of Key Qobad, 89
'Ameliyan, 149
'Andalal, 17
'Andeb, 19, 56
'Aniq, 156
'Arab Bey [Khan] Aghzivar-oglu Shamlu, 201
'Arab Khan, 80
'Araskani lineage, 54
'Archub, 56
'Arishti, 57
'Arshlu, 15
'Askaran, 160
'Askar Bey, 138, 139, 145, 147
'Ata Ollah Khan Shahsevan, 161
'ayyar, 27
'Emad al-Din Beyk, 108
'Eyn al-Mizan, 193
'Ezz al-Din Shirvani, 179
'Isa Khan Gorji, 94
'Omar b. al-Khattab, 41, 57, 77
'Omar Soltan Sa'dari, 148, 163
'Omma Khan, 110, 126, 138, 142, 146, 157
'Oshaqiyan, 189
'Othman b. 'Affan, 42
'Othman Pasha, 79

A

Aba Bakr Qazi, 164
Abahiyan, 189
Abakhiyan, 189
Abaqa Khan, 65, 182
Abarshahreh, 96
Abazeh, 33
Abdalis, 124, 129
Abdal Ostajalu, 131
Ab-e Garm Kalbakh, 36
Ab-e Ghuri, 72
Abivard, 122
Abiyeh Soltan, 76, 85
Abkhazia, 158, 163
Abo'l-Fath Khan, son of Karim Khan, 144
Abovyan, Khachatur, viii
Abu 'Abbas Saffah, 48
Abu 'Ali Rudbari, 190
Abu Bakr Mirza, 74, 79, 94, 95, 96, 99
Abu Ja'far Mansur, 48, 49
Abu'l-'Ala Ganjavi, 174
Abu'l-Fath Khan, 136, 137, 161
Abu'l-Qasem Yusof b. Abi al-Saj, 51
Abu Mohammad Nezam al-Din b. Yusof b. Mo'ayyed, 171
Abu Moslem, 47, 48, 49, 53
Abu Moslem b. Yusof, 57
Abu 'Obeydeh Jarrah, 44, 45, 77
Abu Sa'id, 67, 75
Abu Sa'id Abdal Baku'i, 183
Abu Shahmeh, 98
Abu Taher Shirvani, 184
Abu Turab, 136
Adhar, 170
Afshin, 50
Afzal al-Din b. Ebrahim b. 'Ali Najjar, 175
Aghaj-Machgach, 101
Aghasi Khan, 140, 141, 142, 144, 145, 146, 150
Aghbil, 99
Aghdash, 125, 126, 151
Agher Akhan, 116, 120
Agher Akhan river, 114
Aghtam, 73
Aghvan, 6, 34
Aghzibar, 129
Ahar, 76

Ahmad Amin Khan, 98
Ahmad Aqa, 145
Ahmad b. Chuban, 57
Ahmad Bey, 145
Ahmad Bey Bayat, 156
Ahmad b. Hasan Padshah, 77
Ahmad Khan, 111, 147
Ahmad Khan Abdali, 135
Ahmad Khan Bey Jangta'i, 133
Ahmad Khan Gilani, 106, 118
Ahmad Khan Shahsevan, 139
Ahmad Khan, son of Ulu Bey Usmi, 111
Ahmad Khan Usmi, 112, 113, 127, 129, 130, 149
Ahmad Mirza, 89
Ahmad Pasha, 80, 99, 103, 106, 122
Ahmarlu, 18
Ahran, 36, 37, 44, 48, 99
Ahvaz, 38
Akhalkalak, 146
Akhatalisk, ix
Akhi Farrokh Zanjani, 172
Akhi Juq, 68
Akhi Soltan Chakerlu, 101
Akhsaqeh, 94, 158
Akhsatan, 77
Akhstafeh, 160
Akhti, 37, 48, 52, 53, 99, 112, 143, 153
Akhti-nameh, 37
Akhtipareh, 124, 127
Akhund Eskandar, 188
Akhund Najaf 'Ali Baku'i, 190
Akhundzadeh, vii, viii, x, xiii
Akvakh, 19
Alamut, 59, 97
Alan, xi, 8, 11, 18, 33, 36
Alanjaq, 75, 76
Alans, xi, 6, 8, 11, 29, 33, 34, 37, 41
Albania, 6, 11, 15, 26, 32
Albanus, 13
Al-e Sarkar, 139, 143, 146, 147, 148
Alexander, 27, 29, 31
Alexander I, 157
Alexander Mirza, 101, 159
Algeria, 189
Alkhas-Tav, 72
Alkit river, 104, 108

Allahabad, 188
allahdad, 132
Allahverdi Bey, 138
Allahverdi Khan, 104, 105
Almaq, 72
Alpan, 13, 153
Altai, 12, 17
Alti Aghach, 127
Alvand, 77, 85, 145, 147, 148
Alvand Mirza, 77
Amazone, 29
Amir Aslan Khan Qereqlu, 129
Amir Buynaq Mehdi, 139
Amir Buynaq Morteza 'Ali b. Mehdi b. Morteza 'Ali, 142
Amir Dubbaj, 87
Amireh of Tabarsaran, 143
Amir Hajan, vii, 190
Amir Hamzeh, 111
Amir Hamzeh Khan Ostajalu, 95
Amir Hamzeh Khan Talesh, 99
Amir Hamzeh Usmi, 113, 128, 141, 142, 145, 148
Amir Hatam, 87
Amir Khan, 97
Amir Khan Ghazanesh Mohammad the Toothless, 142
Amir Khan Qajar, 165, 166
Amir Othman Mowsellu, 85
Anak, 34
Anatolia, 16, 25, 33, 74, 85, 86, 87, 149, 190
Andab, 99
Andallal, 130
Andar, 101
Andiya, 99
Anna, Empress, 121, 151
Ansari, Mirza Mas'ud Ishliqi, ix
Ansukh, 19
Anushirvan, 6, 7, 8, 12, 14, 15, 18, 23, 26, 32, 36, 37, 38, 47, 77, 78, 85
Anushtakin, 62
Aqaba Khan, 65, 149
Aqa Keshi Bey, 139
Aqa Mohammad Khan, 146, 147, 149, 150, 153
Aqa Mohammad Khan Qajar, 137, 147, 152
Aqa Mohammad Shah [Qajar], 111
Aqa Razi Bey, 139

Aq Buqa b. Ilkan b. Jalayer, 67
Aqdam, 73
Aqshin, 50
Aq Su, 101, 126, 128, 129, 132, 140, 141, 143, 145, 146, 147, 148, 150, 153, 155, 161
Aq Su Yurt, 95
Aqtam, 145
Aq Ughlan, 160
Aqusheh, 16, 18, 26, 36, 48, 56, 112, 128, 142, 156, 163, 164, 165
Aras, ix, xii, 11, 26, 33, 41, 45, 60, 62, 69, 77, 94, 154, 160, 165, 166
Arasbar, 87, 96, 103
Arash, 90, 94, 108, 125, 127, 128, 132, 138, 140, 144, 148, 179
Aras Khan Rumlu, 79, 92
Archel, 43
Ardabil, ix, xii, 16, 46, 74, 75, 83, 84, 85, 98, 102, 107, 120, 123, 130, 138, 143, 146, 163
Ardashest, 34
Ardashir, 34, 78
Arghi, 34
Arghunay, 100, 101
Arghun Khan, 67
Aristotle, 27
Arjasb, 27
Arkavan, 166, 167
Armenia, 5
Armenian maleks, 138
Armenians, 19
Arpa Chay, 128, 162
Arpa Khan, 67
Arran, 51, 75, 78, 169
Arsalan b. Toghrol, 62, 176
Artanish, 44
Artashes b. Senatrak, 33
Artavaz, 34
Aser Lanbarani, 190
Ash'ath b. Qeys, 42, 77
Ashkabus, 13
Ashkanbar, 96
Ashraf Chubani, 78
Ashur Khan, 80
Ashur Khan Afshar, 132
Aslan Aqa, 165
Aslan Aqa b. Shahmardan, 165

Aslanduz, 161, 166
Asmid, 23
Asrar al-Malakut, 193
Astara, 98, 99, 120, 123, 166
Astarabad, 16, 108, 116, 119, 136, 139, 150
Astrakhan, 22, 72, 113, 116, 152, 153, 159
Atabey Eldegoz, 180, 181, 206
Atabey of Argun Khan, 149
Atabey Qezel-Arsalan Saljuqi, 172
Atabey Yusof, 182
Atal, 7
Atal River, 10, 11, 17, 22, 28, 35, 51, 72
Atal, town, 23
Ataqah, 101
Athir al-Din Akhsikati, 176
Atilla, 9, 17, 22
Atsiz, 63
Avar, 8, 13, 17, 18, 24, 48, 55, 99, 130, 138, 146
Avaristan, 9
Avars, 54
Avoq, 101
Avramov, Semen, 114, 117
Aydin, 189
Aysu, 29
Aytmut, 100
Azad Khan the Afghan, 136
Azaq, 72

B

Baba 'Ali Beyk Kuseh Ahmadlu, 122
Baba-daghi, 12
Babak, xiv, 50
Baba Khalifeh, 95
Bab al-Abvab, 14, 38
Bab al-'Alqameh, 47
Bab al-Hadid, 18
Bab al-Jehad, 47
Bab al-Khoms, 47
Bab al-Maktub, 47
Bab al-Mohajer, 47
Bab al-Saghir, 47
Bab al-Sajasi, 38
Bab al-Shaberan, 38
Baba Rokn al-Din Shirvani, 190
Bab-e Alan, 38
Bab-e Iranshah, 38

Bab-e Kardemanshah, 38
Bab-e Liyanshah, 38
Bab-e Saheb al-Sarir, 38
Badakhshan, 183, 189
Badpay, 27
Badr-e Shirvani, 185
Badr Khan Shah Qoli Khan Ostajalu, 91
Badr Saheb Qadr Shirvani, 185
Baghdad, xii, 37, 49, 50, 52, 58, 60, 61, 62, 66, 67, 68, 69, 70, 71, 73, 74, 86, 87, 89, 121, 122, 188
Baghdad-Kerker, 37
Bahan b. Abi Bakr Qazi, 165
Bahman, 27, 179
Bahram Chubin, 7, 78
Bahram Gur, 14
Bajarvan Mahin Banu, 38
Bakhsaq, 72
Bakhtiyari tribe, 137, 140
Bakr b. 'Abdollah, 41
Balbaleh, 169
Baldeh, 188
Balkh, 27, 36, 44, 109
Ba'lkhani, 149
Baqtolal, 19, 57
Baratashvili, Nikoloz, viii
Barbary Coast, 189
Barda', 23, 28, 29, 38, 41, 46, 51, 67, 130, 132, 169
Bargoshad, 149
Bargoshat, 103, 138
Barij, 25
Barlas emirs, 69
Barmak, 15, 18, 139, 162
Baron Rosen, ix, x, xii, xiii
Baron Shafirov, 122
Barzan, 50
Bash Achoq, 11, 157, 158, 160, 163
Bashli, 9, 15, 100, 110, 111, 128, 130, 143, 151
Baslas, 8, 34
Basra, 137
Batluq, 72
Batu, son of Juji, 17
Bayan, 13, 17, 101
Bayan al-Asrar, 184
Bayan Khan, 13, 17
Bayat, 15, 47, 55, 86, 156, 161
Bayat b. Seraqeh, 55

Bayat Fort, 138
Bayat Qapu, 47
Bayazid, 73
Bayazid Soltan Shamlu, 87
Baydar, 139
Bayt al-Mal, 43
Bektashis, 189
Bektash Soltan, son of Mohammad Khan Mowselli, 101
Belbeleh river, 115
Belghas Beyk Ilisu'i, 140
Bengal, 188
Berdi Bek, 68
Berk-Tav, 72
Berk-Yaruq, 60
Besqal, 16
Bey-kendi, 163
Beylaqan, 78, 177
Beysongor Mirza, 76
Bezenki, 9
Bibi Heybat, 49, 169
Bighord, 86, 88, 91
Bighur, 24
Bileqan, 45, 50, 73, 74
Bileqan Millar, 74
Bilhadi, 18
Bi-navayan, 188
Birakiyan, 188
Bloody Hill, 118
Bodenstedt, Friedrich, viii
Boduq, 18, 127, 153
Bohemia, 17
Bokhara, 130
Bola, 23
Bolach, 141
Bolboleh, 118
Bolghar, 9, 24, 51
Bolnisi, 11
Bonnac, 119
Borhan al-Din Aghtashi, 190
Borhan Amir al-Mo'menin, 60
Borhan Mirza, 79, 89, 90, 94, 99
Boris, son of Fyodor Godonov, 100
Borkeh Khan, 65
Botun Shah, 37
Brahmans, 188

Bulgakov, general, 161
Bulgakov, major-general, 152, 153
Buynaq, 13, 73, 99, 161
Buzchalu, 139, 149
Buzjalu, 149, 160, 163

C

camel-swivels, 124
Carmathians, 51
Caspian Sea, 13
Catherine I, 121
Catherine II, 152, 153
Chaghatay, 16, 18, 105
Chahar Tappeh, 114
Chakerlu, 15, 97
Chamchiyan, 6, 8
Chamghal Beyk, 143
Chamlibel of Koroghli, 155, 162
Chamnaz Khanom, 154
Charandab Soltan Shamlu, 91
Charkay, 72
Charkhi, 163
Chavchavadse, Ilia, viii
Chechen-Tala, 101
Chechi, 164
Cheh, 17
Chehel Nam, 150
Chehel Yurt, 36
Chekam, 9
Chelyurt, 99
Chenaqchi, 160
Chengiz Khan, 63
Cheragh, 12, 18, 130, 143, 156
Cheragh Soltan Ostajalu, 107
Cherkeni, 49
Cherkes, 8, 36, 54, 84, 89, 99, 139
Cheshtis, 189
Chin, 25
Chirkab, 72
Christians, 7, 108, 189
Chuban Shamkhal, 99
Chuban-Tav, 72
Chumlu, 36
Chupan Bey Bingeray Khan, 35
Chupani tribe, 138
Chur, 55

Cimmerians, 26
Circassians, 6, 8
Colchis, 10, 33
Constantinople, 9, 17, 22, 98, 99, 119, 121, 189
Cosis, 33
Cossacks, 23, 114, 116, 120, 152, 165
Count Apraksin, 116
Crimea, 22, 55, 91, 94, 97, 103, 126
Cyrus, 26

D

Dagh-e Shah, 132
Dahdahlu, 115
Dahriyan, 188
Dalv Malek, 108
Danube, 11
Dara, 27
Darab, 189
Daragez, 122
Dar al-Harb, 54
Darband-nameh, xi, xv, 13, 18, 30, 35, 42
Dargah Qoli Bey, 118
Darius, 27
Darvaq, 5, 15, 26, 42, 43, 44, 49, 152
Darvazeh, 29
Darvisha'i, 52
Daryal, 8, 12
Davud Osashi, 190
Deccan, 188
Dedeh Fal, 105
Dekharqan, ix
Delhi, 73, 188
Delshah Khatun, 67
deluge, 21
Dereh-kend, 127
Derreh, 18
Dervish Mohammad Khan, 88, 90
Deveh-batan, 123
Deylam, 52
Dhahabis, 189
Dhu'l-Feqar Khan, 106, 107
Dhu'l-Feqar Khan Qaramanlu, 104
Dhu'l-Feqar Qaramanlu, 80
Dhu'l-Qarneyn, 30, 31, 35
Dilejan, 160
Dioskurias, 26

Divan-e hekmat neh Divan-e 'Aql, viii
divs, 13
Diyarbekr, 60, 74, 83, 86, 189
Diz I, 16
Dniepr, 22
Dolgorukov, xi, xii
Domanisi, 11
Don, 11, 17, 22, 23, 30, 116, 120, 191
Doquzpareh, 127, 128
Dorduqaz, 144
Du Baru, 116

E

Ebrahim Arashi, 190
Ebrahim b. 'Ali Khaqani, 78
Ebrahim Khalil Aqa, 140
Ebrahim Khalil Khan, 159
Ebrahim Khan, 80, 119, 128, 131, 144, 145, 146, 153, 189
Ebrahim Khan Dhu'l-Qadr, 89
Ebrahim Pasha, 97, 119
Ebrahim Sheykh Shah, 85
Egypt, 8, 54, 74, 86, 189
Elburz, 14, 29, 72, 91, 105, 125, 129
Eldar, 99
Eldar Bey, 141, 142
Eldar Khan, 109, 110, 112, 127
Eldar, son of Morteza 'Ali, 127
elephants, 55, 126
Elisabeth, 151
Elisabethpol, 158
Elisiya, 25
Elqas Mirza, 79, 88, 89, 109
Elvand, 143
Emam Qoli Bey, 115, 158
Emam Qoli Khan Darbandi, 160
Emam Qoli Khan Ziyad-oghlu Qajar, 97
Emam Qoli Mirza, 135
Emam Qoli Qereqluy Afshar, 122
Emir 'Ali Shir, 186
Emir Ashraf, 67
Emir Azal, 54
Emir Boqrat, 69
Emir Chuban b. Soltan 'Ali Bey, 54
Emir Ebrahim, 73, 79, 185
Emir Enji, 45

Emir Hajjan, 118
Emir Hamzeh, 47, 57
Emir Hoseyn, 67, 69
Emir Kaghi, 52
Emir Khalil, 79
Emir Khan, 57
Emir Mehdi Vali, 146
Emir Ne'matollah Soltan, 105
Emir Soltan, 57
Emir Soltan b. Biyar b. Seraqeh, 57
Emir Taraqay, 69
Enderey, 15, 35, 36, 48, 73, 100, 114, 138, 142
Enhesar Bey, 164
Enji, 36, 44
Erekle Khan, 139, 147, 154, 158, 159
Erevan, viii, 73, 94, 109, 113, 126, 132, 138, 139, 149, 150, 159, 160, 162, 163
Erhani, 57
Erzenjan, 86
Erzerum, ix, 75, 94, 96, 98
Esfandiyar, 8, 12, 27, 32, 36, 37, 74, 79
Eshaq b. Ebrahim b. Mos'eb, 50
Eshken, 34
Esisheh, 56
Eskandar, 27, 74
Eskandar Bey, 145
Eskandar-nameh, 173
Eskander, son of Qara Yusof, 79
Eslam Geray Soltan, 126
Esma'il Bey, 54, 117, 118, 119, 120
Esma'il II, 93
Esma'il III, 136
Esma'il Mirza, 79, 85, 89, 90
Esm'il Bey Damghani, 160
Estakhr, 26, 77, 85, 98
Ethiopia, 189
Eydeh Bey, 110
Ezekiel, 12, 24

F

Falaki, 174, 178
Falaki Shirvani, 178
Faraj Khan, 80
Farajollah Khan Nasaqchi-bashi, 163
Farajollah Khan Shahsevan, 164
Faramarz, 78

Faramushiyan, 189
Farazman, 33
Farhad Pasha, 86, 98
Farrokh Yasar, 79
Farrokh Yasar Shirvanshah, 84
Farrokhzad, 78
Farrokhzad b. Akhshijan, 77
Fars, 8, 18, 26, 32, 37, 46, 49, 58, 62, 73, 75, 77, 85, 86, 89, 122, 123, 136, 150, 189
Fatemeh Khanom, 137
Fatemeh, sister of Fath 'Ali Khan, 144
Fathabad, 133
Fath 'Ali Aqa, 159
Fath 'Ali Khan, 139, 141, 142, 143, 147
Fath 'Ali Khan Afshar, 80, 132, 140
Fath 'Ali Khan Quseh Ahmadlu, 129
Fath 'Ali Shah, viii, 111, 154
Fath Geray Soltan, 123
Fazel-e 'Eymaki, 190
Fereydun, viii, x, 25, 54
Filanshah, 7, 36, 37, 38, 50, 51, 77
Firas, 25
Firuz, 13, 27, 35, 73, 102
Firuz Qobad, 13
Five Saints, 188
Fort of the Cross, 116, 120
Fowul, 25
Fozuli, 144
Fraehn, 186
Franks, 17, 24
Fyodor, son of Ivan, 98, 100

G

Gamishvan, 163, 166
Ganges, 31
Ganjeh, 26, 33, 52, 60, 69, 73, 98, 99, 103, 105, 108, 113, 121, 123, 125, 126, 132, 138, 139, 140, 143, 147, 149, 153, 154, 157, 160, 162, 167, 169, 170, 171, 173, 187
Garmrud, 155
Gaskar, 120
Gavdushan, 142, 143
Gayomarth, 21
Gazar Hasan, 105
Gelesen Goresen, 91, 138, 151
Gepid, 17

Geray Khan, 110
Geray Khan Shamkhal, 100, 113
Get, 12
Getov, 12
Ghachi, 16
Ghachmaz, 148
Ghadar, 56, 72
Ghani Khan, 124
Ghani Khan Abdali, 129
Gharchub, 19
Ghazanesh, 127, 139, 142
Ghazanfar, 54, 55
Ghazeh, 24
Ghazi Geray Khan, 103
Ghazi Geray Soltan, 96, 97
Ghazi Khan Qomuq, 146
Ghazi-Qomuq, 5, 9, 16, 18, 26, 34, 36, 47, 56, 112, 113, 123, 124, 127, 130, 138, 164, 166
Ghazi Yurt, 100
Ghiyeh-kend, 44
Gholdi Moutain, 57
Ghrim-Shamkhal, 56
Ghubaz, 10
Ghun, 17
Ghunubb, 17
Ghuzz, 60, 61, 63
Gilan, 13, 27, 31, 36, 52, 69, 85, 97, 98, 114, 116, 117, 119, 120, 122, 144, 146, 150, 188
Giorgi VII, 73
Glasenap, general, 161
Gmelin, 143, 151
Gobden, 72
Gog, 25, 30, 31
Gok Chay, 148
Gokcheh-yeylaq, 132
Golbakh, 8
Golbakh-e Qomuq, 9
Golestan, x, 3, 14, 85, 88, 91, 167
Golestan-e Eram, 14
Gonbet, 100
Gorgin Khan, 101, 157
Goshtasb, 27, 32, 36, 78
Goshtasbi, 78
Gowhad Shah Begum, 186
Greece, 14, 24, 31, 189
Gribayedov, viii, ix

Gudovich, Count, 160, 162, 163
Gujarat, 188
Gukcheh Soltan Qajar, 89
Guney, 138, 143
Guragan, 69
Guria, 11
Guríev, general-major, 164, 165
Gutgashynli, Ismail Bey, x
Guyden, 56

H

Habib b. Salameh, 42, 77
Habib b. Salami, 11
Hadehgarar, 31
Hafseh b. 'Omar, 49
Haft Eqlim, 6
Haft Paykar, 173
Hajj Akhund Sharif Shirvani, 190
Hajj Ayub Efendi, 190
Hajj Baba Efendi, 190
Hajj Ebrahim al-'Ordi, 190
Hajji 'Abdol-Qader, 143, 144
Hajji 'Abdol-Qader Khan, 145
Hajji Aqa Qeshlaqi, 144
Hajji Aqa-ye Zolali Shirvani, 190
Hajji Beyram, 105
Hajji Chelebi, 132, 138, 139, 140, 143, 144
Hajji Davud, 112
Hajji Davud Bey, 119, 121
Hajji Davud Moskuri, 80, 112
Hajji Ebrahim Khan Shirazi, 154
Hajji Ghayeb Alpani, 112
Hajji Khan, 80
Hajji Khan Jemeshgezek, 132
Hajji Malek Mohammad, 118, 144, 157
Hajji Malek Mohammad Khan, 118, 144
Hajji Mohammad 'Ali, 138, 139, 141
Hajji Piri, 139
Hajji Rasul Bey, 144
Hajji Sayyed Bey, 146, 150
Hajji Seyf al-Din, 69
Hajji Taqi, 157
Hajji Zeyn al-'Abedin Shirvani, 79, 188
Hajj Mohammad Chelebi 'Aliji Qolhani, 188
Hakim Ma'navi Sheikh Nezami Ganjavi, 171
Halimeh Begom, 84

Halimeh Khatun, 169
Hamadan, 50, 60, 61, 62, 73, 86
Hamamlu, 163
Hameh Sahreh, 96
Hamri, 36, 42, 44, 48
Hamzadiyan, 189
Hamzeh Bey Hezati, 151
Hamzeh Mirza, 94, 98
Hanafi Qarabaghi, 190
Hanafite, 19
Hapshi, 100
Haqayeqi, 175
Harmunas, 26
Harun al-Rashid, 15, 49, 58
Hasan 'Alavi-ye Safavi, 54
Hasan 'Ali Khan, 80, 112
Hasan 'Ali Mirza, 75
Hasan 'Ali Shah, 188
Hasan 'Ali Usmi, 100
Hasan Aqa, 153
Hasan Bey, 54, 75, 76, 84, 120, 121, 156, 164
Hasan Bey Aq-Qoyunlu, 83
Hasan Bey Bayandori Aq-Qoyunlu, 75
Hasan Ilkhani, 67, 69
Hasan Khan, 158
Hasan Khan b. Fath 'Ali Khan, 156
Hasan Khan Moghani, 146
Hasan Padshah, 98
Hasan Pasha, 80, 99
Hasan-Qal'eh, 128
Hasan Sabbah, 59, 61
Hasan Suyi, 160
Hashem, 51
Hashem Khan, 164
Hasin, 44
Hazar Mowt, 189
Hazreh, 16, 84
Hebelel, 56
Hedat, 48
Hedayatollah Khan, 144
Hejran Shah, 36
Heli, 99
Heptaq, 8, 35
Heraclius, 17, 22, 38
Hesan al-'Ajam Khaqani Shirvani, 175
Hesan of the Persians, 175

Hesham, 45, 47, 48
Hesham b. 'Abdol-Malek, 45
Heybat Bey, 118
Heydar Bey Afshar, 131
Heydar b. Kavus, 50
Heydar Khan Afshar, 80
Heydar Pasha, 98
Heydar Qoli Khan, 139
Hezrat, 16
Hikmat al-'Eyn, 186
Himyar, 32
Hodheyfeh b. al-Yaman, 42, 77
Holuliyan, 188
Homay, 27
Homeydi, 18, 49
Horkus, 56
Hormozd, 38
Hormuz, 35, 78, 177, 189
Hoseyn 'Ali Khan, 112, 118, 126, 128, 139, 151
Hoseyn 'Ali Khan, son of Soltan Ahmad Khan, 126
Hoseyn 'Ali Shah, 189
Hoseyn Aqa, 140
Hoseyn Aqa, son of Hasan Aqa, 140
Hoseyn Bey, 88, 135
Hoseyn Bey Dhu'l-Qadr, 106
Hoseyn Khan, 80, 110, 141, 144
Hoseyn Khan Bey, 118, 138
Hoseyn Khan Rudbari, 141
Hoseyn Qoli Aqa, 148
Hoseyn Qoli Bey Qajar, 105
Hoseyn Qoli Khan, 118, 148, 150, 153, 154, 155, 157, 159, 160, 162, 164
Howz, 18
Hulagu Khan, 65, 73, 86, 137, 149
Hun, 8, 9, 12, 17, 24
Hungary, 17
Huri Peykar Khanom, 145
Hurizad Khanom, 154
Hushang, 78
Hushang, son of Kavus, 68

I

Iberi, 11
Iberia, 10, 11, 33, 34
Ibn Fazlan, 186
Ighuriyan, 189

Ikat, 72
Ilaqs, 29
Il Arsalan, 63
Ilisu, 5, 138, 153, 154
Imereti, 11
Iraj, 26
Irak, 26
Iran-e Kharab, 131
Iraq, 21, 38, 47, 49, 50, 58, 60, 65, 67, 68, 75, 77, 86, 89, 98, 122, 136, 144, 149, 150, 182, 188
Irtish, 22
island of Chechen, 114
Isma'ilis, 189
Istanbul, xii, 89, 94, 103, 119
Isthmus of Qom, 9, 72
Italy, 17
Ivan III, 151
Ivan Vasilivich, 91
Ivuros, 11

J

Jabriyan, 189
Ja'far Aqa, 143
Ja'far Barmaki, 15
Ja'far Khan, the son of Sadeq Khan, 137
Ja'far Pasha, 98
Ja'far Qoli Aqa, 161, 165, 166
Ja'far Qoli Aqa b. Mohammad Hasan Aqa, 161, 165
Ja'far Qoli Khan Donboli, 155, 162
Jafeth, 9, 21, 22, 25, 31
Jaghatay, 13
Jahanshah Qara-Qoyunlu, 83
Jalal al-Din, 63
Jalaliyan, 188
Jalayer, 122
Jalayer Turks, 149
Jalqan, 18
Jamalal, 19, 56
Jamal al-Din Mowseli, 177
Jamjameh, 43
JamJam the Great, 43
Jamshid Bey, 201
Jangutay, 13, 146
Jani Bey Khan, 67, 78
jankeh, 99, 100, 158

Jar, 57, 86, 112, 118, 119, 123, 125, 126, 127, 129, 139, 145, 146, 151, 154, 158, 159, 162
Jarak, 19
Jarbelleh, 19
jarchi-bashi, 106
Jarchi Qapu, 47, 141
Jarud, 164
Javad bridge, 132
Javad Gorge, 103, 107
Javad Khan b. Shahverdi Khan Ziyad-oghlu, 147, 149, 158
Javad Khan Ziyad-oghlu, 153
Javad passage, 26, 128
Javanshir, 34
Jayun b. Najm, 49
jazayer, 125
Jebra'illu, 160, 161, 165
Jenkinson, 91
Jeremiah, 24, 31
Jews, 7, 15, 19, 23, 47, 189
Jibir, 164, 165
Jiji tribe, 71
Jineq, 19
Joghrafiya, 193
Jomjuqat, 56, 165
Jonoq, 53
Judaism, 23
Jukh, 130
Jukiyan, 188
Julah, 42
Jurdaf, 48
Justinian, 17, 22

K

Kabul, 188
Kachi Majar, 36
Kadekh, 129
kadkhodas, 128
Kafeh, 89
Kaferi Plain, 113, 154
Kafer-Qomuq, 96, 99
Kaffa, 103
Kaflan Kuh, 128
Kakheti, 125
Kakht, 90, 94, 108
Kakoba, 56

Kalanbar, 96
Kalat, 122, 135
Kalbakh, 37
Kalb 'Ali Khan Ziyad-oghlu, 187
Kalb 'Ali Soltan Qutqashini, 140
Kalhin, 12
Kalisa-kandeh, 125
Kalleh-e Kureh, 53
Kalmyk, 18
Kam, 9, 24
Kamak, 9, 16, 24
Kamakh, 18, 49
Kamari, 9, 24, 25
Kangarlu, 15
Kapuchi, 19
Karakin, colonel, 160
Karak River, 138
Karamazin, Nicholas, xiv, 16
karbas, 55
Karim Khan vakil, 140, 144, 150
Karim Khan Zand, 136
Kartli, 10, 33, 98
Kasamsar, 25
Kashak, 8
Kashf al-Ghara'eb, xiv, 193
Kashkul, 188
Kashmir, 109, 188
Kasog, 8
Katarhun, 34
Kaveh the Blacksmith, 26
Kavekh, 129
Kayani, 9, 25
Kazerun, 137
Kehli, 158
Kelyar-e Qobbeh, 127
Kerkhen, 165
Kerkhi, 56
Kerkhlar Gate, 49
Kerman, 60, 62, 189
Kerman Khatun, 60, 62
Kermanshah, 136, 163
Kesh, 69
Kesran, 37
Ketab-e Asgariyeh, 195
Ketab-e Nasihat, 195
Keychi Bekeh, 145

Keykhaytu, 67
Key Khosrow, 7, 26, 27, 120
Key Qobad Shirvanshah, 78
Keysaniyan, 189
Keyvan, 36, 45
Khabushan, 133
Khachin-Qarabagh, 132
Khachmaz, 96, 123
Khadijeh Bekeh, 141
Khadijeh Bey, 111
Khadijeh Beykom, 83
Khajmaz, 124
Khaksars, 188
Khalaj, 15
Khalifeh Tamleri, 183
Khalifeh-ye Ansar-e Qaradaghi, 80
Khalifeh-ye Ansar-e Qaradaghlu, 97
Khalillu, 15
Khalil Mirza, 76
Khalil Soltan b. Miranshah, 74
Khalkhal, 29
Khalvatiyan, 189
Khamseh, 149, 173
Khan Ahmad Khan, 98, 99
Khan Arkhi Arasbar, 103
Khan Bekeh Khanom, 156
Khan Butay Bey, 164
Khanchupan, 15
Khanlar Aqa, 160
Khan Mohammad, the son of the Usmi, 127
Khan Mohammad Usmi, 100
Khaqan, 23, 35, 37, 42, 45, 51
Khaqani, 62, 78, 174, 175, 176, 178, 179, 180
Khaqan Manuchehr, 77, 170, 174
kharaj, 48, 100, 147
Kharaq, 48
Khasan, 9
Khass Fulad, 112, 124, 126
Khass Fulad Khan, 127, 130, 138, 139, 142
Khatun, 67
Khatuntsev, general-major, 165
Khazar, 22
Khazargan, 13
Khazars, xiv, 7, 14, 16, 22, 23, 29, 32, 35, 38, 41, 42, 43, 44, 45, 46, 48, 49, 51
Khazran-Kuh, 27

Khedhr, 28, 151
Khedhr Bey b. Hajji Bey Qurchi, 152
Khedhr Bey Qurchi, 156
Khenaleq, 18, 89, 127
Khoda-Afarin bridge, 41, 138, 149, 150, 160, 161
Khodad, 111, 112, 138
Khodaverdi, 98
khoms, 43, 44
Khomzaq, 48, 53, 56
Khorasan, 7, 23, 37, 58, 60, 66, 69, 74, 86, 122, 129, 133, 135, 136, 149, 150, 151, 154, 167, 186, 188
Khorramiyan, 189
Khorramkish, 50
Khorramkishan, 59
Khosrek, 124
Khosrow, 34
Khosrow and Shirin, 38, 173
Khosrow II, 34
Khosrow Khan, 80
Khota'iyan, 189
Khoy, 87, 155
Khozeymeh b. Jazem, 49
Khucheni, 18, 164
Khuriyan, 10
Khvajeh Ahmad Mas'ud Sarbadar, 71
Khvajeh Demashq, 67
Khvajeh Mohammad Darbandi, 104
Khvajeh Naser al-Din Mohammad Tusi, 65
Khvarezm, 23, 130
Khvarezm Shah, 62
Kish, 91
Kishavar, 8
Kizliar, 36, 44, 143, 151, 153
Knorring, lieutenant-general, 157
Knov, 48
Kohdom, 87
Komari, 9
Konstandil Mirza, 101
Korak, river, 159
Koralal, 57
Kostak, 100
Kostak-sar, 56
Kothar Shah, 57
Kotliarevskii, general, 166
Krasnoshtekov, 116
Kropotov, general-major, 120

Kubachi, 15, 36
Kuchek Hasan, 106
Kukchay, 146
Kukjeh Yeylaq, 163
Kuklovchi, 112
Kunbet, 101
Kupchi, 18, 48
kupechi, 7
Kur, 5, 6, 11, 13, 14, 18, 19, 26, 33, 37, 45, 48, 51, 57, 65, 71, 73, 78, 94, 96, 98, 99, 103, 116, 117, 119, 120, 123, 128, 131, 132, 141, 143, 147, 153, 161, 165
Kurdestan, 33, 58, 136
Kurekan, 122
Kutvan, 141

L

Lahej, 18
Lahejan, 98
Lahij, 16
Lahjan, 42
Laleh Pasha, 79, 94, 96
Laleh Pasha 'Askar, 79
Langarkonan, 163
Lavand Khan, 90, 94
Laz, 10
Lazeqeh, 8, 38
Lenkoran, 164, 166, 167
Leo the Khazar, 23
Levashev, general-major, 117, 122
Leyla va Majnun, 173
lineage of Espahbadan of Tabarestan, 118
lineage of Hajji Mohammad, 56
lineage of Malek Adi Boduqi, 162
lineage of the Ma'suman, 141
Lisanevich, colonel, 164
Lisanevich, major, 161
Lithuania, 191
Livonia, 191
Lohrasb, 32
Longobards, 17
Lorestan, 137, 140
Lotf 'Ali Khan, 137
Luni, lieutenant, 115
Luri, 126
Lydia, 26

M

Mabahiyan, 188
Machgach, 9, 13, 16, 19, 72, 73, 99, 138
Machin, 188
Machqach, 56, 161
Madariyan, 188
Madi, 25
Magharti, 18
Magog, 25, 30, 31
Maharam-kendi, 164
Mahdevali, 138
Mahmudabad, 71, 75, 85
Mahmud Afghan, 113
Mahmud Bey, 145
Mahmud b. Malekshah, 60
Mahmud Pasha, 80
Mahmud Pasha Jeghal-oghli Beyler-bey, 101
Mahraqeh, 49, 163
Mahsati Ganjavi, 170
Majales, 100, 110, 111, 127
Majame'-ye Ash'ari, 195
Majar, 44
Majd al-Din, 60
Majdhub 'Ali Shah of Hamadan, 189
Majuj, 25
Makuk, 25
Malek 'Ali Arashi, 140
Malek Bey b. Hajji Bey, 162
Malek Farraj, 73
Malek Hamri, 116
Malek Mahmud Seystani, 122
Malek Mohammad Khan Baku'i, 141, 142
Malekshah b. Alp Arsalan, 58
Malekshah II, 62
Malekshah Nazar-Verandeh, 138
Malhamlu, 175
Mamay b. Soltan b. Khan Mohammad, 149
Manaf Bey, 147
Manas, 13
Manaviyan, 189
Mangu Qaían, 65
Mantasha Soltan, 88
Manuchehr Bey, 105
Manuchehr Khan, 80
Maqatir, 18, 49
Maragheh, 18, 52, 65

Mardanshah, 45
Mardavij b. Ziyad, 52
Marwan b. Mohammad, 48
Marzban, 52, 78
Mashhad, 90, 135, 136, 154
Mashqata', 18, 119, 155, 158
Masih, 76, 190
Masih Mirza, 76
Maskanjeh, 16, 124, 153
Maskur, 28, 42, 99, 184
Maslameh, 42
Maslameh b. 'Abdol-Malek, 8, 47, 77
Masqateh, 37
Massagetes, 11, 18, 26
Massagethia, 34
Mast 'Ali, 188
Masub, 12
Ma'sum, 133, 146
Ma'sum 'Ali Shah Hindi, 188
Ma'sum Bey, 54, 55
Ma'sum Khan, 105, 107
Mata'i, 18
Matushkin, general-lieutenant, 120
Matushkin, general-major, 117
Mazandaran, 51, 63, 109, 118, 121, 130, 135, 137
Mazdak, 50
Mazdakiyan, 189
Mazkhan ol-Asrar, 173
Mecheh, 16
Mecheqich, 101
Mecheq river, 101
Medem, general-major, 142, 151
Mehdi Bey, 129, 146, 153
Mehdi Beylu, 150
Mehdi Bey, son of Ahmad Khan Bey Jangkuta'i, 138
Mehdi Khan, 129
Mehdi Khan Khorasani, 80
Mehdi Khan Sardar Khan Qereqlu, 80
Mehdi Qoli Aqa, 160
Mehdivali, 164
Mehrab Mirza, 90
Mehr 'Ali Bey, 145, 155
Mehr 'Ali Khan, 80
Mehtar Dowlatyar, 89
Mehvali, 158
Mekkeh, 16

Meqri, 138
Meshkin, 77, 166, 167
Meskenjeh, 99
Mesopotamia, 29, 86
Miji, 123
Mikael, son of Fyodor, 109
Mikragh, 16, 52
Milesians, 26
Mingrelia, 11, 157, 158
Miranshah, 69, 71, 73
Mir Baqer Bey, 162
Mir Hedayat Bey, 163
Mir Hoseyn Bey, 163
Mir Mostafa Khan, 146, 160, 163, 166
Mir Qobad Soltan, 155
mir-shekar, 107
Mirza Abu'l-Hasan Khan Shirazi, 167
Mirza Abu'l-Qasem, 161
Mirza Adi Gural, 173
Mirza 'Ali Kar-kiya, 98
Mirza 'Askar, 190
Mirza Bey Bayat, 142, 144, 151
Mirza Bozorg Qa'em-Maqam, 160, 164
Mirza Hadi Bey, 157
Mirza Jahanshah, 74
Mirza Kafi Nasiri, 126
Mirza Mohammad Hoseyn Qajar, 130
Mirza Mohammad Khan I, 118, 141, 147
Mirza Mohammad Khan II, vii, 111, 118, 144, 147, 156, 160, 161, 163, 188, 190
Mirza Mohammad Khan Qajar, 166
Mirza Mohammad Khan, son of Dargah Khan, 138
Mirza Moharram Mariz-e Qarabaghi, 190
Mirza Qadi, 163
Mirza Salman, 79, 95, 96, 97
Mirza Sayyed Mohammad Sadr, 136
Mirza Shafi', viii, 159
Mishkat al-Anwar, 194
Mithridates, 32
Miyanaj, 75
Miyaneh, 75
Miyankuh, 132
Miyatulu, 15
Mo'ammari, 28
Mobarakabad, 150
Mo'ezz al-Din Oweys Ilkhani, 68

Moghan, 5, 12, 33, 34, 38, 41, 50, 60, 66, 87, 94, 128, 131, 149, 150, 155, 161, 162, 163, 167, 188
Mogheyreh b. Sho'beh, 42, 77
Mohammad 'Ali Khan, 131, 136
Mohammad 'Ali Khan Qereqlu, 129, 131
Mohammad Amin, 98, 99, 101, 190
Mohammad Amin Khan, 99
Mohammad Amin Pasha, 101
Mohammad b. 'Ammar, 51
Mohammad Bey, 103
Mohammad Bey Zaghuri, 133
Mohammad b. Mosafer, 52
Mohammad b. Takesh, 63
Mohammad b. Toghrol, 62
Mohammad b. Yazid, 78
Mohammad Geray Khan, 94
Mohammad Hasan Aqa, 160
Mohammad Hasan Aqa b. Hoseyn Khan, 145
Mohammad Hasan Bey Qurchi, 138
Mohammad Hasan Khan, 136, 137, 144, 145, 146, 147, 148, 150, 153, 155, 159
Mohammad Hasan Khan Baku'i, 148
Mohammad Hasan Khan Qajar, 136, 137, 144
Mohammad Hoseyn Bey, 143
Mohammad Hoseyn Soltan, 108, 201
Mohammad II, 62
Mohammadi Khan, 80
Mohammadi Mirza, 77
Mohammad Karim Bey b. Hajji Safar 'Ali Bey, 146
Mohammad Khan, 57, 138
Mohammad Khan Bey, 143
Mohammad Khan Beykdeli, 164
Mohammad Khan b. Sorkhay, 151
Mohammad Khan Ghazi-Qomuqi, 140, 141, 142, 147
Mohammad Khan, son of Sorkhay Khan, 80
Mohammad Khan, the governor of Sheki, 88
Mohammad Ma'sum, 47, 112, 138, 141
Mohammad Mirza, 77, 141
Mohammad Mirza, son of Yusof, 77
Mohammad Qadaghi, 190
Mohammad Qadi, 162, 164
Mohammad Qoli Aqa, 147
Mohammad Qoli Khalifeh, 79, 96
Mohammad Qoli Khalifeh Dhu'l-Qadr, 79, 96
Mohammad Qoli Khan, vii, 118, 147, 161
Mohammad Qoli Khan Sa'idlu, 80, 123

Mohammad Reza Bey, 145
Mohammad Reza Khan, 137, 139, 145, 146
Mohammad Reza Khan Shirvani, 137
Mohammad Sa'id Khan, 140, 141, 143, 144, 145, 146, 147
Mohammad Saleh Bey, 107
Mohammad, the Toothless Shamkhal, 142
Mojir al-Din Beyleqani, 180
Mokragh, 53
Mokri Qoli Khan, 80
Mokroq, 57
Molk-e Tumanshah, 8
Molla Aqa-ye Darbandi, 190
Molla Hasan, 95
Mollakendi river, 115
Molla Mohammad b. Najaf 'Ali Baku'i, 188
Molla Panah Vaqef, 190
Moltan, 188
Mongols, 3, 14, 16, 18, 25, 122, 182
Moqtadi bi'llah, 58
Morad 'Ali Soltan Ostajalu, 129
Morad b. Soltan Ya'qub, 77
Moravia, 17
Morroco, 189
Morteza 'Ali, 138
Morteza 'Ali Ma'sum, 141
Morteza 'Ali Shamkhal, 142
Morteza 'Ali, son of Amir Hamzeh Usmi, 112
Morteza Qoli Aqa, 165
Morteza Qoli Khan Qajar, 146, 153
Mosaheb-e Ganjavi, 187
Moses, 28
Moses of Khoren, 6, 9
Mosk, 25
Moskur, 18, 37, 44, 112, 115, 142
Mosque, 47, 189
Mostafa, 153
Mostafa Bey, 143, 145, 147, 148
Mostafa Khan, 150, 160
Mostafa Khan Beykdeli, 136
Mostafa Khan Davelu Qajar, 150
Mostafa Khan Shirvani, 162, 163
Mostafa Khan Taleshi, 162
Mostafa Pasha, 94, 121, 123
Mostahzar bi'llah, 60
Mostanjed bi'llah, 62

Mosul, 47, 49, 61
Mota', 49
Mo'tasim, 50
Mount Fet, 150, 153, 161
Mount Kerkhi, 99
Mount Sinai, 189
Mowlana 'Abol-Rashid b. Saleh Baku'i, 186
Mowlana Kamal al-Din Mas'ud Shirvani, 186
Mowlana Katebi Torshizi, 185
Mowlana Mas'ud-e Shirvani, 186
Mowlana Molla Mirza-ye Shirvani, 187
Mowlana Sayyed Yahya Baku'i, 184
Mowlana Sheikh Molla Yusof Moskuri, 184
Mowlaviyan, 189
Mozaffarabad, 188
Mozaffar Soltan, 87
Muktafi, 51
Muqtadir bi'llah, 51
Muqtafi li'Amrollah, 61
Musa b 'Ali b. Beydu Khan, 67
Musa Khan, 80, 123
muskets, 124
Mustarshid bi'llah, 61
Musta'sam bi'llah, 65
Musuq, 25
Mu'tamid, 51

N

Naderabad-e Afghan, 129
Nader Qoli, 122
Nader Qoli Bey, 122
Nader Shah, 80, 135, 149
Na'eb al-Saltaneh, 159
Naghiya, 13
Najaf, 80, 99, 129, 144, 188
Najaf Qoli Khan, 80
Nakhjevan, 42, 66, 68, 69, 75, 85, 138, 139, 158, 162
Nakhoy, 147
Nakhu, 13
Nanakshahiyan, 188
Naqhshbandis, 189
Naqi Bey, 163
narin-qal'eh, 42, 47, 116, 129
Narin-Qal'eh Qapu, 47
Naser Amir al-Mo'menin, 60

Naseran, 73
Nashaq, 101
Nasib Soltan Shamsh al-Dinlu, 158
Nasrollah Mirza, 132, 135
Naumov, colonel, 114
Nazar 'Ali Khan, 164
Nazar 'Ali Khan Zand, 137, 140
Nebol'sin, general, 162
Ne'matollahi order, 189
Nepluyev, 119
Neshat, 190
Nezam al-Molk, 58, 59
Nezami-ye 'Aruzi, 172
Nik Qadam Tayemini, 130
Noghay, 18
Nokhuy, fort, 144
Noqrat, 35
Noshabeh, 28
Novgorod, 35
Nowruz Bey, 141
Nowsal Khan, 54, 138, 142, 146, 158
Nuh Bey, 156, 159, 164, 165
Nur 'Ali Shah Esfahani, 188
Nurbakhshis, 189
Nur Pasha, 123
Nushirzad, 38

O

Odilu, 15
oil, 47, 48, 51, 78, 101, 149, 183
Okhti, 53
Olameh Soltan Tekkelu, 87
Oljeytu Mohammad Khodabandeh, 66, 183
Olus, 18
Oman, 65, 189
Omm al-Mo'manat, 53
Ommayads, 189
Orbeliani, Grigol, viii
Ordubad, 161
Ordughdi Khalifeh Tekellu, 94
Orozoes, 33
Orus Khan, 69
Ossetians, 6, 8, 159, 161
Ostajalu, 15
Othman Pasha, 79, 94, 95, 96, 97, 98
Otrar, 74

Oudh, 188
Owlad, 130

P

pahlavan, 13
Pakhu Bekeh, 158
Palaseh, 98, 99, 142
Pambak, 163
Panahabad, 138
Panah 'Ali Khan, 139
Panah Bey, son of Ebrahim Khan of Javanshir, 138
Panah Khan, 140
Panah Khan Javanshir, 137
Panah Khan Qarabaghi, 140
Panjab, 188
par aval, 13
Paraval, 126
Parfan, 33
pari, 13
Pari Jahan Khanom, 146, 152, 153
Partaz, 29
Paskevich, viii, ix, x, 190
Paul I, 153, 157
Paulucci, lt. general, 164, 166
Pechenegh, 29, 186
Peri Bazar, 117
Perreh-ye Khalil, 153
Peshang, 45
Peshavar, 129, 188
Peter I, 112
Peter II, 121, 153
Peter III, 151, 157
Peykar Khan Qajar, 79
Peykar Soltan Ziyad-oghlu Qajar, 97
Phanagoria, 26
Pir 'Ali Khan Qajar, 162
Pir Qoli Khan Kuseh, 91
Pir Qoli Khan Qajar, 161
Pishdadi kings, xiv, 25
Piyaleh Bey, 98
Poland, 191
Pompey, 32
Pontus, 8, 32
Portas, 51
Port Said, 189
Prince Buqa, 65

Prince Yashmat, 65
Priscus, 10
Pushkin, vii, viii, ix

Q

Qabalal, 19
Qabaleh, 13, 54, 88, 97, 101, 123, 124, 125, 130, 137, 138, 148, 153
Qabartis, 159
Qaberek, 143
Qabestan, 15, 108, 169
Qabr, 132
Qabrak, 123
Qabuli Khan, 120
Qabus, son of Qeyqubad, 68
Qaderiyan, 188, 189
Qadi, 133, 146
Qadi Mohiy al-Din, 67
Qafqaz, 13
Qahqaheh, 90, 98
Qajar, 15, 149
Qalapur, 136
Qal'eh-ye Ashgbush, 13
Qal'eh-ye Narin, 141
Qalmuq, 114, 139
Qaluq, 143, 151
Qamzaq, 54
Qanbar Bey Guzi Beyklu, 105
Qandahar, 154
Qaneq, 5, 139
Qaneq river, 127
Qanun-e Qodsi, xiv, 193
Qapan, 138, 161
Qaplan Kuh, 80
Qapuchay, 19
Qarabagh, 14, 26, 33, 41, 45, 67, 68, 69, 73, 75, 76, 85, 86, 88, 94, 96, 98, 103, 107, 138, 139, 140, 142, 145, 146, 149, 150, 153, 154, 155, 157, 159, 160, 162, 164, 165, 166, 167, 173, 184, 187
Qarabodagh-kend, 72
Qaraborqa mountain, 149
Qaraburak tribe, 94
Qara Burqa, mountain, 153
Qarachay, 73
Qarachay Bey, 105, 107

Qarachedagh, 76
Qarachi Peykan, 72
Qaradagh, 138, 139, 147
Qarajehdagh, 130
Qarakh, 48
Qara Khan, 141, 146
Qarakhi, 56
Qaraman, 189
Qaramanlu, 15, 97, 108
Qara 'Othman, 75
Qarapiri, 102
Qara Qepek, 95
Qara-Qeytaq, 130
Qara-Qoyunlu, 15, 68, 74
Qara Su, 103
Qarat Gholam, 123
Qara Yusof, 73, 74, 79
Qara Yusof Torkman, 73
Qariz, 153
Qars, 69, 126, 163
Qasani, 141, 145
Qasem Bey, 145, 147, 148, 183
Qasem Bey b. Mansur Khan Bey, 148
Qasem Khan, 148, 153
Qasem Mirza, 91
Qasi, 13
Qatran, 147, 154
Qatrukh, 138
Qavam al-Din Hoseyn, 182
Qazanalp, 100
Qazvin, 96, 97, 113, 117, 154
Qazzaq, 139, 149, 160
Qebchah, 53, 84
Qebchaq, 9, 10, 25, 29, 31, 48, 53, 65, 67, 69, 71, 110, 139
Qerglar Qoli Maësum, 143
qerkhlar, 42
Qerkhlar Qoli Ma'sum, 162
Qerkhler Qapu, 47
Qermunchuk-Shali, 101
Qeyd palace, 47
Qeyqobad, 25
Qeysariyeh, 34
Qeytamas Pasha, 94

Qeytaq, 5, 7, 8, 16, 18, 26, 31, 34, 36, 38, 44, 47, 54, 89, 99, 104, 108, 111, 151, 154, 156, 162, 165
Qeytaq-Lezgis, 131
Qezanesh, 99
Qezel Arsalan, 62, 172, 181
Qezelbash, 84, 85, 88, 90, 91, 94, 95, 96, 97, 98, 101, 103, 106, 108, 112, 170
Qezel-qayeh, 139
Qezelyar, 36, 44
Qezlar, 52, 161
Qiyamat Gate, 79
Qiz Qal'asi, 85
Qobad, 14, 35, 73, 75, 78, 102
Qobarti Minor, 9
Qodyal, 18, 138, 188
Qohestan, 60, 188
Qolhan, 48, 84, 89
Qollar, 156
Qom, 76, 92, 136
Qomari river, 9, 72
Qomishah, 189
Qomuq, 7, 8, 16, 18, 24, 28, 36, 37, 47, 54, 72, 100, 109, 110, 112, 123, 124, 127, 130, 152, 154, 165, 166
Qonbud, 100
Qonduzjeh, 71
Qontal, 29
Qorah, 48, 143, 165
Qorban 'Ali, 90
Qorban Nakhavi, 138
Qoreysh, 16, 53, 128, 131
Qorkh Bulagh, 159
Qorush, 53
Qosar, 99
Qoshunlu, 18
Qotb al-Din Mohammad, 63
Qoveyzijan b. Orus Khan, 72
Qowsar 'Ali Shah, 189
Qriz, 164
Quban, 119
Quban stream, 73
Qunaq kend, 12, 145
qurchi-bashi-ye padar, 88
qurchis, 88, 106
Quriyan, 84
Qutqashin, 125
Quy-su, 15, 36, 49, 72, 100
Quysuybuy, 156
Quyun Ulami, 95

R

Rabi'eh al-Baheli, 42, 49
Ragiyan, 188
Rajgan, 188
Ramaneh, 118
Ran Barzin, 38
Rashed bi'llah, 61
Rashidiyeh tower, 88
Rashid Vatvat, 175
Rasht, 122, 144
Rayan, 188
Refa'is, 189
Res'or, 57
Rey, 29, 60
Reza Qoli Mirza, 123, 127, 130, 133, 135
Ridiyan, 18
Riyaz al-Qods, 192
Riyaz-e Siyahah, 189
Rofuq, 53
Rostam, 13, 26, 179
Rostam b. Morteza 'Ali b. Rostam, 141
Rostam Khan, 149
Rostam Khan Usmi, 105, 107, 108, 109, 152, 153
Rostam Mirza, 85
Rostam Mirza b. Maqsud, 76
Rostam Qadi, 143, 152, 153, 157, 163, 165
Rostam, son of Mohammad Usmi, 104
Rostov, 165, 191
Rotul, 48, 53
Rowzat al-Safa, 9, 21, 27, 38, 45, 60
Rtishchev, general, 166, 167
Rubas River, 26, 44, 85
Rudbar, 29, 111, 155
Rudbar-e Saliyan, 110
Rukal, 18
Rum, 10, 16, 17, 21, 27, 58, 67, 71, 73, 74, 85, 87, 89, 169, 189
Rumiantsev, 119
Rurik, 24
Rus, 7, 16, 24, 29, 35, 51, 52

S

Sabz, 69
Sa'dan, 13, 27
Sadeq Khan Qajar, 166
Sadeq Khan Shaqqaqi, 154
Sadi Jamegan, 189
Sa'dollah Barda'i, 190
Sadr Sa'id al-Masteri, 182
Safi Geray Soltan, 96, 97
Safi Khan Baghayeri, 129
Safi Mirza, 109
Safi Qoli Khan, 109, 112
Safiyan, 189
Sahl b. Sonbat, 50
Sa'id b. 'Amr Harshi, 45, 77
Sa'id Shenazi, 190
Salahshuri, 133
Salam, 26
Sala-Tav, 72
Salavan, 17
Salim Aqa, 151
Salim Khan, 153, 160
Saliyan, xvi, 5, 15, 18, 19, 28, 79, 88, 111, 112, 119, 120, 121, 125, 138, 139, 142, 144, 145, 146, 147, 151, 155, 162
Salman, 42
Salman b. Rabi'eh, 7
Salman Khan Beyler-bey, 97
Salmas, 52, 87
salt, 51, 69
Samandar, 7, 23, 36, 44
Samariyan, 189
Samarqand, 69, 71, 73, 74
Sam Mirza, 80, 94, 109, 131
Samsam, 52
Samuriyeh, 5, 14, 15, 16, 18, 19
Samur river, 84, 96
Saqlab, 24
Sarab, 154, 155
Saraqeh b. 'Amr, 41
sar-'askar, 126
Saratan, 57
Sardar Bey Qereqlu, 129
Sardar Khan, 80, 129
Sardasht, 137, 140
Sar-e Hammam, 53

Saretan b. Oruskhan b. 'Omma Khan b. Firuzshah, 54
Sari, 75, 160
Sarir, 7, 9, 23, 29
Sarkel, 23
Sarmakiyeh, 49
Sartaq, 149
Saru Mostafa Pasha, 113
Saten, 33
Satenik, 33
Sattar Khan Usmi, 145, 148
Sayyed Dhu'l-Feqar Shirvani, 182
Sayyed Ebrahim, 76
Sayyed Ghiyath al-Din Mohammad, 75
Sayyed Hasan Shirvani, 185
Sayyed Khan, 80
Sayyed Yahya Baku'i, 184
Scythians, 11, 26, 31
selahdar-bashi, 105
Senasiyan, 188
Seraqeh b. 'Amr, 77
Sevendok Beyk, qurchi-bashi, 91
Shabaran, 12, 18, 37, 95, 96, 97, 107, 112, 118, 127, 131, 142, 153, 163, 177
Shafi'i, 19
Shah 'Abbas I, 80, 149, 150
Shah 'Abbas II, 109, 187
Shah 'Abbas III, 122
Shah Asan, 37
Shahbal, 13, 47, 48
Shah Ba'l b. 'Abdollah, 47
Shahbani, 37, 52, 124
Shahbaz Bey, 148
Shah Bulaghi, 104, 138, 160
Shahdagheh, 124
Shahdaghi, 125, 130
Shah Esma'il, 16, 79, 84, 85, 86, 90, 94, 122
Shah Mardan Bey, 143
Shah Mir Khan, 99, 101, 103
Shah Nazar Bey Tekkelu Chaghatay, 105
Shah Nazar Tekellu, 107
Shah Qoli Bayat, 105
Shah Qoli Bey Dhu'l-Qadr Mohrdar, 108
Shah Qoli Khalifeh, 91
Shahr-e Abad, 37
Shahr-e Nakhiya, 13

Shahrestan, 52
Shahr-e Turk, 120
Shahriyar, 41, 77
Shahrokh b. Soltan Farrokh, 79
Shahrokh b. Timur, 74
Shahrokh Mirza, 79, 88, 135, 136, 154
Shahrokh, son of Soltan Farrokh, 88
Shah Safi, 109, 110
Shahsevan, 146
Shahsevans, 103
Shah Soleyman, 187
Shah Soleyman II, 136
Shah Soltan Hoseyn, 111, 135, 136, 170, 187, 188
Shah Tahmasp, 16, 79, 84, 87, 88, 89, 90, 92, 104, 117, 119, 120, 121, 122, 130
Shah Tahmasp II, 150
Shahverdi Bey [Soltan] Ostajalu, 201
Shahverdi Khan, 139
Shahverdi Khan Ziyad-oghlu, 89, 138
Shah-yurti, 104
Shamakhi, 13, 18, 54, 74, 80, 85, 86, 87, 88, 90, 91, 94, 97, 98, 101, 103, 104, 105, 107, 112, 113, 119, 123, 125, 126, 127, 131, 138, 139, 141, 142, 169, 175, 178, 185, 188
Shamgir, 52, 147, 150
Shamgir b. Ziyad, 52
Shamkhal, 9, 13, 16, 18, 35, 54, 55, 72, 89, 109, 112, 120, 124, 126, 127, 131, 133, 138, 142, 145, 146, 148, 152, 153, 156, 157, 160, 161
Shamkhal Ma'sum, 143
Shamlu, 15
Shams al-Din Almaleqi, 71
Shams al-Dinlu, 86, 147
Shams al-Din Pasha, 103
Shamshi Khan Qazzaqlar, 101
Shamshir Khan, 99
Shamsh ol-Din Pasha, 106
Shamsi Bey, 98
Shapur, 8, 35
Sharrat, 127
Sharur, 86
Shebut, 19
Shehab al-Din Soltan, 146
Shehab al-Din Soltan Arashi, 148
Shehshpareh, 18
Sheik Abu Eshaq Ebrahim, 54

Sheikh 'Abdol-Karim Qabavi, 190
Sheikh 'Abdollah Khafif, 170
Sheikh Abu'l-'Abbas Nehavandi, 170
Sheikh Abu'l-Qasem Qosheyri, 170
Sheikh Abu Sa'id Abu'l-Kheyr, 170
Sheikh Ahmad, 54
Sheikh 'Ali, 54, 68
Sheikh 'Ali Bey b. Mirza, 141
Sheikh 'Ali Khan, 111, 149, 152, 162, 164
Sheikh 'Ali Ma'sum, 142
Sheikh Baha'i al-Din 'Ameli, 108
Sheikh Ebrahim, 78
Sheikh Hasan, son of Teymurtash, 67
Sheikh Heydar, 76, 84
Sheikh Heydar Safavi, 76
Sheikhi-kand, 165
Sheikh Joneyd, 16, 83, 164
Sheikhlar, 184
Sheikh Mohammad, 54
Sheikh Mohammad Baha'i 'Ameli, 188
Sheikh Naser al-Din, 54
Sheikh Oweys, 67
Sheikh Paydar, 88
Sheikh Safi, 74
Sheikh Safi al-Din, 83
Sheikhshah, 79, 83, 86
Sheikh Shah Elborzi, 53
Sheikh Ya'qub Charkhi Shaberani, 190
Shekufeh Khanom, 154
Sheytan parastan, 189
Shibov, colonel, 116
Shi'ite, 16, 19
Shiraz, 77, 86, 136, 137, 140, 170, 189
Shirin, 38, 144, 173, 177
Shirvan, 5
Shirvand, 6
Shirvanshah, xiv, 37, 38, 54, 68, 69, 75, 77, 85, 178
Shokoba, 56
Sholaver, 149
Shuragel, 163
Shushi, 137, 138, 150, 154, 155, 159, 160
Sigebert, 17
Simun Khan, 98
Sind, 188
Sir Gore Ousely, 166
Sisan, 138

Siyah-Pushan, 188
Siyavosh Bey [Soltan], 201
slave, 50, 52, 75, 130, 135, 174, 176
Sobolev, general major, 152
Sofnan, 49
Sohrab Bey, 143
Sohrab Ma'sum, 143
Soleyman Khan, 158
Soleyman, son of Soltan Mohammad, 62
Soltan Abu Sa'id, 76
Soltan Ahmad, 65, 68, 69, 70, 71, 73, 74, 79, 112, 121, 138
Soltan Ahmad Bey, 158
Soltan Ahmad Jalayer, 69, 73
Soltan Ahmad Jalayer Ilkhani, 69
Soltan Ahmad Usmi, 99
Soltan 'Ali b. Sheikh Heydar, 77
Soltan Bayazid, 68
Soltan Bayazid II, 77
Soltan Bey Bayat, 156
Soltanbud, 76, 165
Soltan Bud, 99
Soltan Fereydun, 78
Soltan Hesan, 166
Soltan Hoseyn, 68
Soltan Hoseyn Beyqara, 186
Soltan Hoseyn Fath 'Ali Khan, 112
Soltan Hoseyn II, 136
Soltaniyeh, 66, 73, 75, 86, 87, 135, 149
Soltan Key Qobad, 54
Soltan Khalil, 71, 79, 88
Soltan Khalil II, 79, 87
Soltan Khalil Shirvanshah, 84
Soltan Mahmud, 11, 58, 60, 62, 66, 71, 114, 121
Soltan Mahmud Saljuqi, 172
Soltan Mas'ud, 11, 58, 61, 62, 180
Soltan Mohammad, 78
Soltan Mohammad Khodabandeh, 66, 94, 98
Soltan Mohammad Khvarezmshah, 182
Soltan Mohammad, son of Sheikh Shah, 88
Soltan Morad, 77, 86, 94
Soltan Morad Khan, 109
Soltan Qarachurlu, 129
Soltan Qutqasheni, 144
Soltan Sanjar b. Malekshah, 60
Soltan Selim, 86, 87
Soltan Shah, 63
Soltan Soleyman, 54, 87, 89, 91
Soltan Ya'qub, 6, 76, 84, 85
Soltan Ya'qub b. Hasan, 6
Sombat, 34, 165
Sombat Mountain, 56
Sorkhab, 36, 88, 178, 182
Sorkhay Bey Ghazi-Qomuqi, 121
Sorkhay Khan, 80, 112, 123, 124, 127, 130, 131, 148, 152, 153, 156, 162, 165
Sorkhay Khan II, 131, 147, 159
Sorkhay Mirza, 109
Sorkhay-ye Shamkhal, 110
Sovar, 49
Soymanov, 116
St. Gregory, 34
St. Nina, 35
St. Sham'un, 169
Su, 26
Sufi Hamid, 169
Sufi Nabi Zarnavaii, 138
Sul, 26, 37, 38
Sulaqchay, 114
Sulaq river, 9, 16, 72, 73, 99, 100, 116, 120, 125, 126
Suluq, 22
Suluqay, 22
Sumokht, 11
Sunnis, 16, 19
Sur, 26, 37, 55
Surakat, 54
Suren, 34
Surhi, 9, 26, 56
Suri, 18
Surkheh-ye Semnan, 136
Syria, 21, 38, 42, 47, 49, 52, 60, 65, 73, 85, 86, 149, 189

T

Tabarestan, 15, 36, 52, 136, 149, 150, 188
Tabariyan, 189
Tabarsaran, 5, 14, 15, 18, 19, 26, 35, 36, 37, 44, 47, 48, 52, 84, 91, 99, 105, 108, 112, 127, 128, 131, 132, 138, 141, 143, 146, 151, 152, 156, 157, 162, 163, 164
Tab-riz, 49

Tabriz, ix, xii, 49, 65, 67, 68, 69, 74, 77, 78, 85, 86, 87, 96, 98, 101, 130, 136, 138, 147, 151, 155, 160, 165, 167, 178, 182
Tadvin-e 'Aliji, 188
Tagh, 9
Tahdhib al-Akhlaq, xiv, 193
Taher Bey, 140
Tahmasp I, 16, 79, 84
Tahmasp II, 113
Tahmasp Mirza, 113, 117
Tahmasp Qoli Khan, 122, 123
Tahmurath Khan, 108
taj, 84, 101
Takesh Khan, 62, 63
Takhlis al-Athar va 'Ajayeb al-Malek al-Qahar, 186
Takht-e Tavus, 95, 160
tala, 8
Taleb Beg, 105
Taleh, 112
Talesh, 85, 95, 98, 117, 144, 146, 156, 157, 159, 160, 162, 163, 166, 167
Tamurath Khan, 105
Tandeb, 56
Tanus, 54
Taqvim al-Boldan, 6
Tarkhu, 13, 36, 44, 48, 56, 73, 99, 115, 142, 160
Tarki, 44, 48, 56, 99, 115, 142, 160
Tarnavat, 160
Tarnavat Fort, 138
Tarsa, 52
Tatar Sin, 96
Tatif, 138
Tat language, 18
Tav, 48
Tavalesh, 88
Tav-Machgach, 101
tax, 37, 41, 54, 73, 128, 130, 133, 138, 145, 159
taxes, 47, 54, 100, 104, 156, 181
Tehran, viii, ix, xii, 135, 137, 151, 154, 189
Tekellu, 15
Teleh, 123, 125, 126, 127, 129
Tepeh Lar, 153
Terek, 6, 36, 72, 99
Terkesh, 151
Terlav, 101, 138
Terlav-oghli emirs, 101

Teymur-Quyi, 100
Tiberius, 22, 33
Tiflis, vii, viii, x, xii, xiii, 8, 11, 61, 65, 94, 103, 126, 130, 139, 150, 158, 165, 166, 190, 193
Tigranes, 32
Tikhonovski, colonel, 162
Timur, 9, 15, 52, 68, 69, 70, 71, 73, 74, 78, 149, 154
Timur-Quye, 73
Timurshah-yolu, 72
Tip, 18
Tiridates, 34
Tiyun Shah, 37
Tizru Soltan Moqaddam, 101
Toghrol b. Arsalan, 62
Toghrol, son of Arsalan, 173, 180
Tokharestan, 188
Tomiris, 26
Toqtamesh Khan, 9, 69, 71
Torkan Khatun, 59
Tormasov, general, 160, 163, 164
Transoxiania, 50, 60, 69, 74
Tsitsianov, general, 149, 157, 159, 160
Tulun, 22
Tumanes, 103
Tumanler, 15, 100
Tumanshah, 15, 36
Tuman tribe, 36
Tumel, 56
Tupkhaneh, 150
Tur, 26
Turan, 26
Turkestan, 14, 16, 22, 73, 86, 122, 137, 149, 176, 177, 188
Turkhaleh, 100
Turkmen, 6, 16, 18, 47, 68, 73, 76, 79, 100, 108, 122, 143, 150, 151
Turkmenistan, 28
Turun, 22
Tush, 55
Tuti Bekeh, 141, 142
Tuz-Machgach, 101

U

Uch Kalisa, 35, 159
Udi, 34

Ujan, 45, 74
Ukraine, x, 119, 191
Ulu Majar, 36, 44
Ulus, 161
Uqa river, 72
Urjamil, 100
Urmiyeh, 136, 140
Urta Bugham River, 115
Usalu, 15
Usmi, 9, 17, 80, 110, 111, 112, 126, 127, 129, 130, 131, 133, 138, 139, 141, 142, 145, 146, 148, 151, 152, 154, 157, 159, 162, 164
Usmi Khan Qeytaq, 201
Ustar Khan, 159
Utemish, 115
Utemish Plains, 73
Utuz-iki clans, 97
Utuz-iki tribe, 103
Uzbeg Khan, 67
Uzun Cherkes, 99
Uzun Hasan, 75, 84

V

Valid 'Abdol-Malek, 42
Varchan, 9
Varingians, 186
Vathiq bi'llah, 51
Venetian Sea, 31
Vis and Ramin, 172
Volga, 11, 17

W

wall of Darband, 6, 18, 30, 31, 36, 38
Warsaw, x
Weteroni, brigadier, 114

Y

Yajuj, 25
Yakhsay, 100, 114, 138
Yalamah river, 115
Ya'qub Mirza, 76
Yarapul, 31
Yasamal, 103
Yaval, 25
Yayq, 22
Yazd, 137

Yazdagerd, 14
Yazdegerd, 7, 36
Yazid b. 'Abdol-Malek, 44
Yazidiyeh, 49
Yazikov, 117
Yeki kend, 110
Yemen, 21, 32, 189
Yengi Qapu, 47
Yengolu tribe, 139
Yermelov, vii, viii, 190
Yersi, 49, 163, 165
Yunan, xi, 27
Yurt Molla Hasan, 97
Yusof Bey, 75
Yusof Khan, 80, 107, 108
Yusof Kuseh, 190
Yusof Pasha Sar 'Askar, 162
Yusof Zarir Qomuqi, 190
Yuvareh Buturlin, 100
Yuzbashi Bey Howzi, 148
Yuzbashi, son Safar 'Ali Bey Howzi, 153

Z

Zabulestan, 188
Zagam, 108
Zaghur, 133
Zahir al-Dowleh Ebrahim Khan, 129
zakat, 55, 66
Zakhur, 19, 48, 112, 113, 138
Zakhuri Mountain, 57
Zaki Khan, 137, 140
Zamtal, 19
Zanganeh, 15
Zang-Zur, 138
Zanjan, 119, 135, 154
Zar Qobad, 13
Zekh, 15
Zerehgaran, 8, 9, 36, 56
Zeyb al-Nisa, 158
Zeyb al-Nisa Begom, 157
Zeydiyan, 189
Zeykhur, 165
Zhentab Mountain, 57
Zimbulatov, lt. colonel, 120
Ziya al-Din Kashi, 102
Zizik, 156

Zobeydeh Khatun, 49
Zohreh Khanom, 110
Zomtal, 57
Zoroastrian, 27
Zovand, 166
Zubov, Count, 152, 153, 157
Zuqar, 56

www.ingramcontent.com/pod-product-compliance
Lightning Source LLC
Chambersburg PA
CBHW081152290426
44108CB00018B/2522